NINTH EDITION

EXTRAORDINARY GROUPS

An Examination of Unconventional Lifestyles

NINTH EDITION

EXTRAORDINARY GROUPS

An Examination of
Unconventional Lifestyles

RICHARD T. SCHAEFER
DePaul University

WILLIAM W. ZELLNER

WORTH PUBLISHERS

Senior Publisher: Catherine Woods
Acquisitions Editor: Sarah Berger
Marketing Manager: Lindsay Johnson
Marketing Coordinator: Jennifer Bilello
Photo Editor: Christine Buese
Photo Researcher: Julie Tesser
Art Director: Babs Reingold
Senior Designer: Kevin Kall
Associate Managing Editor: Tracey Kuehn
Project Editor: Francine Almash
Production Manager: Barbara Anne Seixas
Composition: TSI Graphics
Printing and Binding: RR Donnelley
Cover Photo: © Keren Su/Corbis, *Colored Pencils in Warsaw*

ISBN-13: 978-1-4292-3224-1
ISBN-10: 1-4292-3224-2

Library of Congress Control Number: 2010935768

Printed in the United States of America

First printing

Worth Publishers
41 Madison Avenue
New York, NY 10010
www.worthpublishers.com

To the memory of
William W. Zellner,
a teacher and a scholar

CONTENTS

3   THE SHAKERS   81

4   THE MORMONS   119

PREFACE

Now in its ninth edition, *Extraordinary Groups* has had a most gratifying history. Written by sociologists, using and illustrating sociological principles, the book has also been adopted in various other social science courses, including anthropology, religion, history, and psychology. This interdisciplinary approach is one reason the book has been used in hundreds of colleges and universities, a number that continues to grow.

Another reason for the book's appeal is that it is descriptive and explanatory rather than analytical. True, the description is interwoven with basic sociological concepts, but systematic analysis and inductive reasoning have been left to the discretion of the instructor.

The ninth edition of Extraordinary Groups has undergone the most significant revision since the first edition was published in 1976. The chapters have been re-ordered to approximate the chronological presence of the groups in the United States from the Gypsies (or Roma) in 1498 to the Church of Scientology and the Wiccans in the 20th century. In addition, three groups with very different experiences and membership patterns have been added—the Shakers, the Nation of Islam, and the Wiccans.

All chapters have been updated to reflect the latest events and scholarship. New material includes: Madonna's advocacy on behalf of the Roma; new sections in our chapter on the Mormons titled Contemporary Politics, Fundamentalists, and Global Religion; coverage of the controversy surrounding the death of John Travolta's son, and new sections—Organization and Condemning the Condemners—in the Scientology chapter.

Legal actions continue to affect many of the extraordinary groups covered in this volume. For example, in this edition we consider the Supreme Court ruling that Jehovah's Witnesses have a constitutional right to knock on doors without permits. We continue to consider how the media presents, or misrepresents, extraordinary groups, such as in television programs like *Big Love* (Mormons) and *Amish in the City* and motion pictures *The Craft* (Wiccans) and *The American Gypsy*. Further the hot topic of what constitutes a cult is covered in the Introduction. And Schaefer's own experience attending a meeting with the remaining members of the Shakers is now a part of this edition.

Pedagogical features have been enhanced with the introduction of pictures and captions within the chapter. The glossary of 70 terms has been expanded to 113 terms. Included in these additional terms are ones familiar to the social sciences such as deviance, ethnocentrism, blaming the victim, primary and secondary groups, norms, alienation, stereotypes, and commodification as well as those more specific to extraordinary groups such as spellwork.

As already noted, the addition of three more groups will be apparent to past users. While still maintaining a presence today, the Shakers are primarily a historical story of the nineteenth century that offers another look at the extraordinary practice of communal living underscored by a variation of Christian beliefs. The Nation of Islam is in sharp contrast to the "Judeo-Christian" tradition. The Nation of Islam not only represents a departure from this tradition but also, until very recently, a sharp deviation from the Islamic beliefs brought by immigrants during the 20th century. It is difficult to think of groups staking out more of a departure from conventional traditions than the Shakers and the Nation of Islam. That is, until one turns to Wiccans. Much of seeking to understand this group is to clarify what is not accurate as well as what it is. By adding these three groups, we develop a more complete view of the broad tapestry of social life that constitutes the United States.

Every effort has been made in this edition by the author to maintain the creative and scholarly voices that have been behind the productive publication of *Extraordinary Groups*. The first edition was written by William S. Kephart, longtime professor of sociology at the University of Pennsylvania. Fortunately for tens of thousands of college students, Bill Zellner matched Kephart's passion for groups engaged in unconventional lifestyles, becoming a coauthor with Kephart starting in the fourth edition. I knew Bill Zellner both as an undergraduate and graduate student when I taught at Western Illinois University, which he attended in the latter 1970s. He kept *Extraordinary Groups* alive and fresh for another three editions over a decade.

Acknowledgments

Over the years, the various editions of *Extraordinary Groups* have been strengthened by the thoughtful and perceptive comments of a number of reviewers. I appreciate the input of Lorraine Klimowich, Penny Robinson, Brandy Smith, and the contributions of academic reviewers who offered their thoughts: Carol Apt (South Carolina State University), Bonita Freeman-Withoft (West Chester University), Mark Hartlaub (Texas A&M University–Corpus Christi), Joseph Carroll (Colby-Sawyer College), Jeffery Rosenfeld (Nassau Community College), Brian Moss (Oakland Community College), Michele Titus (College of San Mateo), Paul Demers (University of Nebraska–Lincoln), Richard Jenks (Indiana

University–Southeast), Brian Barry (Rochester Institute of Technology), Feler Bose (Alma College), M.G. Dunn (Roanoke College), Kelly Dagan (Illinois College), Philip Davis (Georgia State University), T. John Alexander (Houston Baptist University), Douglas C. Bachtel (University of Georgia), Antonio A. Chiareli (Union University), Karen B. Martin (Great Basin College), Fred C. Pampel (University of Colorado), and Dennis L. Peck (University of Alabama).

Richard T. Schaefer
schaeferrt@aol.com
www.schaefersociology.net

ABOUT THE AUTHORS

Richard T. Schaefer obtained his M.A. and Ph.D. in sociology from the University of Chicago. His continuing interest in race relations led him to write his master's thesis on the membership of the Ku Klux Klan and his doctoral thesis on racial prejudice and race relations in Great Britain. Schaefer is author of *Racial and Ethnic Groups* (Twelfth Edition, Census Update), *Race and Ethnicity in the United States* (Sixth Edition), *Sociology* (Twelfth Edition), *Sociology: A Brief Introduction* (Ninth Edition), *Sociology in Modules* and *Sociology Matters* (Fifth Edition). His articles and book reviews have appeared in many journals, including *American Journal of Sociology, Phylon: A Review of Race and Culture, Contemporary Sociology, Sociology and Social Research, Sociological Quarterly,* and *Teaching Sociology.* He has served as president of both the Illinois Sociological Association and the Midwest Sociological Society. In recognition of his achievements in undergraduate teaching, he was named Vincent de Paul Professor of Sociology in 2004. Dr. Schaefer has taught sociology for over 35 years. Today he teaches at DePaul University where he continues to learn from his students and appreciate their insights.

William W. Zellner was professor of sociology at East Central University in Ada, Oklahoma. He attended Lafayette College, Missouri Valley College, Moravian College, and Millikin University, earning his B.A. and M.A. at Western Illinois University. His doctoral work was completed at South Dakota State University.

Zellner was author of numerous articles, essays, and books, including *Countercultures: A Sociological Analysis,* and *Sects, Cults, and Spiritual Communities: A Sociological Analysis* (coedited with Marc Petrowsky). He was past president of the Oklahoma Sociological Association, and three times past president of the Association for the Scientific Study of Religion, Southwest. He also served as chairman of an award-winning nine-county community action agency. He had been designated as a resource person for the United States Information Agency to foreign journalists interested in American religious sects and cults. In 1996, he launched his college's inaugural faculty lecture series with the topic "Overview of Countercultures and Extraordinary Groups." He passed away in 2003 shortly after the seventh edition of *Extraordinary Groups* was available to an audience of welcoming readers, students, and instructors.

NINTH EDITION

EXTRAORDINARY GROUPS

**An Examination of
Unconventional Lifestyles**

INTRODUCTION

America is a land of fascinating cultural diversity. Scores of various ethnic groups, hundreds of different religious sects and denominations—the total seems almost inexhaustible. Indeed, it is the tremendous range of associational groups that sets America apart from most other societies.

Out of the multitude of different culture-groups that have appeared on the American scene, we have chosen ten for inclusion in the present volume:

The Gypsies	The Jehovah's Witnesses
The Old Order Amish	The Father Divine Movement
The Shakers	The Nation of Islam
The Mormons	The Church of Scientology
The Oneida Community	Wicca

All of these groups are important in their own right. Just as well-educated persons should have some knowledge of other times and other places, they should also have an awareness of the subcultural diversity within their own society. The only question to be asked is this: Why were these particular groups chosen, rather than others? The answer is threefold.

Sociological Illustration

The first—and most important—reason pertains to sociological illustration. The groups were selected because they illustrate major sociological principles in concrete form. Let us look at some examples.

As used by sociologists, the term *primary group* refers to a small, face-to-face group whose members share experiences, confide in one another, lend mutual support and understanding, and so on. These primary-group needs, as they are called, are deep-seated. They are characteristic of human beings everywhere. In most societies, the basic primary group is the family, and insofar as the personality structure of children is concerned, sociologists feel that the family has a lasting influence.

It stands to reason, therefore, that any culture or subculture attempting to eliminate the family must provide an alternative social mechanism for the satisfaction of primary-group needs. The Oneida Community is a good case in point.

In their attempt to create a utopian society, the Oneidans dispensed entirely with traditional marriage, family, and parental child rearing. All males were permitted to have sexual relations with all females, and all children were raised communally. Undue affection between parents and children—or between a particular man and a particular woman—was severely censured. And because the Oneida community lasted for some fifty years, with a total membership running well into the hundreds, the methods used to promote group solidarity were obviously effective.

Oneidans were all housed under one roof—the Mansion House—a building designed specifically to promote feelings of togetherness. Members ate in a common dining hall and held meetings in a community meeting hall. Activities such as smoking, drinking, and card playing were prohibited, because they were considered to be individualistic or antigroup. Conversely, musical presentations, theatricals, and other group activities were strongly encouraged.

In their day-to-day living, Oneidans totally rejected the concept of private property. They shared their material possessions, their wealth, their mates, and their children. Members held both a common economic philosophy and a common theology. So strong was their we-feeling that they were able to satisfy primary-group needs despite the large size of their community.

Let us look at one more example: *definition of the situation*. As W.I. Thomas, who coined the term, put it, "What men define as real is real in its consequences." And the Old Order Amish provide an excellent illustration, for they have defined the automobile as a threat to their social equilibrium—and they are acting accordingly.

Many permissive changes have taken place among the Amish, but one "contraption" remains taboo: the automobile. Members are not permitted to own them. And despite a variety of pressures, the Amish church has not yielded on this point—and probably never will.

The Old Order Amish have a close-knit family life. They are wedded to the soil, to the church community, and to the horse and buggy. And they feel that the automobile would disrupt their methodical and slow-paced way of life.

True, the Amish may be wrong in their judgment. The automobile might not bring with it the feared aftereffects. But that is irrelevant. They have already defined the situation, and they can hardly change the definition without also changing their entire social perspective.

Other sociological illustrations would include *culture conflict* among the Mormon polygamists; *social control* in the Gypsy community; *cultural theme*, as exemplified by the Father Divine movement; *gender role*, as illustrated by the Shakers and the Nation of Islam; *alienation; assimilation; conspicuous consumption; sanctions; folkways* and *mores; charisma; ethnocentrism; level of aspiration; values;* and *manifest* and *latent function*.

Various chapters in *Extraordinary Groups* contain a number of these sociological concepts around which are woven the threads and cultural fabric of the group in question. By associating the concept with the group or groups involved, the student is thus aided in the learning process.

Diversity

Although we could have selected groups that were fairly similar to each other, such as many of the counterculture communes that materialized between 1965 and 1975, we felt that—in terms of liberal arts values—diversity was much more rewarding. Accordingly, we chose groups that were markedly different from each other.

The Oneidans adhered to a system of strict economic communism, whereas the Mormons believe just as strongly in free enterprise. The Amish are a rural group and the Father Divine movement is urban. Unlike the centuries of history of the Amish, the Church of Scientology is totally a creation of the last seventy years. While the Nation of Islam and the Wiccans both have ties to practices going back more than a thousand years, they are distinct creations of the twentieth century. The groups vary in their outreach. Scientologists make their literature freely available, operate numerous information centers, and make effective use of its voluminous Internet site. The Jehovah's Witnesses and the Mormons gain members through proselytizing, whereas the Amish are content to let God increase their numbers.

Interest

The third and final reason for choosing these particular groups was simply that they are interesting. This we know, because many of the accounts in *Extraordinary Groups* were based on personal experience. For example, author Zellner was born and raised in Pennsylvania, and his fascination and conversations with the Old Order Amish have spanned many decades. Schaefer conducted fieldwork at the primary retreat of the Father Divine Movement and met with Mother Divine on two occasions.

Schaefer attended a meeting (that is, church service) with the three remaining Shakers in 2009 and was audited by a Scientologist in Alaska in 2007 as well. He reached out to the Wiccan community and in 2010 met with a member of a Manhattan-based coven.

Our interest in the Oneida Community also goes back many years; in fact, a number of the surviving members were actually interviewed, as well as their descendants. Interviews and associations with Jehovah's Witnesses were also quite revealing.

We wish we could say that our relationship with the Gypsies was similarly rewarding, but—no pun intended—it was not in the cards. Both physically and conversationally, Gypsies are elusive. A good many of the interviews were out-and-out failures. Fortunately, a few of the interviewees were cooperative. Also, some invaluable fieldwork on the part of other investigators was available.

Sociological principles are not difficult to learn. The trick is to make them meaningful in keeping with the best traditions of a liberal education. And we do hope that a study of the following "extraordinary groups" will result in a meaningful grasp of the subject. Also, in terms of the cultural diversity mentioned earlier, a consideration of these groups may permit us to feel a little less smug about our own way of life.

Cults?

The one word that almost never appears in the ten chapters that follow is "cult." Yet cult is often associated with several of these groups. We have avoided using that term for two reasons.

First, the term cult in the public mind has a very negative connotation that does not have much explanatory value. To call a group a cult serves to disparage it as a belief system not worthy of any respect, much less serious consideration. The term cult connotes that a group is very materialistic with sinister motives behind its leadership and that followers are typically separated from their family and friends, if not kidnapped, undergoing a resocialization program that outsiders decry as brainwashing.

Second recognizing the misuse of the cult label, most scholars in religious studies and the social sciences have abandoned use of the term altogether. Sometimes effort is made to define it very precisely in terms of size, leadership, and relationship to other existing religious groups. In most instances, preference has been shown for speaking of "sects" or "new religious movements" to describe groups that have at times been stigmatized with the cult label.

The absence of the use of "cults," as the reader will see, does not mean that we avoid the controversies associated with the extraordinary groups. Charges of illicit sexual behavior, condoning of crime, cover-ups of embarrassing ventures, and breaking into government offices are a part of the accounts that follow. However, one must keep in mind that our own lifestyle and beliefs always seem normal to us until we stop and realize that many in this society and elsewhere may find our views and even lifestyles to be troubling or bizarre, if not worse.

CHAPTER ONE

THE GYPSIES

- Overview
- Early History
- Challenges to Studying the Rom
- *Marimé*
- Family and Social Organization
- Arranged Marriages and the Bride Price

- Lifestyle
- Economic Organization
- Activities
- Social Control
- Prejudice and Discrimination
- Adaptability: The Rom Trademark
- The Future

Of all the groups discussed in the present volume, the Gypsies are the most "extraordinary." Even for experienced observers, their culture patterns are difficult to grasp. For the fact of the matter is that the Gypsies have a lifestyle that comes close to defying comprehension. The blurb on the dust jacket of Peter Maas's controversial and widely read *King of the Gypsies,* for example, makes the following claims:

> There are perhaps a million or more Gypsies in the United States—nobody knows exactly how many, not even the government. They no longer live in horse-drawn caravans on dusty roads; they live in cities, drive cars, have telephones and credit cards. Yet they do not go to school, neither read nor write, don't pay taxes, and keep themselves going by means of time-honored ruses and arrangements. Gypsies themselves recognize the contrast they make, and they are proud of it.[1]

Given the nature of modern journalism, can this statement be true? The answer is not a simple one, and each of the above points requires some explanation. However, before proceeding further, we should directly address the term *Gypsies*. It is the term generally used to refer to the group, but is not one routinely accepted by the people. The Rom (or Roma) is the most neutral name of this extraordinary group who typically speak a distinctive language called *Romani* (or *Romany*). Many contemporary Rom, especially in Europe, have accepted *Traveler* to refer to

---

[1]Peter Maas, *King of the Gypsies* (New York: Viking, 1975).

themselves since Rom is sometimes reserved for only those who are traced to eastern or southern Europe. *Gypsy*, by contrast, was a name applied to them under the mistaken notion they were Egyptian in origin. Rom almost universally detest the label "Gypsy" and the negative connotations it carries. However, we recognize that Rom is primarily used by those who specialize in the study of these fascinating people, so we will use Gypsy, but remind the reader of the proper use of Rom.

Overview

We will now address the claims of Peter Maas. It is true that no one knows how many Gypsies there are in the United States. One million seems a reasonable estimate, but the real figure will probably never be known. Gypsies move about so much, and many have many different names and aliases. They are generally so secretive given the hostility they encounter that it is difficult to pinpoint the numbers for a given city, let alone for a state or the entire nation.[2]

Gypsies live in cities and drive cars? Indeed they do. They are not likely to be found on farms or in the suburbs. They will not be found on the water. They are urban dwellers—towns and cities—and they reside in nearly all fifty states. At the same time, Gypsies are, and always have been, great travelers. They may be the greatest travelers the world has ever known. As we shall see, traveling serves as an integral part of the Gypsy lifestyle.

As for cars, Gypsies not only drive them but sometimes make their living repairing them. The days of horse-drawn wagons and caravans have long since gone, but Gypsies—as is their wont—have adapted remarkably well to motorized transportation. Indeed, despite the fact that they are a low-income group, Gypsies often drive Cadillacs.

Gypsies do not go to school? Not very often—and not for very long. They feel that formal education is not germane to their way of life and that the American school system would tend to assimilate their youngsters. **Assimilation** is the process through which a person forsakes his or her own cultural tradition to become part of a different culture.

Gypsies neither read nor write? True. A large portion of them are functionally illiterate. They cannot read or write their own language, Romany,

---

[2]Ian F. Hancock, "American Roma: The Hidden Gypsy World," *Aperture* 144 (Summer 1996). Furthermore, there are no census data on Gypsies and only a few thousand volunteer they speak languages associated with them. The estimate of one million in the United States most recently appeared in Mary Beth Marklein, "European effort spotlights plight of the Roma." *USA Today*, February 2, 2005, p. 6A. Language data appear in the report "Languages Spoken, Census 2000" at www.census.gov.

for it is a spoken, rather than a written, tongue. The literacy situation is improving, but so far progress has been slow. In spite of their self-imposed linguistic handicap, however, Gypsies have made a remarkable adaptation to their environment.

In urban United States, public school education has become more common. In fact, beginning in 1965, Roma became involved in creating school and Head Start programs to serve their people, first in San Francisco, then elsewhere, including Oregon and Washington State, then spreading eastward to Chicago and Baltimore.[3]

Gypsies do not pay taxes? Some observers would reply: "Not if they can help it." And it is true that many Gypsies do not pay property taxes because they have no taxable property. They often prefer to rent rather than to buy a dwelling place. Also, many Gypsies work irregularly and have low-paying jobs, so that their income taxes would be negligible. A fair number are on welfare. On the other hand, at least some Gypsies are moving into white-collar occupations, and their tax payments are probably commensurate with those of other white-collar workers.

Gypsies keep themselves going by means of time-honored ruses and arrangements? A complicated question, surely, but then the Gypsies are a complicated people. As is true of all ethnic groups, there are honest Gypsies and there are dishonest Gypsies. Unfortunately, however, many Gypsies continue to believe that all *gadje*[4] (non-Gypsies) are fair game. And more than occasionally this belief does culminate in ruses and petty swindles.

At the same time, Gypsy attitudes toward the *gadje* have been shaped by the *gadje* themselves. As will be shown, Gypsies have not been met with open arms by the various host countries. On the contrary, they have experienced near-universal prejudice and discrimination. There is no question that Gypsy enclaves everywhere are considered **countercultures.** As used by sociologists, the term refers to any group behavioral pattern that arises in opposition to the prevailing culture. Social distance is one way of considering the stigma society puts on the Rom.

Social distance is the tendency to withdraw from a group. It may not involve physical distance. One may associate with members of a group but want to deny them citizenship or perhaps be unwilling to welcome them into the family through marriage. In national surveys, the *gadje* display a great desire to place social distance between them and the Rom.

---

[3]Ian Hancock, "The Schooling of Romani Americans: An Overview." Paper read at the Second International Conference on the Psycholinguistic and Sociolinguistic Problems of Roma Children's Education in Europe, Varna, Bulgaria, May 27, 1992.

[4]Interestingly enough, the Gypsy language has not been standardized. Consequently, most of their terms have a variety of spellings. In the present account, spelling has been adapted to fit the pronunciation. For example, *gadje* is also written as *gaje, gazhé,* or *gawjas.*

Social distance studies in several countries, including the United States, simply confirm the obvious; namely, the Gypsies rank at the absolute bottom of the status scale.[5]

Through it all, the Gypsies have survived. Gypsies always survive. If they haven't exactly flourished, they have in many ways given a very good account of themselves. It is not easy to be a Gypsy. As one writer put it, "Only the fit need apply."[6] In the following pages, the full implications of this statement will become clear.

Early History

Like so many other aspects of their life, Gypsy origins are draped in mystery. As noted earlier, the Gypsies were mistakenly thought to have originated in Egypt. This was a belief that they themselves did little to discourage. In fact, some Gypsies still believe in their Egyptian roots, although it has now been rather well established that their original homeland was India. Romani, the Gypsy language, has its roots in Sanskrit— a classical language of India.

The roots of the Rom are often portrayed as some big mystery as if to add to the mystic stereotype of the people themselves.[7] While some early aspects are still debated, historians agree that they left India sometime after A.D. 1000. Before then they served the Indian militia in a variety of capacities, cooking, erecting tents, mending broken weapons, and attending to the wounded of Indian people who were resisting Islamic warriors. The failure of the people of India in that region to be victorious caused the ancestors of today's Gypsy people to flee, moving quickly across much of the Islamic territory toward Armenia over a period of about fifty years.[8] In another two hundred years, they had basically established themselves in Europe. By the 1400s, they were present in western Europe in France, Germany, Italy, Holland, Switzerland, and Spain. They had distanced themselves both physically and culturally from their roots in Hindu India.[9]

---

[5]Cited in Matt Salo and Sheila Salo, *The Kalderasha in Eastern Canada* (Ottawa: National Museums of Canada, 1977), p. 17; and Tom W. Smith and Glenn R. Dempsey, "The Polls: Ethnic Social Distance and Prejudice," *Public Opinion Quarterly* 47 (Winter 1983): 584–600.

[6]Rena C. Gropper, *Gypsies in the City* (Princeton, NJ: Darwin, 1975), p. 189.

[7]See the discussion in T. A. Acton, "The Social Construction of the Ethnic Identity of Commercial Nomadic Groups," in Joanne Grumet, ed., *Papers from the Fourth and Fifth Annual Meetings, Gypsy Lore Society, North American Chapter* (New York: Gypsy Lore Society, 1985), pp. 5–23.

[8] Ian Hancock, *We are the Romani People* (Hatfield, England: University of Hertfordshire Press, 2002), pp. 7–17.

[9]See Gropper, *Gypsies in the City*, pp. 1–16.

The Gypsies

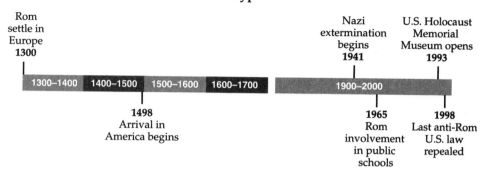

Rom settle in Europe 1300

Nazi extermination begins 1941

U.S. Holocaust Memorial Museum opens 1993

1300–1400 | 1400–1500 | 1500–1600 | 1600–1700

1900–2000

1498 Arrival in America begins

1965 Rom involvement in public schools

1998 Last anti-Rom U.S. law repealed

Some traditions of their origins in the India subcontinent remain among the Rom people, whether they are in Europe or the Americas. Gypsy music displays a musical scale maintained in India. The tribunal for dispute settlement, to be discussed later, is similar to that found among the traditional peoples of India. Gypsies often burn portions of a deceased's possessions with them, which continues to be practiced among some people of India. Even the practice of Gypsies shaking their head from side to side to signify "yes" is a gesture common in India. [10]

The Rom did not remain in Europe alone. The first Rom to come to America accompanied Columbus on his second voyage in 1498.[11] (See the Timetable above.)

Today there are Gypsies in practically every European country. They are also well established in North Africa, the Near East, South America, the United States, and Canada. [12]

As they spread throughout Europe, Gypsies came to be known as— above all else—travelers. "A Gypsy who does not keep on the move," wrote Block just prior to World War II, "is not a Gypsy."[13] Actually, the majority of Rom are sedentary Gypsies, or *Sinte*.

Nevertheless, *Sinte* or no *Sinte*, it was the horse-drawn wagons and gaily decorated caravans that seemed to strike a responsive chord in people of all ages. Jan Yoors, author of one of the most widely read

---

[10]Hancock, *We are the Romani People*, pp. 71–72.

[11]Hancock, "American Roma," p. 20.

[12]Some groups who are often thought of as Gypsies are not in fact true Gypsies, or Rom. These would include the Tinkers of Ireland and Scotland, and the Taters of Norway. The Irish Tinkers, for example, are of Celtic origin, and they speak Shelte, a Celtic dialect. In the present account, we are concerned only with the Rom. Frederik Barth, "The Social Organization of a Parish Group in Norway," in Farnham Rehfisch, ed., *Gypsies, Tinkers, and Other Travelers* (New York: Academic Press, 1975), pp. 285–89; and George Gmelch, *The Irish Tinkers* (Prospect Heights, IL: Waveland Press, 1985).

[13]Martin Block, *Gypsies: Their Life and Their Customs* (New York: Appleton-Century, 1939), p. 1.

books on Gypsy life, ran away as a young boy and lived for many years with a Gypsy group.[14] G. E. C. Webb, another writer, states that "for as long as I can remember, Gypsies have fascinated me. These dark-skinned strangers, indifferent to the rest of the world, mysterious in their comings and goings, traveling the roads with parades of highly colored raggedness, fired my imagination. I was curious about them and wanted to know more. But nobody, it seemed, could tell me more."[15]

Despite these characteristics described by Webb, Gypsies are not a uniform group but rather have cultural differences among them as one might expect, given geographical dispersion and isolation from others on the same continent. The continuing tendency of the *gadje* to maintain a belief in a uniform Gypsy image ironically helps to maintain an ethnic identity among Gypsies across time and distance.[16]

The Gypsy Paradox   There is no doubt that Gypsies fascinate the *gadje*, almost irrespective of the country involved. Novels, plays, operettas, movies, and songs have portrayed—and sometimes glorified—the romantic wanderings of the Gypsy vagabond. Popular pieces like "Gypsy Love Song" have become part of the worldwide musical repertoire.

Yet side by side with the attraction and fascination have come harassment and persecution. This is the Gypsy paradox: attraction on the one hand, persecution on the other. The climax of persecution came during World War II, when the Nazis murdered between a half-million and a million and a half Rom.

Even the Nazi plans to have a "Gypsy-free" Europe have received relatively little attention in history books. In Romani, the event is described as *O Baro Porrajmos,* or the "great devouring," of human life. In the post-war period, there were no relief efforts aimed specifically to assist the Rom survivors, as there were for other nationalities and Jewish refugees. However, finally by 1987, the U.S. Holocaust Museum was having special conferences to share available information about the "great devouring."[17]

Despite worldwide persecution, however, the Gypsies have managed to survive. Gypsies always survive. As Gropper puts it, "For 500 years Gypsies have succeeded in being themselves against all odds, fiercely maintaining their identity in spite of persecution, prejudice, hatred, and cultural forces compelling them to change. We may have something to learn from them on how to survive in a drastically changing world."[18]

---

[14]Jan Yoors, *The Gypsies* (New York: Simon & Schuster, 1967).

[15]G. E. C. Webb, *Gypsies: The Secret People* (London: Jenkins, 1960), p. 9.

[16] Brian A. Belton, *Questioning Gypsy Identity. Ethnic Narratives in Britain and America* (Walnut Creek, CA: AltaMira Press, 2005).

[17] Hancock, *We are the Romani People*, pp. 34–52.

[18]Gropper, *Gypsies in the City*, p. 1.

The Modern Period   Following World War II, urbanization and industrial-ization—together with population expansion—literally cramped the Gypsies' lifestyle. There was less and less room on the modern highway for horse-drawn caravans. Camping sites became harder to find, and the open countryside seemed to shrink. But—as always—the Gypsies adapted. Travel continued, albeit on a reduced scale. Caravans and wagons were replaced by automobiles, trucks, campers, and trailers. Somehow, by one method or another, the Rom managed to get by. And they did so without sacrificing their group identity or their freedom.

Their identity was not maintained without a price, however, for preju-dice and harassment continued. Gypsy nomads were often hounded from one locale to another. The *Sinte,* or sedentary Rom—whose proportion tended to increase—were also met by hostility and discrimination. No Gypsies Allowed signs came more and more to be posted in public places.

The issue was hardly one-sided. From the view of local authorities, Gypsies were using community services without paying their share of the taxes. Indeed, they were viewed as not paying any taxes at all. Additionally, the Rom were perceived as dirty, they would not use indoor toilets, they lied, they cheated, and they stole. Sometimes the charges were true; often they were unfounded. After all, when we are cheated, we say we are "gypped."

Fortunately, the Gypsies also had friends and supporters, and in a num-ber of countries efforts were made to set up camping sites, establish hous-ing facilities, provide legal assistance, and otherwise improve the lot of the Rom. By the 1970s, a number of national and international committees and councils had been organized—with Gypsy representation. The pur-pose of these groups has been not only to protect the interests of the Rom but to dispel stereotypes, combat false portrayals in the media, and act as a clearinghouse for information about Gypsies.

In 2005, eight central European states and a variety of international organizations launched the "Decade of Roma Inclusion." This declaration was to spearhead help but also to bring attention to the Rom as Europe's biggest and poorest minority.[19] In 2009, U.S. Secretary of State Hillary Clinton took the occasion of International Roma Day to call for an end to racial profiling, violence, discrimination, and their human rights abuses toward "Europe's largest ethnic group." In her prepared statement she recalled how as first lady in 1996 she had viewed firsthand the problem faced by the Rom in Eastern Europe.[20]

---

[19]"Europe's Roma: Poor and Unloved," *Economist,* February 5, 2005, p. 50, and David Mayall, *Gypsy Identities 1500–2000: From Egipcycans and Moon-men to the Ethnic Romany* (London: Routledge, 2004).

[20]"Secretary Clinton's Message on International Roma Day" at http://blog.state.gov.index .php/entires/internationa_roma_day/ and "U.S. First Lady in Hungary" at http://www.romnews.com/communityu/modules.php?op=modloadtname=newsoffile= articletside=80.

The Granger Collection, New York

The Roma presence in North America began through immigration from Europe. Here posing for a formal photograph is a group of Gypsies at the Ellis Island port of entry to the United States.

In some ways the Rom do indeed have a difficult life. Their relationship with the *gadje* often takes on the appearance of an interminable contest. At the same time, Gypsies often resist assimilation. They are demonstrably proud that they are Gypsies, an attitude that is unlikely to change.

How many Gypsies are there in the world today? Estimates vary from 9 to 15 million, with the latter figure probably being closer to the truth. (More than half are in Eastern Europe.) [21]

The United States   The first Gypsies to come to what is now the United States arrived in Virginia, Georgia, New Jersey, and Louisiana during the 1500s, although their fate remains unknown.[22] It is known that these early arrivals had been deported from various European countries—hardly an auspicious beginning. Significant numbers of the Rom, however, did not enter the United States until the 1880s and after.[23]

[21]The figure of 15 million Roms was offered by Indian Prime Minister Indira Gandhi at the 1983 International Romani Festival in Chandigarh, India (see http://romani.org).

[22]Ian F. Hancock, "Gypsies," in Stephen Thernstrom, ed., *Harvard Encyclopedia of American Ethnic Groups* (Cambridge, MA: Harvard University Press, 1980), p. 441.

[23]Gropper, *Gypsies in the City,* p. 18; Belton, *Questioning Gypsy Identity*, pp. 69–91.

Up until the 1930s, the Rom followed their traditional traveling and camping patterns, replete with horse-drawn vehicles and colorful caravans. By the 1930s, though—as was true in Europe—the caravan had generally given way to motorized transportation.

The depression of the 1930s saw another significant event insofar as the Gypsies were concerned: the election of Franklin Roosevelt and the introduction of large-scale relief and welfare programs. To take advantage of the situation, the Rom began to flock to the large cities, such as Chicago and New York.[24]

The extent to which they stayed in the cities—and later in the smaller towns—depended on such things as economic opportunities, welfare practices, and degree of police harassment. And because all three of these factors changed from time to time, the Gypsy population in a given city often fluctuated. Nevertheless, the Rom were in the cities to stay, and today there is, for example, an estimated population of 50,000 Gypsies in Los Angeles and 200,000 in California.[25]

Challenges to Studying the Rom

> If you ask a dozen Gypsies the same question, you will probably get a dozen different answers. If you ask one Gypsy the same question a dozen times, you will still probably get a dozen different answers.
>
> —*Anonymous*

Although there are many versions, this adage contains more than a little truth. Gypsies live—and always have lived—in alien cultures, that is, societies hostile to the Rom way of life. The boundaries between Rom and *gadje* are sharp, and the Rom have every intention of maintaining the sharpness. Deception, avoidance, misrepresentation, and lying are part of the Gypsies' arsenal, and they have had hundreds of years to perfect and embellish their defenses. In many ways, investigating the Rom is like trying to penetrate a secret society.

Perhaps the most formidable obstacle the researcher has to face is the avoidance syndrome. The Rom ordinarily do not mingle with the *gadje;* in fact, except for a possible visit to a fortune-teller, most Americans never come into contact with a Gypsy. Almost certainly they never see the inside of a Romani dwelling. Researchers face much the same problem. The fact that researchers are accredited university personnel means little to the Rom. Generally speaking, Gypsies have no intention of divulging their lifestyle and customs to social scientists or to anybody else.

---

[24] Gropper, *Gypsies in the City*, p. 20.
[25] Myrna Oliver, "John Merino: Leader in L.A. Gypsy Council Dies," *Los Angeles Times,* August 14, 1995, p. A12.

Fortunately, we have some excellent field studies, such as those by Anne Sutherland, Rena C. Gropper, and Isabel Fonseca.[26] These investigators not only are trained observers but spent several years among the Rom, learning the language and achieving a fair degree of acceptance. Yet even they experienced great difficulty in gaining rapport with their subjects.

There are difficulties that make it hard to *generalize* about Gypsy life. Practices of the Rom vary depending on their mobility patterns. Some Gypsies have lived in the same domicile for many years. Others move about constantly. Still others travel as the mood strikes them. And customs and lifestyle vary somewhat from one group to another.

Even if all Rom followed similar travel practices, their social structure would be difficult to analyze. Gypsies live in extended families, or *familiyi*, which form part of a larger kinship or cognatic group called the *vitsa* (to be discussed later). The point is that many Gypsy customs may vary from one *familia* to the next, and from one *vitsa* to the next, making it hard, again, to generalize.

One final factor complicates the study of American Rom: their customs often depend on their country of origin. The Romnichals (English Gypsies), for instance, differ from the Boyash (Romanian), and both groups are culturally different from the Arxentina (Gypsies from Argentina and Brazil).[27]

In brief, the Rom in the United States do not present a uniform culture pattern. Because of their kinship structure, their social and economic organization, their geographical mobility, and their nationality differences, it would be difficult to generalize about Gypsies even if they were cooperative—which they are not. (And even the "cooperative" Gypsies pose a problem for the researcher. The Rom often have a working knowledge of their own particular group—but no other. Very few Gypsies have anything like a broad view or a historical picture of their own people.)

Marimé

Central to any understanding of the Rom is their concept of *marimé*. It is *marimé* that is the key to their avoidance of the *gadje*, and it is *marimé* that serves as a powerful instrument of social control, as will be discussed later in this chapter.

Marimé means defilement or pollution, and as used by the Gypsies it is both an object and a concept. And because there is really no comparable

[26]Anne Sutherland, *Gypsies: The Hidden Americans* (New York: Free Press, 1975); Gropper, *Gypsies in the City*; and Isabel Fonseca, *Bury Me Standing: The Gypsies and Their Journey* (New York: Alfred Knopf, 1995). Fonseca's account of current-day Gypsy life in Eastern Europe helped to popularize a view of Gypsy identity (see Mayall, *Gypsy Identities*, pp. 33–35).

[27]See the discussion in Marcel Cortiade, "Distance between Romani Dialects," *Newsletter of the Gypsy Lore Society, North American Chapter* 8 (Spring 1985): 1ff.

term used by non-Gypsies, it is sometimes difficult for the latter to comprehend the meaning. *"Marimé,"* writes Miller, "extends to all areas of Rom life, underwriting a hygienic attitude toward the world. . . . Lines are drawn between Gypsy and non-Gypsy, the clean and the unclean, health and disease, the good and the bad, all of which are made obvious and visible through the offices of ritual avoidance."[28]

The most striking aspects of *marimé* have to do with the demarcation of the human body. The upper parts, particularly the head and the mouth, are looked upon as pure and clean. The lower portions, especially the genital and anal regions, are considered *marimé*. As the Rom see it, the upper and lower halves of the body must not "mix" in any way, and objects that come into contact with one half must not come into contact with the other.

There are countless examples of this hygienic-ritualistic separation. Ronald Lee, who is himself a Gypsy, writes that "you can't wash clothes, dishes, and babies in the same pan, and every Gypsy has his own eating utensils, towels, and soap. Other dishes and utensils are set aside for guests, and still others for pregnant women. Certain towels are for the face, and others for the nether regions—and there are different colored soaps in the sink, each with an allotted function."[29]

Marimé apparently originated in the early caravan period, when—for hygienic purposes—it was imperative that certain areas of the camp be set aside for cooking, cleaning, washing, taking care of body functions, and the like. Also, within the close confines of the wagons and tents, it was important that rules pertaining to sex be carefully spelled out and enforced. As is so often the case, however, over the years the various hygienic and sexual taboos expanded.[30]

Gropper states that "a woman is *marimé* during and after childbirth, and during her monthly period. . . . A *marimé* woman may not cook or serve food to men. She may not step over anything belonging to a man or allow her skirts to touch his things. Women's clothing must be washed separately from men's."[31]

Even such a natural phenomenon as urination may cause difficulties for the Rom. "One old lady called off a visit to a friend because she was indisposed and felt it would be too embarrassing to urinate frequently. Men often go outside to urinate rather than do so in their own homes, especially if guests are present."

[28]Carol Miller, "American Rom and the Ideology of Defilement," in Rehfisch, ed., *Gypsies*, p. 41.

[29]Ronald Lee, *Goddam Gypsy: An Autobiographical Novel* (Montreal: Tundra, 1971), pp. 29–30.

[30]Miller, "American Rom," p. 42. See also Elwood Trigg, *Gypsy Demons and Divinities* (Secaucus, NJ: Citadel, 1973), p. 64.

[31]Gropper, *Gypsies in the City,* pp. 92–93.

Interestingly and—given their conception of *marimé*—quite logically, Gypsy women attach shame to the legs rather than the breasts. Sutherland points out that it is shameful for a woman to have too much leg exposed, and that women who wear short skirts are expected to cover them with a sweater when they sit. On the other hand, "Women use their brassieres as their pocketbooks, and it is quite common for a man, whether he be the husband, son, father, or unrelated, to reach into her brassiere to get cigarettes or money. When women greet each other after a certain absence, they squeeze each other's breasts. They will also squeeze the breasts to show appreciation of a witty story or joke."[32]

Marimé vs. *Melalo*   Mention should be made of the distinction between *marimé* and *melalo*. *Marimé* is pollution or defilement, as just described. *Melalo* simply means dirty, or as Lee describes it, "dirty with honest dirt."[33] Someone who has not had a bath would be *melalo*, but not *marimé*. Hands that are dirty because of manual labor would be *melalo* rather than *marimé*—although they would be *marimé* if they had touched the genitals.

In actual practice, Gypsies tend to wash their hands many times a day—because they may have touched any number of objects or organs that are *marimé*. Miller states that "a working Rom also washes his face and hands whenever he feels his luck leaving him during the day; he washes again upon returning from his work."[34]

The distinction between *marimé* and *melalo* explains why a Gypsy domicile often appears dirty to a non-Gypsy—and vice versa. Some Rom dwelling places, for example, are anything but spic and span. Food scraps, cigarette butts, paper, wrappings—all may be thrown on the floor, presumably to be swept out later. Such a condition is not *marimé* so long as the proper rules of body hygiene, food preparation, and so forth are followed. As one writer puts it, "Americans tend to be shocked at visible dirt, but Gypsies abhor invisible pollution."[35]

The *Gadje:* Definition of the Situation   Not all of the Rom groups follow the same rules and procedures regarding *marimé*. There are also some variations among family groups. The Salos note that families who follow a strict observance pattern have a higher status than those who tend to be lax.[36] But there is one point on which all true Rom are agreed: the *gadje* are *marimé*. Miller writes:

[32]Sutherland, *Hidden Americans*. The quotations in this and the preceding paragraph are found on p. 266 and p. 264, respectively.
[33]Lee, *Goddam Gypsy*, p. 244.
[34]Miller, "American Rom," p. 47.
[35]Gropper, *Gypsies in the City*, p. 91.
[36]Salo and Salo, *Kalderasha*, p. 115.

The *gadje* are conceived as a different race whose main value is economic, and whose *raison d'être* is to trouble the Rom. The major offense of the *gadje,* the one offense that the Rom can never forgive, is their propensity to defilement. *Gadje* confuse the critical distinction between the pure and the impure. They are observed in situations which the Rom regard as compromising: forgetting to wash in public bathrooms; eating with the fork that they rescued from the floor of the restaurant; washing face towels and tablecloths with underwear at the laundromat; relaxing with their feet resting on the top of the table.

Because they do not protect the upper half of the body, the *gadje* are construed as *marimé* all over, head to foot. This condition, according to Rom belief, invites and spreads contagious disease. Rom tend to think of all illness and physical disability as communicable, and treat them accordingly.[37]

Because the *gadje* are *marimé,* relations with them are severely limited. In fact, Sutherland states that "interaction with the *gadje* is restricted to economic exploitation and political manipulation. Social relations in the sense of friendship, mutual aid, and equality are not appropriate." The same author goes on to say that "not only the person of non-Gypsies but items that come into contact with them are *marimé.* Any time a Rom is forced to use *gadje* places or to be in contact with large numbers of *gadje* (for example, in a job, hospital, welfare office, school), he is in constant danger of pollution. Public toilets are particularly *marimé* places, and some Rom go to the extent of using paper towels to turn faucets and open doors."[38]

These differences in the interpretation and implementation of *marimé* illustrate the sociological concept of the **definition of the situation.** Sociologist William I. Thomas coined the term to emphasize the importance of the way any given group views its own social reality. Specifically, this concept refers to people responding not only to the objective features of reality but also to their interpretation of it. If we accept that something is wrong or proper, we will act accordingly regardless of what others outside our group or society might think or believe. In Thomas's words, "What men define as real is real in its consequences."[39]

So Gypsies have defined the *gadje* as *marimé* and therefore as people to be avoided. In one celebrated case police searched the homes of two Gypsy families in Spokane, Washington, even searching babies' diapers, for alleged stolen goods. While all charges were dropped and the police paid a heavy cash settlement, the Rom households found that other Gypsies refused to visit them because the homes had been so defiled by the *gadje.*[40] Later we will consider the Amish, who view the automobile as something to be avoided, in the same way as the Gypsies view the *gadje* as an instrument of defilement.

---

[37]Miller, "American Rom," pp. 45–46.
[38]Sutherland, *Hidden Americans,* pp. 258–259.
[39]William I. Thomas, *The Unadjusted Girl* (Boston: Little Brown, 1927).
[40] For documentary treatment of this episode, review the motion picture *American Gypsy: A Stranger in Everybody's Land.* Find information at www.americangypsy.com.

Barrier to Assimilation   Do not the various rules and prohibitions in-volved in *marimé* impose a hardship on the Rom? In one sense, the answer is yes. The urban world, the Gypsies' major habitat, is seen as "pervasively *marimé,* filled with items and surfaces that are subject to use and reuse by careless *gadje,* polluted, diseased, and therefore dangerous." To avoid the danger, Gypsies must take any number of daily precautions—and there is no doubt that these precautions are time consuming and burdensome. Little wonder, as Miller points out, that "the home is the final bastion of defense against defilement, and the only place that the Rom feel altogether at ease."[41]

At the same time, *marimé* serves as an extremely effective barrier to assimilation. The so-called melting pot in America has boiled unevenly, with some groups being assimilated much faster than others. The Gypsies, of course, would fall at the lower end of any assimilation scale—which is just where they want to be. As the Rom see it, assimilation would be tantamount to group extinction.

Nowhere is this resistance to assimilation more apparent than in Gypsies' attitude toward the *gadje.* The belief that the *gadje* are *marimé* not only serves as a barrier to assimilation but acts as an ever-present sustainer of pride and self-respect. In fact, so pervasive is their negative attitude toward the *gadje* that Gypsies will not assimilate even after death! Nemeth's analysis of cemetery plots and tombstones revealed that the Rom attempt "to maintain distance in the graveyard between themselves and non-Gypsies, and between themselves and outcasts from their own society."[42]

Family and Social Organization

Gypsies maintain a rather complicated form of social organization, and it is sometimes difficult to unravel the various kinship and community net-works. It will simplify matters, however, if two points are kept in mind:

1. Gypsies are not loners. Their lives are spent in the company of other Gypsies. In fact, the term *individual Gypsy* is almost a contradiction in terms. In most of their communities, there are no single-person households, and no households of childless newlywed couples.[43]

2. The Rom are living in an alien culture, and they generally have little inten-tion of assimilating. They are keenly aware of their position, and they are determined to keep an ever-clear line between the *gadje* and themselves. Their social organization is designed to enhance the process of *boundary maintenance.*

[41]Miller, "American Rom," p. 47.
[42]David Nemeth, "Gypsy Taskmasters, Gentile Slaves," in Matt T. Salo, ed., *The American Kalderasha: Gypsies in the New World* (Hackettstown, NJ: Gypsy Lore Society, 1981), p. 31.
[43]Salo and Salo, *Kalderasha,* p. 39.

The *Familia* The heart of Gypsy culture is the *familia*. As Yoors points out, "The inner cohesion and solidarity of the Gypsy community lies in the strong family ties—which are their basic and only constant unit."[44]

The *familia,* however, is much larger and more complex than the American nuclear family. Whereas the latter is generally thought of as a husband-wife-children unit, the *familia* includes spouses, unmarried children, married sons and their wives and children, plus other assorted relatives and adopted youngsters. And because Gypsy couples often have six or more children, the *familia* may easily total thirty to forty members.[45] By the same token, because in many ways the Gypsy world is a man's world, the male head of the *familia* may wield considerable power.

The *familia,* then, appears to be an extended family, but it is actually more than that. Members live together (or close by); they often work together; they trust and protect one another; they celebrate holidays together; they take care of the sick and the aged; they bury the dead. The *familia,* in brief, is close to being a self-sufficient unit. One of the few functions it does not perform is that of matrimony, because marriages between first cousins are frowned upon.

Although the Rom believe in private property and free enterprise, ownership is often thought of in terms of the *familia* rather than the individual. Traditionally, as Clébert notes, "the essential nucleus of the Gypsy organization is the family. Authority is held by the father. . . . [P]roperty belongs to the family and not to the individual. But the family is not limited to the father, mother, and children. It includes aunts, uncles, and cousins."[46]

The *familia* is particularly effective as a *supportive institution.* Whether the problem is economic, social, political, or medical, the various family members unite in their efforts to provide aid. Should a police official, social worker, inspector, tax collector, or any other unwelcome *gadjo* appear on the scene, the intruder will be met with formidable—and generally effective—opposition. Should a family member fall ill, the *familia* will spare no expense in obtaining professional help, especially if it is a serious illness.

As hospital personnel can attest, a full-blown *familia* on the premises creates something of a problem. The Salos write that "illness, especially a terminal illness, requires the supportive presence at the hospital of the entire extended family. Hospitals often balk at the consequent waiting-room crowds."[47]

---

[44]Yoors, *Gypsies,* p. 5.
[45]For an interesting account of the *familia,* see Gropper, *Gypsies in the City,* pp. 60–66.
[46]Jean-Paul Clébert, *The Gypsies* (London: Vista, 1963), p. 129.
[47]Salo and Salo, *Kalderasha,* p. 19.

ZBIGNIEW BZDAK/MCT/Landov

A Polish priest leads a Chicago Roma family in 2007 in prayers in front of a picture of the Blessed Celefino Giménez Malla. A Romanian Roman Catholic lay leader, he is reverently remembered for giving up his life to save a priest during the Spanish Civil War in 1936. In 1997, he was made a saint.

The very structure of the *familia*, of course, creates some problems—housing and otherwise. Landlords do not take kindly to rentals involving a dozen or more persons. Noise, sanitation disposal, complaints by neighbors—all must be reckoned with. Also, by virtue of its size, the *familia* is cumbersome. It is one thing for a Gypsy couple to pack up and move; it is quite another for a large *familia* to "hit the road." And because the Rom obviously like to travel, the extended family presents a mobility problem.

Despite the problems involved, the Rom show few signs of abandoning the *familia*. On the contrary, they seem to thrive on it. In some cases, the size of the extended family has been reduced. In others, the married sons may form their own households. Nevertheless, the *familia* continues to be the center of the Gypsy world. As long as the *gadje* are seen in an adversary context, the *familia* will remain the Gypsies' principal bastion of security. [48]

Unlike all the other extraordinary groups discussed in this volume, the Gypsies are not distinguished from those around them by religious preferences or practices. Most Rom accept the religion of their host countries, which would typically mean some aspect of Christianity or Islam. These formal religious affiliations are supplemented by the traditional beliefs of *Marimé*.

[48]Hancock, *We are the Romani People*, pp. 59–61; Gulbun Coker, "Romany Rye in Philadelphia: A Sequel," *Southwestern Journal of Anthropology* 22 (1966): 98. See also Gropper, *Gypsies in the City*, pp. 60–66.

The *Vitsa* Whereas the *familia* can be thought of as an extended family, the *vitsa* is a kin group made up of a number of *familiyi*. Some Gypsiologists refer to the *vitsa* as a clan or a band, but the important point is that the Rom think of it as a *unit of identity*. Members of the Bimbalesti *vitsa*, for example, would identify with one another—feel a kindred relationship—even though they might all come together very infrequently.

Vitsi (plural of *vitsa*) vary in size from a few *familiyi* to a hundred or more households. Members of a smaller *vitsa* may live near one another and function as a group. The Rom have large families, however, and most *vitsi* tend to grow. The majority of American *vitsi*, therefore, function as a group on only two occasions: at a Gypsy court *(kris)* and at a death feast *(pomana)*, especially if the deceased has been a respected elder.

After a certain point, a *vitsa* may simply become too large, whereupon a split often takes place, usually along sibling or cousin lines. Sutherland cites the Minesti as an example of a large *vitsa* that has recently divided into several smaller *vitsi*.[49] The head of the *vitsa*, incidentally, is generally a respected male elder, although leadership problems do arise—and may be another reason for a *vitsa* to split.

Arranged Marriages and the Bride Price

Gypsies are one of the few groups in America who follow the old custom of arranged marriages. Indeed, such marriages seem to be a cornerstone of the Rom the world over. Matrimony is important to Gypsies, and they are reluctant to place their young people in Cupid's hands. This is not to say that the young are forced into marriage. Although Romani marriages may be arranged, the parents do not arbitrarily impose their will. However, parents do play a major role in the mate selection process, and the arrangements for the bride price, or *daro*, are entirely in their hands.[50]

Gypsy culture stresses the importance of group rather than individual activity. And as Gropper observes, "Marriage for the Rom is quite definitely more than a union of husband and wife; it involves a lifetime alliance between two extended families."[51]

Arranged marriages normally include a ***daro***, a payment by the groom's family to the bride's family. The actual figure varies from less than $1,000 to $10,000 or more. The higher the status of the young woman's *familia*, and the greater her personal attractiveness, the higher will be the asking price.

[49]Sutherland, *Hidden Americans*, pp. 82–83, 194.
[50]Hancock, *We are the Romani People*, p. 72
[51]Gropper, *Gypsies in the City*, p. 86.

Although a *daro* of several thousand dollars is quite common, part of the money is spent on the wedding festivities. The money is also used to pay for the bride's trousseau, to furnish the couple with household equipment, and so on. Additionally, part of the money may be returned to the groom's father, "as a sign of good will."[52]

Weddings themselves are private in that they involve neither religious nor civil officiants. They are, in a very real sense, Gypsy weddings, and are usually held in a rented hall. The festivities—involving ample food and drink—are fairly elaborate, and while formal invitations are not issued, all Gypsies in the community are welcome.[53]

The *daro* has traditionally served as a protection for the young wife. That is, if she should be mistreated by her husband or his *familia*, she can return home—whereupon the money might have to be forfeited.

Whether Gypsy wives are abused more than other wives is doubtful, but it is true that both sexes marry at a relatively young age. Marriages of eleven- and twelve-year-olds are known to occur, although the desired age range is between twelve and sixteen, and "not over 18 for a first marriage."[54] It seems likely, therefore, that many Gypsies are marrying under the legal age, although this fact would cause them no undue worry. The Rom are not overly concerned about marriage and divorce records, birth certificates, and other such documents.

While any two Rom can marry, most marriages involve partners from the same tribal grouping. Young people are also encouraged to marry within the *vitsa*, provided the relationship is not that of first cousin or closer. The Rom feel that by having their youth marry someone in the same *vitsa*—a second cousin, for example—the prospects for a happy marriage will be increased. *Vitsa* members not only have blood ties, but follow the same customs, have the same *marimé* proscriptions, and so forth.

The *Bori*   After the wedding, it is customary for the young wife to live with her husband's *familia*. She is now known as a **bori** and comes under the supervision of her mother-in-law, doing most of the housework.

Contrary to the culture pattern in the United States, Rom girls tend to be *older* than the boys they marry. As Sutherland explains, "It is important that the girl be older than the boy, since after marriage she must be able to perform her duties as a *bori* and make money for her husband; however, her husband need not take many responsibilities until he is fully mature."[55]

---

[52]Sutherland, *Hidden Americans*, p. 232.
[53]Gropper, *Gypsies in the City*, p. 158.
[54]Sutherland, *Hidden Americans*, p. 223.
[55]Sutherland, *Hidden Americans*, p. 223.

Despite the age difference, there is no doubt that many a *bori* has experienced genuine difficulties in adapting to her new role. More than occasionally, she simply gives up and returns to her own *familia*. In many instances, of course, the *bori* is treated well—as it is to everyone's advantage to have a smooth-running household.

The *bori*, naturally, is expected to bear children—lots of them. Birth-control measures apparently are not used. On the contrary, childless marriages are looked upon as a great misfortune.

Once in a great while the roles are reversed, and the boy lives with the girl's *familia*. This situation might occur because the boy was unable to meet the bride price, or because he possessed some undesirable physical or mental trait. Such a person is called a "house Rom," and because he is under the domination of his parents-in-law, he loses the respect of the other men in the community.[56]

Contemporary Changes   Although arranged marriages and the *daro* remain integral parts of Gypsy culture, the system may not be so rigid as it once was. Like society at large, the Gypsy world is witnessing increased freedom on the part of its young people. The Salos note, for example, that at one time young Gypsies were not permitted to date without chaperones being present, a custom that is now often disregarded.

Parents are paying more heed to their children's wishes, and romantic love seems to be gaining in popularity. John Marks concludes that "parents still arrange the marriage, but now some young people fall in love whereas they used to marry without ever seeing each other beforehand."[57] Premarital chastity on the part of the young woman, however, has always been highly regarded—and it remains so.

Elopements are reported to be increasing, and some of the young men "are willing to defend their wives against their mothers."[58] Some adults are openly critical of the traditional marriage system, although others stoutly defend it. Thus far, the number of families that have actually dispensed with the *daro* is relatively small.

Intermarriage   In spite of the above changes, one Gypsy custom has remained unaltered: the prohibition against marriages with the *gadje*. Because the *gadje* are *marimé*, intermarriage with them is also *marimé*. To repeat, this is the Gypsy *definition of the situation*, and they show no signs of relenting on the issue.

---

[56]Sutherland, *Hidden Americans*, p. 175.
[57]Quoted in Sutherland, *Hidden Americans*, p. 219.
[58]Gropper, *Gypsies in the City*, p. 163.

Despite the prohibition, such marriages do take place—much to the chagrin of the Gypsy community. When they do occur, it is usually a marriage between a Gypsy man and a *gadji* (non-Gypsy woman). The frequency of such marriages is a matter of debate. In her study of Barvale, California, Sutherland found that Rom-*gadje* marriages constituted only 5.5 percent of all Gypsy marriages, while a British study found the outmarriage rate there to be 26 percent.[59]

Lauwagie maintains, however, that the Rom-*gadje* intermarriage rate must be fairly high, and that significant numbers of Gypsies are shedding their Rom past and becoming part of the larger community. She argues that the Rom have a substantially higher birthrate than non-Gypsies, and that if this were not the case the Gypsy population would be much larger than it is.[60]

Yet any time intermarriage does occur, offspring and their descendants typically do shed their Rom past. Celebrities whose Gypsy ancestors are typically unknown to even their most ardent fans include actors Yul Brynner, Michael Caine, Charles Chaplin, and Tracy Ullman, as well as musicians Adam Ant and Rolling Stones guitarist Ron Wood. Elvis Presley's parents are both thought to be descendants from Rom in Germany in the eighteenth century. For the record, burlesque performer Gypsy Rose Lee, whose life was the basis of the musical "Gypsy," was born Rose Louise Hovich and has no known Rom roots.[61]

Lifestyle

Although generalizing about the lifestyle of any people is difficult, the Rom do have certain culture traits that set them apart from other groups. At or near the top of the list—and a trait that has been alluded to several times in the present account—is the Gypsies' indomitable love of freedom.

The Rom do not like to be tied down—by schools, businesses, material possessions, community affairs, financial obligations, or any other social or economic encumbrance. Their lifestyle reflects this predilection, and they are quite proud of it. Gypsies also associate freedom with fresh air and sunshine, a belief that goes back to the days of the caravan. In this earlier period, the Rom linked illness and diseases with closed spaces. Fresh air was believed to be a cure-all.

[59]Sutherland, *Hidden Americans*, p. 248; Belton, *Questioning Gypsy Identity*, p. 45.

[60]Beverly Nagel Lauwagie, "Ethnic Boundaries in Modern States: *Romano Lavo-Lil* Revisited," *American Journal of Sociology* 85 (September 1979): 310–37.

[61]A more detailed compendium of famous Rom can be accessed at http://www.imninalv.net/famousgypsies.htm.

Travel and Mobility   Nowhere is the Gypsy love of freedom more apparent than in their fondness for travel. The Rom may no longer be nomads, but they remain a highly mobile people.[62] One important reason for their mobility is the economic factor. While many Rom have a home base, job opportunities may arise elsewhere. Roofing, auto-body repair, carnival work, summer harvesting—all may require periodic travel. In at least some cases, overseas journeys are involved. The Salos report that "the dispersion of the Rom, coupled with an efficient system of communication provided by the *gadje*, allows them to be aware of economic conditions far afield. Some of the Canadian Gypsies have contacts in or first-hand knowledge of conditions in Ireland, Wales, England, Belgium, France, Yugoslavia, Greece, the United States (including Hawaii), Mexico, Australia, and South Africa."[63]

The Rom also travel for social reasons: to visit friends and family, to find a *bori* (bride), to celebrate Gypsy holidays, to attend weddings and death feasts. Illness is a special category, and Gypsies will travel long distances to be with a sick relative.

Predictably, the Rom frequently travel for tactical reasons: to avoid the police, social workers, school authorities, landlords, and the like. This sort of travel—coupled with common name changes—makes it exceedingly difficult for the authorities to track down and identify "wanted" Gypsies. In fact, during their travels, the Rom often pass themselves off as non-Gypsies.[64]

A final reason for travel—and an important one—is simply that Gypsies like to move about. It makes them feel better, both physically and mentally. The Rom associate traveling with health and good luck, and regard settling down as associated with sickness and bad luck.[65]

The Life Cycle   Gypsy children arrive in large numbers, and they are welcomed not only by their *familia* but by the entire Gypsy community. Although they are supposed to show respect for their parents, youngsters are pampered. As John Kearney points out, the maxim "Children should be seen and not heard" was surely never coined by a Gypsy.[66] Corporal punishment is used sparingly—and reluctantly. A Romani child is the center of attention, at least until the next one comes along.

In many ways, Gypsy children are treated like miniature adults—with many of the same rights. Their wishes are respected in much the same manner as those of adults.[67] Subservience and timidity are not highly regarded by the Rom—and children are encouraged to speak up.

[62]Ronald Lee, "Gypsies in Canada," *Journal of Gypsy Lore Society* (January–April 1967): 38–39.

[63]Salo and Salo, *Kalderasha*, p. 76.

[64]Carol Silverman, "Everyday Drama: Impression Management of Urban Gypsies," in Matt T. Salo, ed., *Urban Anthropology, Special Issue* 11 (Fall–Winter 1982): 382.

[65]Sutherland, *Hidden Americans*, pp. 51–52.

[66]John Kearney, "Education and the Kalderasha," in Salo, ed., *American Kalderasha*, p. 48.

[67]Gropper, *Gypsies in the City*, p. 130.

Gypsy children also spend much more time in adult company than do their non-Gypsy counterparts. This would almost have to be the case, because the Rom do not have much faith in formal education. While some government-funded Gypsy schools have been set up in various parts of the country, the Gypsy child's real training comes either at home or in what has been called "participatory education."[68] From the age of eight or nine, boys accompany their fathers on various work assignments, whereas the girls engage in household activities and start to observe fortune-telling routines.[69]

In Gypsy culture, both sexes tend to achieve higher status as they get older. A young man marries, matures, and has children. And as his children grow, his status increases. When he is ready and able to marry his youngsters off, his position in the community is generally secure.

As he grows older, he will be expected to solve family problems and settle altercations. He also acts as a repository for Gypsy traditions and culture. He will spend increasing time and energy "on the affairs of the band rather than on those of his own immediate family. He is becoming an Old One and a Big Man."[70]

A parallel sequence is followed in the case of the Gypsy female. As a young girl she is expected to assist in the housework. Later on—when she marries and becomes a *bori*—she is under the domination of her mother-in-law. But as she ages and has children of her own, she achieves a measure of independence and her status rises accordingly.

In many Gypsy communities, it is the woman rather than the man who deals with outsiders—school officials, social workers, and the like. And if she is successful in this regard, her position in the community becomes one of respect. She, too, is looked upon as a repository of wisdom, especially when it comes to dealing with the *gadje*.

Both sexes look forward to becoming parents, and both look forward to having grandchildren. The latter, it is said, signify true independence, for now the Old Ones have both their children and their children's children to look after them.

Gender Roles   Gender roles are society's expectations of the proper behavior, attitudes, and activities of males and females. These are learned either by observing what adults typically do or by being directed to certain activities or interests. The Rom have sharply defined gender roles. Indeed, Sutherland states that "the male-female division is the most fundamental in Rom society." The gender roles, furthermore, are characterized by separateness. Whether the occasion is a Gypsy function or simply day-to-day activity within the *familia*, men tend to gather on one side of the room,

---

[68]Barbara Adams, Judith Okely, David Morgan, and David Smith, *Gypsies and Government Policy in England* (London: Heinemann, 1975), p. 136.

[69]Gropper, *Gypsies in the City*, p. 138.

[70]Gropper, *Gypsies in the City*, p. 165.

women on the other. The Rom are great talkers, but unless a special situation arises, the conversation will probably not be a mixed one.[71]

This separateness extends even to the marital sphere. Except for having a sex partner and someone besides his mother to cater to his needs, the groom's lifestyle changes very little. "Gypsy marriage is not predicated on romantic love, and the Rom frown on any display of affection between husband and wife. The husband wants the wife to perform services for him, but he continues to spend much of his time with his brothers and cousins. Husband and wife rarely go out together."[72]

Occupationally, also, sex roles tend to be definitive. Women tell fortunes; men are responsible for the physical layout of the fortune-telling parlor. Women cook and take care of the household chores. Men are responsible for the acquisition and maintenance of transportation facilities. In many areas, the women bring in more money than the men. In fact, Mitchell claims that, economically, one Gypsy woman is worth ten men.[73] And while this may be an exaggeration, the women's income seems to be steadier and more reliable than the men's. It is the men, nevertheless, who normally hold the positions of power in the *familia*, the *vitsa*, and the *kumpania* (defined on next page).

Economic Organization

Gypsies have traditionally been involved in marginal and irregular occupations: horse-trading, scrap metal, fortune-telling, blacktopping (repairing driveways), auto-body repair, carnival work, and as musicians.

The Rom are quite willing to use banks, credit cards, charge accounts, and other appurtenances of a competitive economic system, but as a group they are loath to become involved in what they perceive to be the "rat race." Indeed, many Gypsies are quite adept at staying out of the race.

In his Chicago study, Polster found that the Gypsy men did not have steady jobs but worked only when they felt like it. In their Canadian investigation, the Salos concluded that the Rom saw work as a necessity and not as a goal or way of life. The same writers go on to say that "although the Gypsy is ingenious in adapting occupationally, the true commitment of each man is to earn the respect of his people. The pursuit of social prestige among his fellow Rom makes up a significant portion of his life. The Rom must be free to visit, gossip, politick, arrange marriages, and to undertake journeys connected with these activities. The earning of a livelihood is a secondary though necessary activity."[74]

[71]Sutherland, *Hidden Americans*, p. 149ff.
[72]Gropper, *Gypsies in the City*, p. 88.
[73]Joseph Mitchell, "The Beautiful Flower: Daniel J. Campion, *New Yorker*, June 4, 1955, p. 54.
[74]Gary Polster, "The Gypsies of Bunniton (South Chicago)," *Journal of Gypsy Lore Society* (January–April 1970): 142; Salo and Salo, *Kalderasha*, p. 93, also see p. 73.

The Rom face a number of economic and occupational handicaps. Many of their traditional pursuits have dried up. Horse-trading has long been defunct. Metalwork, a traditional Gypsy standby ("Kalderash" actually means "coppersmith"), has largely been taken over by factory methods. Carnival work has been steadily reduced.

The Rom are also penalized by their lack of formal education, because all of the professional occupations require college and graduate training. And finally, a number of jobs—plumber, nurse, certain kinds of hotel and restaurant work—are off-limits to the Rom because of their *marimé* proscriptions.

All things considered, the wonder of it all is not that Gypsies have failed to climb the economic ladder, but that they have adapted as well as they have. In fact, one could argue—as one writer does—that the Rom "fill a gap, albeit marginal, in the *gadje* system of production. They perform needed tasks, such as repair of shopping carts and seal-coating of driveways, that under usual economic conditions are too irregular or unprofitable to be attractive to larger, *gadje* economic enterprises."[75]

The *Kumpania* It is important to note that the Rom alone produce none of their own material needs. These must be procured from the *gadje*. And the procurement is often psychologically as well as materially rewarding: "Economic relationships of Rom with *gadje* are ideally exploitative. *Gadje* are by definition ignorant and foolish. The Rom value governing these relationships may be defined as 'living by one's wits.' The psychological satisfaction of 'putting one over' on the *gadje* is often, at least in anecdotal retrospect, valued even more highly than the actual profit made."[76]

According to Sutherland, "The *gadje* are the source of all livelihood, and with few exceptions the Rom establish relations with them only because of some economic or political motive." The same author points out that economic relations among Gypsies are based on mutual aid, and that they consider it immoral to earn money from other Gypsies. The only legitimate source of income is the *gadje,* and "skill in extracting money from them is highly valued in Rom society."[77]

The economic unit in this "extraction" process is not the *familia* or the *vitsa,* but the *kumpania,* a unionlike organization composed of all male Gypsies living in a particular town or city. An effective *kumpania* would determine the number of blacktopping businesses or fortune-telling establishments to be permitted in the area, whether licensing or political

---

[75]Beverly Nagel Lauwagie, "Explaining Gypsy Persistence: A Comparison of the Reactive Ethnicity and the Ecological Competition Perspectives," in Grumet, ed., *Papers,* p. 135.

[76]Matt T. Salo, "Kalderasha Economic Organization," in Salo, ed., *American Kalderasha,* p. 73.

[77]Sutherland, *Hidden Americans,* p. 65.

protection was necessary, and so on. Such a *kumpania* would have the power to keep out unaffiliated *familiyi*. A loose *kumpania* would lack such power. *Familiyi* could come and go at will, making for an untenable social and economic situation.[78]

The *kumpania* takes on added meaning when seen from the vantage point of Gypsy culture. As part of their effort to maintain a sharp boundary between themselves and the *gadje*, the Rom avoid working with non-Gypsies. If necessary, they will accept employment in a factory or commercial establishment, but this is not their normal practice. Typically, Gypsies operate in terms of *wortacha*, small work units consisting of adult members of the same sex. Thus, two or three men might engage in black-topping or auto-body maintenance. Women might work in small-sized groups doing door-to-door selling or fortune-telling.

Activities

Fortune-Telling   If there is one economic area that has been monopolized by the Rom, it is certainly fortune-telling. Indeed, the terms *Gypsy* and *fortune-teller* seem to go hand in hand—and with good reason.

> [A Rom] girl is expected to be a fortune-teller or reader and advisor, as early as thirteen or fourteen. Fortune-telling is regarded as an appropriate gender role and occupation among Gypsy women, and girls observe their mothers, aunts, and other female relatives performing this tradition every day.[79]

Fortune-telling is not a difficult occupation to learn, overhead expenses are negligible, and—depending on the location—business may be good. Clark cites an old Gypsy saying: "A fortune cannot be true unless silver changes hands."[80] And there have always been enough *gadje* who believe in this aphorism to make crystal gazing, palmistry, and card reading profitable ventures.

On occasion, Gypsy fortune-tellers have been accused—and convicted—of flimflam, or *bujo*. The *bujo* is nothing more than a swindle, whereby a gullible customer is cheated out of a goodly portion of his or her savings. One common ruse is called "switch the bag." In this instance, a bag of fake money or cut-up paper is substituted for a bag of real cash—which the customer had brought to the fortune-telling parlor in order to have the evil spirits or curse on it removed. (In Romany, *bujo* means "bag.") Obviously, these are unusual cases; in fact, many Rom frown on the *bujo* because it causes bad community relations and is likely to bring police action.[81]

---

[78]Sutherland, *Hidden Americans*, pp. 34–35.
[79]Ruth E. Andersen, "Symbolism, Symbiosis, and Survival: Roles of Young Women of the Kalderasha in Philadelphia," in Salo, ed., *American Kalderasha*, pp. 16–17.
[80]Clark, "Vanishing Vagabonds," p. 205.
[81]Mitchell, "Beautiful Flower," p. 46.

At the same time, the *bujo* has occurred often enough to cause many areas to outlaw fortune-telling. Many major cities in the United States, as well as most Canadian regions, have banned fortune-telling. Some observers feel that the illegalization of fortune-telling may be the Gypsies' biggest problem. (Interestingly enough, in 1985, the California Supreme Court, overruling a lower court decision, found that an ordinance prohibiting fortune-telling for profit violated the constitutional right to free speech.)

Legalities aside, the Rom continue to ply their trade, even though they are somewhat restricted in many areas. They often pose as "readers" and "advisors" rather than as seers. And this, in turn, may necessitate a measure of police "cooperation." But by one method or another, the Gypsies survive. Gypsies always survive.

Illegal Activities   What about serious crime—robbery, burglary, rape, murder, and so on—are the Gypsies not involved in these, also? The answer is yes and no. They are seldom involved in crimes of violence, such as assault, mugging, rape, and murder. Stealing is another matter, however, and the police are likely to have strong feelings on the subject.

The blunt fact is that law-enforcement officers who come in contact with them believe that an undue proportion of American Gypsies are engaged in theft. Hancock says that such thinking is as ridiculous as thinking that most every Gypsy is a gifted fiddler.[82] Nevertheless, the belief prevails. The Los Angeles police department actually has a "Gypsy crime investigator." Moreover, without any concern that the show could lead to a consensus boycott of sponsors, the popular network television program, *Criminal Minds* in 2009 aired an episode, "Bloodline," that showed Gypsy households engaged in kidnapping. It is probably impossible to think of another group so routinely characterized as criminal in nature both in fiction and by today's law-enforcement system.[83]

District attorneys and prosecutors are likely to take a similarly dim view of the Rom, for it is both difficult and exasperating to try to send Gypsies to jail. To the Rom, time spent in prison means breaking a variety of *marimé* proscriptions. Consequently, an individual Gypsy will go to almost any length to avoid an actual jail sentence.

Social Control

Romaniya—not an easy term to define—refers to the Gypsy way of life and view of the world. It embraces the Gypsies' moral codes, traditions,

---

[82]Hancock, "American Roma," p. 17; Hancock, *We are the Romani People*, pp. 94–97.

[83] Hector Becerra, "Gypsies: the Usual Suspects," *Los Angeles Times* (January 30, 2006, pp. A1, A2); "Synopsis for 'Criminal Minds'" at http://www.imdb.com/title/tt1256089/synopsis.

customs, rituals, and rules of behavior. *Romaniya* is that which the Gypsies consider to be right and acceptable.[84] It is the glue that holds their society together.

Romaniya is not a set of written rules, however. It is, rather, a built-in aspect of Gypsy culture. And because it is not a written code, the Rom face two problems: (1) Who determines what is and what is not *romaniya?* and (2) How should those who knowingly or unknowingly fail to comply be handled? These questions raise the whole issue of social control.

As used by sociologists, **social control** refers to techniques and strategies for preventing deviant human behavior in any society. **Informal social control** refers to social control that is carried out casually by ordinary people through such means as laughter, smiles, and rituals. **Formal social control** is social control carried out by authorized agents, such as police officers, judges, school administrators, and employers. Sociologically, informal control is considered more important than formal control because it is used all the time to maintain social control, and the Gypsies are a good case in point. The Rom have dispensed almost entirely with formal controls and rely largely on the informal variety.

Gossip, ridicule, and wisecracks, for example, are highly effective because the Rom are a closed society. Individual members cannot escape into anonymity—as is often the case in society at large. In any Gypsy community, therefore, reports and rumors of aberrant behavior lose no time in making the rounds.

Leadership: The *Rom Baro* In most groups, leadership serves as an important instrument of social control, but in this respect Gypsies are not so fortunate. The Rom are not known for their leadership qualities. For one thing, Gypsy leadership is a function of age; that is, the older one gets, the greater knowledge one has of *romaniya*—and knowledge of *romaniya* is a recognized source of power. Almost by definition, then, the Rom seldom have any young leaders.

Another drawback is the tendency for Gypsy leadership to be fragmented. Theoretically at least, each *familia*, each *vitsa*, and each *kumpania* has its own leader. And while there is some overlap—and some real harmony—there is also much bickering and infighting.

Leadership starts in the *familia*, where the head is known as a *phuro*. As the *phuro* ages and as his *familia* grows in size and strength, his standing in the community—and his power—increase accordingly. Should his judgment prove sound, should he show genuine interest in the various members of his *familia*, and should he prove effective in his dealings with

---

[84]Hancock, "Gypsies," p. 443.

the *gadje*, the *phuro* might become the leader of the *vitsa* or of a *kumpania*. He would then be known as a *Rom Baro* or "Big Man."

The Big Man has a dual function: to provide help and services for his followers, and to serve as a liaison with the non-Gypsy community, especially in a political sense. A Big Man rules by persuasion and discussion rather than by coercion, and should his persuasive powers fail, he may be replaced. Also, should he be convicted of a crime, his tenure as a *Rom Baro* may be terminated.

Although there are any number of Big Men in the Gypsy world, there really is no "King of the Gypsies," even though certain individuals often make the claim in order to ingratiate themselves with local authorities. For example, Silverman writes that the "status of King or Queen is invoked when securing hospital rooms or visiting privileges in funeral homes. One informant said: 'Any Gypsy who enters a hospital is automatically a King. They get better treatment. . . . There's no such animal in the Gypsy race as a King. But you go to the newspaper morgues in New York and get old papers, and every time a Gypsy died he was King. There has got to be 1,000 Kings.'"[85]

The most famous (or infamous) American Gypsy leader in modern times was Tene Bimbo, *Rom Baro* of the Bimbulesti *vitsa*. Tene Bimbo pursued power from coast to coast, and in the process he was reportedly arrested 140 times—for everything from petty larceny to murder! "If there are any charges that have not been brought against Tene Bimbo," one newspaper reported, "it is probably just an oversight."[86]

Tene Bimbo died in 1969 at the age of eighty-five, and there has been no *Rom Baro* like him since that time—and there probably never will be. Although his descendants speak fondly of him, and liken him to a modern Robin Hood, most Gypsies are glad that he is no longer on the scene. They feel that he brought unwanted notoriety to the Rom and was responsible for a distorted view of the Gypsy world. (Peter Maas's *King of the Gypsies* was based on the struggle for power that erupted after Tene Bimbo's death.)

The most famous (or infamous) European Gypsy leader in modern times was Ion Cioaba, who "proclaimed himself King of All Gypsies Everywhere but wielded most of his meager influence as a political gadfly in his native Romania . . ."[87] He died in 1997 at the age of sixty-two.

In 1992, he held a coronation ceremony attended by 5,000 Gypsies and a bemused press. At the ceremony, he wore a solid gold crown weighing

[85]Carol Silverman, "Negotiating 'Gypsiness': Strategy in Context," *Journal of American Folk-Lore* 101 (July–Sept. 1988): 261–75.

[86]Cited in Maas, *King of the Gypsies*, p. 4.

[87]Robert Thomas, Jr., "Ion Cioaba, 62, of Romania, Self-Styled King of All Gypsies Dies," *New York Times*, February 27, 1977, Sec. B, p. 10.

13 pounds. Because Gypsies do not regulate who can or can't be royalty, it took only a few months for a rival Gypsy to set himself up as Emperor of All Gypsies.

Thomas described Cioaba as "a portly man who usually shunned traditional Gypsy costumes in favor of a blue business suit, became an outspoken advocate of Gypsy rights, although rarely with much success. For example, he demanded that Germany stop the deportation of Gypsies to Romania and he sought reparations for the thousands of Gypsies who died in the holocaust."[88]

Marimé as Social Control   Although Gypsy leadership may or may not be an effective source of social control, *marimé* has traditionally been a powerful instrument. Indeed, it may just be the most important factor in keeping the Rom in line. The reason is not hard to find, for *marimé* is more than a simple declaration that a person or thing is polluted. A Gypsy who has been declared *marimé* is ostracized by the entire group. Other Rom will have nothing to do with him or her.

Within the confines of their own society, Gypsies are gregarious. They are never really alone. Practically all of their waking moments are spent in the company of other Rom. Talking, laughing, working, arguing, gossiping, and, most important perhaps, eating—all are considered group activities. To be declared *marimé*, therefore, effectively cuts a Gypsy off from the very roots of his existence. He brings shame not only upon himself but upon his family.

Sutherland writes that *marimé* "in the sense of being rejected from social intercourse with other Rom is the ultimate punishment in the Gypsy society, just as death is the ultimate punishment in other societies. For the period it lasts, *marimé* is social death."[89] A permanent *marimé* sentence is not only the most severe form of Gypsy punishment, but if there is no way to win reinstatement, the person involved may actually prefer to end his life by suicide.[90]

The *Kris*   Fortunately for the Rom, *marimé* need not be permanent. Accused Gypsies have the right to a trial to determine whether they are guilty as charged. As used by the Rom, *kris* refers to their system of law and justice, for they do not generally use the legal system of the *gadje.*

---

[88]Thomas, "Ion Cioaba," p. 10. Perhaps Cioaba and activists like him were more effective than previously supposed. It was announced that Germany had created a $1.7 billion fund to compensate victims of the holocaust. The settlement was pressed for by Jewish interest groups. Germany's chancellor, Gerhard Schröder, announced, however, that Gypsies would share in the fund.

[89]Sutherland, *Hidden Americans*, p. 98.

[90]Gropper, *Gypsies in the City*, p. 100.

The *kris* consists of a jury of adult Gypsies, presided over by an impartial judge. Certain judges, or *krisatora*, are known for their wisdom and objectivity and are in great demand.[91] No judge, however, will accept a case unless the litigants agree beforehand to abide by the verdict. In addition to allegations involving *marimé*, *kris* cases include disputes over the bride price, divorce suits, feuds between *vitsi*, allegations of cheating, and competition over fortune-telling.

A *kris* is convened only for serious reasons, because Gypsy trials are time consuming—and expensive. Personnel may come from other parts of the country, and it may be necessary to use a rented hall. In a lengthy trial, "courtroom" supplies may include food and liquor, payment for which must be made by the guilty party.[92]

Because of these factors, a *kris* is not likely to be held until all other attempts at adjudication have failed. Ordinary disputes, for example, may be settled by the *Rom Baro* or by informal debate. And even if these efforts should fail, a *divano*—a public discussion by concerned adults—can be requested.

Is the *kris* an effective instrument of social control? It is hard to say. In most cases, probably yes—but there is a built-in weakness to the system. Presumably, the disputants agree beforehand to abide by the decision. If they do not, theoretically at least, they have no recourse but to leave the Gypsy world. In the last analysis, however, what can really be done with Gypsies who refuse to obey their own laws? As Acton observes, "It is difficult today for any Gypsy group larger than the extended family to exert effective sanctions on their members."[93] Yoors puts it as follows: "The *kris*, or collective will of the Rom, is a structure in flux. . . . The effectiveness of the pronouncements of the judges depends essentially on the *acceptance of their decisions by the majority of the Rom*. There is no direct element of coercion to enforce the rule of law. The Rom have no police force, no jails, no executioners."[94]

[91]In August 1995, John Merino, perhaps the best-known *krisatora*, died in Los Angeles. A third-generation California Gypsy, Merino headed a twelve-member *kris* that meets twice monthly to settle disputes. Merino, a real estate investor and manager, was also captain of the Hawthorn police reserves. He said he wanted his life to send a message "to my people that it is possible to remain a Rom within that rich culture and heritage and yet be accepted in American society." Merino had attended El Camino College. (Oliver, "John Merino," p. A12.)

[92]Gropper, *Gypsies in the City*, pp. 81–102; Hector Becerra and Richard Winton, "Firebombing Linked to Gypsy Feud," *Los Angeles Times*, April 24, 2008, pp. B1, B5; David J. Nemeth, *The Gypsy-American—An Ethnographic Study* (Lewiston, New York: Edwin Mellen, 2002), pp. 109–22.

[93]Thomas Acton, *Gypsy Politics and Social Change* (London: Routledge & Kegan Paul, 1974), p. 99.

[94]Yoors, *Gypsies*, p. 174. (Italics added.)

Prejudice and Discrimination

Prejudice and discrimination are realities that virtually all Gypsies must learn to face—and live with. Prejudice and discrimination are related concepts, but scholars differentiate between them. **Prejudice** is a negative attitude toward an entire category of people. However, discrimination is an action. **Discrimination** is the denial of opportunities and equal rights to individuals and groups because of prejudice or for other arbitrary reasons.

The sad fact is that the Rom have been persecuted in practically every country they have ever inhabited. As was mentioned, the Nazis murdered hundreds of thousands during World War II. Entire *vitsi* were wiped out. Furthermore, Kenrick and Puxon note that during the many months of the Nuremberg war crimes trial, not a single Gypsy was ever called as a witness.[95] Nor was any monetary restitution ever made to the surviving Romani groups.

In 1979, President Jimmy Carter formed the U.S. Holocaust Memorial Council; its purpose was to establish a lasting memorial to all those who suffered and died in Hitler's death camps. It was not until 1987 that a Gypsy was invited to sit on the sixty-five-member council. In a report from the commission to President Carter, "the word Gypsy appears just once, along with Poles, Soviet prisoners of war, Frenchmen, Serbs and Slavs as 'others,' in an appendix. The total number of Romani dead is now estimated to be some 600,000. While this amounts to a tenth of the number of Jewish victims, in terms of the genocide of an entire people, the proportions are nevertheless similar."[96]

Eventually when the U.S. Holocaust Memorial Museum opened in 1993, a Gypsy wagon found in Czechoslovakia was included, as well as a violin of a Gypsy musician who was executed by the Germans and a traditional Gypsy woman's dress. Initial concerns about ignoring the tragedy of the Roma were addressed by various references to the lost.[97]

Although the wholesale slaughter ceased with the downfall of Hitler, Gypsies' problems with prejudice and discrimination continue in both Western and Eastern Europe. Nevertheless, before the fall of the Berlin Wall, Communist bloc states provided a measure of protection for their Gypsy populations.

Since the fall of the Berlin Wall, Gypsies have, perhaps, suffered more than any other group in Europe. For example, in response to hostility in

---

[95]Kenrick and Puxon, *Destiny of Europe's Gypsies*, p. 189.

[96]Ian F. Hancock, *The Pariah Syndrome: An Account of Gypsy Slavery and Persecution* (Ann Arbor, MI: Karoma, 1988), p. 81.

[97]Jeshajahu Weinberg and Rina Elieli, *The Holocaust Museum in Washington* (New York: Rizzoli, 1995).

Romania, many Gypsies did what Gypsies often do: they moved. Of the 91,000 Romanians seeking entrance into Germany during an eight-month period in 1991, 91 percent were Gypsies. The total number choosing Germany as a destination now nears half a million.[98]

For the most part Gypsies are unwanted anyplace in Europe. They serve as scapegoats, often the victims of skinhead and neo-Nazi violence. Their homes are torched. They are occasionally murdered. Even in the Czech Republic, the state purported to have had the smoothest transition from a totalitarian to a democratic structure, significant anti-Gypsy sentiment exists.

While organized anti-Rom feeling has been limited in the United States, it has not been absent. It wasn't until 1998 that New Jersey repealed its anti-Rom law adopted in 1917. This is thought to be the last such measure on the books in the United States.[99]

In Europe especially, Gypsy communities are always viewed as substandard.[100] Such thinking is at the heart at what sociologists define as ethnocentrism. **Ethnocentrism** is the tendency to assume that one's own culture and way of life represent the norm or are superior to all others. In one community, Czech citizens persuaded city government to build a 15-foot wall between their housing and a Gypsy settlement across the street. The mayor of Usti Nad Labem does not apologize for the decision (now on hold owing to the intervention of civil rights groups). "This wall is about one group that obeys the laws of the Czech Republic and behaves according to good morals, and about a group that breaks these rules—doesn't pay rent, doesn't use proper hygiene and doesn't do anything right. . . . This is not a racial problem, it is a problem of dealing with decent and indecent people." The wall was eventually dismantled soon after it was built after pressure by civil rights groups.[101]

The treatment of the Roma in Europe has led to celebrities like the actor Ethan Hawke to speak out on their behalf. The singer Madonna has auctioned personal belongings to a charity supporting Gypsy child education. She drew international attention by speaking in 2009 during her "Sticky and Sweet" concert tour in Bucharest, Romania—the country with

[98]Zoltan D. Barany, "Living on the Edge: The East European Roma in Postcommunist Politics and Societies," *Slavic Review* 53 (Summer 1994): 340.

[99]"The Religion and Culture of the Roma," accessed February 17, 2005, at www.religioustolerance.org/roma.htm.

[100]Henry Kamm, "Gypsies Find No Welcome from Czechs," *New York Times*, December 8, 1993, p. A7 (N).

[101]Jane Perlez, "A Wall Not Yet Built Casts the Shadow of Racism," *New York Times*, July 2, 1998, Sec. A, p. 4; BBC News, "Czech court backs anti-Gypsy wall," April 12, 2000, accessed April 29, 2010 at http://news.bbc.co.uk/2/hi/europe/711211.stm.

the largest Gypsy population. Her concert remarks were largely booed by the thousands present.[102]

Gypsies continue to be seen as totally responsible for their problems, whether it be poverty or the educational challenges their children face. Any shortcomings lying in the larger society are ignored. Sociologists call this "blaming the victim." **Blaming the victim** is portraying the problems of racial, ethnic, and other groups as their fault rather than recognizing society's responsibility. [103]

Among the negative charges aimed at Gypsies worldwide is that they are too generous with their money, harbor strong solidarity, and exhibit loyal family ties whether defined by the immediate family or the broader family group. Yet are these truly negative attitudes?

Sociologists often use the term **in-group,** which refers to a group or category to which people feel they belong, in contrast to the **out-group,** a group to which people feel they do not belong. An in-group is generally characterized by the loyalty, like-mindedness, and compatibility of its constituents. Members refer to the in-group as "we," and the out-group as "they."

Being critical of others for traits for which you praise members of your own group is an example of in-group virtues becoming out-group vices. Sociologist Robert Merton described how proper behavior by one's own group becomes unacceptable when practiced by outsiders. Being family-oriented and having strong kinship ties is typically applauded but when practiced by a group like Gypsies regarded as outsiders it is resented.[104]

Gypsies in the United States continue to face prejudice and discrimination. As already discussed, Gypsies are often viewed as criminal by both the general public and law enforcement. In 2010, Richard Schaefer was told by a woman living in suburban Portland, Maine, that she had begun locking her house because the "Gypsies were coming." A few years earlier, managers of large discount stores in rural areas of Illinois told Schaefer numerous times that they will telephone managers at stores in nearby towns that "Gypsies are on the way."

Why does the persecution continue? Some observers contend that it is a matter of ethnic prejudice, similar to that experienced by African Americans, Latinos, and certain immigrant groups. Others, however, simply feel that the Rom are perceived as nonproductive troublemakers. As one police official put it, "They're nothing but economic parasites." The truth

---

[102] See speech at http://www.hiphopmusic.com/best_of_youtube/2009/08/madonna _gypsies_speech_booed_in_romaniavideo.html.

[103] William Ryan, *Blaming the Victim*, rev. ed. (New York: Random House, 1976).

[104] Robert K. Merton, *Social Theory and Social Structure* (New York: Free Press, 1968); Peter Szuhay, "Arson on Gypsy Row," *Hungarian Quarterly* v36 (Summer 1995): 83.

of the matter can be debated, but that is beside the point. If people *perceive* Gypsies as nonproductive dissidents, then unfortunately for all concerned, prejudice and discrimination might be looked on as justifiable retaliation.

Adaptability: The Rom Trademark

Whether the Rom spend much time thinking about the causes of discrimination is doubtful. Being realists, they expect it. And being Gypsies, they learn to live with it. In fact, being Gypsies, they learn to live with a great many things they do not like or agree with. This, indeed, is the Gypsies' trademark: adaptability.

In addition to coping with discrimination, Gypsies have also had to adapt to a vast panorama of social change. Times change, customs change, governments change—sometimes it seems that nothing is permanent— but whatever the transformation, the Rom seem to make the necessary adjustments. They adapt without losing their cultural identity.

Examples of their adaptation are numerous. Gypsies have long since discarded the Hindu faith of their origins in India. In all their wanderings and migrations, they have simply adapted to the religion—or religions— of the host country. The same is largely true of clothing styles, although as Polster observes, Gypsy women often do wear colorful outfits.[105] And aside from a seeming fondness for spicy dishes, the Rom adapt to the foods and cuisine of the country or area they are living in.

During the days of the caravan, Gypsy nomads camped outside the towns and cities—off the beaten track. When changing conditions forced them from the road, they took to the cities, where they have adapted rather well. Today, most of the American Rom are to be found in urban areas.

When horses were replaced by mechanized transportation, the Rom adapted. Instead of being horse-traders, they learned auto-body repair and motor maintenance. When metalworking—long a Gypsy specialty— was superseded by factory-type technology, the Rom turned to roofing and blacktopping. When fortune-telling became illegal in various places, Gypsies became "readers" and "advisors."[106]

Some Gypsies manage to do well even when they are not "making a living." Despite their literacy handicap, and despite their unfamiliarity with (and disdain for) documentary records, they have learned to adapt to the welfare bureaucracy with—in many cases—remarkable results.

---

[105]Polster, "Gypsies of Bunniton," p. 139.
[106]*American Gypsy: A Stranger in Everybody's Land,* directed by Jasmine Dellal, 1999.

The Future

What does the future hold for the Rom in the United States? Not even a Gypsy with a crystal ball can tell. It is possible, nevertheless, to make some educated guesses.

To begin with, Gypsy activism will probably increase—somewhat. On the international scene, meetings such as the World Romani Congress have had some success in focusing attention on Gypsy problems. Two notable efforts resulted. Gypsies were included in billion-dollar settlements with Swiss banks and German industries guilty of using slave labor during the Holocaust. In the United States, the American Gypsy Organization and other groups have also been established. Such organizations cannot help but have a positive effect on Gypsy–*gadje* relations.[107]

At the same time, Gypsy activism has inherent limits. The American Rom are a low-profile group. They are often difficult to find, let alone activate! They have traditionally resorted to travel and avoidance rather than organization and demonstration. Mass protest, for example—often used by other minorities—would hardly strike a responsive chord in most Gypsy communities.

Looking ahead, the widespread illiteracy that has characterized the Rom will most likely be reduced—somewhat. Schools for Gypsy youngsters have been set up in California; Washington, D.C.; Philadelphia; Chicago; Seattle; and Camden, New Jersey. The trend may continue. As Hancock points out, however, failures have thus far outnumbered successes, and "the majority of Gypsies remain opposed to schooling of any kind."[108]

Assuming that their illiteracy rate is reduced, the position of the Rom in the job market should also improve—somewhat. Even now, there are Gypsies to be found in white-collar and professional positions. Their number is relatively small, however, for the Rom have scarcely penetrated the realm of college and graduate education.

Still, looking ahead, relations between the Rom and the *gadje* may improve—somewhat. In many ways, American Gypsies have cut themselves off from the economic rewards of the larger society. To partake of these rewards they will probably have to change their attitude toward the *gadje,* and the extent to which they will do this can only be conjectured.

The Rom may also soften the rules pertaining to *marimé*—somewhat. In certain Gypsy communities, these rules have already been softened, and if the trend continues, improvements in the relations with the larger society may be one of the by-products. At the same time, most Rom know full well that the concept of *marimé* lies at the heart of the Gypsy world.

---

[107]Hancock, "Gypsies," pp. 444–45; Hancock, *We are the Romani People.*
[108]Hancock, "Gypsies," p. 444.

Without *marimé,* social control would be difficult to maintain. Whether any further erosion of the rules will occur, therefore, remains to be seen.

To sum up, any changes in the Gypsy way of life, or in *romaniya,* will be moderate rather than drastic. The Rom are keenly aware of what they are and who they are—and they are proud of it. And while they may make some changes that will improve their adaptation to the larger society, they will probably not become a functioning part of that society. They will not assimilate. They will not give up their unique identity. They will not renounce their culture. Thus, in all probability they will continue to feel the twin prongs of discrimination and harassment, albeit on a reduced scale.

Exactly how much change the Rom will allow—or what form these changes will take—is debatable. But one thing seems certain: the Gypsies will survive. Gypsies always survive.

KEY TERMS

Assimilation, p. 2
Blaming the victim, p. 33
Bori, p. 18
Counterculture, p. 3
Daro, p. 17
Definition of the situations, p. 13
Discrimination, p. 31
Ethnocentrism, p. 32
Familia, p. 15
Familiyi, p. 10
Formal social control, p. 27
Gadje, p. 3

Gender roles, p. 22
Informal social control, p. 27
In-group, p. 33
Kris, p. 29
Marimé, p. 10
Melalo, p. 12
Out-group, p. 33
Prejudice, p. 31
Romaniya, p. 26
Social control, p. 27
Social distance, p. 3
Vitsa, p. 16

SOURCES ON THE WEB

www.errc.org
The European Roma Rights Centre, based in Hungary, is dedicated to combating anti-Roma discrimination and abuse.

http://romani.org
This website is dedicated to the Rom and their recognition as a people and as a nation.

http://www.gypsyloresociety.org
An international association of persons interested in Gypsy and Traveler Studies; founded in Great Britain in 1888.

www.soros.org/initiatives/roma
A variety of Rom-related initiatives in Europe are outlined at this Web site.

http://www.photomythology.com/
A photo essay of the Rom from California to Italy.

SELECTED READINGS

Andersen, Ruth E. "Symbolism, Symbiosis, and Survival: Role of Young Women of the Kalderasha in Philadelphia." In *The American Kalderasha: Gypsies in the New World*, edited by Matt T. Salo, pp. 11–28. Hackettstown, NJ: Gypsy Lore Society, 1981.
Beck, Sam. "The Romanian Gypsy Problem." In *Papers from the Fourth and Fifth Annual Meetings, Gypsy Lore Society, North American Chapter*, edited by Joanne Grumet, pp. 100–109. New York: Gypsy Lore Society, 1985.
Belton, Brian A. *Questioning Gypsy Identity: Ethnic Narratives in Britain and America*. Walnut Creek, CA: AltaMira Press, 2005.
Clark, Marie Wynne. "Vanishing Vagabonds: The American Gypsies." *Texas Quarterly* 10 (Summer 1967): 204–10.
Clébert, Jean-Paul. *The Gypsies*. London: Vista, 1963.
Cortiade, Marcel. "Distance between Romani Dialects." *Newsletter of the Gypsy Lore Society, North American Chapter* 8 (Spring 1985): 1ff.
Dodds, Norman. *Gypsies, Didikois, and Other Travelers*. London: Johnson, 1976.
Fonseca, Isabel. *Bury Me Standing: The Gypsies and Their Journey*. New York: Knopf, 1995.
Friedman, Victor A. "Problems in the Codification of a Standard Romani Literary Language." In *Papers from the Fourth and Fifth Annual Meetings, Gypsy Lore Society, North American Chapter*, edited by Joanne Grumet, pp. 55–75. New York: Gypsy Lore Society, 1985.
Gmelch, George. *The Irish Tinkers*. Prospect Heights, IL: Waveland Press, 1985.
Gropper, Rena C. *Gypsies in the City*. Princeton, NJ: Darwin, 1975.
Hancock, Ian F. *The Pariah Syndrome: An Account of Gypsy Slavery and Persecution*. Ann Arbor, MI: Karoma, 1988.
_____.*We are the Romani People*. Hertfordshire, England: University of Hertfordshire Press, 2002.
Kearney, John. "Education and the Kalderasha." In *The American Kalderasha: Gypsies in the New World*, edited by Matt T. Salo, pp. 43–54. Hackettstown, NJ: Gypsy Lore Society, 1981.
Lee, Ronald. *Goddam Gypsy: An Autobiographical Novel*. Montreal: Tundra, 1971.
Lockwood, William G. "Balkan Gypsies: An Introduction." In *Papers from the Fourth and Fifth Annual Meetings, Gypsy Lore Society, North American Chapter*, edited by Joanne Grumet, pp. 91–99. New York: Gypsy Lore Society, 1985.
Maas, Peter. *King of the Gypsies*. New York: Viking, 1975.
Marre, Jeremy, and Hannah Charlton. *Beats of the Heart*. New York: Pantheon, 1985.

Mayall, David. *Gypsy Identities 1500–2000: From Egipcyans and Moon-men to the Ethnic Romany.* London: Routledge, 2004.

Nemeth, David. *The Gypsy-American: An Ethnographic Study.* Lewiston: Edwin Mellen Press, 2002.

Okely, Judith. *The Traveler Gypsies.* New York: Cambridge University Press, 1982.

Pippin, Roland N. "Community in Defiance of the Proscenium." In *The American Kalderasha: Gypsies in the New World,* edited by Matt T. Salo, pp. 99–133. Hackettstown, NJ: Gypsy Lore Society, 1981.

Polster, Gary. "The Gypsies of Bunniton (South Chicago)." *Journal of Gypsy Lore Society* (January–April 1970): 136–51.

Rehfisch, Farnham, ed. *Gypsies, Tinkers, and Other Travelers.* New York: Academic Press, 1975.

Salo, Matt T., ed., *The American Kalderasha: Gypsies in the New World.* Hackettstown, NJ: Gypsy Lore Society, 1981.

Salo, Matt, and Sheila Salo. *The Kalderasha in Eastern Canada.* Ottawa: National Museums of Canada, 1977.

Silverman, Carol. "Everyday Drama: Impression Management of Urban Gypsies." In Matt T. Salo, ed., *Urban Anthropology, Special Issue* 11 (Fall–Winter 1982): 377–98.

Sutherland, Anne. *Gypsies: The Hidden Americans.* New York: Free Press, 1975.

Tong, Diane. "Romani as Symbol: Sociolinguistic Strategies of the Gypsies of Thessaloniki." In *Papers from the Fourth and Fifth Annual Meetings, Gypsy Lore Society, North American Chapter,* edited by Joanne Grumet, pp. 179–87. New York: Gypsy Lore Society, 1985.

Yoors, Jan. *The Gypsies.* New York: Simon & Schuster, 1967.

_____. *Crossing: A Journal of Survival and Resistance in World War II.* New York: Simon & Schuster, 1971.

_____. *The Gypsies of Spain.* New York: Macmillan, 1974.

CHAPTER TWO

THE OLD ORDER AMISH

- Early History
- ". . . A Peculiar People"
- The Farmstead
- Leisure and Recreation
- Religious Customs
- Sanctions

- Courtship and Marriage
- Family
- Education and Socialization
- Challenges Facing the Amish
- The Future

The Amish are descendants of the sixteenth-century Swiss Anabaptists. **Anabaptists** is a general term that was applied to those who rejected infant baptism practiced by Roman Catholics and early Protestants. They advocated "believer" baptism or, in other words, baptism by consenting adults, which was a crime in the sixteenth century. Many of the Swiss Anabaptists came to be known as Mennonites because of the strong leadership of Menno Simons. In this sense, the Amish are a branch of the Mennonites, and the two groups have much in common, especially in a historical sense.[1]

Menno Simons was born in 1492 in the Netherlands. He was ordained a Roman Catholic priest, but broke with the church and eventually formed his own movement. His teachings included separation of church and state, adult baptism, and refusal to bear arms or take oaths. He died in 1561.

Although space does not permit an analysis of Menno Simons's theological and secular beliefs, one point should be mentioned. He was a firm believer in the *Meidung*—the shunning or avoidance of excommunicated members. It was the *Meidung* controversy that eventually led to the formation of the Amish.

---

[1]The Amish called themselves Amish-Mennonites until World War II. To file as conscientious objectors (the Amish will not go to war for any reason), they had to fill out a card. They were told by government officials "that they could not write down two religious names, so they dropped the name Mennonites and have been known simply as the Amish ever since." Richard Ammon, *Growing Up Amish* (New York: Atheneum, 1989), p. 17.

Early History

Jacob Amman (also spelled "Jakob Ammann") was a Mennonite preacher. Little is known of his early life, although he seems to have been born in Switzerland in 1656. He rose rapidly in the church hierarchy, and soon became a respected leader. From all accounts, he was a stern and righteous man—not unlike an Old Testament prophet—journeying from place to place, admonishing, exhorting, dutifully defending the faith.

What distressed him most was the fact that some Mennonite leaders were not enforcing the *Meidung*. One thing led to another, factions developed, and in 1693 it became obvious that the *Meidung* controversy was irreconcilable. Those who believed in the ban joined Amman's group and became known as the Amish. The others stayed within the larger Mennonite fold.

When the two groups came to the United States, the schism persisted, as it does to this day. The *Meidung* itself, moreover, remains a key concept. In fact, it would be no exaggeration to say that the *Meidung* is the heart of the Amish system of social control. Details will be discussed in a later section.

What do the present-day Amish think of Jacob Amman? Some members contend that he was overly harsh in both his views and his implementation, although others defend his actions as necessary—given the temper of the times. He is certainly not a revered leader. Indeed, many of the Amish today evidence little knowledge of—or interest in—Jacob Amman.

The reason is not hard to find. Amman was a strong leader with strong convictions, qualities that the Amish tend to de-emphasize. The Amish are devout believers in humility, brotherly love, group discussion, and consensus, and they are suspicious of those with leadership aspirations. Little wonder that their attitude toward Amman is one of ambivalence. Still, it is questionable whether the Amish would have survived as a separate group had it not been for the strong hand and unbending will of Jacob Amman.

The Amish began emigrating from Switzerland and Germany to the American colonies about 1710. They settled on land that would eventually become Pennsylvania, where William Penn was committed to a colony of religious toleration. The Amish as well as Quakers and Mennonites were welcomed.[2]

---

[2]For a comprehensive discussion of this early American period, see John A. Hostetler, *Amish Society*, 4th ed. (Baltimore: Johns Hopkins University Press, 1993). For a look at Amish history and ways of life from an Amish perspective, see Hostetler, *Amish Roots: A Treasury of History, Wisdom, and Lore* (Baltimore: Johns Hopkins University Press, 1989). Included are more than 150 short articles written mostly by the Amish for in-group consumption. Also see Paton Yoder, *Tradition and Transition: Amish Mennonites and Old Order Amish 1800–1900* (Scottdale, PA: Herald Press, 1991).

The Old Order Amish

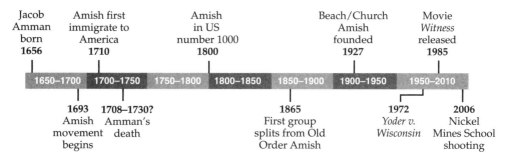

| Jacob Amman born 1656 | Amish first immigrate to America 1710 | Amish in US number 1000 1800 | Beach/Church Amish founded 1927 | Movie *Witness* released 1985 |

| 1693 Amish movement begins | 1708–1730? Amman's death | 1865 First group splits from Old Order Amish | 1972 *Yoder v. Wisconsin* | 2006 Nickel Mines School shooting |

Although they faced the usual hazards encountered by American colonists, the followers of Jacob Amman found an almost matchless opportunity for agricultural development. Climate, soil, rainfall, and topography were excellent. Best of all, the land was cheap and seemed to be in almost limitless supply. The Amish had come upon a farmer's dream, and they proceeded to make the most of it.

They grew and prospered, from a relatively small number of families in the 1700s to thousands in the 1800s. Indeed, the "almost limitless" supply of land in Pennsylvania eventually turned out to be anything but limitless, and to form new settlements the Amish were forced to migrate to other regions. Part of this migration is spurred by population growth. In 1992, the Amish numbered 125,000 in the United States and Ontario, Canada, and by 2009 that number had increased to 233,000 (106,000 are adult baptized members). Today, there are settlements in at least twenty-nine states with the majority being in Ohio, Pennsylvania, and Indiana.[3]

The Amish also have a number of communities in Central America and South America. Paradoxically, there are no Amish in Europe, their original homeland.

Although the secular and religious practices of the Amish show many similarities no matter where they live, there are also some significant regional differences. And although we will try to present a more or less generalized account, special attention will be given to the Old Order Amish of Lancaster County. The Old Order Amish are the conservative wing of the Amish. Beginning in the 1860s, other groups broke away that tended to be a bit more liberal. However, the Old Order Amish are one of the oldest, largest—and certainly one of the most interesting—of all the Amish groups.[4]

---

[3]"Amish Population by State" (2009) and "Amish Population Change" (1992–2008). Young Center for Anabaptist and Pietist Studies, Elizabethtown College. http://www2 .etown.edu/amishstudies.

[4]Readers familiar with Lancaster County will recognize the picturesque names of towns and villages in Amishland: Intercourse, Smoketown, Leola, White Horse, Compass, Bird-in-Hand, Beartow Gap, Mascot, Paradise, and others.

". . . A Peculiar People"

In their olden attire and horse and buggy, the Old Order Amish appear to be driving out of yesterday. Actually, they are more than simply old-fashioned. Conservatism is part of their religion, and as such it permeates their entire life. The Amish recognize they stand apart from the general population. For generations, they have referred to the non-Amish as the **English** or **Englishers.**

The Amish believe in a literal interpretation of the Bible and rely heavily on the statement, "But ye are a chosen generation, a royal priesthood, an holy nation, a peculiar people" (1 Peter 2:9). And because they have been specifically chosen by God, the Amish take great pains to stay "apart" from the world at large. They do this not only by living apart, but by rejecting so many of the standard components of modern civilization: automobiles, radio and television, high school and college, movies, air conditioning, jewelry and cosmetics, life insurance, cameras, musical instruments. The list goes on and on.

This is not to say that the Old Order Amish reject all change. As will be shown later, some of the changes have been fairly far-reaching.[5] But in general, the followers of Jacob Amman resist converting to what they believe to be harmful worldly ways.

Appearance and Apparel   An in-group, defined in Chapter 1, is generally characterized by the loyalty, like-mindedness, and compatibility of its constituents. Members refer to the in-group as "we," and to the out-group as "they." For the Amish, wearing apparel is one of the most distinguishing features of the in-group.

Men's hats—probably the most characteristic feature of their attire—are of low crown and wide brim; smaller models are worn by the youngsters. Coats are without collars or lapels, and almost always include a vest. (An Amishman and his vest are not easily parted.) Wire hook-and-eye fasteners are used on suit coats and vests.

Amish men's trousers deserve special mention, because (1) they never have creases or cuffs; (2) they are always worn with suspenders (belts are unacceptable); and (3) most are without zippered or buttoned flies. Instead, the flap or "broadfall" type is used.[6] Also, with the exception of their shirts, Amish men's attire is predominantly black.

---

[5]Stephen Scott and Kenneth Pellman, *Living without Electricity* (Intercourse, PA: Good Books, 1990).

[6]"When fly closures for pants were introduced in the 1820s," writes Scott, "some considered them indecent. In 1830, the *Gentlemen's Magazine of Fashion* pronounced the fly 'an indelicate and disgusting fashion.' While the larger society eventually accepted this feature, many plain people did not." Among the plain people were the Old Order Amish. See Stephen Scott, *Why Do They Dress That Way?* (Intercourse, PA: Good Books, 1986), p. 114.

William Zellner was once given a workshirt and trousers by an ex-Amishman and found that going to the bathroom requires a measure of planning. The trousers, flapped much like navy bell-bottoms, have seven buttons and snaps to undo. The gray shirt has wire hook-and-eye fasteners.

Following the biblical injunction, Amish women keep their heads covered at all times. Cosmetics and makeup, of course, are prohibited. Dresses are of a solid color—blues and purples are quite common—with (variable) long skirts and aprons. In public, women also wear shawls and capes.

For Amish women, stockings must be black, and shoes are the black, low-heeled variety. Interestingly enough, in recent years young boys and girls have taken to wearing jogging shoes. In fact, the two most popular forms of footwear for the youngsters are jogging shoes and bare feet! For both sexes, all jewelry (including the wedding ring) is unacceptable, because whatever is worn is presumed to be functional. An ornamental exception might be the Amishman's beard, though this does have recognition value: prior to marriage young men are clean-shaven, whereas married men are required to let their beards grow. Mustaches—which in the European period were associated with the military—are completely unacceptable.[7]

Amish males wear their hair long, unparted, in a Dutch bob, with the necessary trimming done at home. Amish females also have their own special hairdo, both cutting and curling being forbidden. Shaving their legs and plucking their eyebrows are also unacceptable.

The Old Order Amish are quite cognizant of the fact that they look different, and they have no intention of changing. On the contrary, their "difference" makes them feel close to one another and accentuates the in-group feeling.

Some observers believe that, because the Amish are thrifty, they deliberately use clothing that never goes out of style. This is not the reason, however. True, the followers of Jacob Amman are indeed thrifty. With the exception of shoes, stockings, and hats, they make nearly all their own clothing. They also wear their clothes until they are literally worn out. But the basic reason they will not change styles is that they consider such change to be worldly—and worldliness has negative connotations.

General Lifestyle   It was Thorstein Veblen, one of the early giants of sociology, who first used the term **conspicuous consumption,** by which he meant the tendency to gain attention through the overt display of one's wealth. But whereas such display might be expected on the part of many Americans, it has no place in the Amish community. Their homes, for example, some of which have surprisingly modern features, would never contain elaborate furniture or fancy wallpaper. Clothes, as we have

[7]The Amish sometimes appear inconsistent in their prohibitions. Thus, wristwatches are forbidden whereas pocket watches are permitted. Sometimes there is a good reason for the seeming inconsistency, and the Amish are well aware of the explanation. At other times, the answer would likely be, "It has always been so."

seen, are plain and functional, and neither sex will wear adornments of any kind.

With their emphasis on humility, the Old Order Amish dislike all types of public recognition. Pride, in fact, is considered a cardinal sin. As a consequence, actions that are more or less commonplace in society at large are seldom encountered in Amishland. Boasting is rare. Having one's portrait painted or picture taken is prohibited; indeed, cameras are completely unacceptable. Such behavior would be considered a sign of self-aggrandizement.[8]

Bicycles, motorcycles, and automobiles are strictly *verboten* in the Lancaster County settlement, and any adult who bought one would be subjected to severe group pressures. The automobile is the best-known case in point, and—as will be shown—the Amish lifestyle is strongly influenced by their being a horse-type rather than an automobile-type culture.

The Old Order Amish are a slow-tempo community. They value such traits as obedience, modesty, and submission, rather than mobility and competitiveness.[9] The hustle and bustle that characterize so much of the society of the English will not be found in Amishland. Seeing an adult Amish person in a hurry would be rather unusual.

In their business ventures, the Amish follow a fairly conservative route. They have no interest in stocks, bonds, or other forms of "speculation." They are staunch believers in private enterprise, however, and will take out mortgages, borrow money from banks, and use checking accounts. Banks consider them excellent customers and excellent credit risks.

The followers of Jacob Amman have no strong interest in politics. Although they do vote—in local more than in national elections—voter turnout is relatively low. Hostetler reports that when they register, most do so as Republicans.[10] The Amish themselves have never held a major office of any kind, for a good reason: the church would not permit it.

The Old Order Amish tend to reject various forms of commercial insurance, including life insurance. However, they do have a fairly comprehensive network of mutual-aid organizations and self-help programs, some of which involve monetary assessments. A sick farmer can count on his fields being tended, and even harvested, by his neighbors.

Medicine and Health   Should an Amish family's barn burn down, up to a hundred neighbors will gather, and in a day or two raise a new barn.

---

[8]For readers who appreciate a mystery, here is one with no immediate answer. The followers of Jacob Amman do not own cameras, and are dead set against having their pictures taken. Yet, on the basis of postcards, brochures, pamphlets, newspapers, magazines, and books, the Amish may well be the most photographed group in America!

[9]Hostetler, *Amish Society*, pp. 185–89, 333ff; Donald Kraybill, *The Riddle of Amish Culture* (Baltimore: Johns Hopkins University Press, 1989), pp. 24–25.

[10]Hostetler, *Amish Society*, p. 000.

AP/Wide World Photos

The Amish make up for the absence of many construction tools by working together to help community members. Here they raise a barn near Tollesboro, Kentucky in 2007.

Barn raisings have attracted nationwide publicity, but Amish construction skills are sometimes put to good use in erecting other kinds of less publicized buildings.

For example, in the late 1980s a young pediatrician, Holmes Morton, discovered that a genetic disease, glutaric aciduria, disproportionately affects Amish and Mennonite children in Lancaster County. Many victims lapse into comas and die within 48 hours. Most of those who survive the initial episode suffer progressive paralysis.

In his efforts to buy building materials to establish a clinic and diagnostic equipment, Morton attempted to take out a second mortgage on his home. But that wasn't necessary. On November 19, 1990, the *Wall Street Journal*, hearing of Morton's efforts, printed a front-page article telling of his dream.[11]

Donations were not solicited; nevertheless, more than 250 readers from thirty-seven states chose to contribute to the project. Two of the donors gave $100,000. Hewlett-Packard Corporation donated diagnostic equipment valued at $85,000. And an Amish farmer donated three prime acres of Lancaster County farmland for a building site.

[11]Frank Allen, "Farm Folks Gather in Strasburg, Pa., against a Plague: Raising High the Roof Beams of Holmes Morton's Clinic Begins to Fulfill a Dream," *Wall Street Journal*, November 19, 1990, p. A1.

On a rainy Saturday in late November 1990, more than one hundred Amish met within a mile of the barn raised for the movie *Witness,* and had their first Amish clinic-raising.

The clinic has become home for the latest in gene therapy, a relatively new medical field. It appears that the Amish have a higher rate of inherited diseases than most communities. Amish in the United States are all descended from just 47 families. Since 1989, Morton's clinic has become one of the most advanced gene research clinics in the country.[12]

At one time all the Amish were reluctant to patronize doctors and hospitals at all, and some members still refuse to do so. In early 1991, for example, four hundred cases of rubella (German measles) had been reported in six Pennsylvania counties, as well as in other Amish settlements. During the previous year, there were only 1,093 such cases reported for the entire United States.[13]

Nevertheless, despite some reluctance to use doctors and hospitals, most Amish now use medical facilities when the situation calls for it. The majority of Amish women, though, have their babies at home, delivered by a midwife.[14]

The insular nature of the Amish community, descended from a limited number of pioneer couples, makes Amish settlements ideal for studying inheritability of disease. From 1976 to 1994, a team of psychiatrists and biologists studied the occurrence of manic-depressive behavior in three generations of Amish families in Pennsylvania. Victims of *manic depression* (or bipolar affective disorder) shift between the extreme emotional states of euphoria and depression. In studying this illness, scientists found that the Amish served as an excellent sample. Their communities keep accurate genealogical records; moreover, many environmental factors that contribute to manic depression, such as alcoholism, drug abuse, unemployment, and divorce, are extremely rare within the Amish subculture.

The findings of the Pennsylvania study suggest a certain hereditary basis for manic-depressive behavior, which is apparently linked to a specific genetic characteristic. The researchers emphasize that this genetic characteristic neither guarantees nor precludes manic depression; they can only report that persons with the characteristic show a *predisposition* for manic-depressive behavior. The researchers did not merely observe the Amish but helped them treat the illness as well as

---

[12]Kate Rudder, "Genomics in Amish Country," posted July 23, 2004, on Genome News Network. Accessed February 9, 2005 (www.genomenewsnetwork.org).

[13]"Rubella Breaks Out in Amish Communities," *New York Times,* March 26, 1991.

[14]Penny Armstrong and Sheryl Feldman, *A Midwife's Story* (New York: Arbor House, 1986); Carol Morello, "Embattled Midwife to the Amish," *Philadelphia Inquirer,* July 23, 1989.

identify the presence of an inherited thyroid disease that contributed to depression.

Being part of a clinical trial and receiving cutting-edge treatment is the exception. Many Amish do not have health insurance and also do not use modern medicine and the services of physicians. Amish in the most traditional communities prefer the more homeopathic or folk forms of medicine. This has led some Amish entrepreneurs to establish health food stores. Generally Amish do not seek out more expensive diagnostic procedures and treatment. Collectively the Amish view of medicine is informed by their conservative rural values, preference for natural antidotes, awkwardness in high-tech settings, and lack of information.[15]

Sadly, even the Amish with their conservative, rural lifestyle are not exempt from AIDS. Lancaster County ranks seventh in Pennsylvania in the number of AIDS cases reported. One preacher told Larry Lewis of the *Philadelphia Inquirer,* "We are not perfect. There is some premarital sex in the sect, probably a small amount of drug use, and some sexual straying."[16] He went on to say that he even knew of an older member of the community who had visited prostitutes at the county seat.

It should be mentioned, in connection with medicine and health, that the Old Order Amish are conservative in death as well as in life. Their funerals are plain: no flowers, no metal caskets, no music, no decorations, no mourning bands, no crepe. Most districts permit embalming, but a few do not. There are no Amish undertakers, however, and even funeral parlors are taboo. The wooden coffin is made by an Amish carpenter, services are held at home, and an Amish bishop presides. The old custom of holding a wake—sitting up all night around the body of the deceased—is still practiced in most areas.

Amish cemeteries are startlingly plain. There are no flowers, no decorations, no elaborate tombstones, and no mausoleums. In fact, there is not even a caretaker, so that the graves sometimes have a run-down look. In general, the only handmade signs are small, uniform headstones, with the name and dates of the deceased—no scrolls, epitaphs, or other inscriptions. Most Amish cemeteries are off the beaten track. For the most part, they are—or were—part of an Amish farmer's land, and there is no charge for the use of burial lots.

As might be imagined, the entire cost of an Amish funeral and burial is only a fraction of that normally spent by the English (non-Amish).

---

[15]"Frequently Asked Questions" and "Health." Accessed on September 9, 2009 at http://www2.etown.edu/amishstudies; Jean Antol Krull, "Family Ties," *Medicine Magazine* (University of Miami School of Medicine, Spring 2004). Accessible at http://www6.miami.edu/ummedicine-magazine/Spring2004/.

[16]Larry Lewis, "The Reality of AIDS Touches Even the Amish: The Sect's Relative Isolation Cannot Shield It from the Pervasive Disease," *Philadelphia Inquirer,* April 12, 1992, p. B1.

The Farmstead

Amish life revolves around the home—literally as well as figuratively. Most inhabitants of Amishland are born at home, they work at or near home, and they socialize at home. Most of their clothing is homemade, and nearly all their meals are eaten at home. Church services are held at one home or another. The Old Order Amish also marry at home, and—as a most fitting finale—their funeral services are held at home.

"Home," however, has a special meaning, for the followers of Jacob Amman are predominantly a rural people, and their traditional dwelling can best be described as a farmstead. Indeed, for most of the Amish in the United States, farm and home tend to be synonymous, a feeling that complements their religious philosophy.

Amish farms are acknowledged to be among the best in the world. In addition to fairly extensive crop acreage, their holdings often consist of large, well-kept houses and barns, stables, springhouses, silos, sheds, and storehouses. And, because the Amish community maintains no homes for the aged, a farmstead may include two, three, or even four generations. Additions are made to the farmhouse as needed. The presence of so many oldsters on the farm, of course, serves as a self-perpetuating conservative influence. At any rate, it is little wonder that some of the larger Amish farms have the appearance of miniature villages.

Basic to the agricultural system is the fact that the Amish do not employ tractors in the field. Whereas such a handicap might seem almost insurmountable to other farmers, the Amish try to turn it to their advantage. True, by using a team of horses instead of a tractor, the Amish farmer spends more time in covering less ground. However, he does not mind hard work. He has ample free labor in the form of his sons. He saves money by not having to buy and replace tractors. And his horses supply him with a rich source of natural fertilizer. As one Amish farmer is reported to have said, "When you put gasoline in a tractor, all you get out is smoke!"

Aside from tractors, the Amish do use a variety of up-to-date farm machinery: sprayers, cultivators, binders, balers, and haymaking equipment. Gasoline engines are permitted, and often a stationary tractor is used as a source of power.

Agricultural failure is infrequent, for the Amish farmer is a master of his trade. He understands the soil, his crops, and his dairy herds, and he loves his work. His farm products are choice, and he is able to sell them for top dollar. And although he may buy food on the open market, much of what he and his family eat is homegrown. In view of present-day food prices, this is a real advantage. Farming also supplies the Amish people with one of their chief topics of conversation.

Economic Development   Until the late 1960s, church members could be excommunicated for being employed in other than agricultural pursuits. This is not the case today. Although farming is their chief occupation, not all Amish are farmers, either because of choice or lack of cultivatable land. Now their work is much more diversified. Although you will not find Amish computer programmers, there are Amish engaged as blacksmiths, harness-makers, buggy repairers, and carpenters. Non-Amish often hire these craftspeople as well.

The movement by the Amish into other occupations is sometimes a source of tension with larger society, or the English. As long as the Amish remained totally apart from dominant society in the United States, they experienced little hostility. As they entered the larger economic sector, however, intergroup tensions developed in the form of growing prejudice. The Amish today may underbid their competitors. The Amish entry into the commercial marketplace has also strained the church's traditional teaching on litigation and insurance, both of which are to be avoided. Mutual assistance has been the historical path taken, but that does not always mesh well with the modern businessperson. After legal action taken on their behalf, Amish businesses typically have been allowed to be exempt from paying Social Security and workers' compensation, another sore point with English competitors.

The Amish entrepreneur represents an interesting variation of the typical ethnic businessperson one might encounter in a Chinatown, for example. Research on ethnic businesses often cites discrimination against minorities and immigrants as a prime force prodding the development of minority enterprises. The Amish are a very different case because their own restrictions on education, factory work, and certain occupations have propelled them into becoming small-business owners. However, class differences are largely absent among the Old Order Amish.

In many of the above instances the jobs are only temporary, to be held until the Amishman can procure a suitable farm of his own. In many other cases, however, the jobs become more or less permanent. This is especially true in the Lancaster County area, where there has been a serious "land squeeze" for some time.

The land squeeze of the late twentieth century and the economic downturn beginning in 2008 pushed more and more Amish to new practices. Occupations other than agricultural became more populated but also caused the Amish to become more vulnerable to the ups and downs of capitalism. Customary reluctance to accept government unemployment was waived in many Amish communities so as to sustain the household.[17]

---

[17]Douglas Belkin, "A Bank Run Teaches the 'Plain People' About the Risks of Modernity," *Wall Street Journal,* July 1, 2009; Joshua Boak, "Hard Times Strike Amish," *Chicago Tribune,* April 19, 2009, sec. 4, pp. 1, 5.

Amish Homes   Describing the typical Amish home of the twenty-first century is not easy. In addition to the usual regional and district variations, the "generational" factor must be considered. Homes of the younger Amish may be noticeably different from those of their parents' generation.

Like the farm, the traditional Amish home is well kept and well run. It is plain, lacking in many of the modern conveniences, in good repair, and solid as an oak. (It needs to be, for untold generations of the same family will live there.)

Most of these houses are fairly large, for several reasons. The Amish have a high birthrate, and at any given time there are likely to be a number of children living at home. Also, Amish farmers tend to retire early in life, and they usually turn the house over to one of their sons while they themselves live in the adjoining *Grossdawdy House*. And finally, as will be shown later, the Old Order Amish have no church buildings. Their home is their church, and services are held on a rotating basis. Houses, therefore, must be large enough to seat the congregation.

In the traditional Amish home, rooms are large, particularly the kitchen, where huge quantities of food are cooked and served. (There is no dining room.) Throughout the house, furnishings tend to be functional, though not drab. The Amish religion does not forbid the use of color. Walls are often light blue, dishes purple. Articles such as bed coverings and towels can be almost any color. Outside the house, there is likely to be a lawn and a flower garden. Fences, walls, posts, and landmarks may also be brightly colored.

Although they love colors, the followers of Jacob Amman do not believe in mixing them. Wearing apparel, fences, posts, buggies—all are of solid colors only. Plaids, stripes, and prints are considered too fancy. For this reason, contrary to popular impression, the Amish never put hex signs on their barns.[18]

Newer Amish houses differ from the traditional variety in a number of ways. They tend to be smaller, and many do not have a "farmhouse" appearance at all. In fact, except for such features as no electrical wiring and the lack of curtains, they often look much like non-Amish houses. In the matter of modern appliances and equipment, the differences between "traditional" and "new" are even more significant.

The Amish have never permitted their members to use electricity furnished by public power lines. The church has been unyielding on this point, and the prohibition has served to restrict the kinds of devices and appliances available to members. Over the years, however, the followers of Jacob Amman have come up with some rather interesting alternatives:

---

[18]Zellner, who grew up in Northampton County, Pennsylvania, says that hex signs are a product of his Pennsylvania Dutch heritage. A variety of signs are sold to bring good fortune or ward off evil spirits. Amish never have used them.

bottled gas, batteries, small generators, air pressure, gasoline motors, hydraulic power. The net result has been a variety of modern devices that have become available to the Amish, not only in their homes, but in their barns, workshops, stores, and offices.[19]

In addition to a fashionable exterior, for example, the contemporary Amish home in Lancaster County is likely to have modern plumbing and bathroom facilities, attractive flooring and cabinet work, and a moderately up-to-date kitchen. The last would include a washing machine, stove, and refrigerator, all powered by one of the nonelectrical sources mentioned above. Amish communities outside Lancaster County may rule out indoor plumbing. On the other hand, Lancaster Amish do not use power mowers or ride bicycles while those elsewhere may. Such is the diversity of Amish interpretations of what constitutes acceptable technology.

The Pace of Change   How significant are the foregoing changes? There is no denying that the Lancaster County Amish have experienced some meaningful alterations, both in their home life and in their employment. Although the reasons may be complicated, many of the changes and modifications have acted as a safety valve; that is, they have given members some necessary leeway, denial of which might have caused internal dissension.

At the same time, the above-mentioned modernization should not obscure the larger picture: *resistance to change* is still one of the hallmarks of Amish society. As discussed above, Amish homes in the Lancaster area, though surprisingly modern in certain respects, are without electricity. There are no light bulbs, illumination being provided by oil lamps or gas-pressured lanterns. And the list of prohibitions remains long: dishwashers, clothes dryers, microwaves, blenders, freezers, central heating, vacuum cleaners, air conditioning, power mowers, bicycles, toasters, hair dryers, radios, television—all are prohibited.[20]

Which parts of modernity will be accepted by the Amish and which will not is difficult to ascertain. When they do change, the change is usually well thought out, with the community assisting the bishop in the decision-making process. Recently, many devout Amish have become avid rollerbladers—a shock to most outsiders.

Sam Stoltzfus, an Amish historian, says, "In-line skates are permissible . . . because they are seen as a newer version of roller skates, a cousin of the ice skate and an improvement over the leg-powered scooter—all long used by the Amish."[21]

---

[19]See the discussion in Kraybill, *Riddle of Amish Culture*, pp. 150–64.

[20]Donald B. Kraybill, *The Amish of Lancaster County* (Mechanicsburg, PA: Stackpole Books, 2008).

[21]David W. Chen, "Amish Going Modern, Sort of, About Skating," *New York Times*, August 11, 1996, sec. 1, p. 10.

Leisure and Recreation

The followers of Jacob Amman work hard; indeed, it is difficult to see how any group could work harder. Recreation and leisure are another matter, however, for in these spheres they have somewhat restricted options. There are a number of reasons for this.

To begin with, the typical Amish farmer and his wife have a limited amount of leisure time. For the husband, the prohibition on tractors means that fieldwork is laborious and time-consuming. And because his wife is denied the use of so many electrical appliances, a number of her routine chores—particularly food preparation—must be done largely by hand.

Also, the Amish do not have a wide range of interests. Except for necessary business trips, they tend to stay away from cities. They feel that city life epitomizes worldliness, and worldliness is linked with wickedness. But this means that the Old Order Amish effectively cut themselves off from much of the cultural life of the English. They do not attend operas, ballets, or concerts. They do not patronize movies or stage shows. They do not go to art exhibits. Generally speaking, they seldom dine out—nor do they go to bars or nightclubs. Attendance at sporting events is strictly prohibited.

At home, the followers of Jacob Amman are similarly restricted in their choice of activities. They do not have television, radio, or stereo. They do not dance, play cards, or attend cocktail parties. They have no pianos or other musical instruments. They are not particularly interested in popular magazines or novels. They are not even permitted that great American invention, the telephone! However, they are permitted to use pay telephones, which abound in Amishland. Also, depending on the district, phones may be found in Amish shops.

The Amish community does not celebrate most American holidays. Memorial Day, Halloween, Labor Day, Veterans Day, Lincoln's and Washington's birthdays, the Fourth of July—all are ignored. Christmas, Easter, and Pentecost are celebrated, although the emphasis is religious rather than secular. Christmas does not involve a Christmas tree, lights, mistletoe, decorations, cards, or Santa Claus. All work is suspended, however, and the children are given presents. Visiting families and friends marks all these religious observances and Thanksgiving.

The Positive Side   Thus far, we have discussed some of the negative side of Amish recreation—things they do not do. But what *do* they do in this connection? Much of their social activity revolves around their home and their religion. Socializing—usually men with men and women with women—takes place both before and after church services. On Sunday evenings, the young people hold "singings," social gatherings that serve as a kind of adjunct to dating and courtship. Certain religious holidays afford opportunities for further socializing, and—as will be shown later— weddings are gala occasions.

Just plain visiting is one of the principal forms of entertainment in Amishland. Church services are held every other week, and on alternate Sundays many families visit (or are visited by) relatives or friends. In spite of some acknowledged restrictions, Amish life is far from somber.[22] The Amish adults and children have as much or more time for face-to-face conversation and relaxing visits with family and friends than most of us because they not spend time watching television, playing video games, and texting on cell phones.

The followers of Jacob Amman are also fond of outings and picnics, and from the amount of food consumed on these occasions, eating should perhaps be classed as a recreational activity! The Amish have a special place in their hearts for animals of all kinds, and it is quite common to see an Amish family enjoying a day at a zoo.

Within their own homes, the Amish do some reading, though they are not a bookish group. They read the Bible, the *Ausbund* (the Amish hymnal), and *Martyrs Mirror*, the story of early Anabaptist persecutions. Farm journals are fairly common, and many families subscribe to local papers. Interestingly enough, there is one Amish newspaper, *The Budget*, put out by a non-Amish publisher.

The Old Order Amish occasionally play games, such as chess and checkers, and the youngsters engage in a variety of sports. Some men chew tobacco, and many districts—including those in Lancaster County—now permit smoking. And although drinking is frowned upon, individual Amish men are sometimes known to "take a nip." Generally speaking, the followers of Jacob Amman evidence a certain degree of tolerance toward drinking, at least on the part of the men.

The Ban on Autos   Another restrictive factor—one of the most striking, in terms of leisure and recreation—is the Amish ban on automobile ownership. The ban is unequivocal, although it is permissible to ride in someone else's car. It is also acceptable to take a bus or taxicab.

Several reasons have been suggested for the ownership ban. It has been pointed out that horses are mentioned in the Bible. It is said that

---

[22]The Amish are not devoid of a sense of humor, and visiting days are often a time for storytelling. If you want to know why the Amish are "genetically bred to be cheap, closer to a dollar bill than George Washington," and for other stories, see Eli R. Beachy, *Tales from the Peoli Road: Wit and Humor of Very Real People, Who Just Happen to Be Amish* (Scottdale, PA: Herald Press, 1992).

Interest in Amish lifestyle is so great that authors and illustrators are beginning to produce children's books on the subject. For a fine example, see Patricia Polacco, *Just Plain Fancy* (New York: Bantam Doubleday Dell, 1990).

automobiles—and their maintenance—are expensive compared to the horse and buggy. The matter of fertilizer (or lack of it) has already been mentioned. Although these factors may be contributory, they do not constitute the real reason. The real reason is that the Old Order Amish feel that automobile ownership would disrupt their entire way of life.

When automobiles first became popular in the 1920s, they were expensive and unreliable. They were, nevertheless, a major invention, and represented a sharp break with the more traditional forms of transportation. Accordingly, they were rejected by both the Amish and the majority of Mennonites. But whereas most Mennonite groups eventually lifted the ban, the Amish community refused to budge, a position they have held to this day.

The followers of Jacob Amman have come under heavy pressure to permit the ownership of automobiles. Horseshoes make grooves in the road, and in a number of areas grooved roads are commonplace. More important, modern highways are dangerous, and buggies have been smashed by oncoming cars, especially at night. State laws require lights on moving vehicles, and the Amish have had to install night lights, powered by under-the-seat batteries. Pressures for automobile ownership have become so great that occasionally an Amish family will leave the church and join the Beachy Amish, a more liberal (but much smaller) group that permits its members to own and drive automobiles.

The ban on cars is one of the key factors that others and the Amish themselves consider important to maintaining Amish identity. Most will suffer great inconvenience and expense to ensure their Amishness if the need arises. Many Amish will accept rides in motor vehicles but not own or drive them.

Both individually and collectively, the Amish are wedded to the soil, to the church community, and to the horse and buggy. The automobile would represent a far-reaching and detrimental change. True, the followers of Jacob Amman may be wrong in their judgment. The auto might not bring with it the feared aftereffects. But that is irrelevant. Just as the Gypsies defined the situation regarding *marimé,* the Amish have defined the situation with regard to the automobile, and they can hardly change the definition without also changing their entire social perspective.

Relative Deprivation   The automobile aside, there does appear to be an imbalance in Amishland; that is, there seems to be an overabundance of work and a scarcity of leisure and recreation. As a consequence, are the Amish not disgruntled? Have they no desire to lead fuller lives?

The answer is no. A large majority of Amish people have no desire whatsoever to lead any other kind of life. They do engage in leisure activities, but even if they did not, it is doubtful whether their outlook would be appreciably dampened. The fact is that they believe wholeheartedly in the simple, uncomplicated, slow-paced way of life, and neither hard work nor the lack of many conveniences disturbs them.

One of the reasons for this can be explained by **relative deprivation,** another concept widely employed by sociologists. Relative deprivation refers to the conscious feeling of a negative discrepancy between legitimate expectations and present actualities. According to this concept, people feel aggrieved not because of what they are deprived of in any absolute sense, but because of what they are deprived of in terms of their reference group.

An employee who receives a $3,000 raise would probably be satisfied if it were known that the amount was as high or higher than that received by others in the department. But if the employee discovered that most of the others had received larger increases, his or her morale would suffer accordingly. Similarly, students are generally satisfied with a B grade—until they learn that the majority of the class received As, with B being the lowest grade given.

Applied to the Amish community, relative deprivation explains a great deal. Most Amish are early risers, day in and day out. They work exceptionally hard, yet are not permitted to own such things as automobiles, television, and air conditioning. But the point is, the entire reference group—all of Amishland—is experiencing the same set of restrictions. A feeling of relative deprivation, therefore, is lacking.

The followers of Jacob Amman are anything but disgruntled. They lack certain conveniences, true, but they all accept this as the will of God. They work hard, but because they generally love their work they do not consider this a burden. As a matter of fact, an Amish family has little trouble operating a 150- or 200-acre farm. The difficulty is not in running a large farm, but in finding farmland large enough to keep the family busy.

Religious Customs

Although outsiders are often unaware of it, the Old Order Amish have neither formal churches nor any kind of central church organization. They have no paid clergy, no missionaries, and no Sunday schools. Yet they are one of the most devout groups in America, and their decentralized church structure—which is simplicity itself—has been remarkably successful.

The Amish are organized into church districts, each district covering a certain geographical area and including a certain number of families. Membership varies, depending on region, but most districts in the United States probably average between 150 and 200 members, including children. When the figure exceeds this number the district usually divides—

a fairly frequent occurrence, because the followers of Jacob Amman have always had a high birthrate.

Held in Amish homes on a rotating basis, the Sunday morning service lasts about three hours. Men and women sit separately, with men occupying the first few rows and women at the rear. (Each district has a set of benches, which are hauled to the designated house ahead of time.) The sermons—almost entirely in German—are quite lengthy, and it is not uncommon to see members start to squirm after the first hour or so, especially because the benches have no backs.

Inasmuch as the Old Order Amish do not permit musical instruments, it is sometimes thought that they prohibit singing, but this is not so. Hymns are an integral part of their Sunday service; in fact, their hymnbook—the *Ausbund*—was first published in 1564 and is the oldest hymnal used by any Protestant group. The hymns themselves—140 in number and written for the most part by Anabaptist prisoners—tell of great suffering and steadfastness. The amazing thing is that the tunes are handed down orally from one generation to the next, for the *Ausbund* has no written notes, only words.

The Clergy   Each Amish district is normally presided over by four clergymen: a bishop, two preachers, and a deacon. The bishop (*Volle Diener*, minister with full powers) is the spiritual head of the district. One could really say "spiritual and secular head," because in Amishland the two spheres tend to blend. In any case, the *Volle Diener* is the head man. He presides at weddings, funerals, baptisms, communion services, and excommunications. He also preaches, although this is not his main job. His main job is to prescribe and enforce the rules and otherwise hold the community together. And because the rules of the church are never written, they are—in point of fact—what the bishop says they are.

The two preachers (*Diener zum Buch*, minister of the Book) assist the bishop at ceremonial affairs such as communion and baptism. But their chief duties are delivering the Sunday sermons, leading the congregation in prayer, and interpreting the Bible. The preachers must be well versed in biblical authority and must be able to stand before the congregation and deliver their sermons without notes or books of any kind.

The deacon (*Armen Diener*, minister of the poor) also assists at the Sunday services and at ceremonial affairs. His chief duties, however, have to do with the day-to-day operation of the district. For example, the deacon serves as go-between during marriage arrangements, he obtains information about reported rule infractions, he tries to settle internal difficulties, he looks after families with problems, particularly those involving widows and orphans, and so on.

The four clergymen are not salaried. They must attend to their farms and their families like any other Amishman. And because the church has no property, no treasury, and no centralized administration, the four officers have their work cut out for them. Women, incidentally, are not eligible for the clergy.

If two or more districts are in "full fellowship" with one another—that is, if they agree on specific rules of conduct, mode of dress, allowable equipment, and so forth—they may exchange preachers on a given Sunday. If the districts are not in full fellowship, there is little or no contact between them. In some areas, such as Lancaster County, the bishops of the various districts meet twice a year to discuss church matters and iron out differences. But this is as close to a centralized church organization as the Amish ever get.

Chosen by Man and God   Old Order Amish clergy are always selected by a "combination of man and God"; that is, they are nominated by a vote of the adult congregation, but the "winner" is chosen by lot. More specifically, if a vacancy should occur in the rank of preacher, the congregation is asked to make nominations. Any member who gets at least three votes has his name entered in the lot. On the day of the selection, a number of Bibles are placed on a table, the number corresponding to the number of candidates. One of the Bibles contains a slip of paper with a biblical quotation. As the candidates walk by, each one selects a Bible, and whoever draws the Bible with the slip is the new preacher. He is thus believed to have been chosen by God.

This is the procedure followed for the selection of preachers and deacons. However, the Amish believe the bishops should have some prior experience, and when a vacancy occurs at this level, the selection is made directly by lot from among the preachers and deacons. Once selected, clergy of all ranks normally hold their positions for life. And although in many ways their jobs are thankless ones, most Amish clergymen apparently consider it an honor to have been chosen.

All the clergy are important; however, the bishop is the central figure, because it is he who determines the character of the district. Although outsiders may see little difference among the various Amish communities, the differences are indeed there, and the bishop is aware of them—down to the last detail. Trimming of the beard, design of women's shawls and aprons, type of hats and bonnets, gadgets on the buggy, tractor usage, house furnishings, barnyard and shop equipment—all come under the careful scrutiny of the *Volle Diener.*

It is easy to see why some Amish districts do not have full fellowship with their neighbors. In some districts, the buggies have gray tops; in others, black tops; in others, white tops; and in others, yellow tops. Districts vary in the tempo of their hymn singing. In some districts, men wear their hair at shoulder length; in others, the hair does not even cover the ears. The style of women's head coverings and the length of their skirts vary. Permissible items in the way of home furnishings also vary. And so on.

"Temporary Visitors"   The followers of Jacob Amman believe strongly that they are only temporary visitors on earth, and that their principal duty is to prepare for the next world. The present world—and all that it connotes—is bad; hence, the Amish try to remain aloof from it. This explains why they insist on being "peculiar"; that is, dressing differently, acting differently, and living differently.

Like most other aspects of their lives, Amish theological beliefs are the essence of simplicity. Because they are on earth for only a short period, the Old Order Amish have little interest in improving the world or making it a better place to live in. Their entire orientation is otherworldly. They believe that the Word of God calls for self-denial and are quite content to make the necessary sacrifices. God, furthermore, is a personal, literal God, and the Bible is a literal transcription of His word. Also—and this is quite important—God is omnipotent. All things are ordered by Him, and nothing happens without His knowledge.

As for personal salvation, the Amish believe in eternal life, which involves a physical resurrection after death. The eternal life, however, may be spent in either heaven or hell, depending on how one lives during one's visit on earth. Members can expect to go to heaven if they follow the rules of the church, for by so doing they put themselves in God's hands.

Although there are no written rules, all the Amish know what is expected of them. Furthermore, there is always the Bible to turn to; in fact, a good many of their customs—including the *Meidung*—are based on specific biblical passages.

Sanctions

The term **sanctions** refers to rewards and punishments employed by a group to bring about desired behavior on the part of its members. What behavior is sanctioned depends on how a group defines acceptable behavior and deviance. **Deviance** is behavior that violates the standards of conduct or expectations of a group or society. Among most groups in the United States, driving an automobile, playing a musical instrument, or going to a motion picture is not only acceptable, but also expected. However, the Amish define proper behavior differently, and in their society each of these acts could be negatively sanctioned. On the other hand, as we will note later, the Amish end formal schooling in the eighth grade. To many this may seem an act of deviance. Famed scholar of the Amish, John Hostetler, was cross-examined by a government official about this practice. The official asked him," Now,

Professor, don't you think that a person needs to get ahead in the world?" Hostetler responded, "It all depends on which world."[23] It is deviance as defined by the world of the Amish that is relevant for the following discussion of sanctions.

Positive sanctions, among the Amish, are quite similar to those used by other communities: membership privileges, group approval, clerical blessings, rites and rituals such as baptism and communion, opportunities for socializing, and, of course, the satisfaction of worshiping God with one's own people.

For *negative sanctions,* the followers of Jacob Amman employ a series of penalties or punishments ranging from the very mild to the very severe. The first step involves informal sanctions: gossip, ridicule, derision, and other manifestations of group disapproval. Such responses are used by groups everywhere, but each Amish community is a small, close-knit unit, and the operation of adverse opinion is particularly effective.

The next step is a formal admonition by one of the clergy. If the charge is fairly serious, the offender might be visited and admonished by both preacher and bishop. The errant member might also be asked to appear before the congregation at large—to confess his or her sin and ask for the group's forgiveness.

The *Meidung*   The ultimate sanction is the imposition of the *Meidung,* also known as the "shunning" or "ban," but because of its severity, it is used only as a last resort. The followers of Jacob Amman have a strong religious orientation and a finely honed conscience—and the Amish community relies on this fact. Actions such as gossip, reprimand, and the employment of confession are usually sufficient to bring about conformity. The *Meidung* would be imposed only if a member were to leave the church, or marry an outsider, or break a major rule (such as buying an auto) without full repentance.

Although the *Meidung* is imposed by the bishop, he will not act without the unanimous support of the congregation. Generally speaking, however, the ban is total. No one in the district is permitted to associate with the errant party, including members of his or her own family. Even normal marital relations are forbidden. Should any member of the community ignore the *Meidung,* that person would also be placed under the ban. In fact, the *Meidung* is honored by all Amish districts, including those that are not in full fellowship with the district in question. There is no doubt that the ban is a mighty weapon. Jacob Amman intended it to be.

On the other hand, the ban is not irrevocable. If the shunned member admits the error of his or her ways—and asks forgiveness of the

---

[23]John A. Hostetler with Susan Fisher Miller, "An Amish Beginning," in David L. Weaver-Zercher, ed., *Writing the Amish* (University Park: Pennsylvania University Press, 2008), p. 35.

congregation—the *Meidung* will be lifted and the transgressor readmitted to the fold. No matter how serious the offense, the Amish never look upon someone under the ban as an enemy, but only as one who has erred. And although they are firm in their enforcement of the *Meidung*, the congregation will pray for the errant member to rectify his or her mistake.

Although imposition of the ban is infrequent, it is far from rare. Males are involved much more often than females, the young more frequently than the old. The *Meidung* would probably be imposed on young males more often were it not for the fact that baptism does not take place until the late teens. Prior to this time, young males are expected to be—and often are—somewhat on the wild side, and allowances are made for this fact. This will be discussed later in the chapter.

Baptism changes things, of course, for this is the rite whereby the young person officially joins the church and makes the pledge of obedience. Once the pledge is made, the limits of tolerance are substantially reduced. More than one Amish youth has been subjected to the *Meidung* for behavior that, prior to baptism, had been tolerated.

Courtship and Marriage

As might be expected, Amish courtship and marriage patterns differ substantially from those of non-Amish society. Dating customs are dissimilar. There is no engagement or engagement ring. There is no fancy wedding. There is no traditional honeymoon, wherein the newlyweds have a chance to be by themselves. And both before and after marriage, a woman's place is firmly in the home. There is no such thing as a women's movement in Amishland. Although their connubial behavior does show some similarity to that of the larger society, the Amish tend to have their own way of doing things.

Dating Practices   Amish boys and girls are much more restricted in their courting activities than are the youth of other groups. For one thing, Amish youth work longer hours; hence, they have less time for socializing. Also, Amish youngsters have a limited number of places to meet the opposite sex. They do not attend high school or college, so they are deprived of the chief rendezvous of American youth. They do not normally frequent fast-food places, shopping malls, movies, bars, dances, rock concerts, summer resorts, and other recreational catchalls. Nor are their families permitted to have automobiles, which places a further limitation on their amorous activities.

Another restrictive factor has to do with the so-called endogamous provision. **Endogamy** refers to the restriction of mate selection to people within the same group. In contrast, **exogamy** refers to marriage outside one's group. Sociologists use the terms with reference to broad groupings such as religion, race, nationality, and social class. But in contrast to the trend in society at large—where exogamous practices seem to be on the increase—the Old Order Amish remain strictly endogamous. Endogamy is a common theme of many of the extraordinary groups discussed in this volume.

Amish parents forbid their young people to date the English. In fact, the only permissible dating is either within the district or between districts that have full fellowship with one another. Endogamy among the Amish, therefore, does serve to limit the number of eligible mates. In outlying districts, this limitation may present some problems.

Amish courtship activities generally revolve around the "singings" held on Sunday nights. These usually take place at the same farm where that day's church services were held. Singings are run by the young people themselves and often involve participants from other districts. Refreshments are served, songs are sung, and there is always a good deal of banter, joking, and light conversation. If he has a date, the boy may bring her to the singing. If he does not, he tries to get one in the course of the evening, so that he may drive her home.

Should the girl permit the boy to drive her home, a dating situation may or may not develop, just as in the outside society. Unlike the larger society, however, Amish youth place less emphasis on romantic love and physical attractiveness, favoring instead those traits that will make for a successful family and community life: willingness to work, fondness for children, reliability, good-naturedness, and the like. The couple themselves, incidentally, tend to avoid any display of affection in public.

Once the couple decide to get married, the young man is required to visit the deacon and make his intentions known. The deacon then approaches the young woman's father and requests formal permission for the marriage. Permission is usually granted, for both sets of parents are probably well aware of developments and may already have started preparations for the wedding.

Marriage   Weddings are the most gala occasions in Amishland, and in Lancaster County alone there are more than a hundred of them each year. Marriage is a major institution for the followers of Jacob Amman, and they go out of their way to emphasize this fact.

The announcement is first made by publishing the banns at a church service, usually two weeks before the wedding. Unless the abode is too small, the wedding is held at the home of the bride. June is not a popular month, as it comes in the midst of planting season. The large majority of Amish weddings take place in November and December, after harvest.

Bill Coleman

Here comes the bride! In a white horse-drawn buggy, no less. The men and women of the community wear their very best as they head to the home where the vows will be exchanged. Typically, weddings are held in late fall so as not to interfere with tending to the crops.

The ceremony itself is not elaborate, although it is rather long, as certain portions of the Old Testament are quoted verbatim. There are no bouquets or flowers of any kind. The bridal veil, maid of honor, best man, photographs, decorations, wedding march—all are missing, though there is a good deal of group singing.

The groom wears his Sunday suit, and the bride wears a white cape and white apron. (The only other time she will ever wear all white is after death—when she is laid out in a casket.) At the conclusion of the ceremony, no wedding rings are exchanged, nor do the couple kiss. The bishop says simply, "Now you can go; you are married folk."

Although the wedding ceremony is unpretentious, the meal that follows is a giant. Enormous quantities of food are prepared, for the entire district may be invited, plus assorted friends and relatives. It is not uncommon to find several hundred people in attendance. Some people, in fact, actually attend several weddings on the same day.[24]

To help in the preparation and serving of the food, women of the district volunteer their services. Kitchens are often large enough to accommodate several cooks at a time. If not, temporary kitchens may be set up. Guests are generally served in shifts.

[24]Stephen Scott, *The Amish Wedding and Other Special Occasions of the Old Order Communities* (Intercourse, PA: Good Books, 1988), p. 13.

When the festivities are over, the couple spend the first night of marriage in the house of the bride's parents. The following morning, after the newlyweds help clean the parents' house, it's off for a two- to three-month trip to the homes of wedding guests. Although for most young people the honeymoon is a vacation whose chief aim is privacy, among the Amish it is merely an extended series of visits with friends and relatives. As guests on the honeymoon circuit, the newlyweds receive a variety of wedding presents, usually in the form of practical gifts for the home.

After the honeymoon, the couple take their place in the community as husband and wife. If it is at all possible, they will settle down to the business of farming. If it is the youngest son who has married, he and his wife may live in his parents' home, gradually taking over both farming and household duties. Even in other instances, however, the young couple will try to live close by, in a house purchased (with considerable parental help) because of its proximity to the parental homestead.

Family

There is an old saying in the Amish community that the young people should not move farther away "than you can see the smoke from their chimney." And it is true that a large majority of the Amish were born in the same county as their parents. Rarely will the Amish sell a farm out of the family. Moreover, about the only time an Amish breadwinner will move from the area is when there is no more land available, or when he has had a deep-seated rift with the bishop. As a result, the Amish family system tends to be perpetuated generation after generation, with little change. The church not only frowns on major change, but—should young couples get ideas—parents, grandparents, and assorted relatives are usually close enough to act as restraining influences.

The Amish family system is at once simple and effective. Both husbands and wives are conscientious workers. They take pride in their endeavors. They are known to be such excellent farmers and workers that outsiders often believe them to be quite wealthy. In a monetary sense this is not so, although many Amish do possess sizable holdings of extremely valuable land.

Because the farm is likely to be an Amish couple's daily concern, they usually have a large number of children to aid in the enterprise. As will be shown later, Amish youngsters are generally exempt from higher education, so that such things as compulsory school attendance laws and child labor laws have limited meaning. Consequently, unlike other children, Amish youngsters are considered to be economic assets. Families with ten or more children are far from uncommon; in fact, the average number of births per couple is around seven.

Role of Women   It is widely understood throughout Amishland that woman's place is in the home. Wives do not lack for kindness and respect—so long as they maintain their subordinate status. As the Amish see it, this duality is simply in keeping with God's wishes: "Man is the image and glory of God; but the woman is the glory of man" (1 Cor. 11:7).

To the outsider, it is readily apparent that the women's movement has no real place among the Old Order Amish. Men make the major decisions, both in the community and in the church. As was mentioned earlier, women are not eligible for the clergy. In addition to their usual household duties, women also perform such tasks as milking cows, mowing the lawn, gardening, and painting walls and fences. In some cases, women can be seen plowing and harvesting with a team of horses. Indications are, though, that Amish men rarely help out with household tasks such as washing dishes, preparing food, cleaning, and the like. This may be changing as women are entering cottage industries and businesses.

Although there are doubtless exceptions, Amish wives seem well adjusted to the patriarchal way of life. Their social roles are not only well defined, but are uniform throughout Amishland. Amish women realize that their English sisters have achieved a much greater degree of equality, yet there is little indication that they desire to change the traditional status quo. They have a substantial voice both in home management and in raising the children. They have an official vote in all church matters, including nominations for the clergy. And—perhaps most important— they have the inner comfort that comes from the knowledge that they are following God's word.

One final note. In any Amish gathering, it can be seen that men tend to associate with men, women with women. The men do not kiss their wives or utter words of endearment in public. From this, it might be inferred that Amish spouses have only moderate affection for one another, but this is hardly the case. What the followers of Jacob Amman object to is not affection itself but any *overt* display of affection. After all, the Amish are a conservative people, and the idea of kissing, fondling, or holding hands in public is distasteful. In private, they are doubtless as affectionate as any other group.

Primacy of the Home   Although the Amish recognize the importance of the school, there is no doubt in anyone's mind that primary responsibility for the socialization of children falls on the parents. If a youngster has difficulty in school, it is the parents who are consulted. If a boy has trouble within the Amish community, the bishop will talk with the parents as well as with the boy. And if a young person runs afoul of the law, the congregation will sympathize with the parents.

Generally speaking, Amish child rearing embodies a mixture of permissive and restrictive philosophies. Infants are more or less pampered and are seldom alone. As soon as possible, they are fed at the family table and made to feel a part of the group. Relatives and friends shower them with attention. Children soon come to feel that they are welcome members of the community, which in fact they are.

As soon as infants learn to walk, they are subject to discipline and taught to respect authority. Although the Amish family is not authoritarian in structure, it is true that great stress is placed on obedience. This is not a contradiction. The obedience is presumed to be based on love rather than fear, on the assumption—unquestioned in Amishland—that parents know best. Spanking and other forms of corporal punishment are quite common, yet the youngsters harbor no resentment. They learn early that such actions are for their own good and are simply manifestations of parental love and wisdom.

Training at home tends to supplement that received at school. Acceptance of traditional values is encouraged, and inquisitiveness discouraged. Cooperativeness rather than competitiveness is emphasized. Children are conditioned to the view that they are all creatures of God, and that therefore they should have deep consideration for the feelings of others. They are reminded—over and over again—of the dangers and evils that lurk in the outside world.

Family Functions   A number of years ago, William F. Ogburn, a sociologist interested in the study of cultural change, made an interesting observation apropos the American family. From the colonial period to the present, he said, the family has been characterized by a progressive *loss of functions.* He went on to list the declining functions as education, religion, protection, recreation, and the economic function. The thrust of his argument was that other institutions had taken over these functions. Thus, the function of religion, once centered in the home, had been taken over by the church. Education had become the province of the schools. Recreation had been usurped by commercialized ventures. The economic function had been lost because the family was no longer a producing unit—owing largely to the fact that child labor laws and compulsory school laws prohibited children from working. Ogburn's conclusion was that, because of these declining functions, the American family had been weakened.

Some sociologists have accepted Ogburn's thesis, others have questioned it, and the issue is far from dead. Some feel that although the family may have lost some functions, it has gained others.[25] The Old Order Amish add another dimension to the debate, for the functions that Ogburn claimed had disappeared from the mainstream of American family life are still being performed by the Amish family.

---

[25]Richard T. Schaefer, *Sociology,* 12th ed. (New York: McGraw-Hill, 2010), p. 316; William F. Ogburn and Clark Tibbitts, "The Family and Its Functions," in *Recent Social Trends in the United States,* edited by Research Committee on Social Trends (New York: McGraw-Hill, 1934), pp. 661–708.

Economically, the Amish farm family is an effective producing unit. Education is still largely a family function, as is recreation. Even religious services are held in the home, and, of course, prayers play an integral part in the life of every Amish family.

In a functional sense the Amish family is a remarkably strong unit. This strength, moreover, is manifest in a number of other ways. Indeed, there is considerable evidence that the Old Order Amish maintain one of the most stable family systems in America. Their birthrate is exceptionally high and is unaffected by social or economic conditions. They have a low infant-mortality rate. Nearly everyone marries, and they seldom marry outside the group. Loss of membership is not a serious problem. Husband-wife-children units are wedded to the land and show strong family and group loyalty. Their farm-type economy has proved both durable and successful.

Illegitimacy and adultery are almost unheard of. Desertion is practically unknown, and no divorces have yet been reported.

Compared to the larger society, the Amish experience fewer problems with the young—and with the old. The youth are seldom in trouble with the law, and, as mentioned earlier, the elderly are cared for by their own families, not public institutions. Orphans, widows, and other dependents are looked after by the community, and no Amish person has ever been on welfare.

One final point that should be mentioned in connection with the Amish family system is their kinship structure, for nothing like it—nothing remotely like it—exists among typical families in the United States. After all, around one-half of American couples do not even sustain their own marriage—they separate or get divorced. Of those who do stay together, one- or two-child families are the norm. As a consequence, the extended family—aunts, uncles, nieces, nephews, cousins—tends to be small in number and limited in function. In Amishland, the opposite is true. The family is clearly the heart of Amish society, and their large kin network functions as a vascular support system.

Education and Socialization

It is commonly believed that the Old Order Amish are against education, but this is not true. What they are against is the kind of education that would tend to alienate their young people and threaten their agrarian, conservative way of life. In Amishland, therefore, schooling is likely to mean reading, spelling, arithmetic, penmanship, and grammar—plus elements of geography, history, and hygiene.[26]

[26]For a detailed account of the Amish educational system, see John A. Hostetler and Gertrude Enders Huntington, *Children in Amish Society: Socialization and Community Education* (New York: Holt, Rinehart & Winston, 1971).

Today, Amish parents are more than willing to have their youngsters attend school—provided it is an Amish school—for the first eight grades. But beyond that they balk. They feel that the years fourteen to eighteen are critical, and they object to having their teenagers exposed to high-school worldliness. Over the years, the Amish community has refused to give in on this point.

In the late 1960s, Amish parents in Wisconsin were arrested and convicted for refusing to send their children to the local high school. After a series of legal battles, the case eventually reached the Supreme Court. In the landmark *Yoder v. Wisconsin* decision in 1972, the Court ruled 7–0 in favor of the Amish parents. Although acknowledging the state's justifiable interest in universal education, the Court declared that there were balancing factors, "such as those specifically protected by the Free Exercise Clause of the First Amendment, and the traditional interest of parents with respect to the religious upbringing of their children. . . ."

The Amish community continues to have school problems in a few states, but the 1972 Supreme Court decision has served to eliminate much of the ill feeling. Now, too, public opinion has swung to the side of the Amish. In Lancaster County, the Amish have worked out an accommodation with state officials on a variety of school-related matters. Any new problems will likely be handled in a similar vein.

The Amish School   Amish schools are a true reflection of the Amish people: unassuming, efficient, economical. There are no frills—no school newspaper, clubs, bands, athletic programs, dances, or class officers. The Old Order Amish have no nursery, preschool, or kindergarten programs; in fact, the large majority of their schools have but one room and one teacher. Average enrollment is about thirty.

Amish communities either build their own schools or purchase them from the state. If they are purchased, certain alterations are made, including the removal of all electrical fixtures. Amish school buildings are heated by wood or coal stoves, and generally do not have indoor toilets. But aside from differences in heating, lighting, and toilet facilities, the Amish school looks much the same as any other one-room school: blackboards, chalk, bolted desks, coat racks, posters and colorful pictures, paper and pencils, and—naturally—homemade artistry adorning the walls.

The Amish teacher, usually a young, unmarried woman, is quite different from her non-Amish counterpart. The typical American teacher is a college graduate who, by virtue of having taken specialized courses in education, has acquired a state-issued teaching certificate. The Amish teacher, by contrast, has not even been to high school, let alone college.

The followers of Jacob Amman are convinced that being a good teacher has no relationship to such things as college degrees and state-issued certificates. They feel, rather, that teaching is a kind of calling, and that the calling is a God-given attribute. The ideal Amish teacher is one who, by her very being, can convey to youngsters the Amish outlook on life. Accordingly, she should be well adjusted, religious, and totally committed to Amish principles.

Although there are exceptions, naturally, most Amish teachers are dedicated individuals. Although they have not attended high school, many of them take correspondence courses. They have their own teachers' association, attend yearly conferences, and subscribe to the Amish teachers' *Bulletin*. They are often required to serve without pay as teaching assistants for a year or so before being assigned schools of their own. And when they are given their own classrooms, they are willing to work at a very low rate of pay.

The Amish teacher is more than "just a teacher." She is also principal, janitor, nurse, custodian, playground supervisor, and disciplinarian. Although Amish children are better behaved than most, disciplinary problems do arise, in which case the teacher applies the usual antidotes: reprimands, lectures, admonitions, keeping children after school, and having them write their "sins" on the blackboard. For serious infractions—such as willful disobedience or leaving the schoolyard without permission—most Amish teachers will not hesitate to use corporal punishment. Amish do not forbid high-school and college attendance but emphasize vocational education. Therefore, Amish education beyond the age of thirteen is most likely to involve apprenticeships or learning skills appropriate to the children's future economic livelihood.

Schoolyard shootings have received considerable national attention, but the Nickel Mines Amish School was in a category of its own. In October 2006, a lone gunman came into the one-room Amish schoolhouse, killing five girls and wounding five others before turning the gun on himself. While the nation looked on, finding no easy answers for the gunman's motive, it admired the compassion shown by the local Amish community. To the killer's family, they brought food and showed unconditional support, and invited the widow to their funerals to share in the grieving. The schoolhouse was demolished four months later, and the surviving children attended a new schoolhouse built 200 yards from the old one.[27]

Values   As used by sociologists, the term **value** refers to the collective conception of what is considered good, desirable, and proper—or bad, undesirable, and improper—in a culture. In fact, values are so basic to those who hold them that they tend to be accepted without question.

---

[27]Donald K Kraybill, Steven M. Nolt, and David L. Weaver-Zercher, *Amish Grace: How Forgiveness Transcended Tragedy* (San Francisco: John Wiley, 2007); Melody Simmons, "After Shooting Amish School Embodies Effort to Heal," *New York Times*, January 31, 2007; Diane Zimmerman Umble and Advid L. Weaver-Zercher, *The Amish and the Media* (Baltimore: John Hopkins University Press, 2008).

Nancy Hoyt Belcher / Alamy

The Amish feel that depiction of faces, whether in photographs or artwork, is an unnecessary celebration of oneself and represents a graven image as forbidden in the Old Testament. Faceless dolls, not necessarily made by Amish, make a nice commodity in the tourist trade.

Most people, furthermore, seem to feel more comfortable when they are in the company of those with a similar value system.

As much as anything else, it is the totality of values that sets one group apart from another, a point well illustrated by the Amish school. It is not simply curriculum and course content that differentiate the Amish school from the public school—it is values. Accuracy, for instance, receives much greater emphasis than speed. Memorization of facts and the learning of (Amish) principles are considered more important than analytical thinking and inquisitiveness.

Amish children receive grades—from A to F—but at the same time they are taught not to compete with one another for top marks. To the Amish, talent—like so many other things in this world—is God-given; hence, it is no disgrace to be a slow learner. In their hierarchy of values, it is more important to do good and to treat others with kindness.[28]

To emphasize that all are alike in the eyes of God, children's dolls are faceless: eyes, noses, mouths, fingers, and toes are missing. The proscription against dolls with features is also consistent in the Amish belief system with the Scriptures that ban making graven images.[29]

[28]Hostetler and Huntington, *Children in Amish Society*, pp. 54–96.
[29]Susan Bender, *Plain and Simple: A Woman's Journey to the Amish* (New York: HarperCollins, 1990), pp. 17–18.

Amish schools are as much concerned with the children's moral development as they are with their mental prowess. Values such as right–wrong, better–worse, good–bad are alluded to over and over again. It is this repeated emphasis on morality—not only by the school but by the church, the home, and the community—that serves to mold the individual's conscience. This fact was mentioned earlier and is worth repeating, for although the threat of the *Meidung* undoubtedly keeps potential wrongdoers in line, it is conscience that is a key element in Amish conformity.

Challenges Facing the Amish

All groups have social problems of one kind or another, and the Old Order Amish are no exception. At the same time, the Amish do have a remarkable record in the "problems" area. Crime, corruption, poverty, divorce and desertion, alcoholism, drug addiction, wife and child abuse—such problems have a low incidence in Amishland. In fact, their low problem rate makes the followers of Jacob Amman wonder what the school controversy was all about. More than one Amish person has said, in effect, "They wanted us to send our youngsters to the consolidated public school and on to high school—but they're the ones with the problems, not us. . . ."

Human nature being what it is, the fact that the Amish have relatively few social problems does not make those that do occur any easier to solve. On the contrary, a given problem may cause more anguish in Amishland than in the larger society. At any rate, the following problems are singled out not because they represent major disruptions, but because they are recurrent headaches that the Amish must somehow learn to live with.

Rum Springa   One of the tasks that the Amish mostly succeed in fulfilling is to rear their children and keep them in the faith. Still, as one might expect, during their teenage years Amish youth often rebel. This manifests itself most vividly when Amish teenagers, especially boys, outwardly exhibit behavior unacceptable to the Amish, such as being disrespectful to their elders or engaging in worldly—that is, English—behavior, such as using a car and living a lifestyle more typical of adolescents in the United States. As scholar of the contemporary Amish Donald Kraybill puts it, "The rowdiness of Amish youth is an embarrassment to church leaders and a stigma in the larger community."[30]

---

[30]Kraybill, *Riddle of Amish Culture*, p. 138.

The allure of the English world has led the Old Order Amish to routinize, almost accept, some worldly activities among their adolescents. Amish youth often test their subculture's boundaries during a period of discovery called *rum springa,* a term that means "running around." *Rum springa* is a common occurrence but is definitely not supported by the Amish religion.

Even if *rum springa* is deviant for the Amish, those engaged in it quickly fall into a routine. Teenage boys pick up girls, signaling them with flashlights from a distance as they wait in cars borrowed from English teens. The girls sneak out and they make their way to a convenience store or gas station, quickly changing clothes and applying makeup. Then the groups of teens head to a prearranged destination to dance to pop music, smoke cigarettes, and drink liquor—hardly the America Jacob Amman envisioned.[31]

Parents often react by looking the other way, sometimes literally. For example, when they hear radio sounds from a barn or a motorcycle entering their property in the middle of the night, they don't immediately investigate and punish their offspring. Instead, they pretend not to notice, secure in the comfort that their children almost always return to the traditions of the Amish lifestyle.

Despite the flirtations with English technology and modernity during *rum springa,* the vast majority of Amish youth "come home," return to the Amish community, and become baptized into the faith. They take this step knowing full well that joining the church as a young adult is for all intents and purposes an irrevocable act. Scholarly studies report 85 to 90 percent of Amish children accept the faith as young adults.[32]

In 2004, UPN aired the ten-week long "Amish in the City" reality program featuring five Amish youths, allegedly on *rum springa,* who move in with six citywise young adults in Los Angeles. Critics on behalf of the Amish community noted that this exploitation showed how vulnerable that Amish are, since no program would be developed to try to show the conversion of Muslim or Orthodox Jewish youth.[33]

Threat of Modernization   Every decade brings a variety of new inventions and technological improvements to society at large, and the Amish must continually fight against the inroads. Automobiles, telephones,

---

[31]Tom Shachtman, *Rumspringa: To Be or Not Be Amish* (New York: North Point Press, 2006).

[32]Richard A. Stevick, *Growing Up Amish: The Teenage Years* (Baltimore: Johns Hopkins University Press, 2007); Shachtman, *Rumspringa,* p. 250.

[33]Bernard Weinraub, "UPN Show Is Called Insensitive to Amish," *New York Times,* March 4, 2004, pp. B1, B8.

electric lights, tractors, radio and television—such things have taken their toll on the followers of Jacob Amman. Every Amish community knows of adult members who have left the fold because of what they felt were unnecessarily strict rules.

In several cases, entire congregations have seceded. Thus in 1927, an Amish bishop, Moses M. Beachy, led a movement away from the main body. As mentioned earlier, members of this group—known today as the Beachy or Church Amish—are permitted to own automobiles and certain other modern conveniences. In 1966, a group known as the New Order Amish began to form. The New Order have installed telephones, permit the use of electricity, and use tractor-drawn farm machinery.[34]

If, as is so often the case, history repeats itself, the Old Order Amish will probably experience further schisms and secessions in the decades to come.

Annoyance of Tourism—Or Is It?   The Amish are a folk society whose way of life until very recently hinged on remaining apart from the rest of the world. For them the influx of tourists into Amishland represented an irritating problem. Today, however, there are a growing number of Amish who welcome tourism with open arms.

State tourism officials got a surprise when they hired a Virginia firm to study tourism in Pennsylvania. It was thought that the Pocono Mountains or the picturesque Allegheny National Forest would top the list. Instead, Amish country was the top draw—over 8 million visitors annually. Outsiders still own most of the businesses in Amish country: motels, guest houses, restaurants, farmers' markets, country stores, handicraft outlets, antique sales, souvenir and novelty shops, discount operations, buggy rides; the list seems endless. Most Amish are content with farming and remain annoyed with tourists. But the Amish population is growing and the land available to them is diminishing. As a consequence, many Amish are now catering to tourists in a variety of ways. Still, only a small fraction of the tourist dollars go to the Amish.[35]

Bus tours—as many as fifty a day—are especially obnoxious to the Amish community. Run by professional tour guides, the vehicles clog the narrow roads, block the horses and buggies, park in front of the schools and farms, and otherwise upset the daily routine. Also, the Old Order

---

[34]Lawrence P. Greksa and Jill E. Korbin, "Key Decisions in the Lines of the Old Order Amish: Joining the Church and Migrating to Another Settlement," *Mennonite Quarterly Review* 74 (November 4, 2002), pp. 373–98; Kraybill, *Amish of Lancaster County,* pp. 42–44.

[35]"Amish Country State's Top Tourist Attraction," *Morning Call,* Allentown, PA, June 2, 1999; Kraybill, *Amish of Lancaster County,* pp. 68–70.

Amish are forbidden to have their pictures taken, but camera-wielding tourists often seem to laugh at the proscription.[36]

The media, as we saw with "Amish in the City," have not always been kind to the Amish. In 1985, the motion picture *Witness,* starring Harrison Ford and Kelly McGillis, was released. Filmed over a ten-week period in Lancaster County, the picture purports to show various episodes in the lifestyle of the Old Order Amish. The Amish themselves objected strongly to the film, feeling that it was an invasion of both their privacy and their religion. They were upset with the depiction of Amish being violent, even if provoked, and of a relationship between an Amish woman and an English man. Nevertheless, the film proved to be immensely popular at the box office. How many viewers were prompted to visit Amishland firsthand will never be known, but the number must have been substantial.

A few Amish families have left the area for quieter pastures. Others operate the hundreds of craft shops and produce stands that now dot the landscape. Some observers feel that large-scale tourism has tended to reinforce cultural identity among the Amish, but this is debatable. In any case, the Amish of Lancaster County are one of the largest tourist attractions in America, and the situation is not likely to change. In most other areas, fortunately, tourism is not nearly so pressing.

Government Intervention   As the nation grows, the web of government becomes more complicated, laws proliferate, bureaucracy increases, and the Amish, no less than other citizens, are confronted with a maze of regulations. The followers of Jacob Amman must now have their children vaccinated and inoculated. Amish dairy farmers have been forced to have their milk inspected according to government regulations. And, though outsiders may or may not be aware of it, the Amish must pay state and federal income taxes, property taxes, and sales taxes.

At one time or another the Old Order Amish have also had run-ins with government agencies regarding such issues as compulsory education, building codes, social security and Medicare, safety devices on buggies, zoning regulations, unemployment insurance, and military conscription.

The last issue—involving draft laws and compulsory military service—deserves special mention, for the Amish are pacifists in a total sense. They will not fight *under any condition.* As Huntington points out, "All forms of retaliation to hostility are forbidden. An Amishman may not physically

---

[36]A number of excellent pictorial accounts of Amish life have been published. Among them are Ruth Seitz and Blair Seitz, *Amish Ways* (Harrisburg, PA: R B Books, 1992); John Wasilchick, *Amish Life: A Portrait of Plain Living* (New York: Crescent Books, 1991); and Leslie Hauslein and Jerry Irwin, *The Amish: The Enduring Spirit* (Godalming, Surrey, England: Colour Library Books, 1990).

defend himself or his family even when attacked. He is taught to follow the New Testament of the Sermon on the Mount."[37]

It follows, of course, that the Old Order Amish will not serve in the armed forces or otherwise fight for their country. And because of their stand, they had some altercations with the authorities during both world wars. Generally, though, their position has been respected by the government. If they were to be drafted today, Amish youth would be allowed to perform alternative service as conscientious objectors.

It would not be correct to say the Amish are apolitical. After the September 11, 2001, terrorist attack, Amish reported being confronted by English about their patriotism. Indeed, to many outsiders, the fact that Amish do not fly the flag seemed suspicious. While they are pacifist, they would declare they love their country and teach their children to respect the flag. In fact, these conservative values led the 2004 campaign of George W. Bush to encourage Amish to get out and vote. While some church leaders still caution against voting, ultimately the church leaves voting up to the individual. However, for many Amish, voting may not be the highest priority. Election Day falls on a very popular day for weddings, and as one Pennsylvania Amish man said, "If I hitch my horse there at the wedding, there's no way I'm going to make it all the way back to vote."[38]

When all is said and done, nevertheless, there is no doubt that the followers of Jacob Amman often find government regulations both burdensome and obstructive. As the record shows, they have had more than their share of bureaucratic grief. And although they have thus far been able to hold their own, the Amish community never knows when trouble will strike again.

Vanishing Farmland: The Number-One Problem?   Many observers feel that the scarcity of farmland is the biggest problem facing the Amish today. Although there is no real shortage of land in the United States, good farmland is extremely scarce in some Amish communities. The reasons are rather obvious. The Old Order Amish are increasing much faster than the population at large, and because most Amish turn to farming, the supply of arable land in a given community tends to become exhausted.

From the Amish point of view, what is the answer?

Aside from subdividing their farmland among one or more of their sons—clearly a limited solution—the followers of Jacob Amman have only two realistic choices. They can relocate or turn to nonfarming occupations. Over the past fifty years, relocation has not been favored.

---

[37]Gertrude Enders Huntington, "The Amish Family," in Charles Mindel, Robert Habenstein, and Roosevelt Wright, eds., *Ethnic Families in America* (New York: Elsevier, 1988), p. 382.

[38]"Bus people," *The Economist*, October 16, 2004, p. 29; Kraybill, *Amish of Lancaster County*, p. 60.

Some have migrated across the country or even to Latin America. Although it now appears that the option to migrate is open, it does not appear that mass migration is on the immediate horizon. What is evident, however, is that the Amish have turned increasingly to other occupations.

The Future

To begin with—and speaking generally—the followers of Jacob Amman are very good in the "problem-solving" area. Some critics have argued that the Amish will not survive in their present form, that they will be gobbled up by high-powered, industrialized society. The Amish, however, have outlasted their critics and in all likelihood will continue to do so.

The aforementioned social problems, although certainly real enough, are somewhat deceptive. The youth problem is actually not so serious as it sounds. True, more than a few of their young people misbehave, and a number even defect to other groups—but this process serves as another safety valve. The Amish know full well that their rules are strict and that certain individuals will be unable to conform. But by giving their young people a certain amount of leeway prior to baptism, it is felt that those who do join the church will prove to be loyal and conscientious members.

In practice, the safety-valve theory seems to work, because—overall—a small percentage of baptized members actually leave the fold. As previously discussed, the Amish population has shown spectacular growth: 5,000 in 1900; 33,000 in 1950; well over 230,000 in 2009.

Tourism seems to be more of a chronic irritation than a major problem. And one way or another, the Old Order Amish have learned to live with it. In fact—ironically enough—although most of the tourist dollars go to the non-Amish, tourism does provide the Amish community with ever-increasing income.

Problems such as government intervention and the threat of modernization are evidently being taken in stride. It is true that the vanishing farmland has more or less forced some Amish men to take other jobs, and this transposition should not be minimized. It is important, however, to look at the *nature* of these jobs. In Lancaster County, for instance, the Amish have not sought blanket entry into the outside job market. On the contrary, their choice of occupations has been highly selective.

As Kraybill points out, many of the men work in craft shops located on or adjacent to the farm. Married women who work—at quilting, baking, craftwork—do so at home. Amish men operate a wide array of shops and small businesses: cabinetry, plumbing, construction, hardware, butchering, machinery repair, masonry, upholstery, furniture, and a variety of retail stores. However, they generally reject factory work as being a bad influence. Indeed, more than 75 percent of those who work away from home are either self-employed or work for an Amish employer.[39]

The same author goes on to conclude that although a third of the Lancaster County Amish have left the farm, "they have not embraced modern work. Nonfarm work is, by and large, local, family-oriented, small-scale, and nestled in ethnic networks. The Amish have retained personal craftsmanship and job satisfaction, as well as a high degree of identity with, and control over, their products. Moreover, they also control the time, speed, and other conditions of their work."[40]

Conclusion   All things considered, the Amish would seem to have a promising future in America. They have handled their problems inimitably and, on the whole, successfully. In the process, they have managed to solidify their identity. Outlook on life, relation to God and the universe, theology, sex roles, clothing styles, love of the soil, separatism, frugality, humility, pacifism, industriousness, attitude toward education—in brief, the basic ingredients of "Amishness"—are much the same today as they always have been.

In the past, the Old Order Amish have sometimes been misunderstood, hassled, fined, and even jailed. Today, they tend to benefit from public opinion. Tourism has brought millions of Americans to the various Amish communities. And as people have come to see and learn about the Amish firsthand, they have also come to respect the Amish way of life. Consequently, in disputes with the government, an Amish community can often count on valuable public support.

The Amish lifestyle, while at variance with larger society, enjoys a bit of nostalgia among contemporary Americans. With the rise of environmentalism and concern over the carbon footprint we leave, many now envy the ability to function so simply today and, even more important, to enjoy life. In fact, the slang term "urban Amish" has entered the vocabulary to refer to those who have none of the technological devices such as television, microwave, or a home computer. Furthermore, the recent bank failures also led to certain admiration by some for the Amish, who seem to thrive without embracing capitalism.[41]

As they look ahead, the Amish in general are quite optimistic, both in a secular and a sacred sense. The latter, of course, is the critical component, for the followers of Jacob Amman have placed themselves in God's hands— permanently—and they have absolutely no doubts about their future.

---

[39]Kraybill, *Riddle of Amish Culture*, pp. 197–205.

[40]Kraybill, *Riddle of Amish Culture*, p. 211.

[41]"Urban Amish," accessed March 16, 2009 at http://www.urbandictionary.com/define .php?term=urban%20amish; Belkin, "A Bank Run," 2009.

KEY TERMS

Anabaptist, p. 39
Conspicuous consumption, p. 43
Deviance, p. 58
Endogamy, p. 60
English (or Englishers), p. 42
Exogamy, p. 61

Meidung, p. 39
Relative deprivation, p. 55
Rum springa, p. 71
Sanctions, p. 58
Value, p. 68

SOURCES ON THE WEB

www.amish.net
This site is intended to serve travelers touring Amish areas—particularly
Pennsylvania, Ohio, and Indiana.

www.thirdway.com
The Third Way Café, produced by Mennonite Media, has information primarily
on Mennonites, but covers the Amish as well.

http://holycrosslivonia.org/amish/
This site of the National Committee for Amish Religious Freedom seeks to defend
the religious freedom of the Old Order Amish religion in the United States.

www2.etown.edu/amishstudies/informativehomepage
Informative fact sheets from a college Amish studies program.

SELECTED READINGS

Altick, Richard D. *Remembering Lancaster.* Hamden, CT: Archon, 1991.
Ammon, Richard. *Growing Up Amish.* New York: Atheneum, 1989.
Armstrong, Penny, and Sheryl Feldman. *A Midwife's Story.* New York: Arbor
House, 1986.
Beachy, Eli R. *Tales from the Peoli Road: Wit and Humor of Very Real People, Who Just
Happen to Be Amish.* Scottdale, PA: Herald Press, 1992.
Bender, Sue. *Plain and Simple: A Woman's Journey to the Amish.* New York: Harper-
Collins, 1990.
Fisher, Sara, and Rachel Stahl. *The Amish School.* Intercourse, PA: Good Books,
1986.
Good, Merle, and Phyllis Good. *20 Most Asked Questions about the Amish and
Mennonites.* Intercourse, PA: Good Books, 1995.
Hauslein, Leslie A., and Jerry Irwin. *The Amish: The Enduring Spirit.* Godalming,
Surrey, England: Colour Library Books, 1990.

Hostetler, John A., *Amish Society*. 4th ed. Baltimore: Johns Hopkins University Press, 1993.

_____, ed. *Amish Roots: A Treasury of History, Wisdom and Lore*. Baltimore: Johns Hopkins University Press, 1989.

_____, and Gertrude Enders Huntington. *Children in Amish Society: Socialization and Community Education*. New York: Holt, Rinehart & Winston, 1971.

Huntington, Gertrude Enders. "The Amish Family." In *Ethnic Families in America*, edited by Charles Mindel, Robert Habenstein, and Roosevelt Wright, pp. 367–99. New York: Elsevier, 1988.

Kraybill, Donald. *The Puzzles of Amish Life*. Intercourse, PA: Good Books, 1990.

_____. *The Riddle of Amish Culture*. rev. ed. Baltimore: Johns Hopkins University Press, 2001.

_____. *The Amish and the State*. Baltimore: Johns Hopkins University Press, 2003.

_____. *The Amish of Lancaster County*. Mechanicsburg PA: Stackpole Books, 2008.

_____ and Steven M. Nolte. *Amish Enterprise: From Plow to Profit*. Baltimore: Johns Hopkins University Press, 1995.

Luthy, David. *The Amish in America: Settlements That Failed, 1840–1960*. Aylmer, Ontario: Pathway, 1986.

Mackall, Joe. *Plain Secrets: An Outsider Among the Amish*. Boston: Beacon Press, 2007.

Morello, Carol. "Embattled Midwife to the Amish." *Philadelphia Inquirer*, July 23, 1989.

Nolt, Steven M., and Thomas J. Meyers. *Plain Diversity: Amish Cultures and Identities*. Baltimore: John Hopkins University Press, 2007.

Schlabach, Theron F. *Peace, Faith Nation: Mennonites and Amish in Nineteenth-Century America*. Vol. 2 of *The Mennonite Experience in America*. Scottdale, PA: Herald Press, 1988.

Scott, Stephen. *Plain Buggies: Amish, Mennonite, and Brethren Horse-Drawn Transportation*. Intercourse, PA: Good Books, 1981.

_____. *Why Do They Dress That Way?* Intercourse, PA: Good Books, 1986.

_____. *The Amish Wedding and Other Special Occasions of the Old Order Communities*. Intercourse, PA: Good Books, 1988.

Seitz, Ruth, and Blair Seitz. *Amish Ways*. Harrisburg, PA: R B Books, 1991.

Shachtman, Tom. *Rumspringa: To Be or Not to Be Amish*. New York: North Point Press, 2006.

Smith, Elmer. *The Amish People*. New York: Exposition Press, 1958.

Smucker, Donovan E. *The Sociology of Mennonites, Hutterites, and Amish: A Bibliography with Annotations, Volume II 1977–1990*. Waterloo, Ontario, Canada: Wilfrid Laurier University Press, 1991.

Stevick, Ruhad A. *Growing Up Amish: The Teenage Years*. Baltimore: John Hopkins University Press, 2007.

Umble, Diana Zimmerman and David L. Weaver-Zercher (eds.). *The Amish and the Media*. Baltimore: John Hopkins University Press, 2008.

Wasilchick, John V. *Amish Life: A Portrait of Plain Living*. New York: Crescent Books, 1992.

Weaver, J. Denny. *Becoming Anabaptist: The Origin and Significance of Sixteenth-Century Anabaptism.* Scottdale, PA: Herald Press, 1987.

Weaver-Zercher, David L. *Writing the Amish: The Worlds of John A. Hostetler.* University Park, PA: Pennsylvania State University Press, 2005.

Wittmer, Joe. *The Gentle People: Personal Reflections of Amish Life.* Minneapolis: Educational Media, 1990.

Yoder, Paton. *Tradition and Transition: Amish Mennonites and Old Order Amish 1800–1900.* Scottdale, PA: Herald Press, 1991.

CHAPTER THREE

THE SHAKERS

On a warm July Sunday morning, I entered the Meetinghouse for worship.[1] I came through the left door, appropriate for men, and sat on a bench directly behind Brother Arnold, at fifty-two the youngest Shaker. Facing directly across from me were benches for the women. Seated on the first bench were Sister Frances, age eighty-three, and Sister June, age seventy. We were seated in the Meetinghouse built in 1794, still bearing the original blue- and white-painted interior and natural wood trim. The room was brightly lit by the sun shining through the many windows—devoid of drapes to allow the outside in. The three Shakers dressed simply but not necessarily in muted colors. The brother wore a leather vest over a white high-collared shirt. The two sisters were in long pastel dresses with a large cotton kerchief folded and draped over the shoulders—a vestige of over two hundred years of modesty.

Just before ten A.M. Brother Arnold sounded the Great Bell, which was from the Alfred, New York, settlement that had ended in 1931. The gathering was totally quiet. Sister June called the meeting (or service) to order by remarking on the beautiful day and asking us to open our 1885 hymnals and join in singing a Shaker melody a cappella (i.e., without musical accompaniment).

That morning in a small settlement on a hilltop 35 miles northwest of Portland, Maine, there were about a dozen community friends, myself

---

[1]The following account is based on a visit to the Sabbathday Lake community in July 2009 by Richard Schaefer. Fieldwork was also completed at the Pleasant Hill and South Union Shaker communities in Kentucky the same year.

and my wife, and all the living members of the United Society of Believers in Christ's Second Appearing. The Shakers (or the Believers) and their friends read from the Old and New Testaments, recited the Lord's Prayer, and gave or asked others to offer testimonials spontaneously on the meeting's theme of "forgiveness." Brother Arnold gave testimony to his father, who had died 21 years earlier to the day. His testimony described his father's unhappiness when Brother Arnold first became a Shaker. The two did not speak for many years afterward. However, speaking to the theme of the service, they eventually forgave each other and resumed a warm relationship.

The group sang a dozen Shaker tunes throughout the one-hour meeting. One community visitor gave testimony to a particularly trying experience in her own home that occurred that morning and caused her to be late. The woman emotionally explained that the biological father of her adopted daughter, age sixteen, had called that morning to say once again that he was not coming that afternoon as planned to meet the daughter he has never seen. Keeping with the theme of the service, she hoped that she could help her daughter find forgiveness. All gathered sat in stillness, unsure of what to say or do. Sister Frances quickly broke out in the well-known melody, "Simple Gifts" ("'Tis the gift to be simple, 'tis the gift to be free . . . To turn, turn will be our delight"), and was joined in song heartily by all present, relieving the anxiety displayed by the visitor.

Following the meeting, everyone greeted each other warmly and Sister Frances made a point of seeking out new faces, such as mine, and making everyone feel welcome!

Mother Ann Lee

The Shaker experience of the twenty-first century has its roots in eighteenth-century England. Although her actual birth record has never been discovered, Shaker tradition says that Ann Lee was born in Manchester, England, on February 29, 1736. She came from a working-class family, and while much of her background remains obscure, there is no doubt that Ann Lee was one of the "common folk." She had no education of any kind, and at an early age was forced to work at menial jobs. From all indications, her working-class origins and bleak childhood were instrumental in shaping both the Shaker economy and the Shaker philosophy.[2]

---

[2]For a good account of Shaker history and lifestyles, see Priscilla J. Brewer, *Shaker Communities, Shaker Lives* (Hanover: University Press of New England, 1986), and Stephen J. Stein, *The Shaker Experience in America: A History of the United Society of Believers* (New Haven, CT: Yale University Press, 1992).

When she was twenty-two, the turning point came in Ann Lee's life, although neither she nor anyone else realized it at the time. She became acquainted with James and Jane Wardley, leaders of a radical religious sect. Originally Quakers, the Wardleys had "seen the light"—that is, came to believe the Christ Spirit would manifest itself a second time in the body of woman—and broke away from the Society of Friends. We will return to the duality in the Shaker view of the sacred as both a man and a woman later in this chapter.

It is difficult to describe a religious meeting of the Wardley group, but it must have been a sight to behold. Starting with a silent meditation so typical of the Quakers, the Wardleyites gradually adopted a more outward expression of spirituality. They would erupt into a paroxysm of shouting, shaking, and talking with the Lord. Because of these "agitations of the body," the group came to be called by a variety of names: jumpers, shiverers, Shaking Quakers, and eventually, Shakers.

These early Shakers retained some of their Quaker practices—such as simplicity of dress and pacifism—but they had no definitive theology or philosophy. And while Ann Lee was welcomed, she had no immediate impact on the group. In 1762, however, an event took place that was to have a lasting effect on both Ann Lee and the Shakers. She married one Abraham Stanley. Being illiterate, both signed the marriage registry with an X.

Sexual Desires   Exactly why the marriage took place is not known, for the couple was obviously not suited to one another, as will be discussed later. Ann had physical difficulties during childbirth. She had four children, all of whom died in early infancy. For the last child, forceps were employed, and Ann Lee's life was in real danger. Although she survived, she was convinced that children signified trouble.

Ann Lee interpreted the childbirth catastrophe as a sign of God's displeasure. In her view, she had given way to temptations of the flesh—not once, but several times. And on each occasion she had been punished severely. Thus, it was sexual desires that were the root of all evil, and unless a person could repress this desire, he or she would have to answer for the consequences. Since sex and marriage were strongly intertwined, marriage per se must be wrong.

Soon Ann started to avoid her husband. By her own confession, she began to regard her bed "as if it had been made of embers." She also took a more active role in the Shakers and began speaking out against sins of the flesh. And while in the beginning not all group members agreed with her, she eventually won them over. Before long, the Shakers were not only condemning all carnal practices, including marriage, but were also criticizing the established church for permitting such activities.

The townspeople of Manchester were quick to react. Allegations of sorcery, heresy, and blasphemy were made, and on several occasions angry mobs attacked Ann Lee. Once she was imprisoned for "disturbing the congregation" of Christ Church, Manchester. Shaker tradition has it that she was treated cruelly, locked in a small cell for two weeks, and left without food. She would have died except for one of her ardent disciples who, during the night, managed to insert a small pipe into the keyhole of her cell, through which he fed her milk and wine. Although the prison story is doubtless an exaggeration, it does show the reverence with which Ann Lee had come to be regarded by the Shakers.

Emergence of a Leader   Predictably, Ann Lee soon found herself the Shaker leader, saint, and martyr all in one. The Shakers had felt for some time that the Second Coming of Christ was imminent, and that it would be in the form of a woman. After Ann Lee's prison experience, they were sure that "she was the one." From that day on, she was known as Mother Ann Lee and invested with a messiahship, a belief that the Shakers hold to this day. In fact, while they accept the term "Shakers," the official name of the organization is the United Society of Believers in Christ's Second Appearing, or Believers for short.

What kind of person was Ann Lee that she could command such devotion and reverence on the part of her followers? Physically, she was a short, thickset woman with brown hair, blue eyes, and a fair complexion. According to her followers, she had a dignified beauty that inspired trust. By all accounts, she was a dedicated, unselfish, thoughtful, and totally fearless individual.

However, as with so many other leaders discussed in the present volume (such as John Humphrey Noyes of the Oneida Community, discussed in Chapter 5 and Father Divine, discussed in Chapter 7), verbal descriptions are grossly inadequate. Ann Lee had a genuinely charismatic bearing, a compelling inner force that made itself felt whenever she was among her followers. In some indefinable way, she was able to make them feel that they were in the presence of a heavenly person.

Beginnings in America

A few months after her release from prison, Mother Ann Lee had a divine revelation in which she was not only directed to go to America, but was assured that in the New World the Believers would prosper and grow. Revelation aside, it was becoming apparent that the Shakers had little future in England or on the Continent. Their physical gyrations and their renunciation of sex had brought them little except physical abuse and legal prosecution. Accordingly, they made plans for their overseas voyage, and in May 1774 Ann Lee and eight of her followers set sail for

The Shakers

1700–1750	1750–1800	1800–1850	1850–1900	1900–1950	1950–2010

Above the timeline:

Ann Lee is born
1736

Ann Lee dies
1784

Lincoln grants the Shakers exemption from draft
1863

Sabbathday Lake becomes the only settlement with living Shakers
1992

Below the timeline:

1774
The Shakers arrive in America

1805
Shaker settlements spread west to Kentucky

1984
PBS airs Ken Burns's documentary, "The Shakers"

New York. Oddly enough, the Wardleys did not accompany her. Odder still—and for reasons best known to himself—her husband did.

Arriving in August, the little band of Believers soon established themselves at Niskayuna, a tract of land just outside Albany. They put up buildings, cleared land, planted crops, and brought in money through blacksmithing, shoemaking, and weaving. But in a spiritual sense, progress was discouragingly slow. Records indicate that by 1779 they had gained but a single convert. Abraham Stanley, moreover, seems to have vanished from the scene.

Some of the group became disconsolate over the failure of Shakerism to make much headway, but Mother Ann preached patience. When the time was right, she would say, new converts would "come like doves." Sure enough, before many months had passed, converts did indeed come streaming in. The most important convert was Joseph Meachem, a Baptist minister and one of the most influential members of the clergy in the area. Meachem not only became an eloquent supporter of Mother Ann, but also ultimately proved to be one of the two or three most influential figures in the history of the Believers.

In spite of her success, Ann Lee faced two difficulties sometimes overlooked by historians. The first pertains to the gender roles of her time. As we saw in the discussion of the Gypsies in Chapter 1, gender roles refer to what men and women are traditionally expected to do. In the 1700s, gender roles were sharply defined. Men and women had quite different roles, particularly in the occupational sphere, and there was little overlap. The professions—for example, medicine, dentistry, law, higher education, the clergy—were male provinces, and any female who sought admittance was suspect. For all intents and purposes, the clergy was entirely male. The fact that Ann Lee was not only the head of her church but believed by her followers to be the incarnation of Christ was a handicap of major proportion.

The second difficulty faced by Mother Ann was the fact that her position on sex and marriage was not popular. True, she was preaching in a period close to Puritanism, yet the Shaker doctrine was extreme even for that day and age. That Ann Lee was able to win adherents in spite of the celibacy rule is a further tribute to her spiritual and charismatic powers.

Persecution and Prosecution

The first decade of the Shakers in North America (1774–1784) virtually coincided with the Revolutionary War. And the Shakers—recently arrived from England—were naturally suspected of being British sympathizers. It was almost inevitable that the followers of Ann Lee would be suspected of formenting trouble, and in 1780 the inevitable happened as people were suspicious of the Shakers' recruitment efforts. Among those jailed were Mother Ann Lee, Joseph Meachem, William Lee, Mary Partington, John Hocknell, and James Whittaker.

Joseph Meachem has already been mentioned. William Lee was Ann Lee's brother. The Hocknells and Partingtons were the only members of the original group to come from the moneyed class; in fact, John Hocknell had supplied most of the capital for the Shakers' passage to America and for the land at Niskayuna. And it was James Whittaker who had reportedly kept Ann Lee from starving to death in an English jail by feeding her through the keyhole. Thus, virtually the entire Shaker leadership was in jail because of alleged British sympathies.

Even after they were released from prison, unruly mobs showered the Believers with indignities and abuse. Fines, expulsions, jail sentences, beatings, clubbings—at times it must have seemed as though God had deserted them. James Whittaker was beaten and left for dead. William Lee had his skull badly fractured by a rock. Mother Ann was stoned and severely mauled on several occasions. And while all three managed to survive, the fact that they died at a relatively young age is attributed to their recurrent exposure to hostile mobs.

The Death of Mother Ann   In September 1783, Ann Lee and her lieutenants returned to Niskayuna, after having been on the road for more than two years. In most respects, their trip had been successful. They had spread the Shaker faith to those who had never heard it before. They had gained a great many converts. They had laid the specific groundwork for at least a half-dozen Shaker societies. By their devotion to principle and refusal to yield to pressure, they earned the sympathy and respect of many Americans who otherwise disagreed with their position.

On the negative side, however, it was obvious that the sojourn had taken its toll. The first to succumb was William Lee, who died only ten months after the return to Niskayuna. He was a strapping young man who had served as a kind of bodyguard to his sister, but the ravages of mob action had taken their toll. His death visibly affected Mother Ann, also in declining health. Two months later, on September 8, 1784, Ann Lee died, although she was only forty-eight years old. Apparently she had had premonitions, because a few days before her death she was heard to remark, "I see Brother William coming, in a golden chariot, to take me home."

The exact cause of Mother Ann's death has been a subject of historical debate. Oral history among the Shakers said she had died after a mob in Petersham, Massachusetts, dragged her down a set of stairs feet first. She was assaulted and her clothes were torn off as the mob attempted to ascertain if she was indeed a woman. Fifty years after her death, her remains were exhumed and moved to a new burial site. At this time it was discovered that she had sustained a fractured skull, seeming to confirm the account she had died at the hands of persecutors of the faith.[3]

Thus ended the short but very remarkable career of an extraordinary person. Through the quiet force of her own personality, she was able to transform a tiny band into a respected and rapidly growing religious body. And while the United Society of Believers in Christ's Second Appearing was not to become one of the major religious organizations, it was to have a prolonged and interesting history. Indeed, the Shakers were to become one of the largest, longest-lasting, and most successful of all the communes in America.

A **commune** is a form of cooperative living in which community assets are shared and individual ownership is discouraged. Today, communes are popularly associated with the hippies and "flower power" of the 1960s, but communes have a long history. Sometimes they are referred to as utopian communities or, reflecting their classless economic system, as communistic. Communism, in its pure theoretical version, takes its lead from communes with no inequality and no distinctions of social rank. Communes, such as the Shaker settlements that developed, are organized so that everyone shares in the decision making and economic output. Later we will examine the nineteenth-century communes of the Oneida community.

The Attractions of Shaker Life

For the next seventy-five years or so, the Believers grew and prospered, eventually expanding into nineteen different societies in eight states— with a reported all-time membership of some 17,000. This figure is

[3]Brewer, *Shaker Communities, Shaker Lives*, footnote 26, p. 240; Anita Sanchez, *Lincoln's Chair: The Shakers and Their Quest for Peace* (Granville, OH: McDonald & Woodward Publishing Co., 2009), p. 31.

especially noteworthy when one considers that most other experimental groups of the period—New Harmony, Brook Farm, the Fourierists, and others—fell by the wayside after a few short years.

Shaker societies imposed strict rules on their members: confession of sins, rejection of marriage, celibacy, manual labor, separation from the world, and total renunciation of private property in favor of a communal, classless economy. Taken collectively, these factors would seem to weigh against a growth in membership. Yet in practice there was a pronounced growth. Why?

Although a combination of factors was involved, several had to do with the latent functions of the Shaker community. According to Merton, many social processes and institutions have a dual function. **Manifest functions** are open, stated, conscious, and deliberate, while **latent functions** are unconscious or unintended.[4]

College fraternities and sororities, for example, have the manifest function of providing food, housing, and camaraderie for interested students. There is also a latent function: the conferring of social status upon those invited to membership. And so it was with the Shakers. Men and women joined manifestly because they believed in the religious orientation of the group, but in a latent sense, the Shaker community provided them with certain rewards not otherwise attainable.

An End to Married Life   There is no denying the fact that some people joined because of an unhappy married life. Today, couples who are dissatisfied have ready recourse to the divorce courts, but it was not always so. In many of the colonies, there was simply no provision for divorce. Even where it was permitted, divorce was a rare occurrence because it was socially unacceptable. For unhappy spouses, therefore, the United Society offered a legitimate way out. A couple could join one of the many Shaker communities, and by following the rules—one of which was that the sexes be segregated—could start a whole new way of life. For some of them sexual abstinence may have been a positive.

Economic Security   The Believers also provided a haven for those women whose husbands had died and who had no real means of support. This was especially true for women with small children. Life insurance was virtually unheard of in this period, and jobs for women were severely limited, both in number and kind. Furthermore, social welfare programs—Medicare, social security, family aid, and the like—were to be hallmarks of the twentieth century, not the nineteenth. At any rate, widows often had a hard time—one reason why converts to the Believers were so often women. Membership lists have always shown a

---

[4]Robert K. Merton, *Social Theory and Social Structure* (New York: Free Press, 1968).

preponderance of females over males, the actual ratio being approximately two to one.

One explicit reflection of how the Believers viewed marriage can be seen in the treatment of widow's last names. A widow relinquishes her husband's name and uses her maiden name, as if to eradicate, as much as possible, all traces of the marriage.[5]

It was not only widows, of course, who were attracted to the economic security provided by the Believers. Some Americans were just not suited to the demands of capitalism. By virtue of such factors as temperament, ability, or outlook on life, they simply had no desire to engage in the day-to-day challenge of a competitive system. Such individuals found a more relaxed atmosphere and a more secure way of life within the confines of a commune.

Sociability   An interviewer, in talking to one of the older Shaker women, asked, "What was there about the Shaker way of life that attracted so many people?" The woman replied almost without thinking, "Well, you knew everybody cared about you. There was good feeling all around, lots of people to be with and talk to. It was a very pleasant association." Shakers were rarely alone. The living arrangements in a typical family dwelling called for several people of the same sex to share the same bedroom. Sometimes the members were grouped by age or occupation, but privacy was at a premium.[6]

Emotionality and Hyperactivity   Another reason for the Shaker success with converts was that some Americans genuinely embraced the emotionality and hyperactivity that were the hallmarks of the United Society's brand of worship. Throughout most of their existence, the Believers engaged in some rather frenzied behavior. And while most of their day-to-day routine was marked by order, steadfastness, and laborious attention to the details of community living, their religious services were something else, as will be discussed later.

Christ on Earth   There were some Americans who also concluded that Mother Ann was indeed the incarnation of Christ. This view of the group's founder as a child of—as well as messenger from—God is an attribute the Shakers share with another extraordinary group, the Father Divine movement, which we will discuss later.

Shaker literature has attributed a number of miracles to Mother Ann Lee. Her gift of healing included mending broken bones and crippled

---

[5]Raymond L. Muncy, *Sex and Marriage in Utopian Communities* (Bloomington: Indiana University Press, 1973), p. 20.
[6]Brewer, *Shaker Communities, Shaker Lives,* p. 69.

joints, curing infections and sores, obliterating cancer, healing lameness, and so on. For those who believed in these miracles, it is easy to see why the United Society came to be accepted as their one true faith. These, then, were the attractions of the Shakers. They are important to consider, since being a celibate group, the only way the Society could grow was by conversion. Conversions were their lifeblood, and for many decades the blood flowed smoothly and with amazing vitality.

Expansion

James Whittaker succeeded Ann Lee as head of the Shakers, and upon Whittaker's death in 1786, Joseph Meachem assumed the leadership. Again, it was a matter of the right person in the right place at the right time. For by now, what the Believers needed above all else was someone to systematize, organize, and set the stage for expansion. Joseph Meachem was that person.

Father Joseph was a brilliant organizer, and one of his first acts was to appoint Lucy Wright to the headship "in the female line." She was an exceptionally intelligent woman and a sound leader in her own right. These two guided the Society for ten years, and following Joseph Meachem's death in 1796, Mother Lucy continued in the top position for another twenty-five years. Joseph Meachem and Lucy Wright were the first of the American-born Shaker leaders.

After the head community was established at New Lebanon, New York, the United Society of Believers grew—both numerically and geographically—for many decades. Some of the settlements were founded and developed with little difficulty. Others, however, were faced with the most deplorable conditions: persecutions and mob violence, topographical handicaps, attacks by Native Americans, inadequate medical facilities, and other perils associated with a frontier environment. Considering the poor roads of the period, Shaker expansionism seems even more impressive. Most of their communities were hundreds of miles from one another.

Civil War   The Civil War was a significant time for the Shakers. As pacifists, their faith precluded service in either the Union or Confederate military. Their beliefs in equality left them sympathetic to the cause to end slavery and therefore to defeat the Confederacy. They enthusiastically welcomed freed slaves to their communities. Two Shaker leaders visited President Lincoln in Washington, D.C., and successfully pled their case for the exemption of all the Shaker men from the draft. In gratitude, the Shakers sent Lincoln a gift of one of their distinctive chairs, which Lincoln acknowledged in written communication as "very comfortable."

Economically, the Civil War devastated the Shaker settlements of Kentucky. Literally caught in movements across their land by both the Northern and Southern armies, the Shaker settlements of Kentucky lost food, wagons, and horses to the war effort. On the other hand, Shaker settlements in New England benefited from the war as Union veterans or widows entered the Believer community seeking the economic and emotional support they lacked in their post-war life.[7]

Counting the Believers   How many people were drawn to the followers of Mother Ann Lee? It is always difficult to provide firm counts of religious groups. First, such data typically originate from the group themselves. Groups may have reasons to overcount members to provide evidence of success or undercount to alloy the fears of their detractors. Second, religious groups vary in whom they count as members. Some count all family members, while others prefer to include only those who have moved through some ritual threshold, such as baptism or confirmation. Often a significant proportion of Shaker settlements, perhaps 20 percent, was composed of children, the elderly, and people with disabilities who were unable to support themselves but were not necessarily devoted to the faith.[8]

In addition, Believers knew that some members were more attracted by the economic support that came from living in the communal setting than by the faith. Lucy Wright, an early follower of Ann Lee, already observed in 1816 that "numbers are not the thing for us to glory in." Rather it was important to maximize feelings of "purity and holiness" among the Shakers.[9]

Following, in chronological order, are the dates, locations, and membership estimates of the various Shaker societies typically made by outsiders drawing upon available data.[10]

[7]Suzanne Thurman, "The Shakers," in vol. 2 of *Introduction to New and Alternative Religions in America*, Eugene V. Gallagher and W. Michael Ashcraft (eds.) Westport, CT: Greenwood Press, 2006), pp. 1–18; and Anita Sanchez, pp. 102–38.

[8]Brewer, *Shaker Communities, Shaker Lives*, p. 89.

[9]Brewer, *Shaker Communities, Shaker Lives*, p. 88.

[10]See Charles Nordhoff, *The Communistic Societies of the United States* (New York: Dover, 1966); Marguerite Fellows Melcher, *The Shaker Adventure* (Cleveland: Western Reserve Press, 1968); Edward Andrews, *The People Called Shakers* (New York: Oxford University Press, 1953). Membership figures are approximations and are based on records of the Western Reserve Historical Society, cited by Andrews, pp. 290–91 and updated from Cathy Newman, "The Shakers' Brief Eternity," *National Geographic Magazine*, September 1989, p. 310.

Date	Location	Total Membership
1787	New Lebanon, New York	3,202
1787	Niskayuna (Watervliet), New York	2,668
1790	Hancock, Massachusetts	548
1790	Enfield, Connecticut	739
1791	Harvard, Massachusetts	500
1792	Canterbury, New Hampshire	746
1792	Tyringham, Massachusetts	241
1793	Alfred, Maine	241
1793	Enfield, New Hampshire	511
1793	Shirley, Massachusetts	369
1794	Sabbathday Lake, Maine	202
1806	Union Village, Ohio	3,873
1806	Watervliet (Dayton), Ohio	127
1806	Pleasant Hill, Kentucky	800
1810	West Union (Burso), Indiana	350
1817	South Union, Kentucky	676
1822	North Union, Ohio	407
1824	Whitewater, Ohio	491
1836	Groveland, New York	793

Like the Divinites (followers of Father Divine), who will be discussed in Chapter 7, the Believers were reluctant to disclose their membership numbers.[11] Nevertheless, in addition to the locations listed, there were at least a dozen other branches and short-lived communities in states as far south as Georgia and Florida. It is certain, therefore, that the membership figure of 17,000 given in standard reference works is a gross underestimation. In fact, on the basis of documentary records at the Shaker Museum and Library, Sabbathday Lake, Maine, total cumulative membership appears to have been about 64,000 different individuals.[12]

The Believers worked hard at gaining converts, despite the fact that their own societies were physically separate from larger society. The Shakers throughout most of their history sought converts enthusiastically and ardently. Each new member vindicated the utopian outlook of this extraordinary group, and the establishment of each new settlement was seen as a step towards the conversion of the earth into the Kingdom of God.[13]

[11]John Whitworth, *God's Blueprints: A Sociological Study of Three Utopian Sects* (London and Boston: Routledge & Kegan Paul, 1975), p. 37.
[12]Written communication from Leonard L. Brooks, Director of the Sabbathday Lake Shaker Museum and Library.
[13]Whitworth, *God's Blueprints*, p. 37.

Economic Organization

For the United Society of Believers in Christ's Second Appearing, a commune built along the lines of economic communism was a natural outgrowth of their religious philosophy. Their reasoning was that in order to practice celibacy, they had to live apart from the world. And to live apart successfully, it was necessary to abolish private property.

Some Shaker leaders also felt that Christian virtues such as humility and charity were best exemplified through common ownership. Throughout the Believers, at least, there would be no rich, no poor; no masters, no slaves; no bosses, no underlings. Such a system, admittedly, constituted what sociologists call an **ideal type;** that is, a hypothetical situation in which all the preconceived criteria are met or where everything goes according to plan. The ideal type has value in that it enables the sociologist to compare the actual situation with the conceptualized ideal. As we will discuss, the Believers came reasonably close to attaining their ideal.[14]

Manual Labor   In both theory and practice, manual labor held an exalted position in the Shaker scheme of things. Exalted. No other word will do. "Put your hands to work and your hearts to God," Ann Lee had been fond of saying, and the Shakers used these words as the cornerstone of their economy.

With the exception of the aged and the infirm, every adult and child was expected to work at some manual task. This applied to the leaders as well as to the group at large. Ann Lee had worked as a mill hand, James Whittaker was a skilled weaver, Joseph Meachem was a farmer, and so on. Shakers held that this was the natural order of things and pointed out that Jesus had been a carpenter, Paul a sailmaker, and Peter a fisherman.

Believers felt strongly that manual labor was not something imposed on individuals. It was, rather, a feeling that came from within, and took the form of a moral commitment. Thus, while there were men and women in charge of the various trades and departments—orchard deacon, cabinet deacon, herb deaconess, and so forth—their job was not to boss or supervise, but rather to handle paperwork, allocate supplies, and otherwise handle administrative matters.

Non-Shakers often have difficulty in understanding just what made the Believers so industrious, since there were no apparent work pressures of any kind. Similarly, some of those who joined the United Society expecting their duties would be easy—the so-called Winter Shakers— could not adjust to the energetic work pattern and soon resigned from

---

[14]Max Weber, *The Theory of Social and Economic Organizations*, translated by A. Henderson and Talcott Parsons (New York: Free Press, [1913–1922] 1947).

the organization. Work was indeed one of the cultural themes of the Believers, as the following expressions—by Mother Ann Lee—indicate:

> You must not lose one minute of time, for you have none to spare.
> The devil tempts others, but an idle person tempts the devil.
> The people of God do not sell their farms to pay their debts, but they put their hands to work and keep their farms.[15]

Ann Lee looked upon idle conversation as time lost from work. Laziness, play, and self-indulgence were to be avoided. In the Shaker view, there are no idlers in heaven. There is no doubt that a fair degree of ethnocentrism pervaded the various Shaker communities. Members were convinced that Mother Ann had pointed the way, and that their lifestyle was superior to any other. As a group, they showed little inclination to mingle with the outside.

The same inner commitment that prompted the Believers to work hard was also responsible for the exceptional quality of their labor. Whether the product was a chair, a table, or a broom, the buyer could be assured of the finest craft. Shaker-made furniture was of top-grain wood, properly cured, functionally designed, joined and fitted to perfection, and constructed for long, tough usage. It was not simply work, but quality work that constituted the Shaker trademark. Even in selling fruits and vegetables, choice quality was maintained. If a buyer bought a basket of apples, he or she knew that each layer would be uniform, with no "plugs" hidden underneath.

Which particular occupation a person followed was left pretty much a matter of individual choice. A number of Believers were skilled at more than one trade and divided their efforts as needed. The total list of skilled roles filled by Shakers approximated that of society at large: carpenter, cabinetmaker, cook, seamstress, farmer, blacksmith, gardener, weaver, metalworker, mechanic, and so forth.

Division of Labor   The early sociologist Émile Durkheim contended that social structure depends on the **division of labor** in society. In other words, divisions within society are based on the manner in which tasks are performed. For example, the task of providing food can be carried out almost totally by a single person, or it can divided among a group of societal members, with each manner of providing food having different consequence for divisions within society.[16]

The way that labor was divided in the various Shaker communities can be seen—retrospectively, at least—as something of a paradox. On the

---

[15]Henri Desroche, *The American Shakers: From Neo-Christianity to Presocialism* (Amherst: University of Massachusetts Press, 1971), p. 228.

[16]Émile Durkheim, *Division of Labor in Society*, translated by George Simpson, reprint (New York: Free Press, [1893] 1933).

one hand, women and children were integral parts of the occupational structure. All youths, in fact, were required to learn a trade. Likewise, all the Shaker women worked, and any number of them achieved positions of real leadership. On the other hand, there is no gainsaying the fact that, positions of leadership notwithstanding, women did "women's work" and men did "men's work"—much as in society at large. Thus, women did most of the domestic chores: food preparation, cooking, sewing and mending, housekeeping, and nursing. Men worked the farms, cut the lumber, made the furniture, engaged in metalwork, and the like.

In all likelihood, one of the reasons that the male–female division of labor followed that of society at large was the Shaker insistence on separation of the sexes. To have assigned jobs without regard to gender, and at the same time to have maintained strict sexual segregation, might well have created insurmountable problems.[17]

Utilitarianism   It goes almost without saying that not all Shaker craftspeople were of equal skill. As in the world at large, some were better than others. The same applied to the various Shaker societies—some were more efficient than others. Throughout the whole of the Believers, however, the basic motif was utilitarianism. Frills, scrolls, refinements, ornaments, elaborations—such things had no place in the United Society.

To be right, a chair had to be light, strong, durable, easy to clean, and comfortable. Building such a chair along straight, simple lines was the mark of Shaker genius. As a former member put it, "Bureaus, chests, and tables were all made with simple, straight lines, but with fine workmanship. There was nothing slipshod about the Shakers. You could depend on it—everything about them, from their religion to the things they produced, was genuine."[18]

Shaker furniture has an esthetic quality all its own: the lines invariably are right, and the viewer perceives them as such. It is interesting that whereas Shaker theology has left no real mark on the world, Shaker music (to be discussed later) continues to be enjoyed and their furniture has become appreciated as a distinctive art form. In today's market, authentic Shaker chairs, tables, cabinets, and other items bring exorbitant prices. For example, the most desirable examples of Shaker furniture now sell in tens of thousands of dollars, including as much as $120,000 for an antique Shaker candle stand.[19]

---

[17]Brewer, *Shaker Communities, Shaker Lives*, p. 28. Also see Lawrence Foster, "Women of Utopia: Life among the Shakers, Oneidans, and Mormons," *Communities: Journal of Cooperative Living*, Spring 1904.

[18]Sylvia Minott Spencer, "My Memories of the Shakers," *The Shaker Quarterly* 10 (Winter 1970): 126–33. See also June Sprigga, *By Shaker Hands* (New York: Knopf, 1975).

[19]Frank Donegan, "Shaker Chic," *Americana* 16 (January/February 1989): 66.

Shaker Inventions   The Believers are also credited with a number of inventions, such as the circular saw, brimstone match, screw propeller, cut nail, clothespin, flat broom, pea sheller, paper seed packers, threshing machine, revolving oven, and a variety of machines for turning broom handles, cutting leather, and printing labels. Oddly enough—with few exceptions—the Shakers did not patent their inventions, believing that such a practice was monopolistic.

No Shaker ever received money for his or her work as an individual, in keeping with the spirit of a commune. This rule extended to church officials as well as to regular members. On the other hand, no Believer was ever in need. When someone wanted a pair of shoes or a new shirt or dress, he or she simply went to the common store and signed for them. At mealtime, members went to the common dining room, where they could eat their fill.

Music   While Shakers obviously did not invent music, it is a part of their legacy. From almost the beginning, Believers incorporated vocal music in their service. Typically, harmony (singing in parts as opposed to melody) and musical instruments were not part of their music. Harmonizing came to be accepted to some degree but musical accompaniment was rarely accepted.

Tens of thousands of Shaker songs were composed, with only a fraction being recorded into hymnals, and many were adapted and sung widely. Best known is "Simple Gifts," written in 1848 by Joseph Brackett in the Alfred community. Later becoming part of Aaron Copeland's 1944 symphony, "Appalachian Spring," "Simple Gifts" was most famously played at the inauguration of President Barack Obama in 2009 by Yo-Yo Ma, Itzhak Perlman, Anthony McGill, and Gabriela Montero.

Assessing the Shaker Economy

Of course, the question that must be asked of any economic experiment is: Does it work? Applied to the Believers, this was a doubly important question, for they were attempting to operate a collectivist economy in the midst of a capitalist system.

Simple questions, alas, do not always have simple answers—and this is certainly true of the issue at hand. The United Society did succeed in working out a rather effective social system. Their day-to-day activities went smoothly, there was a minimum of internal discord, and—considering the size of the various Shaker communities—social cohesion was consistently strong. In assessing their economic efficiency, however, a number of complicating factors arise.

For one thing, it is difficult to tell whether the success of the Shaker economy was due to the socialist factor or to plain hard work. With their zeal and dedication, would not the Believers have been equally successful as a corporate enterprise?

How much of their economic success was due to their religious zeal, and to the fact that their economy and their religion were intertwined? And how much was due to the succession of forceful leaders: Ann Lee, James Whittaker, Joseph Meachem, Lucy Wright, Richard McNemar, and Frederick Evans?

The extent to which these factors were interrelated will probably never be known. However, there is no denying that the collectivist factor, per se, did contribute to their economic viability. Their ready supply of labor, their self-sufficiency, and their ability to deal profitably with the outside world—these were all positive features. And finally, of course, the fact that they paid no salaries and had no stockholders meant that all profit could be reinvested in the society.

It seems likely, therefore, that up to the Civil War, at least, the success of the Shaker economy was due at least in part to its socialist aspects. This was the opinion of most writers of the period.

Lawsuits   As discussed, the early days of the Believers were marked by hostility and persecution. As time went on, however, and the United Society acquired a reputation for honesty, hard work, and devoutness, much of the ill will abated. In place of the persecutions, unfortunately, a new threat arose: the lawsuit, usually brought in the guise of economic recovery.

When a person joined the Shakers, he or she signed a covenant relinquishing all his or her property and permitting the Society to make use of it as it saw fit. Any time a member wished to withdraw, he or she was not only permitted to do so but would have his or her original property returned. If the person had joined empty-handed—as many of the Winter Shakers had—he or she would be given a liberal monetary allowance.

Upon withdrawing, however, some individuals insisted that they be remunerated for their services during the period of their membership. This the Believers refused to do, and in consequence a number of bitter lawsuits were fought. Some of the suits were simply brought by profiteers; others were brought by those who felt they had a just and moral claim. In general, though, the suits were unsuccessful, and the courts sided with the United Society.

Nevertheless, the cases did provoke bitterness, and the allegations often made front-page headlines. The Shakers, like virtually all religions, were subjected to criticism and especially attacks coming from apostates—former members. This is also the case for even established faiths like Roman Catholicism, but when a group is small and not well understood by outsiders, even the most outrageous charges, like those brought in the lawsuits, can come to be viewed as valid.

The suits were so numerous that handling them became one of the trustees' recognized duties. Eventually, the wording of the covenant was tightened and made into a binding contract. The remarkable thing was that, although the trustees were not lawyers, few of the legal challenges to the Society were successful.[20]

Social Organization

Unlike most of the other commune or utopian experiments in the United States, the Shaker venture involved large numbers of men and women spread over many states. At its peak, the United Society of Believers in Christ's Second Appearing owned more than 100,000 acres of land and hundreds of buildings. Caring for these vast holdings was no easy task, but the Shakers managed their affairs with a minimum of bureaucratic involvement. Mistakes were made—some of them serious—yet the Believers must be given a high rating for overall efficiency.

Each of the nineteen Shaker societies was divided into "families" of approximately one hundred members. The families—a rather ironic term—lived separately, worked separately, and were administered separately. Thus, at Niskayuna there were four families; at Hancock and Union Village, six; at New Lebanon and Pleasant Hill, eight; and so on. Although the various families and societies were socially and economically independent of one another, it was commonplace for one group to help another, particularly in time of trouble.

Two male elders and two female elders ordinarily governed each family, and their rule was absolute—subject only to the approval of church headquarters at New Lebanon. The elders were responsible for both the spiritual and temporal order of things within their family. They heard confessions, conducted meetings, enforced rules of conduct, served as preachers, acted as missionaries, and admitted (or rejected) new applicants. The elders were also responsible for economic policy, work assignments, and financial transactions with the outside world. On such matters, however, they customarily appointed assistants in the form of deacons and trustees. The deacons were in charge of the various workshops and food-production centers, while the trustees carried on the business activities with the outside world.[21]

The elders themselves were appointed, or approved, by the church headquarters at New Lebanon, although it was customary for a family to accept an appointed elder by acclamation. Acclamation or no acclamation, however, the United Society of Believers was anything but a democracy. There was no vote. There were no elections. There was no

[20]Thurman, "The Shakers."
[21]Desroche, *American Shakers*, pp. 215–16.

appeal. The family elders, or ministry, were housed in separate quarters, and their decisions were final—albeit on policy matters they normally consulted with New Lebanon.

The central ministry at New Lebanon was also composed of two male elders and two female elders, with the head elder being the official head of the church. This group was self-perpetuating: they not only appointed their own successors, but the head of the church could claim a mantle of divine authority straight back to Mother Ann Lee. The central ministry determined overall church guidelines, printed and distributed rules of conduct, kept its hand on the pulse of the various societies and families, and otherwise molded the disparate Shaker elements into a unified body.

One might think that, with their near-absolute powers, the various ministries would use their position to become oppressively dictatorial. But while there may have been some despotic characters, they seem to have been few and far between. The nature of the Shaker faith—with its stress on humility, confession of sins, and service to God—was such as to preempt the unjust use of authority.

The elders, deacons, and trustees were devout, responsive individuals who nearly always inspired the trust of their followers. And since they had to work at a manual trade in addition to their ministerial duties, their record becomes all the more impressive.

The general membership included persons from all walks of life: doctors, lawyers, farmers, unskilled workers, merchants, artisans. For the most part, though, converts were drawn from the working class rather than from the upper socioeconomic levels. Most of the major religious bodies were represented—Baptists, Methodists, Adventists, Presbyterians, Jews—although there is no record of any Roman Catholic having joined. African-Americans could—and did—belong, and the same was true of the foreign-born. All ages were represented, from the very young to the very old, although in later years the membership of middle-aged and older people was increasing.

At all times, membership in the United Society was voluntary. Shakers believed firmly that any member who wanted to should be permitted to resign. And while some individuals did not find the austerity to their liking, the number of apostates was not excessive. One reason for this was the fact that all applicants were carefully screened and instructed by the elders and, upon acceptance, underwent a period of probation.

Separation of the Sexes

It must be kept in mind that another of the Society's cultural themes was their total renouncement of sex and marriage. Indeed, Believers were quite fond of proclaiming the "joys of celibacy." They looked upon such joys as a mandate from heaven and acted accordingly. Sister Frances Carr of the Sabbathday Lake community today interprets the prohibition of sex in a rather logical straightforward manner. "Celibacy frees us to be able to love and I'm speaking of Gospel love—to love everyone and not be restricted by personal love."[22]

All this fervor notwithstanding, segregation of the sexes was not left to the members' discretion. Printed rules emanated from the ministry at New Lebanon and were carefully enforced by the elders of the various families. It would not be much of an exaggeration to say that never in history were men and women so systematically precluded from physical contact with one another. It was not simply sex that was prohibited, but physical contact of any kind.

Men and women ("brothers and sisters") slept in different rooms on different sides of the house. They ate at different tables in the common dining room. This is a practice that persists into the twenty-first century at the Sabbathday Lake, Maine, community. Believers of different sexes are not permitted to pass one another on the stairs, and—as if this were not enough—many of the dwellings included separate doorways. Even the halls were made purposely wide so that the sexes would not brush by one another. Traditionally, all physical contact was prohibited, including shaking hands and touching. Today this has been modified and Shakers freely shake hands and even give friendly hugs to members of the opposite sex. If coming across a person with a disability, the Believers now offer assistance, though this would have violated the nineteenth-century "do not touch" norm.

Back then men and women were not permitted to be alone together without a third adult present, a rule that applied both to business and social occasions. Wherever possible, all association of the sexes was done in groups. Moreover, brothers and sisters were not even allowed to work together in groups without special permission of the elders.

The children's order was also run along sexually segregated lines. Boys and girls lived in separate quarters and were permitted no physical contact with one another. Boys were generally under the supervision of the brothers, girls under the sisters. It was thus possible for a young child raised in a Shaker family to live virtually his or her entire life without once touching a member of the opposite sex.

While all families were strict with regard to segregation of the sexes, some apparently went to extremes; for example, the elders would spy through shuttered windows or make surprise visits to the dwelling quarters. One of the largest Shaker societies, at Pleasant Hill, Kentucky, went so far as to have watchtowers on the roof.

---

[22]Newman, "Shakers' Brief Eternity," p. 314.

In general, though, relations between the sexes were not marred by untoward incidents. There was little tension, unpleasantness, or antagonism. On the contrary, men and women lived together harmoniously, with a security that comes from inner peace. For example, each brother was assigned a sister who looked after his clothes, took care of his laundry and mending, and otherwise kept a "general sisterly oversight over his habits and temporal needs." In return, the brother performed menial tasks for the sister, particularly those involving heavy manual labor.

Despite the traditional strict segregation of the sexes, a few "backsliders" were able to find time alone. Several cases of fornication have been documented, at least one resulting in a pregnancy. Reports that "backsliders" regretted their decisions bolstered Shaker convictions that theirs was the "right way."

Over the generations, temptation has come not from other Believers but from outsiders. Most publicly, a writer visited the Sabbathday Lake settlement in 2006 to prepare a feature article for the *Boston Globe*. Unbeknownst to her at the time, Wayne Smith, the youngest member of the settlement at age forty-three, was very much attracted to her. A few months after the reporter's article appeared, he indicated to his fellow Believers he was leaving the church, having been a Believer since he was seventeen, to pursue a relationship with her. Two years later they were married. The Sabbathday Lake community was obviously shaken by his departure but helped make his transition from Brother Wayne to citizen Wayne and still speak of him fondly.[23]

A Typical Shaker Day

Days began early in the United Society—four-thirty A.M. in the summer and around five during the winter. At the sound of the morning bell, Believers would arise and kneel in silent prayer. Then the beds were stripped, the bedding placed neatly on the chairs, and the chairs hung on the pegs that bordered the walls. The allotted time for this activity was fifteen minutes, after which the designated sisters would clean the rooms, make the beds, and replace the chairs.

While other sisters prepared breakfast and set the dining-room tables, the brothers performed the morning chores: they brought in the wood, started the fire, fed the livestock, milked the cows, and arranged the day's work.

Breakfast was served at six-thirty, and as with all meals, the brothers and sisters gathered beforehand in separate rooms for a period of quiet

[23]Brewer, *Shaker Communities, Shaker Lives,* p. 140; Stacey Chase, "The Last Standing" (June 23, 2006) and "He Left the Shakers for Lover (February 28, 2010), both in the *Boston Globe.*

prayer. Then, led by the elders, they entered the dining room through separate doors—brothers on the left, sisters on the right. After taking their places at separate tables, the entire congregation knelt for a moment of grace. The food was then served.

Each table seated from four to eight adults—children were served separately—and the bill of fare was ample if not fancy. Dietary matters varied from one society to the next, but in general the Believers preferred dairy products and vegetables to meat. In some societies, meat was not served at all, and pork was forbidden throughout the Believers.

More important than dietary rules, however—which were fairly liberal—were the rules of conduct that governed dining behavior. Good posture was required at all meals; elders were to be served first; members were permitted as many helpings as they wanted, but all food taken was to be eaten—nothing was to be wasted; knives and forks were to be placed in a specified position when the meal was finished; food was not to be taken from the table; meat cut from the platter was to be cut square and of equal part "lean, fat, and bones."

Perhaps most unusual was the rule that forbade all conversation at mealtime. The prohibition was in force throughout all Shaker societies, and if the idea of silent meals seems rather dismal to most of us, all that can be said is that, in the religious atmosphere that prevailed, the Believers apparently took the custom in stride. The practice of silent meals does not seem to have been overly punitive.

After breakfast, each Shaker, including the elders, proceeded to his or her specific work task. Many of the jobs, particularly in the female realm, were rotated. But irrespective of the job, Believers were excellent workers.

The bell for the midday meal sounded a little before noon, and the earlier ritual was repeated. Afternoons were devoted to regular work activity, followed by supper at six. Most evenings were taken up by planned activity of some sort: general meetings, religious services, singing and dancing sessions, Society meetings, and so on. Bedtime was usually between nine and nine-thirty.

Although the Shakers did not all wear similar apparel—as the Amish do—their clothing styles were more or less prescribed. Despite some changes over the years, typical attire for men included broad-brimmed hats, plain shirts buttoned at the throat and worn without neckties, vests and long coats, and dark trousers.

Women wore loose bodices with ankle-length skirts. Aprons were required, as were capes and Shaker bonnets. More than one observer commented on the fact that female attire was deliberately formless, so as not to arouse feelings of lust on the part of the men. By the same token, while both sexes were permitted the use of color, only subdued shades were authorized.

Entertainment for the Believers was rather limited because of their lack of contact with the outside world. Except in a real emergency, members of the Society would not even call in an outside doctor, preferring instead to treat their sick brothers or sisters with herbs, extracts, and whatever Shaker assistance was available. For most members, the only prolonged exposure to the outside world came during their journeys to other Shaker communities. Visiting of this type was one of the high points of their year.

By worldly standards, the United Society of Believers in Christ's Second Appearing was anything but a joyous organization. Daily living was a serious undertaking. The Believers had a regimented existence and a restricted range of opportunities. Their list of prohibitions was a formidable one: no sex, no marriage, no money, no private property; no conversation at mealtime; no outside contacts, and a minimum of entertainment; few visits and fewer visitors. Even household pets were prohibited, because it was feared they would somehow arouse maternal feelings on the part of the young girls. The only pets permitted were cats, used to control rodents.

Order   Rosabeth Kanter, an authority on the subject, believes that order is a common characteristic of utopian communities. She states that "in contradistinction to the larger society, which is seen as chaotic and uncoordinated, utopian communities are characterized by conscious planning and coordination. . . . Events follow a pattern. . . . A utopian often desires meaning and control, order and purpose, and he seeks these ends explicitly through his community."[24]

The Shakers were a good case in point, for in their societies order and purpose were combined to produce a definitive lifestyle. Their buildings, for example, were severely furnished: no rugs, no pictures, no photographs, no ornamentation. Such things were considered dirt catchers, and as the Believers were fond of saying, there is "no dirt in heaven." It is hardly an accident that one of the very first Shaker industries involved broom-making.

Around the walls of every Shaker room were set rows of wooden pegs to hold chairs when the floors were cleared for sweeping. Each outside door had its foot scraper. Orderliness was coupled with cleanliness, with buildings planned for orderly communal living. Most of the rooms had built-in cabinets and drawers, designed by size to hold the necessary tools, supplies, seeds and herbs in the herb shop.[25]

---

[24]Rosabeth Moss Kanter, *Commitment and Community: Communes and Utopias in Sociological Perspective* (Cambridge, MA: Harvard University Press, 1973), p. 39.

[25]Melcher, *Shaker Adventure*, pp. 156–57.

In this scene, typical of Shaker meetings (or services) in the 1840s, men and women gather to march or dance to a Shaker tune in New Lebanon, New York.

The Granger Collection, New York

The Sabbath   Sunday was a special day throughout the United Society. Although it was a holy day, with no work being performed, it was not—as in so many Christian groups—a solemn day. On the contrary, for Shakers of all ages it was a time of spiritual uplift, rejoicing, singing, and dancing. It was as though the quiet, the reserve, the temporal subjugation—traits in evidence six days a week—were released on the seventh day in an outpouring of spiritual ecstasy.

The dances themselves—or "marches," as they were called—ranged from mildly exuberant to highly explosive. Shakers firmly believed that every part of a person should be used in the worship of God. On the mild side were rhythmic exercises in which the participants would march "with their hands held out in front of the body, and with elbows bent, moving the hands up and down with a sort of swinging motion, as though gathering up something in the arms. This motion signified 'gathering in the good.' They also believed in 'shaking out the evil.'"[26]

The following account by a former Shaker gives some idea of what the more volatile dances were like:

> In the height of their ecstasy, Shakers were constrained to worship God in the dance. . . .

[26]Spencer, "My Memories of the Shakers," pp. 126–33. Also see Roger Lee Hall, *Gentle Words: Shaker Music in the 20th Century* (Stoughton, MA: Pine Tree Press, 2009).

The rolling exercise consisted in being cast down in a violent manner, dou-bled with the head and feet together, and rolled over and over, like a wheel—or stretched, in a prostrate manner, turning like a log. . . .

Still more mortifying were the jerks. The exercise began in the head, which would fly backward and forward and from side to side, with a quick jolt, . . . limbs and trunk twitching in every direction. And how such could escape injury was no small wonder to spectators.[27]

There is also some rather convincing evidence that in certain instances both Shaker men and women indulged in naked dancing and naked fla-gellation. No sexual overtones were involved, however, and in any case such behavior was clearly the exception.[28]

Overview   In spite of these extreme forms of behavior—many of which reportedly occurred during the early, formative years of the Society—the Shakers lived a serious life, a life without frills, adornments, or luxuries of any kind. It was also a peaceful, contented life, and this fact puzzled out-siders. But it was clear that the followers of Ann Lee had an inner serenity that was hard to disturb, one they would not have found in society at large.

Understandably, outsiders had mixed feelings about the United Society. On the one hand, the Shakers were resented because they led an "unnat-ural" life, and because they would not vote, participate in public life, or bear arms for their country. On the other hand, they were genuinely admired for their honesty, their spiritual devoutness, and their capacity for hard work. As the nineteenth century wore on, the Believers came to be treated as respected members of the larger community.

Children: A Mixed Venture

There is no doubt at all that children were one of the less successful Shaker ventures. While no children were ever born into the United Society, youngsters of every age were accepted, either as orphans or as children whose parents had converted. When they reached twenty-one, they were given the choice of staying in the Society or leaving. And a large majority chose to leave. Results were so poor that after the Civil War more and more Shaker societies stopped accepting children altogether.[29]

---

[27]Desroche, *American Shakers*, pp. 118–19. Ken Burns has filmed a contemporary version of a modification of the marching that accompanied singing of Shaker songs. See the video clip at the PBS site listed as the conclusion of this chapter.

[28]Thomas Brown, *An Account of the People Called Shakers: Their Faith, Doctrines, and Practice* (Troy, NY: Parker & Bliss, 1812), pp. 322–23, 334–36. Cited in Lawrence Foster, *Religion and Sexuality: Three American Communal Experiments of the Nineteenth Century* (New York: Oxford University Press, 1981), pp. 42–43.

[29]Julia Neal, *The Kentucky Shakers* (Lexington: Kentucky University Press, 1977), p. 81.

More than once, situations involving parents and children resulted in bad publicity for the Shakers. Sometimes one or both parents would leave their children with a Shaker community, with the understanding that they never would see them again. Later, the parents, after re-establishing themselves economically or repairing their marriage, would return for their children. While Shakers did not resist these unexpected returns, sometimes parents, not taking any chances, would make public charges of an alleged kidnapping. In other instances, one parent would join the Shakers, leading to messy and often public custodial battles with the other parent.

There were exceptions, and some children raised in the Shaker lifestyle adjusted happily to their distinctive way of life. Most notable, Sister Frances Carr, now seventy-two, has written widely about her upbringing among the Believers since the age of ten.[30]

Eventually the Shakers came to accept only adults. But the question remains: Why did they not succeed even more with the children? The reasons are not fully understood. The youngsters were given the best of care and were treated with kindness. Corporal punishment was frowned upon. In the 1800s, the idea of public education took hold in the United States, and the Believers followed suit with schools of their own. Their youngsters were taught the "three Rs" in sexually segregated classes.

In day-to-day living, Shaker children followed much the same routine as the adults. Each youngster was taught one or more manual skills. Pride in workmanship was instilled at an early age. Cleanliness was stressed. The sexes were kept strictly apart. Dietary rules and regular dining procedures were observed. Even the clothing was identical with that of the adults; visitors often commented that the children looked like miniature Shakers. And, of course, permeating virtually every aspect of their lives was the inculcation of the religious values laid down by Mother Ann Lee.

Inasmuch as the children were more than adequately cared for, why did so many of them renounce Shakerism? While the answers can be challenged, the fact seems to be that the Believers were a special kind of people. It was not everybody who could renounce normal marital and familial relationships. For an adult to choose this way of life was one thing. But for the average person—especially the average young person— a regimented life without romantic love, sex, or children must have seemed a grim prospect.

Educational Policy   Another factor that must have discouraged young people from remaining in the Shaker fold was the negative attitude of the

---

[30]Sister Frances A. Carr, *Growing Up Shaker* (Sabbathday Lake, ME: United Society of Shakers, 1995); Thurman, "The Shakers," pp. 13–15.

Believers toward education. Although the Shakers themselves tended to gloss over the matter, they were distrustful of most intellectual and artistic pursuits.

Ann Lee said, "Put your hands to work and your hearts to God," a principle that the Believers have followed to the present. But she made no mention of the mind, and the omission also became part of Shaker policy. Education, as carried out in the Society's schools, did not go much beyond the basics of English, arithmetic, and geography. Subjects such as science, literature, foreign languages, history, and the fine arts had little place in the Shaker scheme of things.

It is true that young people in the United Society were given training that many outside youth never received. In addition to learning a manual or domestic skill, Shaker boys and girls were given extensive instruction in religion and the Bible. They were taught humility, honesty, kindness, punctuality, and sincerity. They were cautioned against the evils of the flesh. They were encouraged to promote the happiness of other people and to avoid contention. In brief, as the elders saw it, they were given training in the development of character and moral responsibility.

But for the young boy or girl with real intellectual curiosity—with some feeling for the world of the mind—the United Society must have been a bleak environment. Books, magazines and journals, philosophical debates, abstract ideas, political discussions—all were discouraged. Of higher education there was none. No Shaker youth ever went to college. None ever became a doctor or lawyer. None ever held a significant public office. None ever achieved fame in the natural or physical sciences.[31]

In the arts, the situation was much the same. Poetry, drama, literature, sculpture, painting, symphonic and operatic music—all were missing in Shaker culture. For a youngster with talent along these lines, the path cleared by Mother Ann was painfully narrow.

Reference-Group Behavior Sociologically speaking, a **reference group** is one that people look to for standards of behavior and appropriate conduct, one that can bestow or withhold approval. It is the group against which a person measures himself or herself. For example, a high-school student today who aspires to join a social circle of hip-hop music devotees will pattern his or her behavior after that of the group. The student will begin dressing like those peers, listening to the same music downloads, and hang out at the same clubs. A person will self-evaluate against a particular reference group, and not others or

---

[31]As stated earlier, the Believers did have some doctors, lawyers, and clergy in their midst. However, these were people who converted to the Believers after they had achieved professional status.

even the larger society.[32] For adult Shakers, their own Society was their reference group, and they behaved accordingly.

However, it was a vastly different story for the youth who were taken into the Society. These youngsters did not choose Shakerism. They did not voluntarily look upon the Shaker community as a reference group, and hence they were not overly influenced by reference-group acceptability. While they were largely kept apart from the outside world, they were certainly not immune to its influences.

A young man or woman with normal sexual desires, or with more than a modicum of intellectual or artistic ability, must have found it difficult to remain within the Shaker fold. One would predict that when they were given the choice at age twenty-one of staying or leaving, they would leave. And in practice, as has been mentioned, this is exactly what happened.

Shaker Theology

The theological doctrine of the United Society of Believers in Christ's Second Appearing was neither complex nor extensive. But it was radical, particularly by nineteenth-century standards. The Shakers rejected such concepts as the Trinity, damnation, the Immaculate Conception, resurrection of the body, and atonement. For the most part, they believed in a literal interpretation of the Bible—but they also believed that there were revelations later than the Bible.

Duality: God, Male and Female   In rejecting the Trinity, they held that God is made up of dual elements, male and female, and that this is reflected throughout nature. This view was explicitly expressed by Mother Ann Lee, who perhaps given some of the sorrow she experienced in her own life felt the perspective of women was underappreciated in conventional Christianity. Even angels were believed by Shakers to have a male and female counterpart, and the same was true of Adam. Christ was considered to be a spirit, appearing first in the person of Jesus, male, and—much later—in the person of Mother Ann, female. This male–female duality constituted another definition of the situation, and, in both a secular and a religious sense, the concept permeated the entire Shaker organization. Since women equaled men in their spiritual beliefs, Shakers came to approach daily life expecting

[32]Robert K. Merton and Alice S. Kitt, "Contributions to the Theory of Reference Group Behavior," pp. 40–105, in *Continuities in Social Research: Studies in the Scope and Methods of the American Soldier,* edited by Robert K. Merton and Paul L. Lazarsfeld (New York: Free Press, 1950).

men and women to be equal rather than men to have an edge in authority.[33]

The Believers were convinced that the church's emphasis on common property, pacifism, separatism, and celibacy was based on the right principles, but that later denominations and sects had strayed from the proper path. Violation of celibacy was a good case in point.

The Shakers' position, one from which they would never swerve, was that sin came into the world because of the action of Adam and Eve in the Garden of Eden. This "action," of course, was the sex act and was in direct disobedience of God. Henceforth, it was only by overcoming physical nature and conquering the desires of the flesh that men and women could achieve salvation. And since the Shakers had succeeded in this struggle, they felt that they alone, among the world's peoples, were carrying out God's will.

With regard to the elimination of humanity—a phenomenon that would surely occur if the Shaker dogma of celibacy prevailed—no serious problem was involved. The Believers thought the millennium was at hand, and consequently there was no real reason for the continuance of the human race. In the new order of things, spirituality would take the place of sensuality.

Interestingly, and perhaps contradictorily, the Shakers did not feel that human nature was basically sinful. They believed in Adam's sin in the Garden of Eden, but they also felt that the Lord was too just to penalize all people because of the mistakes of one. In like fashion, they refused to categorize marriage on the part of the world's peoples as sinful. They did feel, however, that non-Shakers were of a lower spiritual order.

Spiritualism   The Shakers were among the forerunners of modern **spiritualism,** the belief that the living could communicate with the dead. Members of the United Society were quite explicit on this point. They contended that they were able to talk—face to face—with their recently departed brethren, as well as with others "born before the Flood."

Communication with the spirit world varied from one Shaker community to the next and also seems to have varied over time, with the 1830s and 1840s being a particularly "vibrant" period. For a while, the religious services were so animated that the elders closed them to visitors. It is easy to see why.

Since the Believers had little entertainment, their religious services tended to take up the slack. After a greeting and some prayers by the elders, the sisters and brothers would form two large circles, one within

[33]Charles Nordhoff, *The Communistic Societies of the United States* (New York: Dover Publications, [1875] 1966), p. 132.

the other. Although the sexes never touched each other at any time, the participants would group and regroup themselves in a variety of intricate patterns—all the while singing, chanting, and clapping hands.

At a certain point in the proceedings, a marked change would sweep over the dancers. A mood of expectancy would prevail. Suddenly there would be a loud "whoosh!" from the group, signifying that the devil was making his appearance. Then, in unison, those present would stamp their feet, shouting and chanting, "Stomp the devil!"

Next, two or three of the sisters would whirl round and round to cries of "Shake! Shake! Shake! Christ is with you!" When the whirlers sank to the floor from dizziness or exhaustion, others would take their places. Midway in the sequence of shaking, jumping, shouting, clapping, and stamping, someone would hold up a hand and announce that Mother Ann was present—with gifts of fruit for everybody. One by one, each member would come forward and receive his or her imaginary basket, then go through the motions of peeling and eating the contents.

Then one of the elders would proclaim that Mother Ann had a message: some nearby Native American chiefs were on their way to join the meeting. The group would then start to chant in a strange tongue and point to the door, waiting for the appearance of the Native Americans.

Hardly was this ritual finished when the brothers and sisters would form parallel rows and begin another sequence of dances and gyrations. This time the Native Americans were reported appearing at the windows, and there was an outpouring of joyous clapping. Then another "Whoosh!" and some more stomping. The devil was loose again.

On and on and on the dances went, sometimes long past the curfew. While there was some variation from one service to the next, spiritual manifestations were more or less taken for granted. Mother Ann Lee was the most frequent visitor, although Native Americans—for whom the Shakers seemed to have a spiritual affinity—were a close second. Other frequent guests included Alexander the Great, Napoleon, George Washington, and Benjamin Franklin.

The visions, hallucinations, messages, apparitions, and communications seemed endless. It was as though the followers of Mother Ann, by ecstatically embracing the spirit world, were able to work off all their worldly inhibitions.

After 1850, spiritualism in the United Society apparently died down—at least there is less of it reported. More than a trace remained for many decades, however, and contemporary Shakers speak of feeling the presence of the spirit of deceased Believers whom they had known, especially during the Sunday meeting. As for the dances, they remained the vibratory signature of the Society for as long as the brothers and sisters had the vitality to stomp the devil. The physical dancing and swirling vanished in the early 1900s and marching during services came to an end by the 1950s.

Decline of the Order

The United Society of Believers in Christ's Second Appearing reached its peak around the time of the Civil War. Thereafter, membership declined, slowly at first, then faster and faster. By the mid-1870s, the Society was forced to advertise in the papers for new members. The following ad, for instance, appeared in several New York newspapers during 1874:

> MEN, WOMEN, AND CHILDREN CAN FIND A COMFORTABLE HOME FOR LIFE, WHERE WANT NEVER COMES, WITH THE SHAKERS, BY EMBRACING THE TRUE FAITH AND LIVING PURE LIVES. PARTICULARS CAN BE LEARNED BY WRITING TO THE SHAKERS, MT. LEBANON, NY.[34]

By the end of the century, whole Shaker communities were folding. By 1925, most of the remaining groups had dissolved.

What had happened to this once strong and spirited group? The answers are not hard to find. To begin with, it was obvious even before the Civil War that the American economy was changing. The old handicraft system, which was perfect for the Shakers, was being supplanted by the factory system. In spite of their emphasis on quality—or perhaps because of it—the Shakers could not compete with modern assembly-line methods. As was mentioned, Ann Lee had been fond of saying, "Put your hands to work and your hearts to God," but she had had no inkling of the tremendous impact of the modern factory.

Transportation and communication were also affecting the lifestyle of the Society. With the advent of the railroad—and later the automobile—it became harder and harder for the Believers to maintain their separatism. The younger members, in particular, found it difficult to resist the various attractions of the outside world.

Leadership in the Society likewise was undergoing change. The original heads—Ann Lee, James Whittaker, Joseph Meachem, and Lucy Wright—were women and men of courage, wisdom, and foresight. Later on, able leadership was provided, but as time went on it seemed that too often the ministry was unable to cope with the problems of a changing society. This was true in both the sacred and the secular spheres.

In the sacred sphere, church leadership was unable either to provide the spiritual guidance necessary to keep Shaker youth within the fold, or to gain a sufficient number of adult converts to make up for the loss of the children.

In the secular sphere, there were too many examples of economic mismanagement. Some of the trustees were clearly unsuited to their jobs. The

---

[34]Quoted in Whitworth, *God's Blueprints*, p. 75.

Shaker group at Enfield, New Hampshire, lost $20,000 because of poor business practices. At Union Village, Ohio, the Society lost $40,000 when one of the trustees absconded with the money. The Shaker branch at South Union, Kentucky, lost over $100,000 because of difficulties stemming from the Civil War. And so it went. A number of branches also lost money because of costly lawsuits. These sums, of course, represent nineteenth-century dollars, not figures adjusted to current dollars.

Another factor that led to the decline of the order was the changing attitude toward human sexuality in society at large. It was one thing to preach against evils of the flesh in the 1700s and early 1800s, when America was still living in the backwash of Puritanism. But by the 1900s, it was evident that fewer and fewer people thought of sex as sin. And with the emergence of more realistic attitudes toward sex, the Shaker position became correspondingly weaker.

Social welfare practices were also changing. Increasingly, various government agencies began to provide assistance for the sick, the widowed, the aged, and the orphaned. And as the whole concept of welfare came to be looked upon as a government obligation, the role of the United Society as a haven for the needy declined.

In a way, Shakerism has always contained the seeds of its own destruction. After all, in the interest of growth—or even survival—celibacy is a self-defeating doctrine. It may represent human subjugation of the flesh, but the end product, biologically speaking, is stagnation. True, the celibate orders of the Roman Catholic Church may persist, but they represent only a small percentage of the membership. With the Believers, the entire organization was involved. And when the rate of conversions declined, the end was just a matter of time.

The Shaker Heritage

What exactly is the Shaker heritage? In their more than two centuries of existence, what have the Shakers done to make us remember them? In some ways, the Shaker venture was an obvious failure; in others, it was a marked success. Where the balance lies depends in part on the personality of the assessor.

On the negative side, the Believers certainly failed in their primary objective: the establishment of a utopia, a heaven on earth. As a matter of record, they failed in both the secular and spiritual spheres. In a secular sense, the Believers simply did not flourish, and nothing can change this fact. Starting around the time of the Civil War, the movement declined inexorably.

Spiritually, the Believers' mark on the world is so faint as to be indiscernible. Their theology is virtually unknown today, their spiritualism is an embarrassment, and their dancing or marching belongs, perhaps, in a similar category. In brief, for all their efforts and sincerity, the Shakers have had virtually no impact on modern religious thought.

On the other hand, there is no doubt that the Believers made some significant cultural contributions to Americana. We must remember that they maintained by far the longest history of communal society in the country's history—from 1787 into the twenty-first century.

Their inventions have already been mentioned. Of equal importance was their stylistic contribution to American furniture. Tables, chairs, cabinets—all bear the functional, workmanlike imprint of the United Society. And in the musical sphere, as mentioned earlier, the Shakers contributed a substantial number of folk songs and spirituals.[35]

Perhaps more than any other group, the Shakers were able to link their name with quality. Their fruits and vegetables were top grade. Their seeds and herbs were the best. Their furniture was fantastically sturdy. Even their buildings were seemingly indestructible. Many are still in use today, having been purchased by outside organizations following the demise of the various Shaker settlements. The buildings are used for schools, museums, state institutions, Roman Catholic orders, and private residences, and most of them are in remarkably good condition, despite their age.

Their hoped-for utopia failed to materialize, yet the Shakers were successful in eliminating many of the social problems that plagued society at large. Poverty and unemployment, crime and delinquency, alcoholism and drug addiction—all were absent in the United Society. This was no small accomplishment, surely, since American society is still beset by these same problems. The point is that the Shakers were able to demonstrate to the world that communal living and separatism could be made to work.

Another contribution of current significance was their insistence on equal treatment for all members. Old, young, rich, poor, Black, White, native-born, foreign-born—nobody felt left out in the Believers. All were treated as equals. And if this practice was not followed in the larger society, the latter at least had the benefit of a working example. The Believers were also able to demonstrate the combined traits of courage and devotion, an amalgam that must have perplexed many of those on the outside. For despite long and harsh treatment, the followers of Ann Lee never once faltered in their beliefs. In the end, it was the outsiders who gave up and stopped the persecution.

Finally, of course, the United Society demonstrated to the world at large the magnitude of their self-restraint. As the contents of the present volume amply attest, America has seen any number of extraordinary groups

[35]Daniel W. Patterson, *The Shaker Spiritual* (Princeton: Princeton University Press, 1979).

with unusual marital and sexual practices. But for an entire organization to abstain from sex on a permanent basis was all but incomprehensible to outsiders. Yet the Shakers not only abstained but gloried in the abstention. As they were fond of proclaiming, "He who conquereth himself is greater than he who conquereth a city."

All things considered, the United Society of Believers in Christ's Second Appearing added a new and interesting dimension to American culture. There has never been another group like them. If a society is enriched by its cultural diversity, then we must give the Shakers a strong plus for their contribution. Whether they can continue as a viable group will be discussed in the following section.

The Present Scene

What is the present status of the United Society of Believers in Christ's Second Appearing? Are they surviving? Growing? Are new members still being accepted? Or is it too late for a spiritual and secular resurgence?

As the various communities closed, assets were auctioned and sold with proceeds reverting to the remaining communities. By the latter part of the twentieth century, with only Canterbury in New Hampshire and Sabbathday Lake in Maine remaining, the cumulative assets were in the millions of dollars. Some believers became concerned over the motives of potential converts, leading the Canterbury Shakers to the unprecedented step in 1957 of refusing to accept new members. This caused a rift with Sabbathday Lake, which continued to welcome new members. Over a period of three decades, perhaps twenty spent a year at the village "trying the life" with only Brother Ted, who died in 1986, and Brother Arnold staying on.

Several former settlements remain, with dozens of buildings. Both buildings and furnishings are in excellent condition. Nearly all of these settlements, however (Hancock, Massachusetts; South Union and Pleasant Hill, Kentucky; Mount Lebanon, New York; Canterbury, New Hampshire) are neither run nor maintained by Believers. They are maintained by historical societies.

Nevertheless, as you saw in the introduction to this chapter, in spite of monumental odds, one "family" of Shakers still exists at Sabbathday Lake, Maine—the farthest north of any Shaker community and for a long time the poorest. It is difficult to characterize the present-day Sabbathday Lake community. On the one hand, the buildings and grounds are in splendid condition. New members are invited to "try the life." To the outsider, Sabbathday Lake may not appear to be a thriving community. Yet there is a group of about sixty loyal volunteers and friends of today's Believers who give a sense of energy to the settlement. Older teens and

AP/Wide World Photos

Friends of the Shakers, a volunteer organization, help with the fall harvest in Sabbathday Lake Village in 2002. On a work day each spring and fall, they help the three remaining Shakers with much-welcomed muscle power, helping to preserve an extraordinary way of life.

twenty-somethings come regularly from a totally different lifestyle to interact with the Shakers and their friends. Prospects for the United Society of Believers numbering in the hundreds may be bleak, but the likelihood of there being Believers is strong for the near future.

On the other hand, rather obviously, membership—numerically speaking—is precarious. Since the mid-1950s, a mere handful of applicants have been accepted, and very few of these have remained. In 1900 there were forty-one remaining Shakers, in 1989 there were nine, and, as noted, today there are only three.[36]

What the future actually holds, of course, no one can say. Only time will tell if far into the twenty-first century the United Society of Believers in Christ's Second Appearing will continue. The Sabbathday Lake Shaker community and its 1,700 acres do not serve as merely a museum or as a restored village. Rather it stands "as a unique example

[36]Jeannine Lauber, "Chosen Faith, Chosen Land," *The Untold Story of America's 21st Century Shakers* (Rockport, ME: Down East, 2009). Data for 1900 from Brewer, *Shaker Communities, Shaker Lives*, p. 238; 1989 from correspondence with Leonard L. Brooks, Director of the Sabbathday Lake Shaker Museum and Library, during the summer of 1989; on Schaefer's fieldwork, 2009.

of an ever-changing response to the world and its demands."[37] Members themselves, however, seem to have little doubt about their survival. They believe that prospects for Shakerism, by definition, are bright. Shakerism, according to the Sabbathday Lake community in 2006, continues as long as one person in a generation, according to Mother Ann Lee, had the saving inner knowledge of the Gospel.[38]

KEY TERMS

Commune, p. 87
Division of labor, p. 94
Ideal type, p. 93
Latent function, p. 88

Manifest function, p. 88
Reference group, p. 107
Spiritualism, p. 109

SOURCES ON THE WEB

http://www.passtheword.org/SHAKER-MANUSCRIPTS/
Includes transcripts of many original Shaker documents and is useful for research.

http://www.pbs.org/kenburns/shakers/
Home page for the 1984 Ken Burns documentary on the Shakers, which includes video clips.

http://www.maineshakers.com/
Describes the site and public areas of the only surviving Shaker community.

http://www.nps.gov/history/nr/travel/shaker/index.htm
A description provided by the National Park Service of contemporary sites of Shaker communities.

SELECTED READINGS

Ald, Roy. *The Youth Communes.* New York: Tower Publications, 1971.
Andrews, Edward. *The People Called Shakers.* New York: Oxford University Press, 1953.

[37]Gerald C. Wertkin quotes Sister Mildred in his foreward to *A Place in Time: The Shakers at Sabbathday Lake, Maine* (Boston: A Pocket Paragon Book, 2006).
[38]*A Collection of Essays by The Shaker Studies Class of 2006* (Sabbathday Lake, ME: Shaker Museum, 2006), p. 3.

Brewer, Priscilla J. *Shaker Communities, Shaker Lives.* Hanover: University Press of New England, 1986.

Carr, Sister Frances A. *Growing Up Shaker.* Sabbathday Lake, ME: United Society of Shakers, 1995.

Desroche, Henri. *The American Shakers: From Neo-Christianity to Presocialism.* Amherst: University of Massachusetts Press, 1971.

Foster, Lawrence. *Religion and Sexuality: Three American Communal Experiments of the Nineteenth Century.* New York: Oxford University Press, 1981.

Gutek, Gerald and Patricia. *Visiting Utopian Communities: A Guide to the Shakers, Moravians and Others.* Columbia, SC: University of South Carolina Press, 1998.

Hayden, Delores. *Seven American Utopias: The Architecture of Communitarian Socialism, 1790–1975.* Cambridge, MA: MIT Press, 1976.

Hutton, Daniel Mac-Hir. *Old Shakertown and the Shakers.* Harrodsburg, KY: Harrodsburg Herald Press, 1936.

Kolken, Diana van. *Introducing the Shakers.* Bowling Green, OH: Gabriel's Horn Publishing Co., 1985.

Lauber, Jeannine. *Chosen Faith, Chosen Land. The Untold Story of America's 21st Century Shakers.* Rockport, ME: Down East, 2009.

Mac-Hir Hutton, Daniel. *Old Shakertown and the Shakers.* Rev. ed. Harrodsburg, KY: Harrodsburg Herald Press, 1987.

Matthaei, Julie A. *An Economic History of Women in America: Women's Work, the Sexual Division of Labor, and the Development of Capitalism.* New York: Schocken Books, 1982.

Melcher, Marguerite Fellows. *The Shaker Adventure.* Cleveland: Western Reserve Press, 1968.

Melton, J. Gordon. *The Encyclopedia of American Religions.* 2 vols. Wilmington, NC: Consortium Books, 1979.

Merton, Thomas. *Seeking Paradise: The Spirit of the Shakers.* Maryknoll, NY: Orbis Books, 2003.

Muncy, Raymond L. *Sex and Marriage in Utopian Communities.* Bloomington: Indiana University Press, 1973.

Murray, Stuart. *Shaker Heritage Guidebook.* Spencertown, NY: Gold Hill Press, 1994.

Neal, Julia. *The Kentucky Shakers.* Lexington: Kentucky University Press, 1977.

Newman, Cathy. "The Shakers' Brief Eternity." *National Geographic* (September 1989).

Nordhoff, Charles. *The Communistic Societies of the United States.* New York: Dover, 1966.

Patterson, Daniel W. *The Shaker Spiritual.* Princeton: Princeton University Press, 1979.

Pearson, Paul M., ed. *A Meeting of Angels.* Frankfort, KY: Broadstone Books, 2008.

Pike, Kermit J. *A Guide to Shaker Manuscripts in the Library of the Western Reserve Historical Society.* Cleveland: Western Reserve Historical Society, 1974.

Richmond, Mary L. *Shaker Literature: A Bibliography.* 2 vols. Hanover: University Press of New England, 1977.

Sanchez, Anita. *Mr. Lincoln's Chair: The Shakers and Their Quest for Peace.* Granville, OH: The McDonald and Woodward Publishing Co., 2009.

Scott, Donald, and Bernard, Wishy, eds. *America's Families: A Documentary History.* New York: Harper & Row, 1982.

Sprigga, June. *Simple Gifts: A Memoir of a Shaker Village*. New York: Alfred A. Knopf, 1998.

Stein, Stephen J. *The Shaker Experience in America: A History of the United Society of Believers*. New Haven, CT: Yale University Press, 1992.

Wagner, Jon, ed. *Sex Roles in Contemporary American Communes*. Bloomington: Indiana University Press, 1982.

Williams, Stephen Guion, and Gerard C. Wertkin. *A Place in Time: The Shakers at Sabbathday Lake, Maine*. Boston: A Pocket Paragon Book, 2006.

Whitworth, John. *God's Blueprints: A Sociological Study of Three Utopian Sects*. London and Boston: Routledge & Kegan Paul, 1975.

Zablocki, Benjamin. *The Joyful Community*. Baltimore: Penguin Books, 1971; Chicago: University of Chicago Press, 1980.

CHAPTER FOUR

THE MORMONS

Of the nearly 1,200 different religions in the United States, none has had a more turbulent history than the Mormons. It would not be much exaggeration, in this respect, to say that the Mormons are in a class by themselves.[1] Born in controversy and vilified throughout most of the nineteenth century, they have nevertheless succeeded in establishing a socioreligious organization of unbelievable vitality not only in the United States but throughout much of the world.

The "Burned-Over" District

The groundwork and foundations of Mormonism were laid out in the 1820s in western New York State. The area came to be known as the "burned-over" district; that is, burned over by the fires of religious ardor. Never in our history has so much religious fervor been packed into one

---

[1]For accounts of the Mormon experience, see Sherri L. Dew, *Go Forward with Faith*, a biography of Gordon Hinckley, the fifteenth president of LDS (Salt Lake City: Deseret Books, 1996). See also Susan Arrington Madson, *Growing Up in Zion: True Stories of Young Pioneers Building the Kingdom* (Salt Lake City: Deseret Books, 1996); Jana Richman, *Riding in the Shadows of Saints* (New York: Crown, 2005); Richard N. Ostling and Joan K. Ostling, *Mormon America: The Power and the Promise* (New York: HarperSanFrancisco, 2000). For reading fun, try Robert Kirby, *Best Loved Humor of the LDS People* (Salt Lake City: Deseret Books, 1999).

geographical area. Bibles, revelations, preachers, and prophets came (and went) with astonishing rapidity.

The Millerites proclaimed that the world was coming to an end. Ann Lee's Shakers renounced sex and marriage, and formed a nearby settlement. Jemima Wilkinson, ruling by revelation, built her colony of Jerusalem. John Humphrey Noyes started the Oneida Community. The Fox sisters, claiming to have communicated with the dead, founded the modern spiritualist movement. All of this occurred in western New York between, roughly, 1825 and 1850. Even the older denominations—Methodist, Baptist, Presbyterian—were torn by schism and dissent.

Into this religious maelstrom came Joseph Smith, Sr., and his wife, Lucy. Lucy Smith consciously questioned many of the accepted faiths of her day such as the Baptist, Methodist, Roman Catholic, and decided that the Presbyterian would be the faith with which to align. Three of her eight children joined her, but Joseph Jr. decided that he needed more time. In genuine perplexity, according to his own account, he turned to the Bible and was struck by the passage in James 1:5: "If any of you lack wisdom, let him ask of God and it shall be given him."[2]

Accordingly, Joseph Smith entered the woods to ask God the all-important question. It was here that he had his first religious experience, for, he wrote, he was visited by both God the Father and His son Jesus Christ. Among other things, he was told that he was to join none of the existing sects, for "they were all wrong." Smith was only fifteen years old at the time, and the visitation remained engraved on him forever.

Smith made no attempt to hide the fact of his heavenly visitation. With the natural exuberance of a teenager, he divulged what had happened, but his story fell on deaf ears. "I soon found," he said, "that my telling the story had excited a great deal of prejudice . . . and though I was an obscure boy of only fifteen, yet men of high standing would take notice sufficient to excite the public mind against me, and create a bitter persecution."[3]

Although he could not know it at the time, Joseph Smith's persecutions would continue as long as he lived. In fact, they would accelerate. But despite the rising tide of troubled waters, he never once recanted or wavered in his spiritual beliefs. His alleged revelations and heavenly visitations continued right up to the day he died.

The Golden Plates   The next visitation came three years later (1823), when Smith was eighteen. This was the most noteworthy of all his religious experiences, because it involved the angel Moroni and the

---

[2]James Coates, *In Mormon Circles: Gentiles, Jack Mormons, and Latter-day Saints* (Reading, MA: Addison-Wesley, 1990).

[3]Joseph Smith, *Pearl of Great Price* (Salt Lake City: Church of Jesus Christ of Latter-day Saints, 1974), p. 49.

discovery of the golden plates. These plates, or tablets, form the very foundation of Mormonism, so let us read Joseph Smith's own account:

> After I had retired to my bed for the night, a personage appeared at my bedside, standing in the air, for his feet did not touch the floor. He had on a loose robe of most exquisite whiteness. . . .
>
> He called me by name, and said that he was a messenger from the presence of God, and that his name was Moroni; that God had work for me to do. . . .
>
> He said that there was a book deposited, written upon gold plates. He said that the fullness of the everlasting Gospel was contained in it. Also, that there were two stones in silver bows—and these stones, fastened to a breastplate, constituted what is called the Urim and Thummim, and that God had prepared them for the purpose of translating the book.[4]

Eventually, Joseph Smith removed the plates from the hill (now known as Cumorah) and took them home. Each of the plates measured eight inches square, and since there were a number of them—the stack was six inches thick—the total weight must have been considerable. Yet young Joseph Smith experienced no difficulty in transporting them, or at least made no mention of the fact. He did, however, have trouble keeping them out of evil hands. "For no sooner was it known that I had them, than the most strenuous exertions were used to get them from me. But by the wisdom of God, they remained safe in my hands, until I had accomplished what was required."[5]

Although the golden plates were written in an ancient tongue, Joseph Smith—aided by the Urim and Thummim—translated them with relative ease. When he had finished, the angel Moroni came and took back both the original set of plates and the Urim and Thummim. The translation, of course, remained on earth and became known as the Book of Mormon.

Considering the theme of the book and the circumstances surrounding the writing, it is little wonder that the Book of Mormon has become a source of contention. Indeed, it is one of the most controversial books ever written. Its author, or translator—only twenty-three years old at the time—remains one of the most perplexing figures in American social history.

Joseph Smith—Man of Controversy

Joseph Smith was born in 1805 in Sharon, Vermont, of old New England stock. Whether any of his early activities foreshadowed other events is a matter of opinion. His grandfather claimed to have had heavenly visions

---

[4]Smith, *Pearl*, pp. 50–51.
[5]Smith, *Pearl*, p. 54.

and actually had his experiences published in book form. Joseph himself was fond of using a "peep-stone," a kind of native quartz or crystal, to locate hidden treasure. And while the digging never unearthed anything of value, the boy did show evidence of lively imagination and—quite important—the ability to lead people older than himself. Use of the peep-stone, incidentally, was a rather common practice of the period.

Although the Smiths were never destitute, Joseph's father had some difficulty earning a living. When they moved to New York, their fortunes did not improve—and neither did young Joseph's luck with treasure hunting. How he would have fared in a competitive economy will never be known, for at an age when most young men were serving their apprenticeships, Joseph Smith was discovering and translating the golden plates. And at an age when most of his childhood acquaintances were starting up in business or agriculture, Joseph was founding a church.

The Mormons

Joseph Smith born 1805	Book of Mormon printed 1830	Brigham Young arrives in Utah 1847	BYU founded 1875	Utah admitted as a state 1896			Tenth temple opens (Los Angeles) 1956	One hundredth temple opens (Boston) 2000 2000–2010
1800–1825	1825–1850	1850–1875	1875–1900	1900–1925	1925–1950	1950–1975	1975–2000	
1820 Smith receives first vision	1844 Joseph Smith killed		1890 Polygamy prohibited	1923 First temple outside U.S. (Alberta, Canada)			1978 Priesthood extended to all males	2008 Mitt Romney campaigns for the presidency

The Book of Mormon   As transcribed by Joseph Smith, the Book of Mormon is a mammoth and fairly intricate work. The present edition runs to 531 double-column pages, divided into fifteen books—Nephi, Jacob, Enos, Jarom, Omni, and so forth. Each book is subdivided into chapters and verses, so that in style it is like the Bible; indeed, a number of Old and New Testament passages reappear verbatim.

The Book of Mormon tells the story of a family who left Jerusalem around 600 B.C. Lehi, the father, was a Jewish prophet who had been notified by God that the city was doomed to destruction. Under Lehi's direction, the family, together with some friends and neighbors, built a small ship and sailed eastward. Their probable route was the Arabian Sea, the Indian Ocean, and the South Pacific, for eventually they reached the western coast of America.

The little group established itself in this New World of promise and soon began to expand and multiply. When Lehi died, the group split into two factions, one following Nephi, the youngest son, the other following Laman, the eldest. The Nephites and the Lamanites eventually became hostile to one another, and fighting ensued. They were, according to the Book of Mormon, forebears of the Native Americans.

In brief, the Nephites advanced and the Lamanites declined, and while both groups had an Israelite background, it was no great surprise when Jesus appeared among the Nephites. Indeed, he taught the same things he had taught in Palestine and set up his church in much the same way. As the Nephites grew and prospered over the years, however, they tended to fall away from Christ's teachings. Prophets such as Mormon—who had kept a chronicle of the Nephites—exhorted them to mend their ways, but to no avail. God eventually lost patience with the Nephites and permitted their hereditary enemies, the Lamanites, to prevail.

The final battles took place around the Hill Cumorah in A.D. 400, and the Nephites were destroyed as a nation. The last remaining Nephite was Mormon's son, Moroni, who took his father's chronicle, wrote the concluding portion, and buried the entire record—in the form of gold plates—on Cumorah. This was the same Moroni who, as a resurrected personage, divulged the hiding place to Joseph Smith.

The idea of a spiritual bridge between the Old World and the New had a natural appeal for people in the United States, especially since there was then much speculation about the origin of Native Americans. And while the account of the Nephites and the Lamanites represents but one small portion of the Book of Mormon, it does illustrate one of the central themes of the book: the cycle of good and evil. Humans follow the commandments of God; hence, they thrive and prosper. But prosperity leads to pride, and pride leads to selfishness and a rejection of God's ways—hence, humans fall. To rise again, they must repent and ask His forgiveness.

Over and over again, in a variety of different contexts and with a host of different peoples, the sequence is repeated: from goodness to prosperity, from prosperity to pride and selfishness, from pride and selfishness to downfall, from downfall to repentance. Repentance leads to goodness, and the cycle starts once more. There is little equivocation or obscurity in the Book of Mormon. Good and evil are portrayed with crystalline clarity. And as more than one commentator has pointed out, it is this clarity that adds to the appeal of the book.

Doubters and Believers   As was mentioned earlier, the golden plates—and the story inscribed thereon—provoked an avalanche of controversy. Critics denounced them as fakes, and Joseph Smith was decried as a mere yarn spinner. If scholars had difficulty with hieroglyphics, how could an uneducated twenty-three-year-old possibly have translated them? The Book of Mormon, furthermore, contains a number of errors. The steel sword of Laban is reported as existing in 600 B.C. (1 Nephi 4:9), long before steel was invented. Cows and oxen are reported in the New World about the same time (1 Nephi 18:25), although the first cattle were actually brought from the Old World by Columbus on his second voyage.

Some critics see the Book of Mormon as a not-too-subtle attempt to paraphrase the Bible. They call attention to similarities in name-style and wording. The phrase "And it came to pass," for example, appears no fewer than 2,000 times.

Defenders of Mormonism reject all the above arguments in no uncertain terms. They believe that because Joseph Smith was a true prophet of God, he had no need of formal education to translate the golden plates. The Urim and Thummim, as instruments of the Almighty, were all that was necessary.

As for the plates themselves, Mormon supporters point out that eleven witnesses testified—by sworn statement—that they had actually seen the plates. A number of these witnesses later withdrew from the Mormon church and renounced their ties completely, but none ever repudiated his sworn testimony concerning the golden plates. To this day, every copy of the Book of Mormon contains a facsimile of the sworn statements, together with the eleven signatures.

As far as archeological evidence is concerned, Mormon defenders claim that it is unclear, that the authorities themselves have differing interpretations, and that new discoveries are constantly being made. It is held that, when all the evidence is in, the account contained in the golden plates will be confirmed. The other criticisms—involving word meanings, grammar, and phraseology—are dismissed as inconsequential points that arise whenever a manuscript is processed for publication.

Most followers believe strongly that the Book of Mormon is an internally consistent document that has stood the test of time. They feel it is beautifully written, eternally instructive, and a true reflection of the word of God. They accept it—along with the Old and New Testaments—as Scripture.[6]

The Early Years

On April 6, 1830, six young men gathered together not far from the Hill Cumorah. In addition to Joseph Smith himself, there were his two brothers, Hyrum and Samuel, as well as Oliver Cowdery, Peter Whitmer, and David Whitmer. All had seen the golden plates—they had so testified— and all had been profoundly moved by the inscribed message. Indeed,

---

[6]Mark Leone, *Roots of Modern Mormonism* (Cambridge, MA: Harvard University Press, 1979), p. 171.

they were gathered for the purpose of founding a church based on that message. The laws of New York State required a minimum of six members for incorporation, and these were the six. When the meeting opened, Joseph Smith announced that he had received a revelation from God which said, "Behold there should be a record kept among you: and in it thou shalt be called a seer, a translator, a prophet, an apostle of Jesus Christ, an elder of the church through the will of God."

By this revelation, and by the unanimous consent of the original six members, Joseph Smith was acknowledged to be a prophet of God and the undisputed leader of the church. Even today, in routine conversation, Mormons refer to him as the Prophet. However, the term *Mormon church* was never adopted, the original designation being simply the Church of Christ. (Outsiders referred to members as *Mormons* or *Mormonites*.) A few years later (1838), the present name was made official: the Church of Jesus Christ of Latter-day Saints. ("Latter-day" refers to the modern era, as opposed to the early period of scriptural history.)

Members of the church do not mind being called Mormons. They use the name themselves. They are more likely, however, to use such terms as *Saints, Latter-day Saints*, or *LDS*.

The church grew rapidly—a thousand members in less than a year. It soon became apparent that, being American in both setting and theology, LDS had a natural attraction for many people. Then, too, in this early period the church was blessed with a number of extremely able, vigorous leaders. In addition to Joseph Smith, a genuinely charismatic leader, there were Oliver Cowdery, Sidney Rigdon, and Parley Pratt. There was also a man named Brigham Young.

Mormon growth, however, was accompanied by prolonged and vicious persecution. In New York State, Joseph Smith was arrested several times for disturbing the peace. To escape harassment, the Prophet and his followers moved westward—to Ohio, Missouri, Illinois—but in each state they encountered real trouble. Raids, attacks by mobs, pitched battles— the trail of persecution seemed endless. Joseph Smith himself was assaulted, beaten, and jailed on a number of occasions.

The end came on June 27, 1844, when a mob stormed the jail at Carthage, Illinois, where four Mormon leaders were being held. Willard Richards and John Taylor managed to escape with their lives, but Joseph Smith and his brother Hyrum were brutally shot to death.

The Aftermath—and Brigham Young

The death of the Mormon leader shocked both the citizens of Illinois and the nation at large. Some of the public thought that the Latter-day Saints would emerge to dominate the religious scene. Skeptics thought otherwise, questioning whether the faithful would survive the death of the Prophet.

As with many religious organizations, the death of the founder provoked a major crisis. The Twelve Apostles of the church prayed about a successor and announced they had received a revelation from God that a reluctant Brigham Young should be the second president of the church. Another group within the church created the *Reorganized Church of Jesus Christ of Latter Day Saints*, now known as the *Community of Christ*. The latter group's leadership was provided by Joseph Smith, III, and Emma Smith (the son and wife of the founder). Other smaller splinter groups broke away at this time, including the *Bickertonites*, the *Strangites*, and the *Church of Christ (Temple Lot)*, some of which still function today.

The Church of Jesus Christ of Latter-day Saints not only survived but grew and prospered. The death of Joseph Smith did not result in a bankruptcy of leadership. On the contrary, LDS had any number of able and enthusiastic people. There was, of course, only one Brigham Young.

Born in 1801 at Whitingham, Vermont, Brigham Young reportedly came from the poorest family in town. Instead of going to school, he worked with his hands. He became a skilled carpenter, painter, and glazier, and—on the side—learned to read and write. He evidenced no special religious leanings until he was twenty-two, when he became a Methodist. A few years later, after reading the Book of Mormon and becoming convinced of its authenticity, he converted to LDS.

In 1832 he met Joseph Smith, and the two had a long talk. From then on, Brigham Young was one of the Prophet's staunchest supporters—and one of Mormondom's most enthusiastic workers. As a carpenter, he helped build temples; as a planner, he laid out whole cities; as a missionary, he achieved a brilliant record in England. His rise within the church was rapid, and following Joseph Smith's death in 1844, he was the dominant figure in LDS for over thirty years. It is difficult to imagine what form Mormonism would have taken without his leadership.

After a short—and uneasy—truce, persecution of the Mormons was resumed. The alleged murderers of Joseph Smith were tried but were acquitted, and from then on things went from bad to worse. Mobs attacked Mormon families. LDS buildings were set afire. Attacks and counterattacks accelerated. At one time, both sides were using artillery pieces. By the end of 1845, it had become obvious that the Latter-day Saints would have to leave Illinois.

The exodus began on the morning of February 4, 1846, and the going was rough. It took the Saints nearly five months to reach Council Bluffs, Iowa, four hundred miles away. But the Rocky Mountains were still five hundred miles distant—and beyond the mountains was another stretch of a thousand miles, most of it unsettled land.

In the spring of 1847, an advance group of some 150 Mormons, headed by Brigham Young and Heber Kimball, set out to blaze a new path. Their success was startling. Known as the Mormon Trail, the new route was eventually followed by both the Union Pacific Railroad and U.S. Highway 30.

The trailblazers pushed on across the Rockies, and on the morning of July 24, 1847, Brigham Young caught his first sight of the Great Salt Lake Valley. He held up his hand and said, "It is far enough. This is the right place." His followers knew what he meant. Thenceforth, July 24 would be celebrated among the Mormons as Pioneer Day, their greatest holiday. Today it is an official state holiday in Utah and is intended to celebrate the pioneer, and not necessarily Mormon, heritage. For example, Pioneer Day now includes an annual intertribal powwow of American Indians to broaden understanding of the area's history.

Polygamy

Once the Salt Lake region was consolidated, the Mormons experienced steady and rapid growth. Like all organizations, they had problems and conflicts. But there was one issue that dwarfed all the others, one issue that almost brought the edifice down. The issue was polygamy, and it is ironic that the very practice that came close to being fatal is the one that, in the public mind, seems interminably linked with Mormonism.

Strictly speaking, **polygamy** refers to plural spouses—husbands *or* wives—whereas **polygyny** refers only to plural wives. However, writers of the period used the term *polygamy* when referring to the Mormons, and somehow the term has persisted. Accordingly, *polygamy* will be used throughout the present account.

How did the Latter-day Saints come to adopt polygamy in the first place? A number of explanations have been offered, most of them false. It has been suggested that plural marriage was used to take care of excess Mormon females. Census figures indicate, however, that—as in most of the West—the Utah area had an excess of males, not females.

It has also been suggested that polygamy was simply a convenient method of satisfying the high male sex drive, yet prurient interests can hardly have been paramount. Before a man could take a second wife, he was required to get the permission not only of his bishop but of his first wife. Only by so doing could he be assured of a sanctioned LDS marriage.

The Latter-day Saints adopted polygamy for one reason and one reason only. They were convinced that the practice had been ordained by God—as revealed through the Prophet Joseph Smith. Virtually all modern scholars are in agreement on this point.

Beginnings   While the history of Mormon polygamy contains numerous gaps, the following information has been fairly well documented. Joseph Smith reported that he had received a revelation from God prescribing polygamy. The date of the revelation is unclear. It was recorded, however, on July 12, 1843, for on that date the Prophet carefully dictated the lengthy revelation, later known as the Principle, to his clerk.

In the early period, polygamy was never publicly admitted; indeed, the revelation itself was locked in Brigham Young's desk for many years. Gradually, however, as more and more of the church hierarchy took plural wives, the element of secrecy was lost. When Orson Pratt and Brigham Young made the public announcement in 1852—based on the Prophet's earlier revelation—the Principle had become a more or less open secret.

By this time, of course, the Mormons had "escaped" from the East and the Midwest. Well beyond the Rocky Mountains, they were—or thought they were—safely ensconced in their territorial domain. Church leaders did not expect that the Principle would go unchallenged. They anticipated some intervention by the U.S. government, but thought that—in the interest of religious freedom—the courts would be on the side of LDS. This was an incorrect assessment.

Nevertheless, for a period of almost fifty years the Latter-day Saints not only practiced polygamy but did so with a fair amount of success. It may well be that this exercise in marital pluralism was the most unusual large-scale experiment in American social history.

The Operation of Polygamy   At the time, there were many misconceptions about Mormon polygamy, and some of them remain. According to the lurid accounts of the eastern newspapers, Mormon patriarchs were simply gobbling up unsuspecting girls in wholesale lots—for lewd and lascivious purposes. And while such charges were obvious nonsense, they did much to inflame public opinion.[7]

The "typical Mormon patriarch" was quite content to have but one wife, for in any group that permits polygamy, most people still practice monogamy. This is because at the marrying ages, males and females are roughly equal in numbers. When there is an excess of one sex, it is usually slight, so that—generally speaking—every plural spouse means that someone else is deprived of matrimony altogether.

What percentage of Mormons actually practiced polygamy? An accurate answer remains elusive. The figure doubtless varied over the years, peaking around 1860. The overall figure—the proportion of Mormon men who ever practiced the Principle—is estimated at 3 percent by LDS. Critics of Mormonism have placed the figure as high as 20 to 30 percent.

[7]Kendall White, Jr., and Daryl White, "Polygamy and Mormon Identity," *Journal of American Culture* 28 (June), pp. 165–77.

When most scholarly calculations are considered, perhaps a fair estimate would be in the neighborhood of 10 to 15 percent. Whatever the figure, one very important fact is often overlooked: namely, that it was the upper-level Mormon men—especially those at the top of the church hierarchy—who were most likely to take plural wives.

A common polygamous practice was for the man to marry sets of sisters, the feeling being that such a procedure would reduce connubial tension. Whatever the reason, Joseph Smith is reported to have married three sets of sisters. Heber Kimball married four sets. John D. Lee married three sisters and also their mother. And so it went.

What about the economic aspect of plural marriage? Was having plural wives (and plural children) an asset or a liability? In many cases, it was a liability. True, an extra wife and children for a Mormon farmer meant that he would have additional help for the farm. But a fair number of Latter-day Saints were not farmers, and even among those who were, there was a point of diminishing returns. A Mormon farmer with fifteen wives and forty-five children could hardly hope to keep them all productively engaged in farming.

Little wonder that so many Mormon polygamists were from the upper economic bracket. Poorer members could hardly afford the practice, a fact of life that was well understood by all concerned. Plural marriage held status advantages for Mormon women as well as for men. Polygamous wives held higher status by their association with the most influential men, and through the sense of serving as religious and social models for others. It wasn't unknown for a first wife to actively encourage her reluctant husband to take a second wife so that they could both reach the highest state of exaltation in the afterlife.[8]

Celestial Marriage   One of the revelatory doctrines promulgated by Joseph Smith and practiced by LDS is **celestial marriage.** According to this concept, there are two distinct types of marriage: one for time and the other for eternity. The former is regarded as a secular marriage that is broken at the death of either husband or wife. Celestial marriage, on the other hand, serves to "seal" a man and woman not only for time but for all eternity. Such marriages are always solemnized in a Mormon temple and include rites and rituals that are never divulged to non-Mormons. Other types of ceremonies—civil or religious—are held to be valid only until death. (Marriages with non-Mormons run counter to LDS policy and are not performed in the temples.)

The point is that celestial marriage dovetailed nicely with polygamy. For example, if a man who had been sealed for time and eternity died

[8]Lawrence Foster, *Religion and Sexuality: Three American Communal Experiments of the Nineteenth Century* (New York: Oxford University Press, 1981), pp. 211–12.

before his wife, the latter could—if she desired—marry another man for time only. Some of the women married to Joseph Smith for time and eternity, later (after the Prophet's death) married Brigham Young for time only, even though they bore him children.

It was also possible to marry for eternity rather than time. A woman who had died without ever having married could be sealed for eternity to an LDS male—after her death. The fact that he might already have a legal wife would make no difference, because plural wives were perfectly acceptable.

Polygamous Households   Living arrangements varied among the polygamous families. In some instances, the wives lived with the husband under one roof. In the larger families, however, there were usually separate dwellings for the respective wives and their children. At any rate, a considerate husband was not supposed to show any favoritism. Hypothetically, at least, he was obligated to spend an equal amount of time with (and money on) each wife. In some cases, evidently, the husband would practice "rotation": he would spend one night with each of his spouses.

The question is sometimes asked whether this sharing of love, as the **Gentiles** (non-Mormons) called it, did not have a sexually frustrating effect on the plural wives. In a strictly factual sense, there is very little information on a subject as sensitive as this. The fact that plural wives voiced no complaint along these lines suggests that the problem was not too significant.

During the nineteenth century, American women, both Mormon and non-Mormon, were regarded as having a procreative function. Birth control was by no means accepted in society at large and is still frowned on by the Mormon church. The point is that sexual intercourse was not considered by most females to be the pleasure-giving activity that it is today. On the contrary, it was more or less openly held to be a "wifely duty."

Sex was not the only problem associated with polygamy. Jealousies, economic disputes, child rearing and in-law conflicts—these too were involved. In a monogamous pairing, for example, there are usually four in-laws, and the resultant problems are a well-known factor in marital discord. Where there were two or six or ten wives, the in-law problem must have indeed been formidable.

Instances of jealousy, also, were fairly common. It was only natural that there would be a certain amount of vying for the husband's attention—and for him to show total impartiality would have required superhuman effort. Conflict apparently occurred when a middle-aged husband took a young woman as an additional wife.

All things considered, it is remarkable that polygamous marriages worked as well as they did, for there is no doubt that some mighty problems existed. And it was the leadership that had to listen to the complaints. In 1860, Brigham Young told how he was often required to listen to accounts of sorrow associated with the institution that were, in his words, like "drinking a cup of wormwood."[9] The Prophet's problems aside, one of the best accounts of Mormon pluralism is by Kimball Young, a grandson of Brigham Young. Through personal interviews, as well as an examination of newspapers, journals, diaries, and autobiographies, Young estimated that about half the polygamous marriages were highly successful, a quarter were reasonably successful, and perhaps a quarter had considerable or severe conflict.

Although there is no satisfactory way to compare these figures with those of monogamous marriages, it does appear that Mormon pluralism frequently presented a stern challenge to the good ship matrimony. According to Kimball Young, "The real problem was that the difficulties could not be easily settled, because the culture did not provide any standardized ways for handling these conflicts. For the most part, these people genuinely tried to live according to the Principle. But when they applied the rules of the game borrowed from monogamy, such as not controlling feelings of jealousy, they got into real trouble."[10]

The End of Plural Marriage

Mormon polygamists had their share of domestic discord—perhaps a bit more than their share. Given time, however, the system of plural marriage probably could have been made to work. The problems were not insurmountable, and the Saints were a dedicated people. Unfortunately for all concerned, the real difficulties were external rather than internal, and as time went on, the situation deteriorated. It soon became apparent that as far as the outside society was concerned, polygamy was creating a lesion of unhealable proportions.[11]

[9]B. Carmon Hardy, *Solemn Covenant: The Mormon Polygamous Passage* (Urbana: University of Illinois Press, 1992), p. 17.

[10]Kimball Young, *Isn't One Wife Enough?* (New York: Holt, 1954), p. 209.

[11]By 1870, there were a small number of non-Mormons in Utah, who complained to the federal government about Mormon activities. Although plural marriage was the most publicized complaint, Cresswell writes that non-Mormon settlers also objected to "the church's economic and political domination of the territory." They further argued that "Utah was devoid of public nonsectarian schools; Utah had a wholly Mormon militia, intimately connected with the church; and the economic life of the territory was collectivist, directed by Mormon authorities. Elections were controlled rather thoroughly by the church hierarchy, and in short, Utah seemed to be an un-American theocracy" (Stephen Cresswell, *Mormons, Cowboys, Moonshiners and Klansmen* [Tuscaloosa: University of Alabama Press, 1991], p. 80).

As portrayed in the Gentile press, Mormonism was a false religion—with many evil connotations. But the target attacked most was polygamy. Over and over and over again the traumas of plural marriage were emblazoned in bold headlines. Some of the stories were factual, but—given the nature of American newspapers—many were the products of reporters' imaginations.

Such stories clearly tended to inflame public opinion. And when that happens, political reaction is sure to follow. In 1862, President Lincoln signed a bill outlawing polygamy in the territories of the United States, and after the Civil War federal agents arrived in Utah. The difficulty was, however, that the agents could not always gain access to church marriage records. Also, Mormon polygamists became adept at scattering and hiding their wives, and—if necessary—themselves.

Brigham Young died in 1877 and was buried in a walnut casket he had designed himself. But even he had not escaped the long arm of the law, having been arrested and jailed on charges of polygamy. However, he was freed after an overnight confinement when he was able to convince the judge that in a *legal* sense, he had only one wife—the first.

After Brigham Young's death, things seemed to go downhill rapidly for the Saints. In 1879, the Supreme Court ruled in *Reynolds v. United States* that the free exercise of religion clause of the First Amendment did not protect the LDS practice of plural marriage. In 1882, a new federal law provided punishment for anyone found living in "lewd cohabitation," and Mormon leaders found themselves going to jail in droves. During a single year, 1887, some two hundred polygamists were imprisoned.[12]

The year 1887 marked the beginning of the end of plural marriage, for in that year the Edmunds-Tucker Act was passed. This bill dissolved the church as a corporation and provided for the confiscation of church property. The cost to the Mormon church was over a million dollars, nearly half of it in cash. And the raids and imprisonments continued. In all, there were 573 convictions for polygamy.

By this time, many Mormons had wearied of the struggle. Then too, LDS leaders—who remained resolute to the end—wanted statehood for Utah, a goal they realized was unattainable so long as polygamy was being practiced.

In 1890, the Supreme Court upheld the Edmunds-Tucker Act as constitutional, a decision that marked the end of the line for plural marriage. Shortly after the decision was handed down, then church president Wilford Woodruff made the following official pronouncement, known in subsequent years as the Manifesto (also called "The Great Accommodation").

[12]Carl Carmer, *The Farm Boy and the Angel* (Garden City, NY: Doubleday, 1970), p. 181. Also see Sarah Barringer Gordon, "The Mormon Question: Polygamy and Constitutional Conflict in Nineteenth-Century America," *Journal of Supreme Court History* 28 (March 2003): 14–29.

Inasmuch as laws have been enacted by Congress forbidding plural marriages, which laws have been pronounced constitutional by the court of last resort, I hereby declare my intention to submit to those laws, and to use my influence with the members of the church over which I preside to have them do likewise. . . .

And I now publicly declare that my advice to the Latter-day Saints is to refrain from contracting any marriage forbidden by the law of the land.[13]

Although the Manifesto caused some internal resentment, both Mormons and non-Mormons were generally glad that the long battle was over. Woodruff's pronouncement was (and is) treated as a revelation. When asked about it, he replied simply, "I went before the Lord, and I wrote what the Lord told me to write." The pronouncement apparently ended the long conflict over plural marriage.

Or did it?

Woodruff's Manifesto put an end to the open practice of plural marriage, and President Benjamin Harrison granted a pardon to all the imprisoned polygamists. In 1896, Utah was admitted to the Union as the forty-fifth state. Nevertheless, for a decade or so following the Manifesto, a few Mormon leaders continued to take plural wives.

In 1902, Reed Smoot, an LDS official, was elected to the United States Senate. There was opposition to his being seated, however, and during lengthy hearings the facts concerning "secret" polygamy came to light. The Mormon church, while not condoning plural marriage, had taken no steps to remove those officials who were continuing the practice.

At the final Senate vote, Smoot was confirmed by a narrow margin, and political opposition to Mormon office seekers came to an end. In fact, over the years, any number of ranking government officials have been Mormons. After the highly publicized Smoot hearings, LDS adopted a policy of excommunicating any member known to practice polygamy, a policy that remains in effect today.

Interestingly, while Mormons no longer practice polygamy on earth, it is expected that polygamy is the norm for worthy male members in the afterlife. "Mormon men are taught that part of the reward that awaits them in the afterlife if they lead a 'pious' Mormon earth life is the opportunity to take on more than one wife after death so that they may become head of their own expansive patriarchies."[14]

---

[13]Joseph Smith, *Doctrine and Covenants* (Salt Lake City: Church of Jesus Christ of Latter-day Saints, 1974), last section.

[14]"The Persistence of Polygamy," *New York Times Magazine*, March 21, 1999, Sec 6, p. 14. Interestingly, the Smoot controversy surfaced in 2009 in the wake of the scandals in Illinois, which involved the governors attempt to sell the Senate seat previously held by President Barack Obama. The U.S. Senate held up confirming the governor's nominee, Roland Burris, recalling the hold-up of Smoot's confirmation over a hundred years earlier.

Organization of LDS

The Mormons have one of the most complicated—and successful—clerical organizations in America. Every "worthy male" is expected to take his place in the hierarchical priesthood. There are now more than a million LDS priests, a figure that far surpasses the number of Roman Catholic priests in the entire world.

A worthy male starts his priestly career at age twelve, when he is admitted to the Aaronic order with the rank of deacon. This is the lowest rank in the priesthood, usually attained a few years after baptism. Chief duties of the deacon include helping at church meetings, collecting fast offerings, and otherwise assisting the higher ranks.

After three years or so as deacon—if all goes well—the boy is promoted to the rank of teacher. This is a kind of apprenticeship, for while teachers do occasionally preach, their primary role is helping their superiors. When he reaches eighteen or thereabout, the boy advances to the highest rank in the Aaronic order, that of priest. The duties of the priest include preaching, teaching, baptizing, and administering the sacraments.

Assuming he has performed his duties in the Aaronic order satisfactorily, the boy is ready for the higher order, the Melchizedek, which also has three ranks—elder, seventy, and high priest. Elders are generally ordained in their early twenties and are invested with authority to take charge of meetings, to bestow certain blessings, and to officiate during rites when the high priest is unable to be present.

Seventies are essentially elders who have been chosen to be traveling missionaries, usually for a term of two years. Top rung in the ascending hierarchy is the rank of high priest. There is no higher priestly rank a Latter-day Saint can aspire to. There are, however, any number of administrative and executive positions available—if the candidate has the necessary qualifications. LDS is a huge operation, and its management requires immense effort.

Wards and Stakes   The Church of Jesus Christ of Latter-day Saints has two forms of administration, horizontal and vertical. Horizontal, in this context, refers to the various ward and stake organizations, whereas vertical refers to the overall administrative hierarchy of the church.

The basic horizontal or geographical unit of LDS is the ward, roughly corresponding to the Protestant congregation or the Catholic parish. Because Mormondom is growing, the number of wards is constantly increasing, the present figure reaching into the tens of thousands.

Although each **ward** contains both priesthood orders—with all the ranks thereof—the ward itself is administered by the bishop. It is he who baptizes and confirms, counsels members, receives contributions, conducts funerals, and so forth. He often gives a prodigious amount of his time, but neither he nor his assistants receive any pay for their work. All Mormons, incidentally, including those at the head of the church, must belong to some ward.

A **stake**—corresponding to the Catholic diocese—is made up of from five to ten wards. At the head is the stake president, who is assisted by two counselors. The president nominates the various ward bishops, holds conferences, and is generally responsible for the management of the wards under his jurisdiction. Although his is also an unpaid job, the stake president—like the ward bishop—spends an enormous amount of time on church-related activities.

The General Authorities   The vertical, or hierarchical, structure of LDS is more complicated than the horizontal. At the top of the Mormon establishment is the first president, also known as "prophet, seer, and revelator"—Joseph Smith's original title.[15] The first president holds office for life.

Because his mantle of authority is believed to be inherited from the Prophet himself, and as his title "revelator" signifies, the first president is the only member of the church empowered to voice revelations. "He is the one who receives inspiration for all of Mormonism, though he is not prone to impose his views forcefully without substantial support from other apostles."[16] The system is theocratic, and authority comes from the top. Indeed, some observers believe that the first president holds more power than any other church leader, including the pope in Roman Catholicism.

In addition to two presidential assistants, there is an executive council of twelve apostles, also appointed for life. "Position in the *Quorum of Apostles* is by seniority: once selected as an apostle, one is at the bottom of the ladder."[17] As apostles die, there is movement up the ladder. On the death of the first president, the senior apostle succeeds to the presidency.

Participatory Involvement   To outsiders, at least, the participatory involvement of Mormons is staggering. There are ward activities and stake activities and temple ceremonies. There are constant family visitations by teachers and bishops. Streams of missionaries flow to faraway

---

[15]The first president of LDS has two counselors. Both are referred to as president. The apostles are selected by the church president and announced without debate, much less any kind of vote.

[16]Philip L. Barlow, *Mormons and the Bible: The Place of the Latter-day Saints in American Religion* (New York: Oxford University Press, 1991), p. xxviii.

[17]Barlow, *Mormons*, p. xxviii.

places, and the conversion rate is high. There are annual and semiannual conferences and visits by the apostles. There are sealings for time and eternity. New religious tracts and publications are constantly being issued. There are weekly social events and Mormon holiday celebrations. There are recreational and musical activities and sporting events. There are a host of subsidiary organizations: women's relief society, young men's and young women's mutual improvement associations, scout troops, the Sunday school union, the genealogical society, the church welfare plan, the Tabernacle Choir, and so on. LDS even has a department of education, which, among other things, administers a series of institutes and seminaries. The church also maintains Brigham Young University, founded in 1875.

From the outside, LDS gives the appearance of being a beehive of activity—which in fact it is. It is no accident that a figure of the beehive, prominently displayed on so many LDS buildings, was chosen to be the state symbol for Mormon Utah. Both literally and figuratively, Mormons are always on the move. In fact, the Latter-day Saints themselves good-naturedly define a Mormon as "one who is on his way to a meeting, at a meeting, or returning from a meeting." Scholars of the Mormon community calculate that practicing members of LDS devote an astonishing twenty hours a week to church-related activities. This participatory involvement is unknown in a large religious group and is more typical of more insular groups, such as the Amish.[18]

In addition to the meetings, there are always new jobs to do, new conversions to make, new challenges to meet. And while the personnel requirements are enormous—it takes hundreds of thousands of dedicated workers to staff the various organizations—the church has never had any recruitment difficulties.

Vitality of the Family

Another feature of Mormon social organization is the strong emphasis placed on family relations. Whether the family member is young, middle-aged, or old—or even deceased—he or she is assured a meaningful place in the kin system. Latter-day Saints are against those things that they feel are harmful to family life. Premarital and extramarital sex are frowned upon, along with abortion, masturbation, indecent language, immodest behavior, birth control, and divorce. While the church mounts no special campaign against these practices, most Mormons seem to have little difficulty abiding by the rules.

---

[18]Ostling and Ostling, *Mormon America*.

There are lapses, to be sure. Some young Mormons do engage in premarital sex, though the incidence is much lower than for non-Mormons.[19] Some LDS marrieds do practice birth control, and in fact the Mormon birthrate has fallen somewhat. However, it is still twice as high as for society at large. Mormons take the biblical injunction to "multiply and replenish the earth" very literally and seriously.[20] Predictably, Latter-day Saints have comparatively few divorces, and the Utah abortion rate is the lowest of any state.

The familistic orientation of LDS is revealed in a variety of other ways. Whereas most Americans are accustomed to pursuing individual interests, hobbies, and activities, Mormons tend to participate as families. Their social life is largely a function of church and family. Ward dances, parties, outings, and sporting events are all attended by families and are designed to encourage the intermingling of different age groups.

Another example: Monday evening is designated as home evening. On this occasion, all members of the household stay home and devote themselves to family recreation, such as singing, games, instrumental music, and dramatics. Surveys indicate that nearly seven of ten LDS families observe the tradition.[21]

The Kin Family Network   In view of the stress on family, it is understandable why kinship plays such an important role throughout Mormondom. Brothers and sisters, aunts and uncles, nieces and nephews, grandparents, cousins, in-laws—all maintain an active and enthusiastic kin relationship. During reunions of the kin family network—one of the Saints' favorite summer pastimes—it is not uncommon to see several hundred people in attendance! Special consideration is often shown to direct descendants of pioneer Mormon families, particularly those whose forebears had direct contact with Joseph Smith or Brigham Young.

However, its emphasis on family and kinship does not fragment the Mormon community. On the contrary, every effort is made to extend and apply familistic feelings to the community at large. One has but to attend

[19]Scott H. Beck, Judith A. Hammond, and Bettie S. Cole ("Religious Heritage and Premarital Sex: Evidence from a National Sample of Young Adults," *Journal for the Scientific Study of Religion* 30[2] [June 1991]: 173–80) conducted a study and reported that "both female and male, White non-Hispanics whose religious heritage was classified as 'Institutionalized Sect' were less likely to engage in premarital sex, even with controls for other factors." The authors included both Mormons and Jehovah's Witnesses in their study groupings as members of institutionalized sects.

[20]Bruce Campbell and Eugene Campbell, "The Mormon Family," in Charles Mindel, Robert Habenstein, and Roosevelt Wright, Jr., eds., *Ethnic Families in America* (New York: Elsevier, 1988), p. 483.

[21]Debbi Willgoren, "For Mormons, No Place Like Home: Monday Night Gatherings Are a Mainstay of Family Life," *Washington Post,* July 8, 1996, p. B1.

any of the ward activities to see the closeness and camaraderie involved. The entire social fabric of Mormonism is designed so that "no one feels left out." And in their routine dealings with one another, this same type of in-group feeling is evident.[22]

Search for the Dead   Before leaving the subject of family, one final observation is in order: the Latter-day Saints' predilection for extending their range of kinship to those long dead. The basic problem is simple. Mormons believe that they themselves are following God's word, as revealed to the Prophet Joseph Smith. But what about those who died without ever hearing the Prophet's revelations?

The answer is also simple. Ancestors who died before the religion was founded in 1830 may be baptized or sealed by proxy. That is, the living person stands in for the deceased during a baptismal or sealing ceremony. The ceremony itself takes place in a Mormon temple, and the deceased is accorded full rites.

Difficulty arises from the fact that, as one goes back in time, (1) the number of ancestors becomes enormous, and (2) they become exceedingly difficult to track down. LDS does not do things halfway, however, with the result that the search for ancestry has become one of the major functions of the church.

The Mormon Genealogical Society, an administrative arm of LDS, is located in downtown Salt Lake City. Additional Family History Centers are maintained throughout the United States and abroad. The amount of genealogical research undertaken at the various branches is staggering. Vital statistics, census materials, church records, poll books, official documents of all kinds—such things are constantly being microfilmed for use by Mormon (and non-Mormon) researchers. And now there is www.familysearch.org, a Web site opened by LDS in May 1999. At its inception, it attracted more traffic than its server could handle. Open to Mormons and non-Mormons alike, the site has a catalog of millions of names. It expects to increase the number by more millions in the near future. The Mormons have records on more than 600 million deceased people.[23]

Ancestral baptism is not without its detractors by non-Mormons. After protests, Jewish leaders reached agreement with LDS that the names of 380,000 Holocaust victims be removed from the Genealogical Institute's lists and that the proxy baptisms of Holocaust victims be halted immediately. Ten years later, representatives of the Jewish community again

[22]Robert Mullen, *The Latter-day Saints: The Mormons Yesterday and Today* (Garden City, NY: Doubleday, 1966), pp. 27–28.

[23]Cf. Kristen Moulten, "Mormon Church Puts Its Genealogy Data Online," AP, Allentown Morning Call, Allentown, PA, May 24, 1999, Sec A, p. 1; www.familysearch.org.

protested the efforts to baptize by proxy other deceased Jews, but the LDS responded that they would not guarantee that this would not occur. Lapses persist, raising the ire of Jews who monitor the process. A related embarrassment occurred in Provo, Utah, in 2009, when a baptism by proxy was performed for Barack Obama's late mother. An LDS spokesman denounced the action, saying it was counter to church policy for church members to submit for baptism names of persons to whom they were not related.[24]

Distinctive Customs

"To us, the greatest day of all time is today." These words, spoken by a former Mormon leader, exemplify LDS philosophy. Few other groups are as present-oriented as the Latter-day Saints. It is not that they disregard or play down the significance of the hereafter. Their emphasis on genealogy, ancestral baptism, and sealing for time and eternity shows the importance they attach to the next world. But the way they prepare for the next world is to keep religiously active in the present one.

Group Identification   Mormons place great stress on cultural and recreational activities, but in both instances the emphasis is on group, rather than individual, participation. Team sports, organized recreation, dancing and ballet, orchestral music, choir work, theater—all such activities are felt to have a religious base in the sense that *they enhance in-group identification.* As we saw in our discussion of the Gypsies and the Amish, an *in-group* is defined as any group or category to which people feel they belong. Simply put, it comprises everyone who is regarded as "we" or "us."

   The in-group may be as narrow as a teenage clique or as a broad as an entire society—say the United States immediately after September 11, 2001. The very existence of an in-group implies that there is an entire out-group that is viewed as "they" or "them." An *out-group,* as previously discussed, is a group or category to which people feel they do not belong. So, most LDS members, see the Church as an in-group and nonmembers, Gentiles, as the out-group. This does not necessarily mean they feel antagonistic to Gentiles, just that they feel apart from them.

   Devout Mormons never forget that they are Mormons. The fact that they are helping to carry out God's word reinforces group identification. Even their *individual* involvements—baptism, tithing, prayer, genealogical research, and certain temple investitures—serve as reinforcement factors.

[24]"LDS Proxy Baptism of Jews Still's an Issue," *USA Today,* April 11, 2005, p. 7D; "The Issue of the Mormon Baptists of Jewish Holocaust Victims," accessed October 14, 2009, at http://www.jewishgen.org/infofile/ldsagree.html.

One of the more interesting of these is the issuance of special undergarments. These derive from one of the temple ceremonies, called the endowments. When they receive their endowments, Mormons are issued a special set of underwear, which they are supposed to wear at all times. Originally the temple garments, as they were called, gave the appearance of a union suit. They were made of knit material and covered the body from ankle to neck. Although they are still worn by devout Mormons of both sexes, the undergarments themselves have been shortened and modified in appearance. They still contain the embroidered symbols that remind the wearers of their temple obligations.

Word of Wisdom   It is a common observation that Mormons do not drink alcohol or smoke, a proscription that derives from one of Joseph Smith's revelations known throughout Mormondom as the Word of Wisdom. Included in the prohibition are tobacco in any form, alcoholic beverages of any kind (including wine and beer), tea, and coffee. LDS has even substituted water for wine in the Sunday communion service.[25]

Although they themselves abstain, Mormons have no objection to drinking or smoking on the part of visitors or outsiders. At the same time, however, the Word of Wisdom makes Mormons uncomfortable at cocktail parties, coffee breaks, and other such gatherings that serve the rest of American society as important occasions for social interaction.[26]

In any case, the Latter-day Saints are convinced they are right, and point to the fact that LDS prohibited smoking long before the surgeon general of the United States and the Royal College of Surgeons of England affirmed that tobacco was a cancer-causing agent. Mormons are permitted to drink hot chocolate, lemonade, fruit juice, and a variety of other nonalcoholic beverages.

But does the membership really abstain, abiding by the Word of Wisdom? The answer is yes, *all worthy* Mormons do abstain. Indeed, abstinence is one of the traits most clearly separating the true believer from the Jack Mormon. The term **Jack Mormon** is commonly used by Saints to refer to a Mormon who is inactive or lapsed. Typically a Jack Mormon plays a marginal role in LDS activities but can become a member in good standing. Failure to contribute time and money to the church also leads to the label or status of Jack Mormon. The Word of Wisdom is looked upon as a commandment. Those who disobey are not considered to be worthy Mormons and are denied admission to the temple—which means that they cannot participate in ceremonies involving sealing, baptism of the dead, endowments, and the like.

---

[25]Smith, *Doctrine and Covenants*, sec. 89, p. 5.

[26]Dean L. May, "Mormons," in Stephan Thernstrom, ed., *Harvard Encyclopedia of American Ethnic Groups* (Cambridge, MA: Harvard University Press, 1980), p. 730.

Legislating Morality   While Mormons do not drink, and they are not strictly opposed to those outside the faith drinking, they do attempt to control the drinking habits of others. There are more than a thousand bars, restaurants, and clubs in Utah serving alcoholic beverages, generating $124 million a year. There are five members of the Utah Alcoholic Beverage Control Commission, on which teetotaling Mormons are well represented.[27]

LDS is often criticized for the influence it exerts over life in Utah, where 71 percent of the population is Mormon. But is this not true of life in any part of the country in which one religious perspective is clearly dominant? For example, the polity of the South clearly reflects the influence of the Southern Baptist Convention. There is also evidence that the Mormons' spirituality may serve to restore the fervor of the non-LDS in Utah. Sociologists Rodney Stark and Roger Finke found that Utah Protestants such as Lutherans, Presbyterians, and Methodists attend church more and contributed more to their church than their non-Utah counterparts.[28]

Tithing   In addition to their adherence to the Word of Wisdom, Latter-day Saints have two other customs that should be mentioned. One is tithing; the other is missionary work. Taking them in order, **tithing** comes from *tithe*, meaning "one-tenth." And in simplest terms, this is exactly what LDS expects: 10 percent of one's income "for the support of the Lord's work."

The 10-percent figure is not based on the income that remains after normal living expenses have been deducted; it is a flat 10 percent "off the top." Tithes are collected by the ward bishops and forwarded directly to the general authorities in Salt Lake City, a procedure that also stems from one of the Prophet's revelations.

The membership does not ask—and the general authorities do not disclose—exactly how much money is collected or what happens to it. However, the two major expenditures are for missionary work and education, including the support of Brigham Young University.

It is true that all Mormons are not full-tithers. Occasionally, members are permitted to give less than 10 percent and still remain in good standing. Others—the inactive group—may give little or nothing. The typical

[27]Drummond Ayres, Jr., "Sober Reality in Utah: Mormons Fulfill Role," *New York Times*, July 22, 1998, Sec. A, p. 2.

[28]"Rights Group Challenges a Church's Restrictions," *New York Times*, May 7, 1999, Sec. A, p. 20; Michael B. Toney, Chalon Keller, and Lori M. Hunter, "Regional Cultures, Persistence and Change: A Case Study of the Mormon Culture Region," *Social Science Journal* 40 (2003): 431–45; Rodney Stark and Roger Finke, "Religion in Context: The Response of Non-Mormon Faiths in Utah," *Review of Religious Research* 45 (2004, No. 3): 293–98.

Amy Toensing/Getty Images

A significant element of the growth of the Church of Jesus Christ of Latter-day Saints has been outreach. Here two Mormon Missionaries say good-bye to villagers after six weeks in Ha'apai as a part of a two-year mission in Tonga.

Mormon, however, not only gives his or her 10 percent but is quite happy to do so. By being worthy members, Mormons maintain their place in the Mormon community, are assured of full temple privileges for themselves and their families, and have the inner security that comes from carrying out the word of the Lord as revealed to the Prophet Joseph Smith.

Missionary Activity   It had aways been Joseph Smith's feeling that Mormonism needed a strong overseas base, and as early as 1837 an LDS mission had been established in England. The actual flow of converts from Europe to America began shortly afterward, but not until Brigham Young took office did Mormon immigration flourish. During the thirty years of his presidency (1847–1877), tens of thousands of converts arrived in the United States, nearly all of whom remained loyal to the church. For some time, the focus of missionary activity has been to convert people outside the United States to LDS, but now the focus has changed: not only to convert people outside the United States, but also have them remain there and create their own wards and stakes.[29]

Like so many other aspects of their religion, the Mormon missionary program is considerably different from that of other groups. It is larger,

[29]Wallace, Turner, *The Mormon Establishment* (Boston: Houghton Mifflin, 1966), p. 69.

more vigorous, more youthful, more systematic—and more successful. Latter-day Saints consider it an honor to be missionaries, and many young Mormons look forward to the time when they will be selected. The selection is made by the ward bishop, who forwards a detailed application to the missionary committee in Salt Lake City. The applicant must be young (nineteen or twenty), of good character, and worthy in the eyes of the church. Also he or she (or his or her family) must be able to afford the cost, for the expenses incurred during the fieldwork are not borne by LDS.[30]

Either sex may apply, although males outnumber females by a margin of about four to one. If an applicant is accepted by the committee, he or she receives a "call," a letter with a territorial assignment. This may be in any one of the fifty states or abroad, but in either case the young missionary is expected to stay for the stipulated period of time, usually one-and-a-half or two years. Before departing for his or her post, the missionary spends four to eleven weeks in Salt Lake City attending a training course.

Those who have been approached by Mormon missionaries may have wondered how these young people manage to learn so much about Mormonism in so short a time. But the fact is that they have been trained in Mormonism all their lives. The short intellectual period in Salt Lake City is merely to explain the operational details.

Once they have reached their assigned areas, the young emissaries work hard making cold calls knocking on people's doors. It is not at all uncommon for them to put in eight to ten hours a day, seven days a week. They operate in pairs, living together and visiting the homes of potential converts together. They have strict rules of conduct and are not permitted to date during the missionary assignment and calls home are limited to about twice a year.

When they discuss Mormonism with potential converts, the missionaries are sincere but not insistent. They patiently and systematically explain their point of view in accordance with a routine mapped out by LDS authorities. They leave pamphlets and other literature, and often make return visits to the same home. The work is occasionally tiring and—like all door-to-door efforts—more than occasionally discouraging. Nevertheless, most missionaries are happy in their assignments. There are over 60,000 of them in the field at any one time and when their tour is over, memories of their experience will undoubtedly remain with them for the rest of their lives.[31]

[30]Coates, *In Mormon Circles,* p. 138; Kirk Johnson, "Door to Door as Missionaries, Then as Salesman," *New York Times,* June 12, 2009, pp. A1, A16; Rick Phillips, "'De Facto Congregationalism' and Mormon Missionary Study: An Ethnographic Case Study," *Journal for the Scientific Study of Religion* 47 (No. 4, 2009); Rodney Stark, *The Rise of Mormonism* edited by Reid L. Neilson (New York, Columbia University Press, 2005).
[31]Coates, *In Mormon Circles,* p. 141.

Hard work aside, is the missionary effort successful? Indeed it is. First, the conversion rate is fantastically high. The number of yearly converts is reported to be in the neighborhood of 300,000. This is what accounts for much of the phenomenal growth of LDS. Second, Mormon missionary efforts have been so successful that in many parts of the world permanent missions have been established—Canada, Mexico, ten nations in Europe, three countries in Africa, ten countries in South America, six in Asia, six in Oceania, and six in Central America and the Caribbean. In fact, 138 Mormon temples have been erected or are under construction.

Owing in part to effective proselytizing, the Church of Latter-day Saints is now emerging as a "world" church. There is no doubt, however, that all of Utah benefits from visits made by Mormon converts to holy sites within the state—yet another positive latent function of the missionary effort. As evidence of the effect of tourism, Hudman and Jackson note that "more than two million Mormons visit Temple Square yearly, combining the elements of the pilgrim's devotion with modern tourism for pleasure."[32]

Sociologist Anson Shupe observes yet another interesting latent function of Mormon missionary efforts: "Both the Federal Bureau of Investigation and Central Intelligence Agency eagerly recruit Latter-day Saints. Overseas missions have provided many male missionaries with valuable foreign-language experience and contacts."[33] Shupe goes on to say that, apart from their language skills, Mormon recruits are valued for their sobriety, patriotism, and respect for authority. Mormon attorney Reed Slack notes how patriotism is fostered by church doctrine: "Modern prophets, modern scriptures, and modern revelation proclaim that the Constitution was divinely inspired. . . . The answer to why the Constitution was inspired lies in the Mormon belief that the Americas are the site of the New Jerusalem, the land of Zion. . . . The divine inspiration for the Constitution came through the foreordination of the Framers and through the influence of the Light of Christ acting upon them."[34]

Contemporary Politics

Mormons have emerged into the political limelight in a big way in the twenty-first century. Former Massachusetts governor Mitt Romney campaigned for the Republican nomination in the 2008 presidental

[32]Lloyd E. Hudman and Richard Jackson, "Mormon Pilgrimage and Tourism," *Annals of Tourism and Research* 19 (1992): 120.
[33]Anson Shupe, *The Darker Side of Virtue* (Buffalo, NY: Prometheus Books, 1991), pp. 124–25.
[34]Reed D. Slack, "The Mormon Belief of an Inspired Constitution," *Journal of Church and State* 36 (1994), pp. 37, 39.

race. While he ultimately lost that bid to John McCain, his yearlong effort brought as much attention to his Mormonism as to his position on social issues.

During his campaign, commentators often attempted to explain the Mormon faith to the public—half of whom, surprisingly, didn't think Mormons were Christians, despite the words "Jesus Christ" in the church's name. Not surprisingly, polls at the time showed that 43 percent of citizens would not vote for a Mormon. Clearly the LDS church and many Mormons were taken back by the virulent anti-Mormonism. In some ways it was reminiscent of the anti-Roman-Catholic attacks encountered by John F. Kennedy during his 1960 campaign.[35]

Romney ultimately found himself, more often than he probably wished, saying that his values were rooted in the "Judeo-Christian tradition" and that Jesus Christ was his "personal Savior." Both pronouncements are not typical of members of the Mormon church and probably reflected a desire to use language familiar to evangelical Christians. In the wake of Romney's defeat, many Mormons took a positive view that Latter-day Saints were now better and more accurately understood by the general public.[36]

While Romney may not have been on the ballot in 2008, the LDS church was actively campaigning. Californians passed Proposition 8, which banned same-sex marriage. As pro-gay marriage supporters sought to understand the defeat, they quickly focused on the role of the Mormon church in helping to pass the ban. The church directly spent little on the effort but definitely encouraged members to work actively to pass the Proposition 8 ban and spend millions of dollars in contributions. Probably most significantly, the LDS leadership called on individual churches to mobilize the faithful with such campaigns as "Thirty People in Each Ward," referring to how many volunteers were desired, and "More than Four Hours per Week," the expectation for time devoted to stop gay marriage. Fueling the controversy is the long-standing church position that it is not welcoming to gays and lesbians who are in active same-sex relationships. Entering into heterosexual-founded families is central to Mormon faith and practice.[37]

[35]Other Mormons have made runs for the presidency: Mitt Romney's father, George, in 1968; Morris Udall in 1976; Orin Hatch in 1999. These campaigns did not get as close to victory as Mitt Romney, and, perhaps, that is why Mormonism escaped as sharp a scrutiny as in 2008.

[36]Daniel E. Campbell and J. Quinn Moson, "The Religious Test," *USA Today,* January 22, 2002, p. 9A; Jonathan Dorman and Lisa Milla, "Mitt's Mission," *Newsweek,* October 8, 2007.

[37]Lisa Duggan, "What's Right With Utah," *The Nation,* July 13, 2009, ed. 22, pp. 16, 18, 20; David Von Biema, "The Storm Over the Mormons," *Time,* June 22, 2009, pp. 48–53.

Mormon Challenges

All large organizations have their problems, and LDS is no exception. In fact, in a historical sense the Mormons have probably had more than their share. That they have managed to solve most of them is due to good management, plus—always—the conviction that God is with them. Of the problem areas that remain, seven seem to merit particular attention.

The Intellectuals   In view of the origin and nature of Mormonism, the church has a special problem with the intellectual element. That is to say, intellectuals are by definition challengers. They challenge accepted beliefs and try to apply a so-called rationality to various issues. Through their critical insights, they are able to provide concepts—new ways of looking at things—not obtainable from other sources.

The Mormon church, on the other hand, is based on revelation. It is active rather than contemplative; it maintains a set of long-cherished beliefs; and, of course, it holds to the view that the Book of Mormon and the Bible (correctly translated) are literally true. As a result, disagreements between LDS and the intellectual members of the church crop up every now and then.

Academics and women, especially academic women, are fueling fires of discontent within the Mormon community. From time to time, Brigham Young University (BYU) professors are denied tenure or not rehired for reasons, many argue, involving conflict with church teachings. Mormons unaffiliated with the LDS-supported university who publish research unacceptable to the church have been subjected to disciplinary actions. These can range from being "disFellowshipped"—which allows one to retain membership but be unable to enter a temple—to the ultimate sanction of being excommunicated.

If the church is to change, the change will be slow. Boyd Packer, a church leader, told a Mormon conference in 1991 that "feminists pose a serious threat to the faith, along with homosexuals, and so-called intellectuals and scholars."[38]

Women's Role   LDS does not prohibit its female members from joining the labor force, and Mormon women are to be found in all walks of life, including the professions. At the same time, there is no doubt—in terms of priorities—that the church leaders feel that "woman's place is in the home." President Gordon Hinckley noted in October 1996, "It is well-nigh impossible to be a full-time homemaker and a full-time

---

[38]Dirk Johnson, "As Mormon Church Grows, So Does Dissent from Feminists and Scholars," *New York Times,* October 2, 1993, p. 1; Travis Reed, "Mormon scholar suspended from church" *Chicago Tribune* (December 13, 2004), p. 17.

employee. To you [women] I say do the very best you can. I hope that if you are employed full time you are doing it to ensure that basic needs are met and not simply to indulge a taste for an elaborate home, fancy cars and other luxuries."[39]

Although they have their own organization within the church, women are not permitted to ascend in the LDS hierarchy. All Mormon leaders, from ward bishop to church president, are—and always have been—male. Some Mormon women have resented their exclusion and have complained. A few have even been excommunicated for "preaching false doctrine, and undermining church leadership because of their public statements."

This, then, is the problem: although the large majority of Mormon women seem to be quite satisfied with the role accorded them by the church, some are clearly dissatisfied. There is no denying that the women's movement has had some impact on Mormon women, and it is equally apparent that it has had some impact on the church. During 1990, in a rare revision of the endowments, the church dropped wording that required women to pledge to obey their husbands; now, like the men, they must only vow to obey God.[40] It would be an exaggeration to say, however, that the women's movement has had a critical impact on either Mormon women or the church.

The Race Question   Mormons have a mixed history with people of color, to say the least. First, their settlement of Utah was marked by violent confrontations with Native Americans—ironic given the Prophet Joseph Smith's teachings of Jesus' appearance among the indigenous peoples of North America.

Second, the Church banned Black men from the priesthood beginning in 1852. Brigham Young's pronouncement came from his teaching the "curse of Cain," stating that God marked the descendants of Cain with black skin and they would be persecuted forever. The Book of Mormon implies in several places that white skin is pure and black skin is vile. While Black men were welcomed into church membership it took a revelation from God—reported by church president Spencer W. Kimball on June 9, 1978—to drop the racial ban in the priesthood. The pronouncement also brought the church in line, using its past rulings of granting priesthood to Black people in the Pacific who were not of African descent.

---

[39]Vern Anderson, "Mormon President Says Moms Should Stay Home with Kids," *Associated Press,* October 7, 1996.

[40]The endowment ceremony is a Mormon prerequisite for living in the highest level of heaven. It has remained mostly intact since Smith's revelations. In the same 1990 revision, LDS made another interesting compromise with the world: clergy of other religions are no longer portrayed in the ritual as paid agents of Satan.

The LDS reversal on race made sense given the LDS's success in developing countries, as represented by Brazil with its racially mixed population. By 2000, non-English-speaking members became the majority worldwide.

The history of past exclusion weighs heavily, and racist doctrine still is to be found in Mormon historical texts used today by church leaders, and efforts to have them officially repudiated have been ignored. African-American church members number a miniscule 10,000 today. Blacks and Latinos wield little influence in the church's upper echelons. LDS members are still discouraged from crossing "racial lines in dating and marriage," although this is supposed to be for reasons of compatibility and not a scriptural commandment. Outside the United States, however, Latinos and non-Whites have become very visible among the LDS.

Mormons are hardly unique among Christian faiths in the United States in having a racist legacy that echoes in the present. Yet the LDS failure to repudiate the past in its totality serves to separate it from major Protestant faiths.[41]

Inflexible Process of Succession   LDS presidents serve for life, most followers believing that they are chosen by God. At death they are replaced by the senior apostle from the quorum of twelve. The twelve are the only members who cannot retire. This process guarantees a gerontocracy, or rule by elders. Critics argue that by the time these leaders come to office, they are too old to serve.

Ezra Taft Benson assumed the presidency at age eighty-six in 1985. He died May 30, 1994, at ninety-six. Benson served as Secretary of Agriculture during the Eisenhower administration. During his lifetime, he was at the forefront of many conservative causes. A vibrant man until he suffered a stroke, Benson served more than half his presidency severely incapacitated, barely able to communicate.

Steve Benson, a Pulitzer prize-winning cartoonist, is Benson's grandson. During a visit in 1993, he said his grandfather said "virtually nothing" to him. He further said that despite their close relationship, "my grandfather looked at me quizzically, as if he were examining me."

Steve Benson resigned from the church because it appeared to him that church hierarchy was projecting a false image that his grandfather was capable of governance. In response to Benson's condition, Gordon Hinckley, then first counselor to the president, assured the public that

[41]Richard N. Ostling and Joan K. Ostling, *Mormon America: The Power and The Promise* (San Francisco; HarperCollins, 2000), pp. 99–112; Margaret Ramirez, "Mormons' New-Time Believers," *Chicago Tribune*, July 24, 2005, pp. 1, 17; Armand L. Mauss, *All Abraham's Children: Changing Mormon Conceptions of Race and Lineage* (Urbana: University of Illinois Press, 2003). LDS membership is 98 percent White non-Hispanic, according to Bary A Kosmin and Ariela Keysar, *American Religious Identification Survey 2008, Summary Report*, March 2009, accessible at www.americanreligionsurvey-aris.org.

there was no leadership problem in the church, that "the apostles all possess priesthood power to be prophets, seers and revelators, but only the president has the authority to receive revelations from God for the church." He went on to say that "when the president is ill or not able to function fully . . . his two counselors together comprise a Quorum of the First Presidency."[42]

On the day after Ezra Taft Benson's death, LDS publicly heard the voice of a living prophet for the first time in five years. Senior apostle Howard Hunter was named president. In apparent reference to feminists and scholars, he asked that "Mormons treat each other with more kindness, more courtesy, more humility and patience and forgiveness."[43] He wanted them back in the fold. Hunter, eighty-eight when he assumed the presidency, was not to see his hope come to fruition. He died March 3, 1995, having served only nine months.

Little more than a week later, Gordon Hinckley became the fifteenth president of the Church of Latter-day Saints. An experienced administrator, Hinckley had served three presidents as counselor and had often acted as the voice of the church in the absence of these presidents. Hinckley served for 12 years—the longest term in church history—as president until his death in 2008 at the age of 98. At this time Thomas Spencer Monson, at 80 years old, assumed the position. Monson was the youngest man to assume the position since 1973.

The Apostates   Over the years, LDS has had its share of trouble with apostates—those who have left the fold. During the nineteenth century, much of the anti-Mormon propaganda could be traced to disgruntled Mormons. Some of the apostates were simply individuals who had become dissatisfied with certain policies of the church. Much more serious, however, were those who, finding themselves unable to accept church doctrine, defected as a group to pursue their own set of religious beliefs.

A number of such withdrawals occurred after polygamy was officially proclaimed in 1852. The most significant was that of the Josephites, who rejected not only the doctrine of plural marriage but also the leadership of Brigham Young. The Josephites held that church leadership should have followed a hereditary line, and that the rightful heir, following Joseph Smith's death, was his son Joseph Smith, III.

Organized in 1852, the Josephites grew steadily, if not spectacularly, and at the end of the decade proclaimed themselves the Reorganized Church of Jesus Christ of Latter Day Saints, with Joseph Smith, III, as head. Today

---

[42]"Mormons' Inflexible Process of Succession Questioned," *Associated Press, Saturday Oklahoman and Times,* July 31, 1993, p. 12.

[43]"The Prophet's Mantle," *Economist* (June 11, 1994): A24.

it is a large, active organization, with some quarter-million members. In 2001, the church took on the new name of Community of Christ.

The relationship between LDS and the Community of Christ is amicable enough. Indeed, the two groups have much in common, including their founder, Joseph Smith. Like LDS, the Community hierarchy includes a president, twelve apostles, and a quorum of the seventy. The church likewise relies on the nonsalaried services of elders and priests for the handling of their local congregations. Most important, perhaps, both accept the Book of Mormon as divinely inspired. The original manuscript, dictated by Joseph Smith from the controversial golden plates and written in longhand by Oliver Cowdery, is owned by the Community of Christ church and kept in a temperature-and-humidity-controlled bank vault in Kansas City.

On the other hand, there is little likelihood that LDS and the Community of Christ will bury their differences and unite; the division is too pronounced. In addition to the leadership factor just mentioned, the Community of Christ does not maintain a volunteer missionary system. Also, they have no secret temple rites of any kind, no endowments, no special undergarments, no sealings, and no celestial marriage. The temples—and the meetings—are open to the public. In recent years they have allowed women to be priests.

Conflicts with intellectuals, gender rules, recognition of African-Americans, aging leadership, and criticism from those who proclaim their loyalty to Joseph Smith but are outside the church are a continuing challenge and an embarrassment to LDS.

The Fundamentalists

Just as the official adoption of polygamy created a number of schisms within the Mormon church, the 1890 Manifesto announcing an *end* to plural marriage had the same effect. Small groups of Mormons—or more accurately, ex-Mormons—have continued to practice plural marriage, even though it is against both the law and the tenets of LDS. These "Fundamentalists," as they are called, have had the unfortunate effect of prolonging the association between Mormonism and polygamy. Hence, it is little wonder that they are denounced by LDS.

After the Manifesto was proclaimed, some of the fundamentalists migrated to Mexico, but others stayed in the United States—mainly in remote areas of Arizona, Utah, and California—where they have continued their polygamous practices.

Exactly how many fundamentalists there are is not known, because their operations are generally underground. Estimates in 2010 of plural marriage have edged upward, placing the number at 38,000 people. The largest of the polygamist groups is the Fundamentalist Church of the Latter-Day Saints (FLDS), numbering about 10,000. This estimate of 38,000 overall can be variously viewed as very small compared with the millions involved in the various mainstream Mormon faiths; it can also be viewed in absolute numbers as a very large number of faithful engaged in an illegal activity. Regardless, there may well be more living in plural marriage now than 120 years ago, when it was practiced legally in Utah. As noted before, the term *deviance* is used to describe behavior that violates social norms—the expectations of a society. For someone growing up in the FLDS community—relatively closed to the outside world—polygamy seems normal, so for their young men and women, having multiple wives is the expectation. Not to engage in polygamy for them is deviant. But as seen by larger society and the broader Mormon community, these Fundamentalists are devout but misguided and certainly deviant.[44]

A number of observers—including, perhaps, most LDS members—look upon the Fundamentalists as deviants, and of lower socioeconomic status. Fundamentalists themselves say that they come from all walks of life. They also claim to be devout rather than deviant. In point of fact, they seem to be both.

Fundamentalists contend that just before he died in 1887, First President John Taylor (Brigham Young's successor) called together five of his followers and told them that the practice of polygamy must, at all cost, be retained. His message had great impact on the five men for two reasons: in defense of the Principle, he himself had spent the last years of his life in hiding, and because he was president of the church at the time, the five men felt that his counsel was based on revelation.

Polygamy Today   Whatever the rationale, there is no denying that the spark of polygamy is still very much alive—despite the fact that the pluralists have long since been cut off from the Mormon church. The Fundamentalists may have some sort of clandestine organization, although not too much is known about it. From time to time they publish and distribute literature, and every so often the popular press runs an exposé of their plural marriages. But responsible information is hard to come by.

The reason for our dearth of knowledge is twofold. In the first place, despite their agreement on the Principle, the Fundamentalists are not united or organized into one cohesive organization. They are spread over several states and Mexico, and their geographical area encompasses

---

[44]Melissa Merrill, *Polygamist's Wife* (Salt Lake City: Olympus, 1975), p. 116; Elise Soukup, "Polygamists, Unite!" *Newsweek,* March 20, 2006, p. 52; Scott Anderson, "Polygamy in America: One Man, Five Wives, 46 Children," *National Geographic* 34 (February 2010), pp. 34–59; Mirian Koktuedgard Zeitzen, *Polygamy: A Cross-Cultural Analysis* (Oxford, England: Berg, 2008), p. 89.

thousands of square miles. A number of different sects are involved, most of them quite small. Indeed, many of those who adhere to the Principle do so as individuals; that is, they have no connection with *any* group or organization.

The second reason for the lack of information is that polygamy is illegal, and those involved never know when the authorities will crack down. To circumvent possible court action, most polygamists take but one *legal* wife. Subsequent marriages—and some polygamists are reported to have as many as eleven wives—are performed by some sort of religious officiant, and do not involve a marriage license.[45] Utah, in turn, has made cohabitation a felony—provable merely by the presence of children.

High Profile Cases   Plural marriage with its sensational aspects continues to fascinate the media and the public. National television from the *Oprah Winfrey Show* to the *Jerry Springer Show* devotes programs to it. While the LDS denial of any relationship to such arrangements is regularly noted, the embarrassment to the church is apparent. Recently the national spotlight was shone on it when a disaffected Mormon who proclaimed his vision as polygamist snatched fifteen-year-old Elizabeth Smart from her Salt Lake City home. The last thing the Mormons want is to continue to be associated with plural marriage. But as long as Fundamentalism exists, that association seems inevitable.[46]

In April 2008, a massive raid on an FLDS compound in El Dorado, Texas, received global attention. The state seized custody temporarily of 416 children amid cries of abuse and child marriages. Television footage of crying mothers in conservative dress outside courthouses all across Texas led to countercharges that the state has acted hastily, with, ironically, concerns coming from feminists. Ultimately cases of sexual abuse, neglect, and "marriages" with girls as young as twelve moved through the legal system.[47]

The seriousness of the cases in El Dorado was matched in publicity by a more trivial event. Two years earlier, HBO launched "Big Love," which has had five seasons through 2010. This drama follows a family with a man, his three wives, and his eight children who belonged to fictional

---

[45]James Brooke, "Utah Struggles with Revival of Polygamy," *New York Times*, August 23, 1998, Sec 1, p. 107.

[46]White and White, "Polygamy and Mormon Identity." While legal intevention is infrequent, the polygamy question has sparked the formation of two interesting groups, Tapestry Against Polygamy (www.polygamy.org) and The Women's Religious Liberty Union. Tapestry is a self-help group that seeks to free women from polygamy, while the Union's aim is to deter those who would interfere with the happiness of women involved in polygamous marriages.

[47]"Texas Department of Family and Protective Services," *Annual Report* 2008 (Austin: State of Texas, 2008), p. 9; Mary Zeiss Stange, "What Does Texas Church Raid Say about Us?" *USA Today*, May 12, 2008, p. 119.

fundamentalist Mormon group, "The United Effort Brotherhood." The Church of Jesus Christ of Latter-day Saints denounced the series as soon as it was launched for its endorsement of polygamy as well as its depiction of sacred endowment ceremonies.[48]

Mormonism Today

Irrespective of what criteria are employed—total membership, rate of growth, wealth, devoutness, education, vigor—the Church of Jesus Christ of Latter-day Saints has an extraordinary record. There is no evidence, furthermore, that its various activities are diminishing, either in scope or tempo. On the contrary . . .

Business and Financial Interests   To say that the Mormon church is wealthy would be a clear understatement. A number of observers, including *Time* magazine, believe that on a per capita basis, LDS is the richest church in the world. For example, the church carries hundreds of millionaires on its rolls. Apart from individual wealth, the church has enormous organizational wealth.

Time estimates that the Mormon church is an empire worth at least $30 billion. Among its holdings is the 312 thousand-acre Deseret Cattle and Citrus Ranch near Orlando, Florida. Apart from the income it generates as the top beef ranch in the United States, the real estate is valued at nearly $900 million. As part of its agribusiness complex, the church also owns fifty other farms.[49]

LDS real estate holdings include much of the property around church headquarters in downtown Salt Lake City. The Polynesian Cultural Center is the number-one visitor attraction in Hawaii. LDS owns Brigham Young University in Provo, Utah, and several smaller educational institutions.

Then there are the church's media holdings. Again according to *Time*, it owns sixteen radio stations and one TV station that, combined, generated $162 million in 1996. It owns Deseret Books, a publishing house with thirty chain outlets in Utah. Its newspaper, *Deseret News*, has a circulation of 71,000 as of 2008. LDS owns choice hotels and motels, department stores, insurance companies, and skyscrapers

[48]"Church Responds to Questions on HBO's Big Love" (http://newsroom.lds.org/ldsnewsroom/eng/commentary/church-responds-toquestions-on-hbo-s-big-love), press release, The Church of Jesus Christ of Latter-day Saints, June 3, 2006; Jennifer Dobner, "HBO Vs. The Mormons In Battle Over Temple Ceremony" (http://www.huffingtonpost.com/2009/03/10/hbo-vs-the-mormons-in-bat_n_173707.html), *Huffington Post*, March 11, 2009.

[49]David Van Biema, "Kingdom Come," *Time*, August 4, 1999, vol. 150, no. 5, pp. 50–54.

Lynn Seldon/www.DanitaDelimont.com

Mormons in good standing are married (or "sealed") within a temple, such as the Salt Lake City Temple, dedicated in 1953.

in New York and Salt Lake City. The list could be extended.

The Mormon church has been powerfully successful. This is a safe statement, despite the fact that no yearly financial statements are released. The economic prosperity of LDS stems from a generous and enthusiastic tithing system, plus sound business practices. The money generated is used for the maintenance and continued expansion of the church.

Welfare All Mormons are not rich, naturally. Most of them belong to the broad middle class. And, of course, there are some at the lower end of the economic ladder. LDS, however, takes care of its own needy, who seldom have to depend on public relief. The system employed is most effective, for it permits those in need to be helped without drawing on general church revenue.

The program has two main features. First, each stake has one particular welfare project. Some stakes have farms, others have orchards, others have canneries or factories, others raise cattle, and so on. All project labor is performed without charge by LDS members. Each stake has a quota, and the interchange of commodities takes place on the basis of administrative conferences.

Turner, who studied the distribution system, shows how extensive the program is: "Peanut butter comes from Houston; tuna from San Diego; macaroni from Utah; raisins from Fresno; prunes from Santa Rosa, California; soup from Utah; gelatine from Kansas City; toothpaste and shaving cream from Chicago; orange juice from Los Angeles; grapefruit juice from Phoenix and Mesa; sugar from Idaho."[50]

---

[50]Turner, *Mormon Establishment*, p. 123.

The second half of the welfare program involves "fast money" contributed by LDS members. On the first Sunday of the month, each Mormon family skips two meals. The estimated price of the meals is then given as a welfare contribution, most of the money being used for items not obtainable from the exchange program, such as clothing, razor blades, light bulbs, and so forth. Although the fast money collected from each family may not seem like much—perhaps fifteen to twenty dollars a month—the LDS welfare program takes in millions of dollars every year by this method.

All the welfare items, both produced and purchased, are stocked in the various bishops' storehouses scattered throughout Mormondom. The storehouses—some 150 of them—resemble fair-sized supermarkets, except that no money changes hands. The needy simply present a written order from the ward bishop, whereupon the necessary supplies are dispensed. (If money is needed, there is a special bishop's fund available.)

Some contend that no Mormon ever goes on public relief, and while this may be true in some wards, it is probably not true in all. Also, in spite of the obvious success of its welfare program, it is doubtful whether LDS could handle the need that would arise, say, in the event of a major depression. But then, neither could most other groups. All in all, the Mormon welfare program is one of LDS's more successful undertakings.

Education   For some reason, the general public seems unaware that LDS places great stress on education. But the fact is that the Mormons founded both the University of Utah—the oldest university west of the Mississippi—and Brigham Young University.

One of the two major educational efforts of the Latter-day Saints is their system of seminaries and institutes. The seminaries are programs held as supplements to high school, and the institutes are socioreligious centers for Mormon college students. There are well over 2,000 institutes and seminaries in the United States and abroad, and at any one time some 100,000 Mormon youth attend them. These programs are used "to bridge the critical period of life when young Mormons must make the transition from the blind faith of their childhood to the reasoned acceptance of the faith the church hopes they will achieve."[51]

The second major thrust of the Mormon educational program is in higher education itself. Utah leads the country both in the percentage of college enrollees and in the percentage of college graduates. Latter-day Saints are justifiably proud of this accomplishment, and of the fact

---

[51]Turner, *Mormon Establishment*, p. 123.

that they have supplied the presidents for many colleges and universities outside Utah. (The number of eminent people who have been Mormons—corporation heads, scientists, engineers, governors, senators, presidential cabinet members—is too great to attempt even a partial listing.)[52]

Brigham Young University (BYU), of course, is the capstone of the Mormon educational effort. The buildings and campus are magnificent, and—in terms of physical plant—would probably rank at or near the top of U.S. colleges and universities.

In the last fifty years, enrollment has gone from 5,000 to well over 35,000, making Brigham Young the largest church-related university in the nation. Tuition at BYU is low—just a little more than $4,290 a year. (For non-LDS, the tuition is $8,580.) And although the university receives no federal aid of any kind, building and other expenses present little problem. As elsewhere in Mormondom, tithing supplies fuel for the educational machinery.

BYU is primarily an undergraduate institute, although it does offer a doctorate in 26 fields. The large majority, about 98 percent, of the student body are Mormons, and they come from all fifty states as well as over 120 foreign countries.

Why the stress on education? The impetus can be traced to a revelation of Joseph Smith's in 1833: "The Glory of God is intelligence, or, in other words, light and truth." This motto, encircling the figure of a beehive, can be seen on university literature and letterheads.

While BYU is a major university in every sense of the word, it is still a *Mormon* educational institution. The campus is organized into wards and stakes, as is Mormondom at large. Also, student attire and behavior are conservative, in keeping with the tenets of the church. The men, for example, are not permitted to wear beards, while for women "the no-bra look is unacceptable." The BYU Web site proudly notes that *Princeton Review* consistently ranks the university as the most "stone-cold sober" school in the United States.

A Global Religion

During World War I, LDS membership stood at approximately half a million. At the outbreak of World War II, the number had risen to around a million. Today, total membership is more than 13 million. Clearly, church

---

[52]Mormon celebrities include Stephenie Meyer (author of the *Twilight* series), Fox News television host Glenn Beck, singer David Archuleta (runner-up on *American Idol* in 2008), Richard Paul Evans (author of *The Christmas Box*), football quarterback Steve Young, and professional golfer Johnny Miller.

membership is not only growing but accelerating. The majority of LDS membership now lives in foreign countries, with the greatest conversion increase in South America.[53]

There is nothing secret about this phenomenal rate of increase. The Mormon church grows because it wants to grow. The Latter-day Saints have not only a high birthrate but a low death rate. On the average, they live several years longer than other Americans. (This they attribute to their prohibitions against alcohol, caffeine, and tobacco.)

So great has the success been that today's scholars of religion are asking: Has this faith, which numbered in the thousands in the 1850s, now merged as a global religion? Obviously, the reach of its membership is global. But is it a truly globalized faith, or do overseas members basically belong to a Salt Lake City entity?

Worldwide practitioners of Roman Catholicism and Islam, for example, often adopt customs of the local culture into their religious practice, and even into worship rituals not found elsewhere. This has yet to happen with the Church of Jesus Christ of Latter-day Saints. For example, Mormons have had great success in Nigeria but proceed as they would in Utah, even though they could easily accommodate dancing and the rhythms of local drum tunes.

Some the aspects of Mormon faith that other devout Christians find baffling if not blasphemous seem to be very attractive in some cultures. Converts are attracted to a faith in which divine revelations did not just occur in the distant past but in which the flow of messages from God continue. Believers may conduct baptisms for their dead ancestors. Upon their own death, the faithful look forward not only to eternal life but to an eternity linked with their spouses. In Muslim cultures, the LDS teaching that the covenant began with Abraham but that the message of Jesus was distorted, only to be connected by a later prophet (Joseph Smith rather than Mohammad), strikes a familiar chord.[54]

Mormon missionaries are received but do encounter hostility from the wealthy when they seek members among the poor or disposed indigenous

---

[53]As with other religions (including some of the extraordinary groups discussed in this volume), membership estimates are based on information released by the groups themselves (Amish and Father Divine do not even do that). According to an independent national survey, 3,158,000 people in the United States self-reported as members of the Latter-day Saints in 2008—the same proportion of the general religious population as in 1990. By comparison, the LDS declared U.S. membership at 5.8 million. See Kosmin and Keysar, *American Religious Identification Survey 2008;* Ellen W. Lindner, ed., *Yearbook of American and Canadian Churches 2009* (Nashville: Abingdon Press, 2009).

[54]Douglas J. Davies, *An Introduction to Mormonism* (New York: Cambridge University Press, 2007); "A Modern Prophet Goes Global," *The Economist,* January 6, 2007, p. 37; Mary Jordan, "The New Face of Global Mormonism," *Washington Post National Weekly Edition,* November 26, 2007, pp. 20–21; Seth Perry, "An Outside Look in Mormonism," *Chronicle of Higher Education,* February 3, 2006, pp. B9–B11.

people. This hostility may stem from a general fear among the wealthy of any emerging organization among the more powerless. Yet on a more general level, despite attracting millions of followers, in order for the Mormon faith to become a truly global religion it will need to shed the stigma of being an outsider religious group of fanatics in many people's eyes.[55]

The Latter-day Saints have had more than their share of challenges. They have been criticized for not assimilating, for not caring enough about the larger community. They have been troubled by apostates and plagued by polygamy. They have been rebuked because of their position on women. And they have been condemned by other denominations for stealing their members.

In the early days, of course, persecution was rampant. Time after time, in state after state, entire Mormon settlements were forced to flee. LDS leaders were jailed, and substantial amounts of church property were confiscated. Despite the many problems, however, both old and new, the long-term vitality of the movement has remained unimpaired in the United States and now worldwide. If anything, the tempo has increased. The fact is that Mormonism is more than a religion or a set of theological beliefs. For most of its members, it is a whole way of life.

KEY TERMS

Celestial Marriage, p. 129   Polygyny, p. 127
Gentiles, p. 130   Stake, p. 135
Jack Mormon, p. 140   Tithing, p. 141
Polygamy, p. 127   Ward, p. 134

SOURCES ON THE WEB

www.lds.org/
Official information about the Church of Jesus Christs of Latter-day Saints, their scriptures, magazines, general conference talks, temples, events, and stake/ward calendar.

http://www.cofchrist.org
The second largest group to follow the Book of Mormon is the Community of Christ, whose leadership for over a century was directly descended from the founder and faith's prophet.

---

[55]Stark, *Rise of Mormonism*, p. 12.

http://www.nps.gov/mopi/index.htm
The National Park Service maintains this site to identifying historical sites along the trail taken by the early Mormons from Nauvoo, Illinois, to Salt Lake City, Utah.

http://mormonconspiracy.com/cult.html
As with all active extraordinary groups, the detractors on the Internet are widespread. This is but one example.

SELECTED READINGS

Alexander, Thomas, and Jessie Embry, eds. *After 150 Years.* Midvale, UT: Charles Redd Center for Western Studies, 1983.

Arrington, Leonard. *Brigham Young: American Moses.* New York: Knopf, 1985.

Barlow, Philip L. *Mormons and the Bible: The Place of the Latter-day Saints in American Religion.* New York: Oxford University Press, 1991.

Bushman, Richard L. *Joseph Smith and the Beginnings of Mormonism.* Urbana: University of Illinois Press, 1988.

Carmer, Carl. *The Farm Boy and the Angel.* Garden City, NY: Doubleday, 1970.

Clark, Annie Turner. *A Mormon Mother: An Autobiography.* Salt Lake City: University of Utah Press, 1969.

Coates, James. *In Mormon Circles: Gentiles, Jack Mormons, and Latter-Day Saints.* Reading, MA: Addison-Wesley, 1990.

Cresswell, Stephen. *Mormons, Cowboys, Moonshiners and Klansmen: Federal Law Enforcement in the South and West, 1870–1893.* Tuscaloosa: University of Alabama Press, 1991.

Davies, Douglas J. *An Introduction to Mormonism.* New York: Cambridge University Press, 2003.

Decker, Ed. *What You Need to Know about Mormons: Conversations with Cults.* Eugene, OR: Harvest House, 1990.

Dew, Sheri L. *Go Forward with Faith.* Salt Lake City: Deseret Books, 1996.

Foster, Lawrence. *Religion and Sexuality: Three American Communal Experiments of the Nineteenth Century.* New York: Oxford University Press, 1981.

_____. *Women, Family, and Utopia: Communal Experiments of the Shakers, the Oneida Community, and the Mormons.* Syracuse, NY: Syracuse University Press, 1991.

Gates, Susa Young. *The Life Story of Brigham Young.* New York: Macmillan, 1930.

Hardy, B. Carmon. *Solemn Covenant: The Mormon Polygamous Passage.* Urbana: University of Illinois Press, 1992.

Heinerman, John, and Anson Shupe. *The Mormon Corporate Empire.* Boston, MA: Beacon Press, 1985.

Ison, Jim. *Mormons in the Major Leagues: Career Histories of Forty-Four LDS Players.* Cincinnati, OH: Action Sports, 1991.

Krakauer, John. *Under the Banner of Heaven: A Study of Violent Faith.* New York: Doubleday, 2003.

Leone, Mark. *Roots of Modern Mormonism.* Cambridge, MA: Harvard University Press, 1979.

Madson, Susan Arrington. *Growing Up in Zion: True Stories of Young Pioneers Building the Kingdom.* Salt Lake City: Deseret Books, 1996.

Maus, Arnold L. *All Abraham's Children: Changing Mormon Conceptions of Race and Lineage.* Urbana: University of Illinois Press, 2003.

Merrill, Melissa. *Polygamist's Wife.* Salt Lake City: Olympus, 1975.

Morris, Carroll Hofeling. *"If the Gospel Is True, Why Do I Hurt So Much?": Help for Dysfunctional Latter-day Saint Families.* Salt Lake City: Deseret, 1992.

Mullen, Robert. *The Latter-day Saints: The Mormons Yesterday and Today.* Garden City, NY: Doubleday, 1966.

Nibley, Hugh. *Tinkling Cymbals and Sounding Brass.* Salt Lake City: Deseret, 1991.

Ostling, Richard N., and Joan K. Ostling. *Mormon America: The Power and the Promise.* San Francisco: HarperCollins, 2000.

Porter, Blaine. *Selected Readings in the Latter-day Saint Family.* Dubuque, IA: Brown, 1963.

Schow, Ron, Wayne Schow, and Marybeth Raynes, eds. *Peculiar People: Mormons and Same-Sex Orientation.* Salt Lake City: Signature Books, 1991.

Shupe, Anson. *The Darker Side of Virtue.* Buffalo, NY: Prometheus Books, 1991.

Stark, Rodney. *The Rise of Mormonism.* Edited by Reid L. Neilson. New York: Columbia University Press, 2005.

Stegner, Wallace. *The Gathering of Zion.* New York: McGraw-Hill, 1964.

Tobler, Douglas F., and Nelson B. Wadsworth. *The History of the Mormons in Photographs and Text: 1830 to the Present.* New York: St. Martin's, 1989.

Turner, Wallace. *The Mormon Establishment.* Boston: Houghton Mifflin, 1966.

Turpin, John C. *The New Stress Reduction for Mormons.* Covenant, 1991.

West, Ray B., Jr. *Kingdom of the Saints.* New York: Viking, 1957.

Whalen, William. *The Latter-day Saints in the Modern-Day World.* New York: Day, 1964.

Whipple, Maurine. *This Is the Place: Utah.* New York: Knopf, 1945.

Young, Kimball. *Isn't One Wife Enough?* New York: Holt, 1954.

CHAPTER FIVE

THE ONEIDA COMMUNITY

Imagine a few hundred Christian people following a dynamic leader, living together in a true economic communist society, with no concept of personal wealth or even property. Add to this that all adult men and women are collectively married. Heterosexual experience did not recognize any notion of "partners." Free love replaced romantic love. Childbearing occurred only as permitted by a committee of older members to conform to a program of selective breeding to produce perfectionist offspring. Place all this in rural New York of the mid-1800s, and you have the extraordinary Oneida Community.

Most readers are familiar with the term **culture,** which refers to the totality of learned, socially transmitted customs, knowledge, material objects, and behavior. People in a society, whether it be the United States or Bulgaria, share a common culture. Less familiar, probably, is the concept **subculture.** Subculture is a segment of society that shares a distinctive pattern of mores, folkways, and values that differs from the pattern of the larger society. Residents of a retirement community, a street gang, and members of a marching band are all examples of a subculture.

In this chapter, we will consider an extraordinary subculture, the Oneida Community, sharing an unusual set of religious beliefs and following an individual with unusual personal magnetism, John Humphrey

Noyes. He exercised what is referred to as **charismatic authority.** This refers to power made legitimate by a leader's exceptional personal or emotional appeal to his or her followers. Max Weber believed charismatic authority often allowed the leader to advocate dramatic changes in social behavior.[1]

Noyes was able to lead and inspire without relying on the established rules or traditions. He was an astute judge of character. He could "read" his followers with uncanny accuracy, knowing when to praise and when to blame. He knew when—and to whom—to delegate authority. Noyes always knew the mood and temperament of his community. And Oneida was "the lengthened shadow of this one extraordinary man, reflecting his complex personality and concerns."[2]

On the one hand, as will be shown, Noyes was an original thinker, a sound judge of human nature, and an exceedingly versatile individual. On the other hand, he was capricious, unpredictable, and at times given to making errors in judgment. Little wonder that social historians have been hard pressed to depict the "real" John Humphrey Noyes.

Background

Unlike most of the other leaders discussed in the present volume, John Humphrey Noyes was of upper-class origin. His mother, Polly Hayes, was a cousin of Rutherford B. Hayes, the nineteenth president of the United States. His father was John Noyes, a U.S. congressman from Vermont and a successful businessman.

Not much is known about the boyhood of John Humphrey Noyes. One of eight children, he was born in 1811 at Brattleboro, Vermont. In 1821, his family moved to Putney, a small town ten miles to the north. Redhaired, freckled, and somewhat self-conscious about his appearance, he was noticeably shy around girls. With members of his own sex, however, he showed clear evidence of leadership. He entered Dartmouth at fifteen, a typical college age at that time, and was eventually elected to Phi Beta Kappa.

Upon graduation, Noyes worked as an apprentice in a New Hampshire law firm. However, it soon became obvious that he was not cut out to be a barrister, and he returned home to Putney. Up to that time, he certainly had no thoughts of founding a subculture, and he had probably never heard of a place called Oneida.

---

[1]On charismatic authority, see Max Weber, *The Theory of Social and Economic Organization.* Translated by A. Henderson and T. Parsons (New York: Free Press, 1947, originally published 1913–1922).

[2]Lawrence Foster, *Women, Family and Utopia: Communal Experiments of the Shakers, the Oneida Community and the Mormons* (Syracuse, NY: Syracuse University Press, 1991), p. 77.

John Humphrey Noyes (1811–1886), the charismatic leader of the Oneida Community.

The Granger Collection, New York

The early 1830s found the country caught up in a frenzy of religious rejuvenation, and, as luck would have it, a four-day revival was held in Putney in September 1831. Noyes attended, listened—and succumbed completely. To those who knew him, he suddenly seemed to come alive with ideas, spiritual enlightenment, and visions of eternal truth. Although religion had not heretofore been a major part of his life, it was obvious that he had found his calling. Henceforth he would devote himself to disseminating God's word. A few weeks later he enrolled in theological seminary—first at Andover, then at Yale Divinity School.

At Yale, Noyes acquired the reputation of being a radical, and although he was granted his license to preach in 1833, he was not a success. At one point, for example, he declared himself to be without sin—for which heresy he was called before the theological faculty. He refused to recant, whereupon he was denied ordination and his preaching license was revoked.

The Putney Association

Jobless, penniless, and now looked on as a religious oddity, John Humphrey Noyes did not appear to have much of a future, but there were several things in his favor. He was only twenty-three years old. He had an inner flame that was inextinguishable. He was already making a few converts, and soon he would make more. In an oft-quoted statement, he said, "I have taken away their license to sin, and they keep on sinning. So, though they have taken away my license to preach, I shall keep on preaching." Events were to prove the statement more prophetic than Noyes realized.

For the next few years he traveled through New York and New England, living on a shoestring and spreading the doctrine of **Perfectionism:** people could be without sin. Although the concept did not originate with him, Noyes's brand of Perfectionism was genuinely new. And while, over the years, he introduced a number of additions and refinements, his basic theological postulate remained unchanged: Christ had already returned to earth in a *second* coming—in A.D. 70—so that redemption or liberation from sin was an accomplished fact. Given the proper environment, therefore, man could lead a perfect, or sinless, life.

This was a radical notion, of course, and while he made some headway in spreading the gospel of Perfectionism, the existing churches turned a deaf ear to his teachings. Noyes returned home in 1836, sobered by his experience. He would spend the next dozen years in Putney, incorporating Perfectionism into the most radical social experiment America had ever seen.

Things started off innocently enough. Noyes's first converts in Putney were members of his own family: his sisters, Charlotte and Harriet, his brother, George, and his mother. (His father rejected the whole idea.) Other converts trickled in, one here, one there. In 1838, he married Harriet Holton, granddaughter of the lieutenant governor of Vermont. She not only was a convert but remained a loyal Perfectionist all her life. By 1844, however, adult membership was still only about two dozen, although other small groups of followers were scattered throughout New England.

During the early years, the Putney Perfectionists were not a communal organization. Members lived in individual houses and worked at individual jobs. They had resources; in fact, they were incorporated for $38,000, the money coming largely from the estate of Noyes's father. Gradually, they developed a type of social organization referred to as a **commune.** As discussed in Chapter 3, the commune is a form of cooperative living where community assets are shared and individual ownership is discouraged.

Communes are usually organized with everyone sharing equally in the decision making just as they share equally in earthly possessions. But even before they adopted the communal style of life, one thing was clear: the Putneyites were not a democracy. John Humphrey Noyes was both the leader and the binding force. And while he often gave the impression of operating through discussion and persuasion rather than by proclamation, there was no doubt in anyone's mind—including his own—about who made the rules.

In 1844, the Putney Perfectionists adopted economic communism as a way of life. They commenced to share their work, their food, their living quarters, and their resources. Their children began to attend a communal school. And once every day, for a protracted period, they met together for Bible reading, theological discussion, and a sharing of religious experiences.

Following his marriage to Harriet Holton in 1838, Noyes fathered five children in six years. Unfortunately, all but one were stillborn, a fact that was to have utmost significance. The Perfectionist leader grieved deeply, not only for the lost children but for their mother. Was this to be woman's lot in life, to bear children year after year, whether or not they were wanted? To suffer, to mourn, to be kept out of the mainstream of daily activity—all because of nature's imperious call? He thought not, but what could be done about it?

The Shakers, as we saw in Chapter 3, had solved the problem of childbirth—to their own satisfaction, at least—by practicing celibacy. Noyes rejected this rather drastic solution, although he realized that, whatever the answer was, it would have to include some sort of birth control. He finally hit upon the novel idea of *coitus reservatus,* or, as he called it, **male continence.** It was not necessary, he said, for a man to reach ejaculation during the sex act. With a little practice, he could enjoy sex relations without attaining the climax that might lead to conception.

In his widely quoted pamphlet *Male Continence,* published in 1872, Noyes had this to say:

> Now we insist that this whole process, up to the very moment of emission, is *voluntary,* entirely under the control of the moral faculty, and *can be stopped at any point.*
>
> In other words, the *motions* can be controlled or stopped at will, and it is only the *final crisis of emission* that is automatic or uncontrollable. . . . If you say that this is impossible, I answer that I *know* it is possible—nay, that it is easy. (pp. 7–8)

As it turned out, Noyes's contention was correct, at least insofar as the Perfectionists were concerned. Throughout the whole of the group's existence, *coitus reservatus* was used—and used successfully.

In 1846, the group began to share spouses. As might have been predicted, once the Perfectionists began the practice of spouse sharing, the word soon spread. Actually, there was never any attempt—then or later—to keep the matter a secret. In his numerous sojourns and talks, Noyes often alluded to the fact that his brand of communism involved sexual as well as economic sharing.

Nevertheless, to the citizens of Putney, right was right, and wrong was wrong—and sex outside marriage was wrong. It was the 1840s, and marriage meant one man and one woman, joined in the sight of God and legally recorded in the town-hall registry. The followers of John Humphrey Noyes, quite obviously, not only were living in sin but were more or less flaunting the practice.

One thing led to another. Finally, irate citizens met in protest and demanded action. In October 1847—amidst rumors of mob violence—John Humphrey Noyes was indicted in Vermont by a grand jury on grounds of adultery. He was released, pending trial, on $2,000 bail. Had the trial been held, the Perfectionist leader would almost surely have been found guilty. However, after much soul-searching and discussion—and on the advice of his lawyer—Noyes fled to New York. As he explained it later, the reason for his flight from Vermont was not to escape justice, but to save his followers and others from the mob violence that was clearly imminent. Oddly enough, though he probably caused more shock and outrage than any other religious leader of his time (with the probable exception of Joseph Smith, founder of the Mormons), John Humphrey Noyes was never to stand trial for his unorthodox—and illegal—practices.

Oneida

All during his stay in Putney, Noyes had made periodic forays into the hinterland to gain converts. His various publications had helped to spread the word. By 1847, when the Perfectionists' sexual system became operative, the popular press was also giving John Humphrey Noyes and his followers a good deal of publicity. When Noyes left Putney, therefore, other Perfectionist centers—rather loosely organized—were available to him. One such spot was a fairly large tract of land along Oneida Creek in New York State (about 35 miles east of Syracuse). Their newly found "promised land" was also near the Canadian border, which could prove convenient in case of future prosecution.

Formerly a reservation belonging to the Oneida Indians and now the site of a sawmill, the property was owned by Jonathan Burt, an ardent follower of Noyes. Burt had come upon hard times and was quite willing to turn over his land to the Perfectionist cause. Noyes was attracted to the site and wasted no time in reassembling the little flock of Putneyites. Burt and his associates stayed on. Other small groups of followers joined them. They cleared land, made their own implements and furniture, and held discussions. Working as farmers, they were able to buy up adjoining properties. Before long, their Oneida holdings totaled nearly six hundred acres. And in spite of adverse conditions, membership continued to grow. By the end of the first year, 1848, there were eighty-seven persons living in the Community. A year later, the number had more than doubled. (See the Timeline on page 168.)

From the very beginning, the mission of the group was made crystal clear. With the help of Almighty God, as expressed through the person of John Humphrey Noyes, they were going to create a heaven on earth. Indeed, in his own words, Noyes had said, "God has sent me to cast up a highway across this chaos, and I am gathering out the stones and grading the track as fast as possible."[3] There was never any doubt about their utopian goal. Nor was there any doubt about how they were going to attain it.

[3]Spencer Klaw, *Without Sin: The Life and Death of the Oneida Community* (New York: Penguin, 1993), p. 10.

The Mansion House   During their first winter at Oneida, the little group of Perfectionists lived in the existing dwellings: Jonathan Burt's homestead plus some abandoned Indian cabins. Top priority, however, was given to the construction of a communal home. John Humphrey Noyes believed that, in actual day-to-day living, true communism could best be achieved by having all members live under one roof. This was the way the Perfectionists lived throughout the rest of their existence.

In the summer of 1849, the first communal home was built. No one knows how it got the name Mansion House, but it was a wooden affair and was constructed by the entire Community. Membership grew so rapidly, though, that in 1862 the wooden structure was replaced by a brick building. In subsequent years, wings were added as needed, and the building still stands in its entirety. Noyes helped in the planning of both the original and the present building, and both were exceptionally well thought out.[4]

Although most adults had small rooms of their own, the building as a whole was designed to encourage a feeling of togetherness rather than separateness. To this end, *group facilities* predominated: a communal dining room, library, concert hall, recreation area, picnic grounds, and the like. It was in the Big Hall of the Mansion House that the regular evening

Syracuse University Library Department of Special Collections
Oneida Community Collection. Oeida Community Mansion House.

The Mansion House, pictured in 1870, was the focus of life in the Oneida Community in New York and where virtually all its members lived. It is still maintained as a historical site and a tourist attraction. A few descendants of members of the Community still live there.

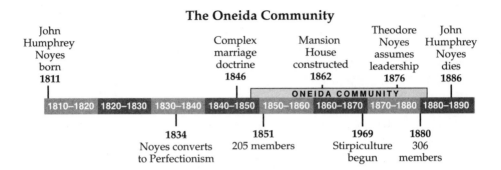

The Oneida Community

| | | | Theodore | John |
| John Humphrey Noyes born 1811 | Complex marriage doctrine 1846 | Mansion House constructed 1862 | Noyes assumes leadership 1876 | Humphrey Noyes dies 1886 |

| 1810–1820 | 1820–1830 | 1830–1840 | 1840–1850 | 1850–1860 | 1860–1870 | 1870–1880 | 1880–1890 |

ONEIDA COMMUNITY

| 1834 Noyes converts to Perfectionism | 1851 205 members | 1969 Stirpiculture begun | 1880 306 members |

meetings were held, and it was here that Noyes gave most of his widely quoted home talks.

Over the years, the Perfectionists developed a lively interest in the performing arts, and—although most of the talent was homegrown—they were able to organize such activities as symphony concerts, choral recitals, and Shakespearian plays. Occasionally, outside artists were invited to perform, but on a day-to-day basis the Community was more or less a closed group, with members seldom straying far from home.

Primary-Group Interaction

All of us have certain emotional needs: to talk, to be listened to, to socialize, to share experiences, to exchange banter, to elicit sympathy and understanding, and so on. These needs, for most people, are best satisfied within the dimensions of a small, face-to-face group, such as the family, the clique, or the friendship circle. These groups are characterized by intimate, face-to-face association and cooperation. Sociologists refer to such groups, therefore, as **primary groups.** By contrast, **secondary groups**— such as the large corporation, the business firm, or the government bureau—are formal, impersonal groups in which there is little social intimacy or mutual understanding. For the most part, members tend not to relate to one another in an emotionally meaningful way.

With several hundred people living under one roof, the Oneidans had an interesting problem in human relations: how to enjoy the benefits of

[4]During August 1993, William Zellner had the opportunity to visit the Oneida Mansion House and commented: "Before an initial visit to any place, we all have expectations as to size, shape, general appearance, etc. I found the Mansion House larger than I had expected, certainly as large a house as I have ever seen. Individuals' rooms, on the other hand, were much smaller than I had envisioned, so small that a submariner would be uncomfortable in the setting. I should not have been surprised, however, as the focus was on group living, and people were expected to be around others most of the time, not alone in their rooms. The buildings and grounds were immaculately kept." For a virtual tour of the Mansion House, see www.oneidacommunity.org.

primary-group association in an organization that had already grown to secondary-group size. They had the advantage, naturally, of believing both in John Humphrey Noyes and in the tenets of Perfectionism, but these convictions alone would hardly account for the operational smoothness that prevailed.

Their success is explained by the fact that they worked out an amazingly effective system of interpersonal relationships. Practically everything the Perfectionists did was designed to play down the "I" in favor of the "we." Members ate together at a common dining table, worked together at common tasks, and played together in a variety of recreational pursuits. They shared their property. They shared their sexual partners. And they shared their children.

In their day-to-day activities, they were ever on guard against things that might become "antigroup." Thus, tea, coffee, and alcoholic beverages were taboo. At the dining table, pork products, including bacon and sausage, were never served; in fact, meat of any kind appeared infrequently. The Perfectionists reasoned that proclivities such as coffee drinking and meat eating might become habitual and hence distractive. By the same token, dancing was encouraged because it was a group activity, whereas smoking was prohibited because it was too individualistic.

From an outsider's view, some of the prohibitions seem excessive. An interviewer was told, for example, of an episode involving all the girl children. There were several large dolls that, like other material things in the Community, were shared. Around 1850, some kind soul thought it would be better if each of the little girls had a doll of her own, and this plan was put into effect. Unfortunately, it developed that the youngsters spent too much time with their dolls and not enough on household chores. Accordingly, on a specified date, all the girls joined hands in a circle around the stove, and one by one were persuaded to throw their dolls into the fire. From that time on, dolls were never allowed in the nursery.

Often overlooked is the fact that the religious practices of the Oneidans also served to reinforce primary-group association. It is true that the Perfectionists dispensed with most of the formal aspects of religion. They maintained no church or chapel, held no prayer services, and had no paid clergy. Neither baptismal nor communion services were utilized. Because there was no marriage, there were no weddings. Death was played down, and there were no formal funeral arrangements. Christmas was not celebrated as a religious holiday, although in deference to outsiders, no work was performed on that day.

At the same time, religion was a central part of the Oneidans' daily lives. This was the whole point. Rather than have special religious celebrations or special days set aside for worship, the Perfectionists believed that every day should involve religious awareness. They were avid readers of the Bible and loved to discuss the various parables. They believed in Perfectionism. And they believed that by listening to John Humphrey Noyes—and following his teachings—they were listening to the voice of God.

The Big Hall   Every night, the Oneidans met in the Big Hall to combine the sacred and the secular. Women brought their sewing and knitting, and both sexes sat in groups around small tables. The program was conducted from in front of the stage by one of the senior members. A hymn was sung, passages from the Bible were read, and if he was present, Noyes would give one of his home talks. The talks themselves, involving as they did the secular application of Perfectionist theology, were one of the highlights of the evening—so much so that if Noyes was traveling, the talk was read by someone else. Also included in the nightly program were news and announcements, lectures, dancing, comments and suggestions by members of the audience, business reports, and so forth. The evening meetings can thus be seen as another means of promoting group solidarity. According to the weekly *Oneida Circular* of July 17, 1863, the meetings were "the most cherished part of our daily lives."

Noyes, incidentally, was no prude. He enjoyed entertainment and activities of all kinds, and encouraged his followers to do the same. Even on this point, however, he insisted on *group* involvement: a glee club rather than a soloist, a band or orchestra rather than a recital, a play or an operetta rather than a monologue, and so on.[5]

Although by modern standards such entertainment might seem rather tame, there is no doubt that the system worked. The Oneidans were clearly successful in their efforts to establish a primary- rather than a secondary-group atmosphere. Both in their conversation and their publications, "the family" was a constant reference point.

One of the oft-told stories of the Community pertains to the time a visitor was shown through the Mansion House. "What is the fragrance I smell here in this house?" the stranger asked. The guide replied, "It must be the odor of crushed selfishness."

Decision Making

All organizations have a power structure and a decision-making process, and the Oneida Community was no exception. However, the Perfectionists had a special problem because (1) they were all housed under one

---

[5]John Humphrey Noyes played the violin vigorously in the Community's twenty-piece band, but, alas, a number of listeners observed, not well. Pictures of the all-male band show a wide variety of instruments, from clarinets to violas to snare drums.

roof, and (2) they were attempting to combine the social and the economic. They solved the problem by employing a combination of the democratic and the autocratic.

Committee Work   In keeping with their emphasis on group solidarity, the followers of John Humphrey Noyes might have been expected to arrive at decisions on a democratic basis. And in one sense, there was ample opportunity for discussion. The Community *Handbook*, for example, states, "In determining any course of action or policy, *unanimity* is always sought by committees, by the Business Board, and by the Community. All consider themselves as one party, and intend to act together or not at all. . . . If there are serious objections to any proposed measure, action is delayed until the objections are removed. The majority never go ahead leaving a grumbling minority behind" (p. 17).

True enough, but what these lines refer to were the day-to-day operational decisions. Major decisions, as well as Perfectionist doctrine and Community policy, were made by Noyes.

Rosabeth Moss Kanter believes that *order* is a common characteristic of utopian communities. She states that "in contra-distinction to the larger society, which is seen as chaotic and uncoordinated, utopian communities are characterized by conscious planning and coordination. . . . Events follow a pattern. . . . A utopian often desires meaning and control, order and purpose, and he seeks these ends explicitly through his community."[6]

Order in the Oneida Community at the upper echelon was embodied in Noyes. And it was Noyes's intention that order in the lower echelons would be embodied in the committee system. Such was rarely the case.

On operational matters, members were indeed encouraged to speak out at the evening meetings. Moreover, there were a sufficient number of committees and departments to enable everyone to have a real voice in the day-to-day management of the Community. In this respect, the trouble was not that members had insufficient authority, but that they had too much. There were no less than twenty-one standing committees and forty-eight different departments. Such things as heating, clothing, patent rights, photographs, haircutting, fruit preserving, furniture, music, dentistry, bedding, and painting all involved a committee or a department. There was even a department for "incidentals."

The committees and committee heads met; departments and department heads met; the business board met. The Community itself met nightly. In a given thirty-day period, there were probably more

---

[6]Rosabeth Moss Kanter, *Commitment and Community: Communes and Utopias in Sociological Perspective* (Cambridge, MA: Harvard University Press, 1973), p. 39.

managerial discussions in the Oneida Community than in any other organization of comparable size in the United States.

Ultimately, the Perfectionists wasted too much time thrashing out details and inaugurating meaningless change. In fact, change was almost an obsession with them. They changed the work schedule, the meal schedule, and the number of meals per day, discussing endlessly which foods to serve and which to prohibit. (The debate over whether to serve tea, for example, took several years. They finally decided to permit only a brew made from strawberry leaves.) The prohibition against smoking was also years in the making. The Perfectionists liked to change their jobs and their way of doing things. They even had a habit of changing their rooms.

The Central Members   Noyes was the acknowledged leader of the Community, ruling benevolently but firmly and basing his authority on divine inspiration. As his son Pierrepont put it, "The Community believed that his inspiration came down what he called the 'link and chain'—from God to Christ; from Christ to Paul; from Paul to John Humphrey Noyes; and by him made available to the Community."[7]

On their part, the Perfectionists were quite content with the arrangement. They acknowledged that Noyes was God's representative on earth. As a matter of fact, such acknowledgment was one of the preconditions for membership.

Nevertheless, Noyes was away a good part of the time, and in his absence important decisions had to be made—on some basis other than the twenty-one committees and forty-eight departments. The system employed was the utilization of "central members." These were a dozen or so men and women who more or less served as Noyes's deputies. They were all older, dedicated individuals, many of whom had been with John Humphrey Noyes at Putney.

This, then, was the leadership process: Noyes made the major decisions, with the cooperation of the central members. These decisions encompassed economic policy, sexual matters, relations with the outside, admission of new members, childbearing and child rearing, and, of course, Perfectionist doctrine. Day-to-day operational details were handled by committees and departments, in consultation with the general membership.

The Oneida Community was hardly a model of functional efficiency. Yet the Perfectionists' system worked. Up to the very end, the Community functioned with scarcely a major quarrel. What they lost in operational efficiency, they gained in their primary-group associations and in their feelings of closeness to one another.

[7]Pierrepont B. Noyes, *My Father's House: An Oneida Boyhood* (Gloucester, MA: Peter Smith, 1966), pp. 132–33.

Role of Women

Because there were a number of divergent forces at work, the role of women must have presented something of a challenge for the Perfectionists. On the one hand, they believed in equality. Concepts of rank and privilege were foreign to them; they were communists. On the other hand, in society at large, women held a clearly inferior position. They were generally excluded from higher education, from the professions, and from public office. All but the most routine jobs were closed to them. When the Oneida Community was founded in the spring of 1848, a wife had no legal control over her own personal property, and the right to vote was more than seventy years away. Indeed, the first Women's Rights Convention—at Seneca Falls, New York—had not yet been held.

To complicate matters, John Humphrey Noyes—in this sense, at least— was a product of his times, for he, too, believed in man's innate superiority over woman. Thus the community did not acknowledge that, inherently, women were the equal of men. However, as far as the allocation of jobs was concerned, the Community was ahead of society.

In practice, the Oneida women did work usually performed by women, but they also handled jobs that were normally reserved for men, such as being lathe operators. They did the cooking, washing, sewing, mending, and nursing, and were responsible for child care, but they also worked in various business and industrial departments. They held jobs in the library and on the Community newspaper. In a number of other areas, they worked side by side with the men. And they were well represented on the various committees, including that of the central members.[8]

There were a number of adult educational programs within the Community, and women as well as men were encouraged to take part. Subject matter included mathematics, science, music, and foreign languages. At one time, the Perfectionists even discussed plans for establishing a university. And while the plans never materialized, there was no doubt that women would have been admitted to the same courses as men. The point is worth mentioning because at the time, in 1866, in all the United States only Oberlin College admitted women.

Yet it would be a mistake to interpret the Perfectionists as concerned with restructuring gender roles. Their primary focus was the totally new way of looking at society and religious commitment.

---

[8]Marlyn Klee-Hartzell, "'Mingling the Sexes': The Gendered Organization of Work in the Oneida Community." *The Courier* 28 (Fall 1993); Lawrence Foster, *Religion and Sexuality: Three American Communal Experiments of the Nineteenth Century* (New York: Oxford University Press, 1981); Lawrence Foster, "Women and Utopia: Life among the Shakers, Oneidans, and Mormons," *Communities: Journal of Cooperative Living* (Spring 1994), pp. 53–56.

The New Attire   Male members of the Oneida Community dressed much like anybody else, but visitors were caught off guard when they first saw the women's attire. It was John Humphrey Noyes, never one to accept a conventional practice if he could find an "improvement," who first pointed to the impracticality of the standard female attire. "Woman's dress is a standing lie," he wrote in the first annual report of the Community in 1848. "It proclaims that she is not a two-legged animal, but something like a churn, standing on castors!"

He went on to suggest a change: "The dress of children—frock and pantalettes—is in good taste, not perverted by the dictates of shame, and well adapted to free motion." Accordingly, three of the women embarked upon a daring stylistic venture. Following Noyes's suggestion, they proceeded to cut their skirts down to knee length and to use the cut-off material to fashion pantalettes, which reached to the ankle. After a demonstration and discussion at one of the evening meetings, the new garb was adopted forthwith. Thereafter, it was the only attire worn by the women of the Community.

In addition to short skirts and pantalettes, the Oneida women bobbed their hair. Their reasoning was that long hair took too long to fix and was not functional. The new style was quite satisfactory, although some outsiders thought the coiffure too brazen. Oddly enough, although the Oneida women first bobbed their hair in 1848, the custom was not introduced to the outside world until 1922. According to comments made in interviews, the distinctive appearance of the Oneida women was another factor that served to strengthen their we-feeling.

Membership and Secession

All groups face the problem of numbers. Some, like the Amish and Mormons, show fantastic rates of growth. Others, like the Father Divine movement, lose members so rapidly that survival becomes a problem. The Oneida Community fell between these two extremes. Once they were fully established, their numbers remained fairly constant. Dissolution—in 1881—had nothing to do with loss of membership. In fact, the Perfectionists had much more trouble keeping people out than keeping them in.

What was the total membership of the Community? It depends on what is meant by "total." Available records indicate that at any given time, there were around three hundred members. When deaths and secessions are taken into consideration, total all-time membership was probably in the area of five hundred. There were roughly equal numbers of males and females, although there were somewhat more females at the older age levels.

At one time or another, there were seven branches, all under the leadership of John Humphrey Noyes. In addition to the main group at Oneida, there were smaller branches at Willow Place, New York; Cambridge, Vermont; Newark, New Jersey; Wallingford, Connecticut; New York City; and Putney, Vermont (reopened four years after Noyes departed). The branch at Wallingford, Connecticut—with about forty-five members—survived until the very end.

Except during the early Putney period, the Perfectionists did little or no active proselytizing. Yet they had no difficulty in attracting members. In some years, they received as many as two hundred applications. Over and over again, the *Oneida Daily Journal* reported requests for membership (evidently more male than female), but in most cases the applications were turned down.

The reason for the steady stream of membership applications is not hard to find. The Oneidans were a successful group—and word of their success traveled fast. Their own publications, as well as the popular press, afforded them wide coverage. Noyes himself journeyed and lectured extensively. And, of course, visitors to the Community could not help but be impressed by what they saw. The total number of visitors must have been staggering. The *Circular* reports that on one day—July 4, 1863— between 1,500 and 2,000 persons visited the Community.[9]

Applicants who were admitted were carefully screened, and once accepted they went through a probationary period for a year or so. The idea was to determine not only whether the newcomers could adjust to Community life, but whether they possessed the necessary devoutness. Over the years, most new members adjusted very well. Educational and recreational programs abounded, work was not excessive, and relations both within the Community and between the Community and the outside world were generally pleasant.

Unlike the Father Divine movement, the Oneida Community was not primarily of lower- or working-class origin. They had more than their share of skilled artisans and (especially in later years) professionals. After the Perfectionists were on a solid footing, their ranks came to include any number of lawyers, dentists, doctors, teachers, engineers, accountants, ministers, and business managers. Also, many of the children born in the Community eventually went on to college and professional school.

Sociability   What was there about life in the Oneida Community that attracted so many people? Oneidans were rarely alone. There was a caring atmosphere and a good feeling all around—lots of people to be with and talk to. Even their working arrangements reflected sociability. On a

[9]Constance Noyes Robertson, ed., *Oneida Community: An Autobiography,* 1851–1876 (Syracuse, NY: Syracuse University Press, 1970), p. 71.

typical work day, Community members would rise between five and seven-thirty and proceed to the dining hall. Following breakfast, there was a short period of Bible reading, after which members would go to their assigned jobs in the trap factory, the mill, the farm, or elsewhere. A square board with pegs—each peg containing a member's name—was located near the library, and at a glance it was possible to tell each person's whereabouts. Dining hours changed over the years, but the Oneidans came to prefer a two-meal-a-day schedule, with dinner being served from three to four. After dinner there were adult classes in French, algebra, science, and other subjects, followed by the evening meeting. By nine or ten o'clock, most of the Community had retired.

While they were working, the Perfectionists were also social. Men and women worked side by side, and there was constant talking and laughing. During an interview, one former member made the following comments: "As children, we loved to visit the various departments they used to have: the laundry, the kitchen, the fruit cellar, the bakery, the dairy, the tailor shop. The thing is that small groups of people worked side by side in most of these places, and they were able to talk with each other as they worked. It was this sort of thing, year after year, that gave rise to a kindred spirit."

Secession   While most of those who joined Oneida were satisfied with their decision, some were not. Each year a few individuals left—for a variety of reasons. Some were unable to adjust to the sharing of sexual partners. Others became discontented with the economic philosophy. Still others found themselves disturbed by Noyes's brand of Perfectionism.

In isolated cases, individuals joined for the wrong reason and soon became disillusioned. For example, from time to time Noyes would renounce orthodox medical treatment in favor of faith cures. He himself was alleged to have cured a woman who was both crippled and blind. Those whose hopes for a miracle cure were not fulfilled were natural candidates for secession.

In general, those who left the group were likely to be from the more recent additions. Veteran members seldom withdrew. The actual number of seceders is not known, but the figure was probably not high. Those who left were permitted to take with them whatever property they had brought, and those who had nothing were given a hundred dollars.

The Oneidans were not plagued with legal suits based on property rights. And unlike the Mormons, the Perfectionists seldom had to contend with apostates who spread untrue stories. In all the many decades of their existence, there were only two embarrassing experiences. One member, William Mills—for reasons that will be explained later—was asked to leave, refused, and had to be forcibly evicted. Another member, the highly unstable Charles Guiteau, left the Community in 1867 after a short stay. Fourteen years later, Oneidans were dismayed to learn that the same

Charles Guiteau had assassinated President James Garfield. (Guiteau was subsequently hanged.)

By and large, however, those who left did so with goodwill. A number of them actually came back and rejoined the Community. For the fact was that, on a day-to-day basis, the Oneidans were a happy group—more so, perhaps, than almost any of the other groups discussed in this book. In fact, Noyes taught that "unhappiness was, if not a sin, a serious deficiency."[10]

Even those who eventually voted to disband the Community had kind words and pleasant memories. The following remarks occurred during a personal interview: "I was too young to remember much. But as I grew older and asked my relatives about the Community days, their faces would light up. My own folks were 'come outers'; that is, they thought the thing had gone on long enough and weren't too sorry when the group broke up. But even they loved to talk about the 'old days' and how much they missed them. They were wonderful people and they had wonderful times."

Mutual Criticism

One technique used by the Perfectionists had an important bearing on high morale—and low secession. Social control is an element in the dynamics of all the groups discussed in this volume, but this technique is unique to the people of Oneida. The technique was **mutual criticism.** Mutual criticism is the practice of bringing a member who was being reprimanded in front of either a committee or sometimes the whole Community to be criticized for his or her action.

Mutual criticism apparently originated during Noyes's seminary days, when a group of students would meet regularly to assess one another's faults. The criticisms were carried on in a friendly but forthright manner, and all the participants—including Noyes—were pleased with the results. Response was so gratifying that Noyes instituted the practice at Putney. It was continued at Oneida and remained in effect throughout the whole of the Community's existence.

The technique of mutual criticism changed over the years. Sometimes the person involved simply stood up at the evening meeting and was criticized by each member of the group. As membership grew, however, the system proved unwieldy, and committees were appointed to conduct the criticism. Frequently Noyes added his own comments. But irrespective of the method, the goal remained the same: to bring about self-improvement through the testimony of impartial witnesses.

For certain members, understandably, criticism was traumatic. It is not easy for sensitive persons to listen to their own faults examined in public.

[10]Klaw, *Without Sin*, p. 7.

A few Perfectionists, in fact, left the Community rather than submit to what they felt was unwarranted censure. The large majority, however, looked on the criticism not as a personal attack but as an impersonal expression of group opinion, an expression aimed at maximizing group morale.

Initially, mutual criticism involved those who were believed to be failing in the spiritual realm, or whose individuality was too pronounced. After the "treatment," they were expected to show some improvement. As Estlake, one of the Perfectionists, put it, "Mutual criticism is to the Community what ballast is to a ship."[11]

As time went on, however, the technique of mutual criticism came to be employed whenever a member genuinely desired self-improvement. In this instance, the person would volunteer, and although no records were kept, mutual criticism evidently grew in popularity to the point where most sessions were voluntary. But voluntary or otherwise, the technique was effective.

All the Perfectionists were subject to mutual criticism, including the central members. The only exception was John Humphrey Noyes, who was never criticized by the Community. On occasion, however, he did undergo self-criticism.

Perhaps the most bizarre feature of mutual criticism was the fact that death did not necessarily put a stop to the process. Deceased members whose diaries or letters were found to be incriminating might find themselves being subjected *in absentia* to a "rousing criticism."

Aside from occasional excesses such as the above—and these were the exception rather than the rule—there is no doubt that mutual criticism was beneficial. It enhanced both individual morale and group cohesion. By its very nature, of course, most criticism was negative: it was aimed at revealing a person's faults. Noyes recognized this fact, and sporadic attempts were made at introducing "commendatory criticism," but the idea never took hold.

Economic Communism

One of the principal features of the Oneida Community was its total adherence to economic communism. From beginning to end, the Oneidans rejected all forms of personal wealth and private property. They never once had second thoughts about the correctness of their economic path.

Everything was jointly owned, including such things as clothes and children's toys. Pierrepont Noyes wrote: "Throughout my childhood, the

---

[11]Allan Estlake, *The Oneida Community: A Record of an Attempt to Carry Out the Principles of Christian Unselfishness and Scientific Race-Improvement* (London: George Redway, 1900), p. 58.

private ownership of anything seemed to me a crude artificiality to which an unenlightened Outside still clung. . . . For instance, we were keen for our favorite sleds, but it never occurred to me that I could possess a sled to the exclusion of the other boys. So it was with all Children's House property."[12]

On the subject of clothes, the same author states: "Going-away clothes for grown folks, as for children, were common property. Any man or woman preparing for a trip was fitted out with one of the suits kept in stock for that purpose."[13]

How did the Oneidans make out financially, in view of the fact that they were operating a communist economy in a capitalist society? The answer is, very well. Very well indeed, as we shall see. There are, however, some qualifications.

For the first ten years or so, the Community had more than its share of economic woes. Almost everything the Oneidans tried seemed to fail. They started in agriculture, but although they had a number of experienced farmers in their midst, they somehow could not compete successfully in the open market. They next tried light manufacturing, turning out such products as outdoor furniture, baskets, slippers, and bags, to no avail. Then came commercialism, and the Perfectionists set about peddling such wares as silk thread, pins and needles, and preserved fruits and vegetables. Again they lost money.

A few of the lines showed a small profit, but overall, expenditures outstripped profits year after year. At one time, members agreed to sell their watches to reduce losses. In fact, if it had not been for the $108,000 brought in by those who joined the Community, the Oneidans would have gone bankrupt. They were losing an average of $4,000 a year.

They failed for several reasons. In some of their endeavors they lacked experience. In others, they had some unfortunate setbacks, such as a fire that destroyed supplies of goods. But the chief reason for their failure was that they were spread too thin: seven different branches in four different states. Accordingly, Noyes decided to retrench. All the branches were phased out except Oneida and Wallingford—with the bulk of the economic operation remaining at Oneida. As it turned out, this was a wise move. But there was a wiser one just around the corner.

Traps   In 1848, shortly after their founding, the Community admitted to membership one Sewell Newhouse. A north woods hunter and trapper, Newhouse was a legendary figure even before he joined the Perfectionists. More or less a loner, he knew every foot of the wilderness surrounding Oneida Lake. And he knew hunting and trapping. Around Oneida, his fame equaled that of Davy Crockett.

[12]Noyes, *My Father's House*, pp. 126–27.
[13]Noyes, *My Father's House*, pp. 126–27.

Aided by his prodigious strength, Newhouse made his own traps by using a blacksmith's forge, anvil, and hand punch. He made an excellent product and had no trouble selling his traps to local woodsmen. He had no real desire to make money or establish a business, however, and between sessions of trap-making, he would invariably disappear into the north woods for a prolonged period.

Why Newhouse joined may have been a mystery, but his effect on the Community was indelible. At first, no one thought of using the traps as a basic Community product. Among other things, their manufacture involved a secret process of spring tempering, which Newhouse was reluctant to reveal. Under Noyes's patient prodding, however, Sewell Newhouse finally relented, and by the late 1850s the Oneida Community was turning out traps by the hundreds.

Demand for the product grew rapidly. To meet the orders that were pouring in, the Oneidans were forced to use assembly-line methods. In fact, whenever there was a deadline on a large order, the entire Community—including the children—would pitch in. And even this was not enough. By 1860, the Newhouse trap not only had become standard in the United States and Canada but was being used all over the world. Many professional trappers would use no other brand.

By this time, of course, the Perfectionists could not possibly handle all the orders themselves. They began to hire outside workers, the number eventually reaching several hundred. The trap factory, located near the Mansion House, developed into a typical industrial plant of the period. By the late 1860s, the Community was turning out close to 300,000 traps a year. During one record-breaking period, they actually manufactured over 22,000 traps in a single week.[14]

Interestingly enough, once they had "turned the corner" with the trap business, their other products—canned vegetables and preserved fruit, bags, silk thread—proved to be valuable sidelines. So, too, did their tourist business. As the fame of the Perfectionists grew, the number of visitors—with their admission fees—also grew.

Later on, in 1877, the Community began to manufacture silverware. Although there were some ups and downs, this business also proved successful. In 1881, when the Community disbanded, the industrial component was perpetuated under the name of Oneida Ltd.

It is often said that John Humphrey Noyes was the indispensable man insofar as the Perfectionists were concerned, an assertion that is doubtless true. Without him, there would have been no Community, and after he was gone the Community fell apart. But one question remains. How

---

[14]According to the *Oneida Community Daily Journal* of November 5, 1866, if it hadn't been for a mechanical defect, they would have been able to turn out 80,000 traps that week!

successful would Noyes have been if it hadn't been for a crusty old woodsman named Sewell Newhouse?[15]

Self-Sufficiency and Ethnocentrism   Once trap-making had made the Oneidans' economic base secure, the Perfectionist brand of communism worked rather well. The Oneidans built their own homes; made all their own clothes, including shoes; did their own laundry; raised their own food; and provided their own services. They did all these things, furthermore, at a remarkably low cost.[16]

Like the Old Order Amish, the Oneida "family" performed functions that were disappearing from society at large. They provided their own recreation and their own religious services. They ran their own school, and—even though they occasionally practiced faith healing and krinopathy (mutual criticism directed at physical illness)—they had their own doctors and dentists. The Perfectionists also had their own "social security benefits," which included child care, full employment, old-age assistance, and the like.

Functionally, economically, and socially, the Oneida Perfectionists were close to being a self-sufficient community. This self-sufficiency not only enhanced their in-group solidarity but also gave rise to ethnocentric feelings. As noted in our consideration of Gypsies, *ethnocentrism* is the tendency to assume that one's own culture and way of life represent the norm or are superior to all others. The Oneidans were building the best traps. They also invented a popular type of mousetrap and the lazy Susan. They were making money. Visitors were flocking to their doors, and there was a steady stream of new applications. Little wonder that John Humphrey Noyes and his followers felt that their way of life was superior to that found on the outside. As one of the members put it, "It was never, in our minds, an experiment. We believed we were living under a system which the whole world would sooner or later adopt."[17]

Work: A Cultural Theme   As with the Shakers, work was a cultural theme among the Oneida Community. While a certain amount of inefficiency was acknowledged, the Perfectionists were not idlers whose chief preoccupation was socializing. On the contrary, they were good workers. Their methods simply did not include regimentation, time clocks, quotas,

[15]A "Newhouse/Oneida" bear trap (eleven inches by thirty-six inches) was advertised in the October 1989 *Shotgun News* for $350. In February 2005, these traps were selling for $595 on eBay.

[16]*Bible Communism: A Compilation from the Annual Reports of the Oneida Association* (Brooklyn, NY: Oneida Circular, 1853), p. 16.

[17]This statement was made by Pierrepont Noyes's mother-in-law, and is quoted in Noyes, *My Father's House*, pp. 17–18.

The Oneida Community was an industrious group but the division of labor was along gender lines—here, women make bags to be sold while men observe. Note the short hair and the trouserlike garments worn under relatively short skirts. Both of these were considered inappropriate by society at the time.

and the like. As Robertson puts it, "From the beginning, the Community believed in work; not legally—that is, work forced upon the worker as a duty—but work freely chosen, as they said 'under inspiration.'"

When there was work to be done, the Oneidans did it—without coercion. For the smaller projects, one of their most effective innovations was a cooperative enterprise known as the bee. "The bee was an ordinance exactly suited to Community life. One would be announced at dinner or perhaps on the bulletin board: 'A bee in the kitchen to pare apples'; or 'A bee to pick strawberries at five o'clock tomorrow morning'; or 'A bee in the Upper Sitting Room to sew bags.'"[18]

For the larger tasks—a building project, an influx of visitors, an important industrial order—a much larger proportion of the membership would turn out. All of the above, of course, was in addition to the daily work assignments. Generally speaking, while the Perfectionists never claimed to be a model of economic efficiency, their system worked.

[18]Robertson, *Oneida Community*, pp. 47, 103.

The economic aspects of the Community have been discussed in some detail because most of the other sixty-odd communist experiments then under way in America failed because of economic difficulties. Along with the Shakers, the followers of John Humphrey Noyes succeeded. Despite the fact that the accumulation of material wealth was not their primary concern, the Oneida Community—at the time it disbanded—was worth some $600,000. In 1881, this was no small amount.

Level of Living   On a day-to-day basis, the Perfectionists did not bask in luxury, but neither did they lead a Spartan existence. They ate well, in spite of their dietary prohibitions. They were amply clothed, although, like the Amish, there was no conspicuous consumption, a term coined by Thorsten Veblen which sociologists use to describe the purchase and display of material objects well beyond what one needs or, perhaps, even can use. If a man needed a suit, he would go to the Community tailor and—in accordance with a budgetary allotment—get measured for a new one. The same procedure was followed for other needs.

Members could, if they wished, travel or visit on the outside, but few availed themselves of the opportunity. There were too many attractions at home: recreation and entertainment, adult education, a well-stocked library, social and sexual privileges, opportunities for self-expression in the musical and performing arts, physical comforts (the Mansion House even included a Turkish bath)—all this in addition to the spiritual enlightenment provided by John Humphrey Noyes.

Even in the matter of work assignments, the Oneidans were given every consideration. There was no such thing as demeaning labor. Members were respected for the spirit with which they did their work rather than for the work itself. Menial tasks, such as cleaning and mending, were generally rotated. Special skills and abilities, on the other hand, were amply rewarded. Those with writing aptitude were assigned to the Community newspaper, those with a love for children worked in the children's department, and so on.

Complex Marriage

The world remembers the followers of John Humphrey Noyes not for their social or economic system, but for their practice of complex marriage. Right or wrong, just as the term *Mormon* brings to mind polygamy, so the term *Oneida* conjures up thoughts of the "advanced" sexual practices of the Community. It was Noyes himself who coined the phrase "free love," although because of adverse implications the phraseology was discarded in favor of **complex marriage.** Complex marriage is the state in which every man and every woman are married to each other. They could engage in sexual intercourse, but were not attached to one another as couples.

According to Noyes, it was natural for all men to love all women, and for all women to love all men. He felt that any social institution that flouted this truism was harmful to the human spirit. Romantic love—or "special love," as the Oneidans called it—was harmful because it was a selfish act. Monogamous marriage was harmful because it excluded others from sharing in connubial affection. The answer, obviously, was group marriage, and throughout the whole of their existence, this was what the Oneidans practiced.[19]

Over and over again, on both secular and religious grounds, John Humphrey Noyes criticized monogamy and extolled the virtues of complex marriage: "The human heart is capable of loving any number of times and any number of persons. This is the law of nature. There is no occasion to find fault with it. Variety is in the nature of things, as beautiful and as useful in love as in eating and drinking. . . . We need love as much as we need food and clothing, and God knows it; and if we trust Him for those things, why not for love?"[20]

Although he did not say it in so many words, Noyes hoped that the sharing of partners would serve as yet another element in the establishment of group solidarity. That he was able to succeed in this realm—despite the fact that the bulk of his followers had Puritan backgrounds—attests to his leadership capacity.

The system of complex marriage was relatively uncomplicated. Sexual relations were easy to arrange inasmuch as all the men and women lived in the Mansion House. If a man desired sexual intercourse with a particular woman, he simply asked her. If she consented, he would go to her room at bedtime and stay overnight. Once in a while, because of a shortage of single rooms, these arrangements were not practicable, in which case the couple could use one of the "social" rooms set aside for that purpose.

Sexual Regulations   Sex is never a simple matter (among humans, at least), and from the very beginning, complex marriage was ringed with prohibitions and restrictions. Other modifications arose over the years. By the early 1860s, a fairly elaborate set of regulations was in force, so that

---

[19]Noyes himself may have had a "special love," Mary Cragin, the wife of one of his early followers. According to Foster, Mrs. Cragin was the first to inspire Noyes in the direction of complex marriage. Following her death in a boating accident in 1851, "Noyes proved almost inconsolable. For more than a year, nearly every issue of his newspaper contained fulsome tributes to her character, examples of her writing, and the like" (Foster, *Women, Family and Utopia*, p. 112).

[20]Quoted in Robert Parker, *Yankee Saint: John Humphrey Noyes and the Oneida Community* (New York: Putnam, 1935), pp. 182–83.

throughout most of the Community's existence, sexual relations were not nearly so "free" and all-encompassing as outsiders believed.

As early as Putney, Noyes taught that sex was not to be considered a "wifely duty," that is, something accepted by the female to satisfy the male. Noyes also went to great pains in his discourses to separate the "amative" (sex for pleasure) from the "propagative" (sex for reproduction) functions of sex. It was only when the two were separated, he said, that the true goals of Perfectionism could be attained. In practice, this meant that men, through male continence, could have sexual intercourse up to, but not including, ejaculation. (Women, of course, could achieve sexual climax at any time.)

There were two exceptions to the nonejaculatory rule: (1) when the man was having intercourse with a woman who was past menopause, and (2) when a child was desired. Authorization for childbearing involved a special procedure and will be discussed in the following section. However, by permitting men to achieve ejaculation only with postmenopausal women, the Perfectionists not only were employing a novel method of birth control—effective, as it turned out—but were using an ingenious method of providing older women with sexual partners.

The *Handbook* also points up the desirability of courtship, and there is no doubt that in the Oneida Community sustained courtship was the order of the day. Men were eager to win the women's favor, so they acted accordingly. And the women evidently found it refreshing to be wooed by the men.

As in society at large, the men were apparently more enthusiastic than the women, at least in a strictly sexual connotation. The practice of having the man ask the woman for sexual relations, therefore, was soon replaced by a new system.

Use of a Go-between   Under the new system, the man would make his request known to a central member—usually an older woman—who in turn would pass on the request. In practice, the use of a go-between served a number of purposes. It spared the women—it was they who suggested the system—the embarrassment of having to voice a direct refusal or conjure up an excuse. As one of the interviewees said, "Sex relations in the Community were always voluntary. There was never any hint at coercion. But after they started using a go-between, it made things easier for everybody."

Employment of a go-between also gave the Community a measure of control over the sexual system. For example, the Perfectionists were ever on guard against two of their members falling in love—special love, as they called it. So if a particular couple were having too-frequent relations, the go-between would simply disallow further meetings between them. In the matter of procreation, too, it was important that the Community be able to establish paternity. And while this was not always possible, the go-between greatly facilitated the identification process.

The Oneidans considered sex to be a private matter. Aside from the particular go-between involved, "who was having relations with whom" never became common knowledge. Indeed, the subject itself was taboo. Public displays of affection, vulgarity of any kind, sexual discussions or innuendos, immodest behavior—all were forbidden. During the many decades of their existence, the Perfectionists had but one unpleasant experience along these lines.

William Mills was accepted into the Community during the early 1860s. A rather vulgar person, it soon became obvious that he was a misfit. The women would have nothing to do with him. As a consequence, he started to cultivate the friendship of teenage girls. Breaking the Perfectionist taboo, Mills would discuss sexual matters openly with them, asking them about their amours and boasting of his own. The situation soon became intolerable, and he was asked to leave. He refused. The central members were in a quandary: from time to time others had been requested to leave, but none had ever refused. After several discussions, it was decided—in an almost literal sense—to take the bull by the horns. According to Robert Parker, "Mills found himself, one winter night, suddenly, unceremoniously, and horizontally propelled through an open window, and shot—harmlessly but ignominiously—into the depths of a snowdrift. It was the first and only forcible expulsion in the history of the community."[21]

In a burst of vituperation, Noyes said of Mills, "He is the representative of that species of parasites which works its way through the vitals of families and society by bare power of jackass-will and brazen effrontery, without lubrication of any kind except canting pretences of extraordinary piety."[22]

Taken collectively, the regulations concerning sex were designed to permit maximum freedom for the individual without jeopardizing the harmony of the group as a whole. This involved a delicate balance of rights and responsibilities, and Noyes was well aware of this fact. He strove mightily to keep sex "within bounds," and whenever there were excesses, he moved to correct them.

To take one example, the original procedure had been for the man to go to the woman's room and remain all night. Some of the women evidently complained that the practice was too "tiring," and Noyes saw to it that a change was made. Henceforth, the man would stay for an hour or so and

---

[21]Parker, *Yankee Saint*, p. 223.

[22]Klaw, *Without Sin*, p. 13. Noyes could be quite colorful with words, if not just plain corny. Klaw cites as an example the following metaphor, "As a man is said to know a woman in sexual intercourse, why not speak of the telescope with which he penetrates her heavens, and seeks the star of her heart," *Without Sin*, p. 17.

then return to his own room. This was the procedure followed through-out most of the Community's existence.

Along these same lines, the Perfectionist leader constantly inveighed against the so-called fatiguing aspects of sexual intercourse. Instead of advocating *coitus reservatus* (that is, male continence), for instance, he could have endorsed *coitus interruptus*—both being equally effective as birth-control techniques. But Noyes was convinced that ejaculation had a debilitating effect on the male; hence, he preached against its danger.

He was also against *coitus interruptus* on theological grounds, because the practice is condemned in the Bible. That is, when Onan had inter-course with his deceased brother's wife, he refused to ejaculate in the nat-ural fashion. Instead, he "spilled it on the ground, lest that he should give seed to his brother. And the thing which he did displeased the Lord" (Gen. 38:9–10).

Additionally, Noyes totally rejected all forms of contraception. For rea-sons best known to himself, he looked upon them as "machinations of the French" and refused even to consider them. To be acceptable, birth con-trol had to include a strong element of (male) self-control.

Interestingly enough—and in spite of some rather questionable logic—John Humphrey Noyes's ideas about sex and birth control proved work-able. His goal was to provide complex marriage with a spiritual base, and he apparently succeeded. Throughout the whole of the Community's existence, there were no elopements, no orgies, no exhibitionism. Nor was there any instance of homosexuality, sadism, masochism, or any other sexual activity that would have been considered reprehensible by the standards then current.

Ascending Fellowship   Complex marriage did pose one problem that Noyes went to great pains to solve: how to keep the older members of the Community from being bypassed in favor of the younger members. True, it was only with postmenopausal women that men were allowed to achieve ejaculation, but this restriction provided an inadequate answer to the problem. The real answer was to be found in the princi-ple of **ascending fellowship**—the practice of older "godly" male mem-bers being in a special group called the Central Committee. They could pick a virgin of about the age fourteen for whom they were spiritually responsible.

According to the elaborate procedures of the principle of ascending fellowship, members were ranked from least to most perfect. Any fol-lower who wished to improve, therefore, was advised to associate with someone higher on the spiritual scale. (Noyes taught that a high-ranking person would not in any way be downgraded by associating with a person of lower rank.) Because it took time and experience to achieve high spiritual rank, those at the upper end of the scale were nearly always the older, more mature members. It was these older Perfectionists, rather than the younger members, who were thus held up as the desirable partners.

How did this elaborate sexual system operate? Noyes's son Theodore in a 1892 letter offers this insight:

> But now to come closer, and take the bull fairly by the horns. In a society like the Community, the young and attractive women form the focus toward which all the social rays converge; and the arbiter to be truly one, must possess the confidence and to a certain extent the obedience of this circle of attractions and moreover, he must exercise his power by genuine sexual attraction to a large extent. To quite a late period father filled this situation perfectly. He was a man of quite extraordinary attractiveness to women, and he dominated them by his intellectual power and social "magnetism" superadded to intense religious convictions to which young women are very susceptible. The circle of young women he trained when he was between 40 and 50 years of age, were by a large majority his devoted friends throughout the trouble which led to the dissolution [of the Oneida Community between 1879 and 1881].
>
> . . . I must suppose that as he grew older he lost some of his attractiveness, and I know that he delegated the function [of initiating young women into sexual intercourse] to younger men in several cases, but you can see that this matter was of prime importance in the question of successorship and that the lack of a suitable successor obliged him to continue as the social center longer than would have otherwise been the case and so gave more occasion for dissatisfaction.[23]

There is no doubt that age was shown great respect in the Community. This is the way Noyes wanted it, and this is the way it was. In addition, the fact that younger men were encouraged to have sexual relations with older women served to strengthen the birth-control measures that were used.

Complex Marriage: Unanswered Questions

Although we give the broad outlines of the sexual system employed by the Perfectionists, a number of questions remain unanswered. To what extent did the women refuse sexual requests? Was a go-between really used, or was this a formality that was easily bypassed? Did women as well as men initiate sexual requests? Was not the factor of jealousy a

---

[23]Private correspondence cited in Lawrence Foster, "Free Love in Utopia: How Complex Marriage was Introduced in the Oneida Community," 2002 International Conference, Center for Studies on New Religions, "Minority Religions, Social Change, and Freedom of Conscience," Salt Lake City, June 2002.

problem? Did members have difficulty adjusting sexually to a large number of different partners? Researchers have attempted to find answers to these questions, but they have had only limited success. One of the interviewees made the following points: "I grant the questions are of sociological interest, but look at it from our view. If somebody came to you and asked questions concerning the sex life of your parents and grandparents, you'd have a tough time answering. The same with us. When the old Community broke up, there was a natural reluctance to discuss sex. Former members didn't discuss their own sex lives, and naturally their children and grandchildren didn't pry."

During the decades of the Community's existence, many of the Oneidans were in the habit of keeping diaries. Diary keeping was evidently much more common in the nineteenth century than it is today. Some of the Perfectionists also accumulated bundles of personal letters. After the Community broke up, and as the members died over the years, the question arose as to what to do with all these documents.

Because so much of the material was of a personal and sexual nature, because names were named, and inasmuch as a number of the children and grandchildren were still living, it was decided to store all the old diaries, letters, and other personal documents in a specially constructed fireproof storage vault at Oneida Ltd. The corporation, concerned about the sensitive nature of the material it was holding, decided to destroy the truckload of documents in the mid-1940s.[24]

While there is little doubt that the burned material would have shed much light on the sexual behavior of the Perfectionists, the action taken by the company is understandable. Oneida Ltd. is not in business to further the cause of sociological research, and regardless of how much the material might have benefited social scientists, there was always the possibility that the contents would have proved embarrassing to the company or to some of the direct descendants.

The diary-burning episode has been mentioned in some detail to show how difficult it is to answer sexual questions of the kind posed earlier. The interview information presented here should be thought of as a series of clues rather than as a set of definitive answers.

To what extent did the Oneida women refuse sexual requests? The company official who had examined some of the material to be burned reported that there was nothing therein to suggest a high refusal rate. Another male respondent stated that he had been informed by an old Community member that the man "had never been refused." One female interviewee felt that refusal was a problem "in some instances." Most of those interviewed, however, had no specific information to offer. The

[24]Lawrence Foster, *Free Love in Utopia* (Urbana: University Press, 2001), pp. x–xii.

overall impression given is that female refusal was not a major issue, although it probably arose from time to time.

Was a go-between really used, or was this a formality that was easily bypassed? None of those interviewed had any direct evidence to offer. All that can be said is that there were no *reported* instances where the rule was broken. Because the matter was never raised by the Oneidans themselves, it is doubtful whether a real issue was involved. Given the religious orientation and *esprit de corps* of the members, there is every reason to suppose that the stipulated procedure was followed.

Did the Oneida women, as well as the men, initiate sexual requests? This question drew a generally negative answer from all the respondents. Several said they knew of some coquetry on the part of certain women, but they had never heard of anything more direct. Two of the older female respondents stated that there was one known case where a woman went to a man and asked to have a child by him. In this instance, however, the implication is not clear, because the Perfectionists differentiated sharply between amative and procreative aspects of sex. All reports considered, it appears that the Oneida women were no more disposed to assume the role of active partner than were women in society at large.

Noyes himself constantly preached against the dangers of male jealousy. On one occasion, he remarked: "No matter what his other qualifications may be, if a man cannot love a woman and be happy seeing her loved by others, he is a selfish man, and his place is with the potsherds of the earth."[25] On another occasion—referring to a man who was becoming romantically involved with a particular woman—he said: "You do not love her, you love happiness."[26]

It is likely that male jealousy was at most a minor problem, though it did receive a certain amount of attention. Female jealousy was evidently no problem at all. It was not mentioned by any of those interviewed, nor, so far as could be ascertained, was the matter ever raised during the Community's existence.

Did the members of the Community have difficulty in adjusting sexually to a large number of different partners? The Oneidans were encouraged to have sex with a variety of partners but were not supposed to become emotionally involved with any of them. Respondents had little or nothing to report on this matter—which is unfortunate, because the question is an intriguing one.

---

[25]W. T. Hedden, "Communism in New York, 1848–1879," *American Scholar* 14 (Summer 1945): 287.

[26]Quoted in Raymond Lee Muncy, *Sex and Marriage in Utopian Communities* (Bloomington: Indiana University Press, 1973), p. 176.

Stirpiculture

Because John Humphrey Noyes had so many other "advanced" ideas about life on earth, it was predictable that he would not overlook the subject of children. It will be remembered that Noyes introduced *coitus reservatus,* or male continence, to spare the Oneida women from being plagued with unwanted children—as they were in the world at large. He also felt that the Oneidans needed time to prove themselves—in both a financial and social sense—before children were permitted. Accordingly, when the Community was founded, the Perfectionist leader announced that there would be no children until further notice. As it turned out, "further notice" stretched for a period of twenty years (1848–1868), during which time the prohibition remained in effect.

By the late 1860s, however, it was evident to both John Humphrey Noyes and the general membership that the ban should be lifted. There was much discussion within the Community, and the Perfectionists wondered when the announcement would be made and what form it would take. On his part, Noyes had given the matter a great deal of thought. He was ready to lift the ban on children, but he was not ready to endorse a system of uncontrolled births such as that found in the outside world.

John Humphrey Noyes read widely on the subject of propagation. He studied Francis Galton's works on hereditary improvement. He read Charles Darwin's *On the Origin of Species.* And the more he thought about it, the more he became convinced that a scientific breeding program could be adapted to the needs of the Oneida Community. Although the word *eugenics* was unknown—it was coined by Galton in 1883—eugenics was precisely what Noyes had in mind. In 1869, the Perfectionists embarked on their program, the first systematic attempt at eugenics in human history.

Eugenics is the study of methods to improve inherited characteristics. In recent years, eugenics has focused on genetic engineering and efforts to reduce certain inheritable diseases such as hemophilia. However, there is great controversy over the scope of even this aspect of genetic engineering, since it requires value judgments about what are undesirable human traits and what steps should be taken (e.g., terminating pregnancies in which fetuses show such genetic markers).

Eugenics in the popular mind often raises the horrors of some kind of Nazi experiment of creating a master race. While the Oneidans' practices were not of this magnitude, their selective breeding program was yet another very controversial aspect of the lifestyle practiced by the followers of John Humphrey Noyes.

Noyes called his selective breeding program **stirpiculture** (from the Latin *stirps,* meaning "root," "stock," or "lineage"), and from its inception there was no doubt about the goals, methods, or enthusiasm involved. The goal was crystal clear: biological improvement of the Oneida Community. In the words of the *Circular:* "Why should not beauty and noble grace of person and every other desirable quality of men and women, internal and external, be propagated and intensified beyond all former precedent by the application of the same scientific principles of breeding that produce such desirable results in the case of sheep, cattle, and horses?"[27]

The methods were also made explicit: only certain persons would be permitted to become parents. The selection would be made by a stirpi-culture committee, headed by Noyes, and the committee's decision would be final. There would be no appeal. And even though this meant that the majority of Oneidans might never become parents, there was no objection from the membership. On the contrary, the Perfectionists endorsed every facet of the program.

At the start of the eugenics program, fifty-three women and thirty-eight men were chosen to be parents (stirpicults). Over the years others were added, so that eventually about one hundred members took part in the experiment. Approximately 80 percent of those who took part actually achieved parenthood. During the decade or so that the program was in effect, fifty-eight children were born, and there were four stillbirths.

There were also a dozen or so accidental conceptions. Despite their pledge, a few of the "unchosen" individuals did their best to achieve parenthood—with some success. For instance, there was a passage in one of the burned diaries in which a man—referring to his sexual encounter with a particular woman—wrote, "She tried to make me lose control." In general, though, both the men and women who were bypassed seem to have accepted their lot willingly enough.

The precise method of selection used by the stirpiculture committee was never revealed. Throughout most of its existence the committee was composed of central members, and presumably they judged applicants on the basis of physical and mental qualities. Most of the candidates applied as couples, although on occasion the committee suggested certain combinations.

John Humphrey Noyes was the chief figure in the stirpiculture process. The concept was his, the committee was his, and it was he who served as chief judge and policymaker. The records show, for example, that the fathers were much older than the mothers, a fact that reflects the principle of ascending fellowship. Noyes felt strongly that the qualities necessary for fatherhood could be acquired only through age and experience. And while this was an erroneous, Lamarckian view, it was adhered to. In fact, a number of men in their sixties were chosen as stirpicults. Noyes

[27]Quoted in Robertson, *Oneida Community*, p. 341. See also Martin Richards, "Perfecting People: Selective Breeding at the Oneida Community (1869–1879) and the Eugenics Movement," *New Genetics and Society* 23 (April 2004): 47–71.

himself fathered at least ten of the children, so that evidently he was not averse to self-selection. The principle of ascending fellowship was less applicable to women, naturally, because of the menopause factor.

What were the results of the stirpiculture program? Was it successful? Were the offspring really superior? Most observers thought so. During the entire program, no mentally or physically disabled children were ever born, no mothers ever lost. Compared with children on the outside, the Oneida youngsters had a markedly lower death rate. A number of them went on to achieve eminence in the business and professional worlds. Several wrote books. And nearly all of them, in turn, had children who were a credit to the Community. How much of the program's success was due to the eugenic factor will never be known, because the children presumably had a favorable environment *as well as* sound heredity.

Surprisingly few children were born in the stirpiculture program. In view of the high birthrate that prevailed in society at large, the fact that the stirpiculs produced only fifty-eight live children is difficult to understand. *Coitus reservatus,* practiced by the Oneida males for so many years, may have had an unaccountable effect on their fertility, although this is probably a far-fetched explanation.

The most likely answer is that John Humphrey Noyes was fearful of the effects of multiple childbirth on the health of women. Remember, his own wife, in the pre-Oneida period, had had four stillbirths, and his outlook on life had been shaped by her experience. Nearly all the female stirpiculs, for example, were authorized to have but one child. A handful had two children, and only two women had three. If there were other reasons for the Perfectionists' low birthrate, they have not come to light.

Child Rearing

According to Noyes's teachings, all adults were supposed to love all children and vice versa, and the entire program of Community child rearing was based on this philosophy. Excessive love between children and their own parents was called "stickiness" and was strongly discouraged.

In practice, Oneida children were anything but neglected. For the first fifteen months they were under the care of their own mothers. After that, the youngsters were moved to the Children's House, where they were raised communally. There they were taught to treat all Community adults as they would their own parents, and there they received their formal education. There too they were introduced to John Humphrey Noyes's brand of Perfectionism.

A fair amount of published material exists on the Community child-rearing program. Evidence indicates that the program was patently successful. The following question-and-answer session—although totally fictitious—is based on factual information. The answers are those a Community spokesman might have given, say, in the 1870s.

Q. Where do the Oneida children live?

A. In the Children's House. Originally this was a separate building. However, in 1870 a south wing was added to the Mansion House, and the children have been there ever since.

Q. Do the youngsters have their own facilities?

A. Yes. The south wing was designed with this in mind. The children have their own nursery, sleeping quarters, schoolrooms, playrooms, and so forth.

Q. Who is in charge of the children?

A. I suppose you could say the whole Community. But if you mean who is in charge of the Children's House, there are a dozen or more adults whose full-time job is looking after the youngsters.

Q. Are all these adults women?

A. No. Most of them are, but we do believe in having a show of male authority.

Q. What about the children's education?

A. They are taught the same subjects as other children. But they also receive an equal amount of on-the-job training in the various departments. And when we have a bee, they often join in like everybody else.

Q. Do you use outside teachers?

A. No, we have our own.

Q. Do the children like school?

A. Do children anywhere?

Q. How is their religious instruction handled?

A. They meet for an hour a day—in prayer, Bible reading, discussions of Perfectionism, confession of faults, and so forth.

Q. How do the children like this type of training? Is it effective?

A. The only thing they like about it is when the hour is over! At the same time, whether they like it or not, we think it is effective.

Q. Do they have their own dining facilities?

A. No. We believe in bringing them into the life of the Community as early as possible. After the age of two, they eat in the regular dining room. And after the age of ten, they are permitted to sit at the same tables as adults.

Q. Do the youngsters know who their real parents are?

A. Of course.

Q. Whose name do they take?

A. Their fathers'.

Q. Are they permitted to associate with their parents?

A. Oh, yes. They spend a certain amount of time with their parents every week. However, we try to get the children to think of all Oneida adults as their parents.

Q. Doesn't this work a hardship on the children? Isn't there a natural desire to establish a bond of personal affection?

A. Perhaps so. It depends on how a child is conditioned. We think that under our system, a young person gets more love and understanding than on the outside.

Q. It's hard to believe the Oneida youngsters don't yearn for their own parents.

A. Well, one little girl did. She would stand outside her mother's window and call to her, even though her mother wasn't supposed to answer. That was an exceptional case, however.

Q. And you contend that under the Perfectionist system, the children are happy?

A. We do. But why not ask them?

Q. Do you not have problems of discipline?

A. Of course, and both the adults and the children spend a good deal of time discussing the matter. On the whole—since we're a tightly knit group—we probably have fewer disciplinary problems than they do on the outside.

Q. There are reports that Oneida children are afraid of visitors. . . .

A. As a matter of fact, some of the younger children are. They usually grow out of it, but we're not entirely satisfied with that end of it.

Q. Are the adult members of the Community happy at being separated from their children?

A. Well, they knew the rules when they joined. However, they are not really separated. They have the love of their children and the pleasure of their company, without the day-to-day burden that plagues most parents.

Q. Is there any likelihood that the Perfectionists will ever change their system of child rearing?

A. None whatsoever. As far as we're concerned, the system has proved itself. It's here to stay.[28]

The End of the Road

All good things must come to an end—or at least, so it must have seemed to the Oneidans by the late 1870s. John Humphrey Noyes had been expounding his Perfectionist views for almost fifty years. Communal living—at both Putney and Oneida—had been successfully practiced for more than forty years. There was no doubt that, sociologically, the Perfectionists had established a genuine subculture. But now the currents were going against them. There was no single reason. The causes ran together like foam on the ocean. Nevertheless, the tide was inexorable.

---

[28]This hypothetical "Q & A" was developed by William Kephart, *Extraordinary Groups*, 1st ed. (New York: St. Martin's Press, 1976). Also see Susan M. Matarese and Paul G. Salmon, "Here's to the Promised Land: The Children of Oneida," *International Journal of Sociology of the Family* 13 (Autumn 1983), pp. 35–43.

Outside Pressures   By and large, outsiders who lived in the vicinity of Oneida were favorably disposed toward the Community. The Perfectionists were known to be honest, industrious, and law-abiding. Moreover, as time went on, Oneida was recognized as a growing source of employment. Unfortunately, as the Oneidans' fame grew, so did their "notoriety." Free love, complex marriage, scientific breeding—such things were more than nineteenth-century America could accept. And so the pressures grew—from isolated editorials and sermons in the 1860s to a concentrated barrage in the 1870s. Two of the attackers, in particular, are worthy of mention.

Anthony Comstock, self-appointed watchdog of American morals, was in a special position to hurt the Oneidans. A member of Congress from New York, he sponsored the omnibus state law forbidding immoral works. He also organized the New York Society for the Suppression of Vice. Most important, in 1873 he persuaded Congress to enact a federal obscenity bill which, among other things, forbade the dissemination of all literature dealing with birth control. As fanatical a reformer as the country had ever seen, Comstock succeeded in tarring the Perfectionists with the brush of vice and obscenity. His followers found the Community an easy—and rather defenseless—target.

Less well known than Comstock, but even more effective, was Professor John Mears of Hamilton College. Whereas Comstock was against "obscenity" in any form, Mears's sole obsession was the Oneida Community. Week after week he wrote to the newspapers, gave public talks, and preached Sunday sermons—all against the "debaucheries" being practiced by John Humphrey Noyes and his followers.[29]

Methodists, Presbyterians, Baptists, Congregationalists—all took up the cry. Committees were appointed, conferences held, legal action demanded. Anthony Comstock's help was solicited. And while some editorials were fair, others joined in the diatribe against the Oneidans.

Internal Pressures   Meanwhile, back at the Community all was not well. Dissent was not only in the air; it was stalking the corridors and invading the rooms. Behind closed doors, small groups of Perfectionists voiced their complaints. And while there is no doubt that outside pressures were a contributing factor, it was the internal dissension that really destroyed the Community.

To begin with, the nature of Perfectionism was changing. The deeply religious orientation gave way to an emphasis on social science, then in its infancy. Bible reading and sermons were superseded by talks on self-improvement and social engineering. Noyes himself seems to have initiated the trend, announcing in the *Circular* that that publication would no

[29]Quoted in Parker, *Yankee Saint*, p. 268.

longer be a "strictly religious" paper.[30] While some in the Community went along with the change, others—particularly those in the older age groups—felt that the whole basis of their life was being violated.

Problems, too, were arising with the young people. Three in particular are worthy of mention: (1) Acceptance of John Humphrey Noyes as the ultimate authority came to be resented, especially by those who went to college and returned to live in the Community. Not unnaturally, they demanded a larger role in the decision-making process. (2) The principle of ascending fellowship began to be questioned. Young men and women objected to being paired off sexually with the older members. And (3) those who failed to qualify for parenthood under the stirpiculture program took umbrage at the fact.

The Townerites   At the evening meeting of April 21, 1874, Noyes made an important announcement. (How important, even he did not realize.) Twelve new members—remnants of the defunct Free Love Society of Cleveland—were being admitted into the Community. Their leader was a minister-turned-lawyer, James W. Towner.

A man of some talent, Towner became a divisive force almost immediately. Those with complaints—a growing number, it seems—found him a ready listener. And although a majority of the Perfectionists remained loyal to John Humphrey Noyes, Towner succeeded in winning over a fair minority of the membership. In retrospect, he seems to have been a shrewd operator who was out to gain control of the Community for his own ends. While he failed in the attempt, he succeeded in dividing the Oneidans into two factions, Noyesites and Townerites.

The Townerites complained that Noyes was too autocratic, and they wanted an equal voice. While the entire story is much too long to relate here, an important part centered on a strictly sexual matter.[31]

According to the principle of ascending fellowship, young people were required to have their first sexual encounter with the older, more spiritual members of the Community. Noyes evidently reserved for himself the right to initiate the young girls, although as he grew older he sometimes delegated the authority to one of the central members. However, the Townerites questioned his authority to make the decision, and the controversy became bitter.

Although Noyes exercised the rights of "first husband" for many years, he did so only with girls who had reached menarche (first menstruation). The catch was that some of the girls reached menarche at a very early age—as low as ten in some instances, with a range of ten to

---

[30]Parker, *Yankee Saint,* p. 274.
[31]Robertson, *Oneida Community,* p. TK.

eighteen, and an average age of thirteen.[32] The Perfectionist leader's exercise of first-husband rights, therefore, provided the Townerites with a powerful weapon. If legal charges were brought, Noyes could be accused of statutory rape; in fact, Towner was rumored to be gathering evidence against the Perfectionist leader. Towner denied the allegation, but the argument continued.

Lack of Leadership   Where was John Humphrey Noyes all this time? As Comstock and Mears mounted their attacks, as internal dissension accelerated, as Towner succeeded in tearing the Community apart— what was the Perfectionist leader doing? Unbelievable as it may seem, the answer is: nothing. After battling all his life for what he believed in, John Humphrey Noyes—for no known reason—seemed to give up. He left the Community for extended periods of time, and even when he was there, he seemed to withdraw more and more from a position of active leadership. Little by little, the central members were permitted to make both operational and policy decisions. Unfortunately, they were not qualified to do so.

The Perfectionist leader not only withdrew from Community life, but the decisions he did make were disastrous. He permitted Towner to join, probably the worst decision of his entire career. He changed the Community's focus from the sacred to the secular—another misjudgment. And he made no provision for succession of leadership, other than to recommend his son Theodore for the job—still another bad decision. It was not only Noyes's spirit that waned, but his judgment as well.

The Breakup   In 1877, Noyes resigned. One of his last acts was to appoint a committee to succeed him, headed by Theodore, who actually directed the Community for the next few years. But the group was too far gone to be saved by anyone—least of all by Theodore. Theodore, a Harvard graduate, was a devout Darwinist who saw no reason to seek the creator.[33]

On June 22, 1879, John Humphrey Noyes left the Oneida Community, never to return. He left secretly in the middle of the night, aided by a few close friends. And he left for the same reason that he had fled Putney thirty-two years earlier: to escape the law.

Noyes felt that Mears or the Townerites were about to bring charges against him on grounds of statutory rape, and in view of his vulnerability he decided to leave New York State. Actually, he may have been

---

[32]Ely van de Warker, "A Gynecological Study of the Oneida Community," *American Journal of Obstetrics and Disease of Women and Children* 17 (August 1884): 795.

[33]Klaw, *Without Sin*, p. 225.

overcautious. The Townerites could hardly have brought charges inasmuch as they were guilty of the same offense. And because Mears was exceedingly unpopular in the Community, he could hardly have gathered the necessary evidence. Nevertheless, Noyes left for Canada, from where—through emissaries—he kept in touch with Oneida.

In August, he sent word to the Community recommending that they abandon the practice of complex marriage. The recommendation satisfied both the Noyesites and the Townerites and passed without a dissenting voice. Shortly thereafter, a large number of monogamous marriages took place within the Community. Where it was possible, mothers married the fathers of their children. In the case of some of the younger women, Noyes more or less arranged the marriages.

For a while, the Oneidans continued to live communally, but it was clear to both insiders and outsiders that the end was imminent. Dissension prevailed. The aging Noyes remained more or less isolated in Canada. No new leader appeared. During 1880, plans for dissolution were discussed and approved, and on January 1, 1881, the Oneida Community officially ceased to exist. Yet some members continued to reside in the Oneida area well into the 1930s as more conventional households. About half of the remaining adults married outsiders. Yet the marriage of Noyes's son and granddaughter (by different women) raised some eyebrows even among Oneida Community descendants.

The Aftermath   Although the group dissolved itself, it did not—in a literal sense—go out of business. For in spite of the wrangling and dissension mentioned above, the economic side of the Community held up surprisingly well: its net worth was $600,000. At the time of dissolution, a joint-stock company was formed—Oneida Ltd.—and the stock was apportioned among the members.

Like most business organizations, Oneida Ltd. has had its ups and downs. On the whole, however, the company has grown and prospered. For the first fifty years or so, the enterprise was managed—in whole or in part—by Pierrepont Noyes, a son of John Humphrey and an extremely able businessman. It was under his direction that the company phased out the traps and concentrated on silverware.

In 1960, P. T. Noyes—son of Pierrepont and grandson of John Humphrey—took over the presidency. And in 1967, the company was accepted for listing on the New York Stock Exchange with the simple designation "Oneida." During the late 1970s, the company diversified: copper wire and cooking utensils were added to the silverware lines. In 1981, P. T. Noyes retired as chair and chief executive and for the first time, an outsider headed Oneida. Today, Oneida Ltd. is a worldwide organization with thousands of employees.

The expanding global economy of the twentieth and twenty-first centuries has caused Oneida to refashion itself. It has diversified to include glassware and decorative crystal. Manufacturing moved abroad and it operated only one production facility in the United States at Oneida, which was closed in 2005. Oneida was the last remaining stainless steel flatware manufacturer in the United States. This has left about 400 employees at administrative offices in Oneida. Yet it oversees sales of about $400 million annually, and continues to have high name identification among consumers.[34]

What about the other phases of Community life following the breakup? A few members left the area entirely, never to return. A handful of the older members went to Canada, where they could be near their former leader. Towner's influence declined sharply, and a year after the breakup he and some twenty-five of his followers left for California. Many of them prospered, although they made no attempt to live communally. Towner eventually became a county court judge.

John Humphrey Noyes stayed in Canada with a few of the faithful. Most of his time was spent in Bible reading and—most likely—reminiscing. He died in 1886, at the age of seventy-four. He was buried at Oneida in the Community cemetery, his simple headstone identical to all the others.

Most of the ex-Perfectionists remained in the Oneida area. Some stayed on in the Mansion House, in private apartments. Others moved to nearby houses. The majority of the men retained their positions with Oneida Ltd., many becoming officers, a pattern that has persisted for years. The Mansion House, over the years, served as a kind of social headquarters for the Oneidans and their descendants. While the social function today is minimal—an occasional wedding, a funeral, an anniversary celebration—the building is still in excellent condition, set among fourteen acres. Inside the Mansion House, there are rental apartments as well as eight bed-and-breakfast guest rooms available to the public, giving them access to the Big Hall and a small museum. Five minutes away, amid the fairways of a golf course, is the Oneida Community Cemetery, where Noyes and many of his followers are buried. Back in the Mansion House, one can still see the one remaining tiny bedroom where complex marriage was practiced. As one walks around the grounds and the Mansion House, one can only imagine the fascinating memories the place holds.[35]

---

[34]Constance L. Hays, "Why The Keepers of Oneida Don't Care to Share The Table," June 20, 1999, Sec. 3, p. 1. Also see www.oneida.com and specifically at that site "Q & A—Sherrill Factory Announcement," accessed February 24, 2005; and Richards, "Perfecting People," pp. 60–61.

[35]Beth Quinn Barnard, "The Utopia of Sharing," New York Times (August 3, 2002), pp. D1, D8.

A Contemporary Assessment

Was Oneida a success or a failure, a rewarding venture or a waste of time? Was John Humphrey Noyes a genius, an egomaniac, or simply a religious eccentric? Writers collided over these questions a hundred years ago— when the Community was still in existence—and there is still disagreement. Perhaps there always will be.

In a sociological sense, the Perfectionists were anything but failures. They not only lived together, communally, for many decades, but developed an economic base that was strong enough to spawn a multimillion-dollar corporation. Furthermore, they were able to provide society at large with a genuinely new perspective.

As the term is used by both anthropologists and sociologists, **cultural relativism** is the viewing of people's behavior from the perspective of those people's own culture. As a distinct subculture, the Oneida Community provides a good example of the significance of cultural relativism. That is, when the Community was flourishing, most Americans did not agree with the Perfectionist value system. Noyes's brand of communism, after all, had limited appeal. At the same time, it drove home to many Americans—firsthand—the realization that there were viable lifestyles other than their own.

This lesson is not lost even today. Students who read about the Oneida Perfectionists surely have a keener awareness of a completely different way of life even if we still consider it difficult to understand how hundreds of people came to accept the teachings of Noyes. Most of us show little willingness to relinquish personal property, renounce conjugal love, or reject parenthood. The Community certainly anticipated a time when sexual relationships could be discussed openly and raised the possibility that what is "proper" sexual behavior could be debated. Yet if one gives some serious thought to the Oneidans, their lifestyle becomes—if not attractive—at least understandable. Through understanding comes tolerance, the great lesson of cultural relativism.

KEY TERMS

Ascending fellowship, p. 187
Charismatic authority, p. 162
Commune, p. 164
Complex marriage, p. 183
Cultural relativism, p. 201
Culture, p. 161
Eugenics, p. 191

Male continence, p. 165
Mutual criticism, p. 177
Perfectionism, p. 163
Primary group, p. 168
Secondary group, p. 168
Stirpiculture, p. 191
Subculture, p. 161

SOURCES ON THE WEB

www.oneidacommunity.org
Information aimed at tourists visiting the Mansion House of the Oneida
Community.

http://library.syr.edu/digital/guides/o/OneidaCommunityCollection/
Syracuse University maintains the Oneida Community Collection; some of it is
accessible online.

http://www.crjc.org/heritage/V04-1.htm
A detailed description of the Putney Village Historic District with numerous references to the Noyes family.

SELECTED READINGS

Burridge, Kenelm. *New Heaven, New Earth: A Study of Millenarian Activities.* New
    York: Schocken, 1969.
Carden, Maren Lockwood. *Oneida: Utopian Community to Modern Corporation.*
    Baltimore: Johns Hopkins University Press, 1969.
Cross, Whitney R. *The Burned-over District: The Social and Intellectual History of
    Enthusiastic Religion in Western New York 1800–1850.* Ithaca, NY: Cornell Univer-
    sity Press, 1950.
Estlake, Allan. *The Oneida Community: A Record of an Attempt to Carry Out the Prin-
    ciples of Christian Unselfishness and Scientific Race-Improvement.* London: George
    Redway, 1900.
Fogarty, Robert. *Special Love/Special Sex: An Oneida Community Diary.* Syracuse,
    NY: Syracuse University Press, 1994.
Foster, Lawrence. *Religion and Sexuality: Three American Communal Experiments of
    the Nineteenth Century.* New York: Oxford University Press, 1981.
_____. *Women, Family and Utopia: Communal Experiments of the Shakers, the Oneida
    Community, and the Mormons.* Syracuse, NY: Syracuse University Press, 1991.
_____, ed. *Free Love in Utopia: John Humphrey Noyes and the Origin of the Oneida
    Community.* Compiled by George Wallingford Noyes. Urbana: University of
    Illinois Press, 2001.
Handbook of the Oneida Community. Oneida, NY: Office of the Oneida Circular, 1875.
Hayden, Dolores. *Seven American Utopias: The Architecture of Communitarian
    Socialism, 1790–1975.* Cambridge, MA: MIT Press, 1976.
Kephart, William M. "Experimental Family Organization: An Historico-Cultural
    Report on the Oneida Community." *Marriage and Family Living* 25 (August
    1963): 261–71.
_____. *The Family, Society, and the Individual.* Boston: Houghton Mifflin, 1981.

Klaw, Spencer. *Without Sin: The Life and Death of the Oneida Community*. New York: Penguin, 1993.

Levine, Murray, and Barbara Benedict Bunker. *Mutual Criticism*. Syracuse, NY: Syracuse University Press, 1975.

Muncy, Raymond Lee. *Sex and Marriage in Utopian Communities*. Bloomington: Indiana University Press, 1973.

Nordhoff, Charles. *The Communistic Societies of the United States*. New York: Dover, 1966.

Noyes, Corinna Ackley. *Days of My Youth*. Oneida, NY: Oneida Ltd., 1960.

Noyes, George Wallingford. *John Humphrey Noyes: The Putney Community*. Syracuse, NY: Syracuse University Press, 1931.

Noyes, Hilda H., and George W. Noyes. *Male Continence*. Oneida, NY: Office of the Oneida Circular, 1872.

_____. *Essay on Scientific Propagation*. Oneida, NY: Oneida Community, 1873.

_____. "The Oneida Community Experiment in Stirpiculture." *Eugenics and the Family* 1 (1923): 374–86.

Noyes, Pierrepont B. *A Goodly Heritage*. New York: Holt, Rinehart & Winston, 1958.

_____. *My Father's House: An Oneida Boyhood*. Gloucester, MA: Peter Smith, 1966.

Parker, Robert. *A Yankee Saint: John Humphrey Noyes and the Oneida Community*. New York: Putnam, 1935.

_____, ed. *Oneida Community: An Autobiography, 1851–1876*. Syracuse, NY: Syracuse University Press, 1970.

Robertson, Constance Noyes. *Oneida Community Profiles*. Syracuse, NY: Syracuse University Press, 1977.

Thomas, Robert. *The Man Who Would Be Perfect: John Humphrey Noyes and the Utopian Impulse*. Philadelphia: University of Pennsylvania Press, 1977.

Walters, Ronald G. *American Reformers, 1815–1860*. New York: Hill & Wang, 1978.

CHAPTER SIX

THE JEHOVAH'S WITNESSES

- Millenarian Movement
- Charles Russell
- Witnesses and the Federal
  Government
- Organization
- Finances
- What Witnesses Believe

- Social Characteristics
- Gaining Converts and
  Maintaining the Faith
- The Religious Perspective
- The Meetings
- Concluding Observations

Most Americans in the twenty-first century separate their religious and secular lives, and there is relatively little condemnation of competing religious ideologies. But there are certain religious groups that are often thought of as being beyond the pale.

One such group is the Society of Jehovah's Witnesses, now numbering 1 million in the United States and worldwide another 6 million. Americans exhibit a range of attitudes toward the Witnesses from indifference to derision to occasional hostility. Yet the group continues to grow and prosper, not only through natural increase but also through proselytizing.

Why have they been so successful? To answer this question, it is necessary to know the group's history, understand their belief system, and examine the "supports of faith" that bind them together.[1]

[1]Because Witness ideology conflicts in many ways with the ideologies of mainstream Christianity, it is difficult to find unbiased accounts of Jehovah's Kingdom. The most recent literature is much like past literature. Writers interested in the Witnesses tend to focus on interpretations of Scriptures. Some, mostly Witnesses, argue the correct posture of the Watchtower Bible and Tract Society; others, often apostates, argue the opposite. Membership estimates are drawn from Eileen W. Linder, *Yearbook of American and Canadian Churches 2009* (Nashville: Abingdon Press, 2009), Table 2; "Membership and Publishing Statistics," accessed at http://www.jw-media.org/people/statistics.htm on October 16, 2009. The Jehovah Witnesses may offer an interesting case of a religious group that *under*reports its number of followers. The number reported by an independent national survey was 1.9 million—almost twice the number reported by the Witnesses as self-identified as members. See Barry A. Kosmin and Ariela Keysar, *American Religious Identification Survey 2008, Summary Report* (March 2009), accessible at www.americanreligionsurvey-aris.org.

Included in the apostate literature is *In Search of Christian Freedom* by Raymond Franz (Atlanta: Commentary Press, 1991), a former member of the governing body of Jehovah's Witnesses and a nephew of Frederick Franz, immediate past president of the Society. Also see David A. Reed, ed., *Index of Watchtower Errors*, comp. Steve Huntoon and John Cornell King.

Millenarian Movement

The Jehovah's Witnesses are an example of a millenarian movement. A **millenarian movement** is a group of people who look forward to a dramatic change, after which all will be perfect. Obviously, such beliefs have their own biases about what constitutes a perfect future.

Typically, millenarian movements are associated with a prophecy about this imminent change, which is frequently delivered by a charismatic individual. Millenarian movements have included the Ghost Dance practiced by the Plains Indians and the cargo cult of the South Pacific. While many religions speak about a better future at some vague point in time in the future, millenarian movements may also describe a remaking of society and can be very specific about when this prophecy will occur. Special times to expect the arrival of the new millennium create great anticipation and even serves as an effective recruiting tool as the day arrives. But what happens if the prophecy fails to materialize? We will see how such events unfold with the Jehovah's Witnesses.

Charles Russell

Charles Russell, founder of the Jehovah's Witnesses, was born in 1852 in Allegheny, Pennsylvania, now a part of Pittsburgh. Both his parents, Joseph L. and Eliza Russell, were of Scottish-Irish descent. The Russells were religious people, members of the Presbyterian church. Eliza Russell died when Charles was nine, so it is difficult to know how much religious influence she had on her precocious child. As to child and father, it is probable, at least in a religious sense, that the son had greater influence on the father than the father on the son.

An exact date does not appear in Witness literature, but sometime during his adolescence, young Charles left the Presbyterian church and joined a Congregational church, ostensibly because its attitudes were more liberal.

Joseph Russell, a haberdasher, owned a chain of five shops. After only a few years of formal education, Charles joined his father in business. By day, Charles sold shirts; at night, he studied the Bible. He was most interested in the prophetical books, particularly Daniel. By the time he was fourteen, he was on the streets with colored chalk writing Scripture verses on the sidewalk. Nevertheless, at age seventeen, Russell encountered a

(Grand Rapids, MI: Baker Book House, 1990). For commentary, see Matthew Alfs, *The Evocative Religion of Jehovah's Witnesses: An Analysis of a Present-Day Phenomenon* (Minneapolis, MN: Old Theology Book House, 1991); Andrew Holden, *Jehovah's Witness: Portrait of a Contemporary Religious Movement* (London: Routledge, 2002).

spiritual crisis. He found himself no longer able to accept the concepts of eternal punishment and predestination. Surely, he believed, a good and just God would offer a plan of salvation for all of humankind. And certainly a loving God would not eternally damn even the worst of his children. For a period of time he rejected religion.

During Russell's youth, there was an industrial depression. Foreseeing a revolution on the horizon, he declared that "the old order of things must pass away, and the new must supersede it. . . . The change will be violently opposed by those advantaged by the present order."[2] Russell wrote: "Revolution world-wide would be the outcome, resulting in the final destruction of the old order and the introduction and establishment of the new."[3] His words share the tone of the *Communist Manifesto*, but there is no evidence that he ever read Karl Marx.

During his religious renunciation, which lasted about a year, Russell stated: "I'm just going to forget the whole thing and give all my attention to business. If I make some money, I can use that to help suffering humanity, even though I cannot help do them any good spiritually."[4] By the time he was thirty, he had accumulated $300,000, a fortune in the 1880s. There is no indication that any of this money was used to aid humanity in a secular sense. Russell soon showed, however, that he was quite willing to use his fortune when it came to the expansion of his religious beliefs.

The Millerites   Russell's return to faith came as a result of his contact with the Second Adventists, or Millerites, a group founded by William Miller in 1829. Millerite membership was, for the most part, confined to the Middle Atlantic states, and most followers were economically disadvantaged. Miller preached that the Second Coming of Christ would occur in the 1840s, thus proclaiming a millenarian movement. The failure of this prophecy, of course, was already evident by the time Russell encountered the group. Russell believed the Millerites were "called of God," but had miscalculated the date for the Messiah's return. The Millerites were the only religious group Charles Russell did not denounce during his lifetime.

After Miller's death, his followers recalculated and decided Christ's Second Coming would occur in 1873 or 1874. In 1870, Russell organized a Bible study group in Pittsburgh. He and his group—there were only six members—determined that the Second Coming would occur later, and that Christ's return would be invisible. To set the record straight, Russell published, at his own expense, 50,000 copies of a booklet entitled *The*

---

[2]Quoted in Barbara Grizzuti Harrison, *Visions of Glory* (New York: Simon & Schuster, 1978), p. 43.

[3]Harrison, *Visions of Glory*, p. 43.

[4]*Yearbook of Jehovah's Witnesses* (New York: Watchtower Bible and Tract Society of New York).

The *Watchtower,* said to be published in 168 languages, is one of the main communication vehicles among Witnesses. It is also distributed to non-members to attract them to the faith. The Witness shown here is pictured in front of the Bethel, the Witness headquarters in Brooklyn, New York.

Object and Manner of the Lord's Return. An early convert was his father, Joseph, who lent Charles both emotional and financial support.

Russell's following began to grow, and in 1879 he began publication of a periodical called *Zion's Watch Tower and Herald of Christ's Presence.* The new magazine had an impact. By 1880, some thirty congregations were established in seven states. Also, in 1881, the Zion's Watch Tower Tract Society was organized as an unincorporated body in Pittsburgh. Stipulated in the organization's charter was the intent to "disseminate Bible truths in various languages by means of publication of tracts, pamphlets, papers, and other religious documents." Society pamphlets sold for five cents, books for twenty-five cents. Potential converts with no money were given the literature free. This practice has not changed.[5]

By 1909, the organization had grown so large that it was decided to move its headquarters to Brooklyn, New York. The original building on the site was the home of the noted abolitionist Henry Ward Beecher.

---

[5]The Jehovah's Witnesses until 2000 were officially incorporated as Watch Tower Bible and Tract Society of New York, Watch Tower Bible and Tract Society of Pennsylvania, and International Bible Students Association, Brooklyn. Now the organization's work is conducted by the Christian Congregation of Jehovah's Witness (to supervise educational activities), Religious Order of Jehovah's Witness (to manage staff in full-time service), and Kingdom Support Services (to administer building construction and maintenance).

Personal Characteristics   Charles Russell was a small, thin man with an ascetic demeanor. A spellbinding speaker, he possessed charm and appeared to enjoy meeting people. He welcomed the press and photographers, and a large pictorial account exists of his ministry. He studied the Bible, and quoted Scripture readily in support of his beliefs. In his later years, his long white beard gave him the appearance of a sage patriarch. He was, indeed, a genuinely charismatic leader.

Russell was a workaholic. It is estimated that in the forty years of his ministry, he traveled a million miles, delivered 30,000 sermons, and wrote more than 150,000 pages of biblical exposition. While doing this, he managed a worldwide evangelistic ministry that employed more than seven hundred speakers.

Hints of Scandal   The Witnesses had to overcome several scandals during their formative years, but none was as far-reaching and caused as much disruption as Russell's marital difficulties. In 1879, Charles Russell married Maria Ackley. No children were born to the union. In the early years of the marriage, Maria Russell worked side by side with her ambitious husband, answering correspondence and addressing women's groups in his stead. But by 1909, the marriage had deteriorated to such a point that she sued for divorce, alleging, among other complaints, that Pastor Russell, as he had become known, had sexual relations with female members of the congregation. Russell always denied these charges, but the divorce was granted.

During his ministry, Russell's endorsement of dubious products (such as wheat with "marvelous properties" and cancer cures) received much press attention and caused some loss of Society membership. Russell was often sued and was quick to use the courts in retaliation. He had unshakable faith in the invincibility of his own rightness. Because he was quick to attack Christians of every denomination, it is not surprising that those he denounced were often eager to attack him. His belief that only he understood the Bible made him anathema to most religionists of his time. On October 31, 1916, the stormy life of Charles Russell came to an end. While on a nationwide lecture tour, he died unexpectedly of heart failure in a Pullman car near Pampa, Texas.

Charles Russell, the moving, dynamic organizer of the Jehovah's Witnesses, is now but a footnote in the history of the organization. Today, the faith, which is heavily involved in publishing, does not even reprint his works. When a knowledgeable elder was asked how it all began, he answered, "It began in Pennsylvania when a group of Bible students wanted to learn the 'real truth.' They studied the Bible just as we are studying." Then, as though it were an afterthought, he added, "One of them, Charles Russell, was probably a little more prominent than the others."

The Jehovah's Witnesses

Witnesses and the Federal Government

Judge Joseph Rutherford (1869–1942) was elected president of the Jehovah's Witnesses shortly after Russell's death. Within a few months of Rutherford's election, his convictions were tested. At the beginning of World War I, there was much pro-war sentiment in the United States. The Witnesses do not believe in war for any reason; also, they do not believe in silence when secular beliefs conflict with the Witness worldview.

In 1917, Rutherford and seven other Witness leaders were indicted for violation of the Espionage Act. The Witnesses were charged in federal court with "the offense of unlawfully, feloniously and willfully causing insubordination, disloyalty and refusal of duty in the military . . . by personal solicitations, letters, public speeches, distributing and publicly circulating throughout the United States of America various publications."[6] The Witnesses argued that they owed allegiance to no person, flag, or nation; they owed allegiance only to Jehovah. They were "of another world."

Rutherford and his followers were convicted, and all but one were sentenced to serve twenty years in the federal penitentiary at Leavenworth, Kansas; the seventh man received a ten-year sentence. The Witnesses began serving their sentences in June 1918. A petition for a new trial was filed, and in March 1919 all of the jailed Witnesses were released on bail. By then the war was over, and the government chose not to retry the case. Many people considered the jailing of the Witnesses a travesty of justice, and Society membership grew rapidly in the decade that followed.

Rutherford, like Russell, was a prolific writer. He proclaimed the group's name to be henceforth "Jehovah's Witnesses" and the use of the name "Jehovah" as the personal name of God as a major point of doctrine and faith.

[6]Alfs, *Evocative Religion of Jehovah's Witnesses*, p. 17.

Despite the central roles of Miller and Rutherford, the Witnesses deemphasize individuality and stress the importance of the "group." Since the death of Rutherford in 1942, none of their publications bears an author's signature. When knowledgeable Witnesses are asked about authorship, the usual response is that the article in question was probably written by a committee of Bible scholars.

Following Rutherford's death, Nathan Knorr (1905–1977) was elected third president of the Society. He, too, had to stand up for Witness pacifist beliefs in the face of a draft. During the First World War, Witness leaders had been jailed; the government took a different tack during the Second World War. Instead of jailing a few leaders, more than 4,000 of the rank and file were arrested and jailed for failure to comply with draft laws. The Witness argument continued to be that they were "of another world."

Harassment of Witnesses on other issues was evident as well. During the war, Witness children were targeted in public school systems. Harrison, an ex-Witness, describes in her book, *Visions of Glory*, a grade school experience: "Having to remain seated . . . during flag salute at school assembly was an act of defiance from which I inwardly recoiled. . . . Not saluting the flag, being the only child in my school who did not contribute to the Red Cross, . . . and not bringing in tinfoil balls for the War Drive did not endear me to my classmates. I wanted to please everybody—my teachers, my spiritual overseers, my mother; and, of course, I could not."[7]

Many Witness children were expelled from public schools for failing to conform to the system's expectations, and the Witnesses brought court suits in response to the expulsions. A 1940 Supreme Court decision, *Minersville v. Gobitis*, held that children who did not salute the flag were subject to expulsion. In 1943, the issue was returned to the Supreme Court in *West Virginia v. Barnette*. The Court ruled that the previous case had been "wrongly decided," and it was a Fourteenth Amendment violation to force children to salute the flag.

Following Knorr's death in 1977, Frederick Franz was elected president. Little conflict existed between the Witnesses and the outside world during his leadership. However, no draft occurred during his tenure as president, and no attempt was made to bring the flag-saluting incident back into court. The Witnesses have not changed their minds on these issues.

For several years, Franz, who died in December 1992 at the age of ninety-nine, was incapable of fully participating in the day-to-day affairs of the Society. The Witnesses believe, however, that all major decisions should be the consequence of a committee process, and because all the members of the governing committee are considered competent Bible

[7]Harrison, *Visions of Glory*.

scholars, it matters little if one committee member—even the president—requires a reduced workload.

Deformation Thesis   The progress of groups and organizations, including those with a spiritual basis, is influenced by what takes place in larger society. Sociologists have advanced the **deformation thesis** to describe the dynamic and rapid shifts in organizational form and activities of groups and organizations in response to societal influences. The word "deformation" is taken from engineering and refers to how an object changes shape—that is re-formed or deformed—in response to a physical force. Similarly, organizations are reshaped by how others react to it.

In the case of the Witnesses, the reactions by outsiders have often been critical and the group has had to devote resources—time and money—to defend itself. One example is in the 1940s *Gobitis* and *Barnette* U.S.-flag salute cases. Costs assumed in these legal battles created a defensive culture or siege mentality within the organization, an attitude in which administrators and leaders feel their actions are subjected to severe criticism by those outside the organization. Members were prepared and ready for attacks to their faith. Missionaries and ministers were given crash courses in civil rights. Procedures were created to report incidents to headquarters. We can see similar preparedness patterns with the Latter-day Saints and the Scientologists.

The deformation thesis is ultimately realized when religious groups like the Jehovah Witnesses that protect antiworldliness are forced to engage nonbelievers in public-relations efforts. Witnesses would just as soon be allowed to spend their time with like-minded folk or seeking converts rather than justifying their very existence. Public relations, not to mention legal efforts, are undertaken not so much to convert others but to persuade them to let the already faithful worship as they please.[8]

In the decades following Russell's leadership, press coverage of Witness events had not been encouraged. Witness positions were simply Witness positions, and the Society exhibited no concern for public image. However, at a Minnesota district convention attended by William Zellner, there was a pressroom set up and staffed by elders who could quote Scripture in support of any Witness viewpoint. The existence of the press center may have been significant, evidencing a sensitivity to the "other world," a sensitivity that has not existed in the past.

Witnesses and Other Governments   Jehovah's Witnesses have been the victims of prejudice and discrimination in a number of countries. As part

---

[8]Pauline Cote and James T. Richardson, "Disciplined Litigation, Vigilant Litigation and Deformation: Dramatic Organization Chase in Jehovah's Witnesses," *Journal for the Scientific Study of Religion* 40 (March 2001), pp. 11–25.

of Nazi extermination policies before and during World War II, Witnesses were sent to death camps along with Gypsies (Roma), gays and lesbians, and Jews. About 3,200 Witnesses were sent to concentration camps for their refusal to sign a document renouncing their faith.

Currently in Russia and in neighboring Georgia, prosecutors are trying to prohibit the Witnesses from practicing their religion "under a law that gives the courts the right to ban religious groups found guilty of inciting hatred or intolerant behavior."[9] Charged with making a decision, a panel of experts has been appointed to review Witness literature.

Organization

During the early years, the Society's work was carried on by a board of directors. Anyone who donated ten dollars to the Society was eligible to cast one vote at board elections. Contributors could cast one additional vote for each ten-dollar increment contributed above a minimum donation. During his lifetime, Russell was the Society's unquestioned leader, and voting for the presidency was perfunctory.

In 1944, the Society's charter was amended to remove monetary contributions as a means of access to the governing body. Today, a governing body currently made up of nine men meets weekly in Brooklyn, New York, to make both secular and religious decisions.

At the next echelon are district and circuit overseers. Charged with the responsibility of visiting each congregation twice each year, these men (there are no women overseers) often accompany local Witnesses on home visits, ostensibly to help them with proselytizing techniques. When leadership positions open, all baptized male Witnesses over age twenty are eligible for consideration.

At the head of each local congregation is a presiding overseer chosen from among the elders. This is a rotating position, the appointment not to exceed one year. The transience of the position fortifies the authority of the New York Society, emphasizing that no one man at the local level is indispensable.

Headquarters   The Witness headquarters complex in Brooklyn, like the branch offices of the Jehovah's Witnesses, is called Bethel (House of God). Residents at the Brooklyn Bethel, including married couples, live two to a

---

[9]Arin Gencer, "Jehovah Witness Tells L.A. Audience of Defying Nazis," *Los Angeles Times,* May 26, 2006, p. 133; Terence Neilan, "World Briefing," *New York Times,* June 29, 1999, Sec. A, p. 6; Michael Ochs, "Persecution of Jehovah's Witnesses in Georgia Today," *Religion, State and Society* 30 (No. 3, 2002), pp. 239–76; William Zellner, "Of Another World: The Jehovah's Witnesses" (Ph. D. diss., South Dakota State University, 1981), pp. 60–61 and Joel Engardo "Russia's bans on Jehovah's Witnesses" *Washington Post* (December 9, 2010).

room. Baths and toilets are shared. Most of the needs of the Bethelites are met within the confines of the complex, which includes its own barber shop, tailor shop, laundry, and bakery. Food and housekeeping services are provided. The rooms are pleasant and the food is good. Staff members, including the president of the Society, receive a monthly stipend of ninety dollars for personal needs. A few Witness detractors make much of the fact that headquarters personnel travel first class when on tour. It would seem, though, that Witness leaders move about in no greater style than leaders of other religious organizations.

The Society also owns and operates a number of farms, including a 1,698-acre farm near Wallkill, New York, which provides most of the food required by the more than 3,500 headquarters workers. Witness farmworkers produce a large vegetable crop, maintain a herd of beef cattle, raise broiler chickens and laying hens, and milk a dairy herd. They also process what they produce. Eight hundred workers are required to operate the farm, processing facilities, and the two large printeries located on the farm.

The printing operation at Wallkill produces the magazines *Watchtower* and *Awake!* It is difficult to know just how much printed material is produced by the Jehovah's Witnesses. *Awake!* in 2008 claimed an average printing of 36 million copies. Similarly, *Watchtower* reported an average printing of 39 million copies in 174 languages. Each magazine is produced semimonthly. The printeries at Wallkill, which produce the magazines, are not nearly as large as the Bethel printeries, which produce books and pamphlets, and where six of the ten multistory buildings are devoted to production of the written word.

Patterson Farm   In 1984, the Witnesses bought a 670-acre dairy farm in Patterson, New York, to build an educational center. The campus is the major educational institution for the church's missionaries and staff. It is equipped to teach, feed, and house 1,600 people at a time. Presently, there are about 1,300 on the campus.

The school was built the Jehovah's Witness way. During the building process, an estimated five hundred workers plied their trades, from engineers to architects, carpenters, draftsmen, concrete workers, plumbers, electricians, and laborers—all volunteers. These workers, from every part of the United States, received the same ninety-dollar-per-month stipend as the headquarters' workers.

Today, there are six apartment houses two to five stories high with more than six hundred apartments, garage space for eight hundred cars, a 144-room motel, and a kitchen big enough to serve 1,600 people at one sitting. There is an office building, a classroom building, and several service buildings.

The various properties of the Jehovah's Witnesses are so vast that a tour business has developed to take the faithful to see the various sites. An eleven-day bus tour takes in New York City properties, Wallkill, Patterson Farm, a Canadian branch and, reflecting the tragic history of Jehovah's Witnesses in Germany, the U.S. Holocaust Memorial Museum in Washington, DC.[10]

Finances

Each year, the Society places a notice in an issue of the *Watchtower* soliciting contributions. To facilitate planning, the notice asks contributors to specify how much the Society can expect to receive and when contributions will be made. Collections are not taken at the Kingdom Halls,[11] and the elders do not solicit money from the pulpit. Every Hall has a contribution box, but contributions from this source seem to be few and far between. Most donations come from self-imposed tithes.

Classified as a charitable religious organization, the Society is not required to make public its financial statements. Many denominations, similarly exempt, choose to make public disclosures of income and assets; that the Witnesses do not may be linked to past problems with tax collectors. The most notable of these occurred in 1971, when the state of New York enacted a law permitting taxation of property not exclusively used for religious purposes. The Society paid $2 million, under protest, to the city of New York. On July 11, 1974, tax exemption was restored to the Society by the New York State Court of Appeals. The court's written decision stipulated that the Society was organized exclusively for religious purposes within the meaning of the statute.

The Witnesses are trying to be good neighbors at the new Patterson facility. The church voluntarily put the Patterson Motel on the tax rolls. Witnesses have about twenty houses in the community, all on the tax rolls. When the church built five-story structures on the Patterson campus, the fire department said they could not provide services because they did not have the equipment to fight fires in tall buildings. The Witnesses responded by buying them a new truck.[12]

Charity Members of other faiths, legislators, and the public in general do not understand the Witness position on charity. There are no charitable entities within Witness organizational structure: no hospitals, no

---

[10]Harold Faber, "Jehovah's Witnesses Build Center on Dairy Farm," *New York Times,* April 4, 1991, p. 28; Mary McAleer Vizard, "Watchtower Project Grows in Patterson," *New York Times,* April 18, 1993, p. R9; Janis Harris Consulting at http://www.bethel-tours.com/.

[11]Kingdom Halls are places for education and worship. Witnesses do not use the term *church.* A body of believers is termed a *congregation.*

[12]Vizard, "Watchtower Project Grows," p. R9.

clinics, no food programs. The Society believes that the last days are so near that all available funds must be spent on the "promulgation of the truth"—that is, spreading Jehovah's word.

The edict to be charitable permeates Society literature. Charity is up to the individual, however; it is not viewed as an organizational responsibility. Aid usually involves services such as baby-sitting, shopping or providing transportation for the elderly, and reading Scriptures to the infirm. It is difficult to know the private transactions of the Witness in-group, but it is probable that they help each other financially as well.

Construction   Erecting new buildings is not a problem for most Witness congregations, which are willing to expend their own time and energy. For example, a Minnesota congregation has a new Kingdom Hall, built almost entirely by the members, many of whom are skilled laborers. Nothing was spent for outside help. When the congregation had difficulty planning and installing the electrical system, a call for assistance was sent to nearby congregations, and the problem was resolved quickly. When the building was dedicated, members of the congregations who lent assistance were honored. Great pride was felt in the accomplishment. An investment of time and labor is apparently more rewarding than a monetary contribution.

Financing construction of Kingdom Halls is a relatively simple matter. Congregations need only finance the cost of building materials; there are no labor costs. The elimination of labor costs creates built-in equity for the lender. For example, a Kingdom Hall valued at $100,000, minus the cost of labor, may necessitate only a $50,000 loan. There is almost no risk for the lender. The parent Society maintains a list of bankers and institutional investors eager to invest in Kingdom Halls.

Witness congregations save money in many ways. For example, they do not hire janitors. In most congregations, janitorial and maintenance duties are assigned to Bible study groups on a rotating basis. Most Witnesses are skilled or semiskilled laborers, so maintenance is never a problem for them, and thus, the Kingdom Halls are well cared for.

What Witnesses Believe

In the Beginning   Before earth there was heaven and in heaven was God (Jehovah) and he was alone. His first creation was a son, the Archangel Michael. Michael "was used by Jehovah in creating all other things." Michael's first creations were other spirit sons for God, angels numbering in the millions. Among these sons was Lucifer, who would later be called Satan, which means "Resister."

After creating the earth, Jehovah said to Michael, "Let us make man in our image."[13] His purpose was to create a perfect paradise (Eden), for a perfect man (Adam) and woman (Eve). Adam and Eve, in turn, were expected to bear perfect children, who would live according to Jehovah's laws and glorify him.

The Fall   It was Jehovah's intent that humans should live in perfect harmony with their environment and never die. Lucifer was put in charge of Eden. Jealous of Jehovah, he wanted followers who would adore him. To accomplish this, he had to alienate Adam and Eve from God. While Jehovah rested at the beginning of the seventh day (Genesis 2:2), Lucifer found the fatal flaw in Adam and Eve.[14]

Jehovah had given Adam a single prohibition: Do not eat the fruit of the tree of knowledge of good and evil, or you will die. Satan, using a snake as a medium, persuaded Eve to eat the fruit. She then seduced Adam, and he, too, ate the fruit. Jehovah's punishment was death to Adam and Eve, and death for all of their kind yet to come.

Witnesses do not attribute the Fall to the sex act. Interestingly, original sin is tied to intellectual freedom. Eve's act led to freedom of choice, which didn't exist before the forbidden fruit was eaten. Before the Fall, Adam simply obeyed Jehovah's laws, as he had been commanded: "The woman was the first human sinner. Her temptation by God's adversary . . . was not through an open appeal to immorality of a sensual nature. Rather, it paraded as an appeal to the desire for supposed intellectual elevation and freedom. . . . He [the snake] asserted that eating the fruit from the proscribed tree would result, not in death, but in enlightenment and godlike ability to determine for oneself whether a thing was good or bad."[15]

The Ransom   Jehovah loved Adam despite his failure, and chose to release Adam's children from the death penalty. Viewed by the Society as the head of a theocratic legal system, even Jehovah must act according to law. Humankind could be released from the certainty of death, but only through a legal ransom. Witnesses define *ransom* as an exact corresponding price. Adam was a perfect man, therefore a perfect man had to be sacrificed to redeem humankind.

Witnesses reject the concept of a Holy Trinity—the idea that Father, Son, and Holy Spirit are one. Jesus is believed to be God's first son, the

[13]*Insight on the Scriptures*, vol. 1 (New York: Watchtower Bible and Tract Society of New York, 1988), p. 527.

[14]All biblical references in this chapter are from the *New World Translation of the Holy Scriptures* (New York: Watchtower Bible and Tract Society of New York, 1971).

[15]*Insight on the Scriptures*, vol. 2 (New York: Watchtower Bible and Tract Society of New York, 1988), p. 963.

Archangel Michael. Because Adam was human, Michael was sent to earth in human form. As Jesus, he was capable of sin, but to pay Adam's "ransom," he had to live a sinless life. After the Resurrection, he was restored to a spiritual being.

Prophecy Failure   The most important date in early Witness chronology is 1914. Witnesses believe that on October 4 or 5 of that year, Christ fought the devil in heaven, won the battle, then hurled Satan and his demons to earth. Russell and early Witnesses thought that Christ would establish his earthly kingdom in that same year. When Christ did not make a visible appearance, the date for his advent was recalculated to 1918. Despite the recalculation and Russell's charisma, there was some decrease in Society membership in the years that followed.

Judge Rutherford, Russell's successor, studied the Scriptures and concluded that the Society had erred. It was decided that Christ had established his "invisible heavenly kingdom" in 1914 but that he would not establish his "earthly kingdom" until after a "generation had passed." A generation was defined as the life span of all those living in 1914 who were old enough to understand the horrors of that year. The Society cites the beginning of World War I, along with other disasters that occurred in that year, as proof that an angered Satan, cast out of heaven, was displaying his wrath.

Witnesses believed that an infant would not have understood the horrors of 1914 but, perhaps, a precocious child of three or four years would. If there was to be a second prophecy failure, it could not occur until the Witnesses were convinced that all those who understood the events of 1914 were dead.

With the generation that was alive in 1914 rapidly disappearing, the *Watchtower* magazine reported in November 1995 that all timetables pinpointing exactly when Armageddon would take place were merely speculative. Jesus said that "no one knows the day or the hour."

Woodward and Engardio observe, "The year 1914 still marks the beginning of the last days [for the Witnesses]. But those who hoped to witness the battle of Armageddon and the establishment of God's kingdom on earth will have to wait. Henceforth, any generation that experiences such calamities as war and plagues like AIDS could be the one to witness the end times. In short, the increasingly middle-class Witnesses would do well to buy life insurance."[16]

Eschatology   Eschatology is the part of theology that considers the final events of the world. Often referred as "end of the world" predictions, eschatology, when practiced, proclaims the coming of a new world, a new

[16]Kenneth L. Woodward and Joel P. Engardio, "Apocalypse Later: Jehovah's Witnesses Decide the End Is Fluid," *Newsweek*, December 18, 1995, p. 59.

life. Christian eschatology is concerned with the Second Coming of Christ, the resurrection of the dead, the last judgment, and the effect of human existence on the completion of history.

Russell's final dispensation, "The World to Come," begins with the "Millennial Age." Christ, and those already in heaven, are waiting to begin the battle of **Armageddon**—the final, decisive battle between good and evil. Armageddon in religious writings refers to an epic battle associated with the end of time as we know it. Purification of sin is thought to occur at this time. Satan will be defeated in the battle and cast into an abyss for a thousand years, a millennium.

Witnesses believe that only 144,000 people "have the heavenly hope" (Revelation 14:1) to rule with Jesus in heaven. Along with Witnesses eligible for heavenly service are the prophets David, Abraham, Moses, and Noah. All who will serve have already been chosen, and only a handful of those, known as the "remnant," remain on earth.

Witnesses do not believe in a fiery hell. Most of the billions of people who will die before the battle of Armageddon will be turned to dust, from which they will be resurrected. The few who will not return are those who in life were "willfully wicked." Witnesses view the "willfully wicked" as those who knew the will of Jehovah but defied him. There appears to be no consensus among Witness rank and file as to who had been "willfully wicked," but the number is deemed small. Adam and Eve, Judas, and Nimrod are certain to remain in dust. All others returned from the dust will live in an earthly paradise ruled by Jehovah.

Since the failed prophecy of 1914, leaders of Jehovah's Witnesses have become involved in the failed prophecy. In 1966, the governing body issued a major proclamation that traced the history of humankind beginning with the creation of Adam and that the 6,000-year anniversary would come in 1974. The proclamation continued on "how appropriate" it would be for the Jehovah God to make this point the "jubilee" and proclaim liberty throughout the world.

While not specifically a declaration of another prophecy, many Witnesses interpreted the proclamation this way and began to treat 1975 the way Witnesses two generations earlier had treated 1914. The faithful were reported as doing everything from selling property to avoiding having children as the year approached. When 1975 came and went, membership dropped significantly and evangelistic efforts enjoyed little success. Since these events, the leadership of the Witnesses has avoided statements that could be interpreted as yet another prophecy.[17]

[17]Andrew Holden, *Jehovah's Witnesses: Portrait of a Contemporary Religious Movement.* (London: Routledge, 2002), p. 98; David L. Weddle, "Jehovah's Witnesses," in *Introductions to New and Alternative Religions in America*, Vol. 2, pp. 69–70, edited by Eugene V. Gallagher and W. Michael Ashcraft (Westport, CT: Greenwood Press, 2006).

Paradise   By the end of the millennium, humankind will have reached a perfected state; vice, disease, corruption, and death will disappear from the earth. But at the end of the millennium, Satan will be freed from his bondage. He will gather demons around him, and together they will try to persuade humankind to follow them. Witnesses believe that few will. After experiencing paradise, how could humankind want to lead an immoral and degrading life? Satan's small army will be defeated, and a second judgment day will follow.

Jehovah's first judgment, after Adam's failure, was against all of humankind. The final judgment, following the destruction of Satan, will be of individuals. All those deemed unworthy will be condemned to eternal dust. Even this untoward group will not have to suffer the agonies of a tormenting hell.

After the millennium, Christ will return a perfected earth to Jehovah. Jehovah will become an active king in his theocratic system. Survivors of the final judgment will live in harmony with their creator in paradise for eternity. There is little speculation as to what life will be like in "the Ages to Come." Most Witnesses simply believe that it is beyond the power of mortals to comprehend all the goodness Jehovah has in store for them.

Social Characteristics

Voting Behavior   Most Jehovah's Witnesses do not vote. The faith argues for an antiworldly stance (that is, noninvolvement), citing Jesus who says of his followers, "They are not of the world, just as I am not of the world" (John 17:14). Those who do ordinarily confine their ballots to local issues such as zoning, taxes, and school board elections. At a group meeting in Minnesota, an elder was asked if he didn't think it was in the interest of the Society for members to vote for national candidates who might best represent Witnesses' moral convictions. His response was that it didn't make much difference who was elected, because nothing would change. Satan's evil plan would be followed until Jehovah establishes his Kingdom on earth. The wife of the congregation's presiding elder ended the conversation when she asked the interviewer, "If you were a citizen of France, would you expect to vote in Great Britain's elections?" The interviewer said he would not. "Well," she continued, "we are citizens of Jehovah's Kingdom. Not only should we not want to vote, we really don't have the right to vote."[18]

Typically Witnesses' not voting attracts little attention. Yet in 2008 at Wimbledon, reporters were all over the tennis player Serena Williams, a

---

[18]Zellner, "Of Another World." All subsequent references to the "Minnesota study" were extracted from this thesis.

Witness, when she said she would not vote for Barack Obama because we "don't get involved in politics." Sometimes the keeping out of politics can have more tragic implications: *Watchtower* reported in 1968 that hundreds of Jehovah's Witnesses in the African nation of Malawi had their homes destroyed when they refused to buy a political membership card as required by law.[19]

Sexual Attitudes   Witnesses do not consider sex to have been the downfall of Adam and Eve. But this has not led to "liberated" sexual attitudes. Masturbation is considered self-love, and most Witness children are told early and often about the Scriptures that forbid the practice of self-adoration. Witness children are warned that masturbation can inhibit a happy marriage, noting that it is a man's responsibility to ensure that his wife derives pleasure from the sex act. If a habit of premarital masturbation develops, one thinks only of oneself, and it becomes difficult to satisfy a partner. Witnesses take the position that masturbation can lead to homosexuality. Homosexual behavior is considered an unnatural abomination and is grounds for **disfellowship.** *Disfellowship* is the Witness term for excommunication. Homosexuals are counseled before action is taken against them.

During his two-year study of Minnesota congregations, Zellner found that two young women were disfellowshipped from one of the congregations, each deemed guilty of fornication; both were living unwed with a male friend. On several occasions, "brothers" visited and counseled the errant "sisters." Members of the congregation all felt the sisters were censured fairly, but all hoped the women would repent: Society doors are opened to repentant sinners.

Note, the brothers counseled the women. Sisters are considered the weaker vessel; their position in the Society is one of support. In the Minnesota study, a rather stable, seemingly strong young woman was asked if she resented the secondary role assigned women by the Society, if she didn't think it was unjust that she couldn't counsel, in an official way, those who faltered, or that she couldn't hold a leadership position in the church. "Oh, no!" she replied, and looked at the interviewer with a somewhat puzzled expression. "Women are not emotionally strong enough to handle those kinds of things."[20]

Detractors of extraordinary groups point to alleged excesses of celebrity members as examples that the particular faith is not serious about its

---

[19]Jacob Leibenluft, "Why Don't Jehovah Witnesses Vote?" *Slate* (June 26, 2008), accessible at http://www.slate.com/id/2194321; "The Malawi Incident;" *Watchtower*, February 1, 1968, pp. 71–79 accessible at http://www.jwfiles.com/malawi.htm.
[20]Zellner, "Of Another World," p. 62. Also see Kyria Abrahams, *I'm Perfect, You're Doomed: Tales from a Jehovah's Witness Upbringing* (New York: Touchstone, 2009).

lifestyle. The Witness lifestyle suggests a conservative demeanor and utmost civility, especially when in public. Tennis professionals Serena and Venus Williams's clothing on court tends to be provocative, but they note, when questioned, that of course they dress conservatively when attending Kingdom Hall services. Similarly, Serena Williams's profanity-laden outburst at the 2009 U.S. Open match led many to fault her religious convictions. Interestingly, such parallels are rarely drawn about members of mainstream religious groups (consider John McEnroe, a practicing Roman Catholic).[21]

Witnesses recognize Jehovah's biblical commandment to be fruitful and multiply. Members are, however, permitted to practice birth control. Witnesses are opposed to abortion, so birth control must not include the use of intrauterine devices (IUDs), on the grounds that these devices act to abort the egg after fertilization has occurred. Such methods as the pill, a diaphragm, or prophylactics may be used at the discretion of the individual. Jehovah's Witnesses' family size tend to be a bit larger than typical families.[22]

The Society suggests that young Witnesses consider singleness—celibate singleness—as a viable alternative to marriage. Missionaries are particularly encouraged to give extra thought before marrying. The Society warns that marriage could limit their ability to carry out their duties properly. The Society further makes the point that, with Armageddon so near, there is no need to hurry parenting; it might be better to wait and bring children into a perfected world.

Marriage and Family   In its ideal form, the Witness marriage is the kind of marriage that was supposed to have existed in the United States before the sexual revolution of the 1960s. The husband is responsible for meeting the family's economic needs, whereas the wife is responsible for maintaining and caring for the home. A good wife defers to her husband on all matters of importance. Many Witness texts, however, such as *Happiness, How to Find It,* suggest that the husband—to promote marital happiness—give in to the wife on unimportant matters.

In practice, the familistic orientation of the Witnesses is very similar to that of the Mormons. Families are encouraged to do things together or with other Witness families. Congregational functions are to be attended by all members of the family, and families are encouraged to work together, play together, and worship together. There are no separatist bodies within the Society—no men's groups or women's groups.

[21]Juliet Lapidos, "Serena Williams Swears to God," *Slate* (October 16), accessible at http://www.slate.com/id/2228410/.
[22]The Pew Forum on Religion and Public Life, *U.S. Religious Landscape Survey 2008.* (Washington, DC: Pew Research Center, 2008), p. 68.

The Society does, however, recognize that some married couples are so mismatched that it is impossible for them to live together. Charles and Marie Russell were such a mismatch. In such cases, separation is condoned, but divorce is permissible only on the scriptural ground of adultery.

The Society recommends that women whose husbands live outside the Kingdom defer to their spouse on all matters except those that contradict Jehovah's teachings. It is thought that if a wife continues to exhibit a "sweet nature," the husband may eventually mature.

Integrated Community   The Witnesses evidently do not practice racial discrimination, and Society literature clearly denounces the practice. On several occasions during the Minnesota study, an observer attended meetings (they are never called services) in a racially mixed urban neighborhood. The congregation reflected the makeup of the larger community. Intermarriage is quite common, and it is not unusual to see a White grandparent making a fuss over a Black grandchild. The interactions within this congregation clearly showed that racial harmony is the norm. Male African American Witnesses are eligible for, and do attain, leadership roles in the organization's hierarchy.

Nationally Jehovah's Witness is one of the most diverse religious traditions in the country. In 2008, 48 percent were White, 22 percent Black, and 24 percent Latino. Witnesses are more likely than others to be foreign born.[23]

Medicine   On the basis of their interpretation of a number of scriptural injunctions, for example Acts 15:29 (that Christians abstain from things offered to idols, from blood, from things strangled, and from sexual immorality), Jehovah's Witnesses do not accept blood transfusions, regardless of medically defined need.

However, this does not mean they categorically reject the medical profession. The Society does not object to the use of medicinal drugs, inoculations, internal medicines, or necessary surgery, provided blood transfusion can be avoided. The ban against the use of blood is also based on Leviticus 17:10: "God told Noah that every living creature should be meat unto him; but that he must not eat blood, because the life is in the blood." Witnesses cite the current AIDS epidemic as proving this long-held belief to be correct.

In the middle of the twentieth century, Witnesses seemed to take stronger prohibitions as different blood components such as red cells, white cells, platelets, and plasma were better understood. It was not just whole blood transfusion that was being questioned. Transfusions of any of kind were prohibited. Then in 2000, the group citing biblical ambiguity, indicated that individuals are free to decide whether to use different

[23]Pew Forum, *U.S. Religious Landscape,* pp. 44, 47.

transfusion therapies as they related to hemophilia. In 2004 the prohibition was again altered to allow fractions of a blood component, which freed devout Witnesses to accept many types of treatments drawing upon donated and stored blood. Criticism of this stance, almost entirely coming from outside the faith, notes that any support based on biblical foundation has vanished and, furthermore, these "clarifications" in *Watchtower* continue to show ignorance of medical technology. Regardless of the pronouncements, the teachings remain to avoid transfusions and to seek "bloodless surgery."[24]

The proclamation of blood transfusions has been advanced since 1945, and since 1961, members who accept a transfusion are subject to banishment from the faith. Kidney dialysis is permitted as long as the blood continually circulates, and hemophiliacs are allowed certain specific blood treatments.

Some hospitals recognize the Witnesses' position and beginning about 2005, the American Medical Association urged medical personnel to consider alternative forms of care when treating Witnesses that normally would require transfusions. Nonetheless, cases involving minor children or pregnant women in danger of placing the fetus in peril occasionally reach courts, where the emotional matter is settled on a case-by-case basis.[25]

Witnesses do not believe in faith healers. Such individuals are considered absolute frauds. The Society acknowledges that a select few, prior to Christ, had the ability to heal, as did Christ and the apostles, but the gift was lost with the death of the last apostle.

Education   At one district convention, a Witness speaker encouraged young people of ability to attend trade schools and stay away from colleges, insisting that college instruction contradicts Jehovah's teachings. Society literature directs the Witness father to train his sons to use their hands. When he repairs his car, his son should be allowed to help. Daughters should be trained by their mothers and taught to sew, cook, and maintain a clean house. At one Bible study, a well-attired young man had the floor. "No, you won't find much of man's education in this room," he said. "You won't find no bachelor's degrees, no master's degrees. This is not what we seek. Our education is of God's word."[26]

Witnesses place little value in insights beyond the scope of their religion. One need only have reading skills sufficient for comprehending the Bible

[24]Richard N. Ostling, "Jehovah's Witnesses Get New Transfusion Directive," *Chicago Tribune*, February 3, 1006, p. 8; *Watchtower*, June 15, 2004; "Associated Jehovah's Witnesses for Reform on Blood," accessed October 16, 2009 at http://www.ajwrb.org/index.shtml.

[25]Weddle, "Jehovah's Witnesses," pp. 79–80; M. B. Sutherland, "Balancing Patient Care and Religious Connections," *Chicago Tribune*, July 15, 2006, sect. 4., pp. 1, 5.

[26]Zellner, "Of Another World," p. 66.

and Witness publications. Witness apostate David Reed, formerly a Society overseer, writes that "although most outsiders are unaware of such a restriction, Jehovah's Witnesses know well that they are forbidden to read the literature of other religious organizations. They have been told that 'it would be foolhardy, as well as a waste of valuable time, for Jehovah's Witnesses to accept and expose themselves to false religious literature that is designed to deceive.' And they have been taught that 'reading apostate publications' is 'similar to reading pornographic literature.'"[27]

Holidays   The "Memorial of Christ's Death," the observance of the death of Christ, is the only Witness holiday (occurring on Passover eve annually). It is not a festive occasion, but a very solemn meal of unleavened bread and wine. There is no thought of the bread and wine as symbolic of the body and blood of Christ. Only those who are convinced that they are part of the "remnant" (those still living who will ultimately rule in heaven with Christ) actually partake of the meal; all others simply pass the bread and cup. When members are asked how they know they are part of the "remnant," the response is always, "You just feel it." Only two persons in a Kingdom Hall in Minnesota, where an observer regularly attended meetings, felt justified in eating the meal.

The Witnesses find reasons for not celebrating other holidays. The Easter rabbit and Easter eggs are pagan symbols of fertility; New Year's celebrations are debaucheries; Halloween is associated with Catholicism's celebration of the dead; secular holidays, such as Labor Day, Independence Day, and Columbus Day, glorify humans.[28]

Witnesses do not celebrate Christmas, do not accommodate it, but do acknowledge the event. What's the distinction? Accommodation would suggest they try to incorporate some elements of it. For example, some Jewish-Christian interfaith couples participate in what has been called Christmaka, in which elements of Chanukah and Christmas are both celebrated in the household. Jehovah Witnesses do not do that. No Christmas decorations are present or gifts exchanged in a Witness household. Yet, Jesus' birth is still acknowledged among Witnesses. For example, the December 2009 issue of *Awake!* featured a picture of a children's nativity pageant accompanying an article entitled "What Kind of Star Led the 'Wise Men' to Jesus?" Yet the article dealt mostly with astronomers' views about whether a star guided the "wise men." Taking selected scientific theories, the Witness publication concludes that if this "popular Christmas story" were true, the star was most

[27]Reed, *Index of Watchtower Errors.* The author quotes two *Watchtower* sources: May 1, 1984, p. 31, and March 15, 1986, p. 14.

[28]Ron Rhodes, *Reasoning from the Scriptures* (New York: Watchtower Bible and Tract Society of New York, 1985), p. 179.

likely from "Satan the Devil," trying to lead Jesus or the wise men into the hands of Herod.

Witnesses do not celebrate their own birthdays. They contend that the only birthday celebrations mentioned in the Bible (those of a pharaoh of Egypt and the Roman ruler Herod) ended in misery. While the birth of Christ may be a joyful occasion, Witnesses do not partake in the celebration since they contend we do not know the precise day and, anyway, Christmas has been overtaken by secular images.

Gaining Converts and Maintaining the Faith

Why people join and maintain membership in a group that is often deprecated is an interesting question. The answer has remained somewhat elusive. Witnesses themselves are often less than cooperative. The few studies we do have contain little more than demographic data. The important issues, such as how members of the Society come to agree on rules, definitions, and values, are not addressed.

In the Minnesota study, Zellner went beyond collecting demographic data, and chose, instead, to observe Witnesses as they function in the

Jehovah's Witnesses baptize those "of a responsible age" who have made a conscious decision to join the religion. Baptism is done by full water immersion and is taken to be a sign of one's devotion to God. As with many such baptisms, this one pictured in a St. Louis public park involves many people taking this step. After baptism, primary duties expected of a Jehovah's Witness include regular attendance at Kingdom Hall meetings and evangelism.

day-to-day world. He attended meetings and participated in a home Bible study. Questions were asked in a conversational way and recorded later. Often, the questions did not have to be asked. Witness converts, like most other religious converts, have a penchant for comparing their former unfulfilling lifestyles to their new, much-improved life situation. The questionnaire that follows contains typical answers. The respondent was a forty-nine-year-old white female identified by the pseudonym Kate Williams.

Q. What is your marital status?
A. Widow.
Q. Do you have any children?
A. Eight.
Q. Are they members of the group?
A. Three participate fully. Five are, at this time, living outside of Jehovah's Kingdom. It is difficult to raise children in Satan's world. They are sent to school and taught by teachers who know nothing about Jehovah, or have rejected him. Then when they get a job, they are surrounded by more people who either don't know or won't accept Jehovah's word. It is my sincerest hope that all my children will eventually enter Jehovah's Kingdom.
Q. How long have you been a member of the Jehovah's Witnesses?
A. Twenty-six years.
Q. How did you first encounter the group?
A. They came to the door when we were living in California. I wasn't at home the first time they came, but I remember my husband was very excited about their visit. We studied over the literature for many hours.
Q. Were you at a time in your life when you were experiencing some sort of unusual strain?
A. We had not been living in California very long, and we were having some difficulty getting adjusted to that way of life. We felt we were surrounded by godless people.
Q. Do you feel that a pattern for life is important?
A. Everyone should have direction in life. My husband and I both felt that need.
Q. Did your becoming a Jehovah's Witness fulfill that need?
A. Most definitely.
Q. Did you believe in the existence of God before encountering the Jehovah's Witnesses or would you have considered yourself an agnostic or atheist?
A. My husband and I both believed in God. We went to a Lutheran church before moving to California.
Q. Before attending formal group [Witness] meetings, did you form a close tie with one or more of the Witnesses?
A. We liked the people who came to our house, and we began attending meetings right away. We went to the Kingdom Hall and met people who wanted to live according to God's will. It was very different from what we had previously experienced in California.

Q. How many hours a week do you spend in organizational activity?

A. Twenty-two to twenty-three hours a week. [This included attending meetings and proselytizing.]

Q. How long was it before you moved from verbal agreement with the group to commitment, attending regular meetings, and so on?

A. We began right away.

Q. Do you seek to gain new members for the group? How?

A. Of course. We are obligated to spread the word. When I feel that I can talk to someone at work, or someone in the neighborhood, I talk to them about Jehovah. Also, I go door-to-door like all Witnesses who are able.

Q. Do you subscribe totally to the belief system of the Jehovah's Witnesses or do you have some doubts or disagreements?

A. I believe totally.

Q. Do you consider membership in the group the most important aspect of your life?

A. Yes, I do. I have brought at least ten people into the "new system." If my life wasn't fully committed, I couldn't have done that.

Kate Williams is an extremely pleasant woman and her claim of conversions is probably accurate. Most Witnesses are not nearly so successful at bringing new members into the group despite their dedicated activity.

There are more than 7 million Witnesses worldwide, and their further growth is more or less guaranteed by the process of natural increase. Witnesses, however, are not content with only that kind of growth. Because they believe that the end is near, the Society has defined its mission as bringing as many as possible into the "new system" before Armageddon.

On three occasions, Zellner spent half a day with a Jehovah's Witness who was proselytizing. He was not convinced that the Witness liked the idea of his tagging along. Because Zellner had not completed his home Bible study, the elder felt Zellner's training was inadequate to the task. It was only after Zellner assured the elder that he would be friendly, but leave the Bible talk to him, that the elder reluctantly allowed him to go along.

Two of the trips were to working-class neighborhoods, the other to a middle- to upper-middle-class area. Very few doors were opened to the pair, and what little success they did have was in the working-class neighborhoods. The Witness making the calls was employed by a janitorial service. When he got his foot in a door, he not only talked about the Bible, but about his family and job as well. He had much in common with most of the working-class people to whom he spoke—shared backgrounds, experiences, and problems.

Not surprisingly, a proselytizing butcher does not attract a college student; rather, he or she tends to attract a carpenter or a plumber. A working-class housewife is more likely to develop rapport with a widow working in a school lunchroom than she is with a banker. As a group, Jehovah's

Witnesses have similar social-class backgrounds, one of the consequences of the proselytizing process.[29] According to a national survey, Jehovah's Witnesses tend to be more working class. About 42 percent earn less than $30,000, compared to 31 percent for the general population. Seven out of ten have no college compared to half of the country as a whole.[30]

Bonding   Forming an "affective bond" (an emotional relationship) with one or more members of the group is the keystone to conversion for most Witnesses. Kate Williams's response to the survey question "Before attending formal group meetings, did you form a close tie with one or more of the Witnesses?" was typical. Thirteen of the eighteen Witnesses interviewed had their first encounter with the Society when Witnesses called on them at their homes. All of the Witnesses interviewed reported having formed an affective bond with one or more Witnesses before becoming active in the group.

Bonding is more important than dogma. The differences between Witness dogma and conventional Christian dogma are not emphasized in the proselytizing process. What is emphasized are the similarities. Zellner made the following observations concerning his home Bible study program:[31]

> It was several months before my instructor revealed that Christ was not God incarnate, long after an affective social bond, under ordinary circumstances, would have been formed. It would have been very difficult to break a strong interactive bond based on that one bit of information. The dogma comes in bits and pieces.
>
> I was never lied to, but when I did not initiate the "hard" questions associated with doctrinal differences between the Witnesses and normative Protestant denominations, the differences were not revealed until my instructor thought I was ready for the "truth."[32]

There are no half-hearted Witnesses. The price for not buying wholeheartedly into the belief system, after a reasonable length of time, is possible loss of interaction and the cutting of affective bonds. The potential convert must accept Society teachings or risk losing interaction in the form of primary-group relationships.

---

[29]There are notable exceptions. Rock star Michael Jackson was once a Jehovah's Witness, as was Mickey Spillane, the creator of the fictional detective Mike Hammer, and President Dwight D. Eisenhower. Other members with differing levels of activity include the singer Prince, the late singer Selena, actor Terrance Howard *(Crash)*, the Wayans brothers and sisters, supermodel Naomi Campbell, and Evelyn Mandella (first wife of Nelson Mandela).

[30]Pew Forum, *U.S. Religious Landscape,* pp. 56, 60.

[31]Zellner was working as a Pinkerton security guard during the course of his "participant observation" of the Jehovah's Witnesses. He did not reveal to the Witnesses that he was a sociologist.

[32]Zellner, "Of Another World," pp. 101–2.

Meaningful bonds are apparently formed very quickly. Kate Williams responded to the survey question "How long was it before you moved from verbal agreement with the group to commitment, attending regular meetings, and so on?" that she and her husband began attending meetings right away. This was not an unusual response. Of the eighteen Witnesses interviewed, most became active in a period varying from a few weeks to a few months; only one held out as long as six months.

Need for Certitude   A "need for certitude" is a necessary, but not sufficient, condition for conversion to the Jehovah's Witnesses. All eighteen converts felt that their lives lacked direction before encountering the group, all felt that a pattern for life was important, and all felt that their conversion satisfied this need. The Witness belief system is conformity-demanding.

Prescriptions for action cover every situation. Converts are told exactly what is required of them in family situations or job situations, and how to act in the presence of nonbelievers. The Society provides a way to cope with the suffering and inequities of Satan's world. The plan meets the human need for certitude, provides light beyond death, and becomes the convert's *raison d'être*.

Anomie   First used by Émile Durkheim and now a part of the standard sociological vocabulary, the term **anomie** refers to a sense of powerlessness or worthlessness, leading eventually to a feeling of alienation. An anomic person feels left out of the mainstream of society, and because of this state of normlessness, an individual's survival comes into question. At least, this was Durkheim's belief.

As applied to people who join the Jehovah's Witnesses, *anomie* is perhaps too strong a term. Note, however, that five of the eighteen converts had just moved to a new community where they had no family and few or no friends. Four had weak or nonexistent family ties even before they encountered the Jehovah's Witnesses. Family ties, in most cases, suffer further strains after conversions. For those who feel a need for primary-group relations, the Society offers access to such relationships with like-minded people.

Shared Values before Conversion   The convert must accept new religious dogma, but most share similar social values before conversion. Society literature merely confirms and refines what most converts already believed about the world.

Also, most converts share many of the Society's social values before encountering the group. For example, the Society generally rejects voting; only two of the Witnesses interviewed voted before joining the group. Most were fundamentalists, and believed the Bible should be taken literally. All believed that the male should be dominant in the family unit. The Society emphasizes that people should work with their hands and strongly denounces higher education; all the converts worked with their hands before joining the group. The Society provides support for those who, for whatever reason, are not well educated in the traditional sense. Joining the Society adds group affirmation and justification for a lifestyle already chosen.

The Religious Perspective

Sociologists recognize three major problem-solving perspectives: religious, psychological, and political. Most people employ all three in their efforts to resolve life's problems. There are those, however, who tend to rely only on one perspective. Members of a radical political party emphasize a political problem-solving ideology, whereas people who buy self-help books from supermarket shelves tend to use the psychological perspective. Devoutly religious people almost exclusively answer life's questions with religious explanations. All eighteen Witnesses interviewed believed strongly in God and had a religious problem-solving perspective before joining the movement.

House Calls   Conversionist religious groups do not convert atheists or agnostics. Any door-to-door vacuum cleaner salesperson can relate to this argument. Rarely does a salesperson knock on a door to have it opened by someone who shouts, "Hey! That's just what I was looking for!" Salespeople must knock on many doors; when they find one open, they must sell first themselves and then the sweeper. For the vacuum cleaner salesperson to have a chance, the potential customer must have a rug. For the Witness proselytizer, the customer's rug must be a religious problem-solving perspective.

Jehovah's Witnesses are believers; there is no doubt about that. Zellner discusses the rejection Witnesses encounter when seeking converts door-to-door: "I will never forget the few field trips I made with a Witness proselytizer. Next to no-one-at-home, I considered polite indifference a good call. After the Witness introduced himself, the occupant usually said, 'I'm a Presbyterian, Catholic, Jew, or whatever.' What the prospect meant was 'I'm not open to a new religious outlook,' and doors closed to us very quickly."[33]

Proselytizing and perceived persecution are important "supports of faith." The Witnesses uniformly perceive the rejection they encounter in their missionary work as persecution; this common feeling creates internal cohesion and a strong we-feeling. They are convinced that the world

[33]Zellner, "Of Another World," p. 106.

is on the brink of the millennium, the time when Satan's strength is on the increase. They talk endlessly about those they meet who are in poor spiritual condition, and the many good people deceived by Satan.

Cold calls, knocking on the doors of strangers, has even forced the Witnesses into court. In the wake of 9/11, communities started to require permits for door-to-door calling. However, in the 2002 Supreme Court decision *Watchtower Bible and Tract Society v. Stratton*, the justices supported the Witnesses' right to knock on doors without permits. It was decided that to restrict their ability to do so would be a violation of their First Amendment rights.[34]

Past Relationships   Most Jehovah's Witnesses more or less sever relations with the outside world; meaningful relationships occur only within the microcosm. In response to the survey question "Did your becoming a Witness cause a strain between you and other family members?" only two of the eighteen converts reported any degree of normality in family relationships, and both felt there was room for improvement. Many had tried to convert relatives but had given up. All hoped their relatives would someday understand "the truth."

In response to the question "Did your joining the group strain relationships between you and your friends?" all eighteen Witnesses reported changing friends after joining the Society; a few reported having few or no friends before membership. The new friends were, of course, Jehovah's Witnesses.

Alienation   Eleven converts reported that they had, at one time or another, been chided at their workplace because of their beliefs. Through interaction, Witnesses share common definitions of situations, and all felt sorry for their tormentors. For the convert, religion is a matter to be taken seriously and never joked about. There is no question that Witnesses are alienated in most situations outside the microcosm, yet it is alienation with hope—not hope that they will someday fit in, but a hope that someday the rest of the world will join them.

Group Membership   As previously noted, the Society effectively promotes primary-group relationships. When the Sunday meetings are over, Witnesses do not leave their religion at the Kingdom Hall. They consider themselves "of another world," and spend as much time as possible in their self-created microcosm. In many ways, they are social isolates: most are alienated from their families, and most have few friends outside the group. What they do have is each other, and they interact much like an extended family.

---

[34]Joel P. Engardio, "Opening the door for us all," *USA Today*, May 6, 2007, p. 13A.

Argot   Argot is the special language peculiar to a group. The Witness microcosm has a special language, uniquely its own, which adds to the desired feeling of separation of "us" from "them." Only a few examples need be cited to illustrate the depth and richness of this language.

Witnesses always refer to God as Jehovah, in the belief that he would prefer his people call him by his name. They note that "Jehovah"—not "God"—appears 6,961 times in the original Hebrew Scriptures.

"Sheep and goats" is a commonly used term in the argot. A sheep is a person receptive to a Witness proselytizer, a goat is not. Biblical justification for this usage rests in Matthew 24:32: "And all the nations will be gathered about Him, and He will separate the sheep from the goats."

"In the truth" is another common argot term. This means an understanding of Jehovah's plan, and a willingness to live by it. A Baptist or Pentecostal might ask, "Are you saved?" A Witness would ask, "Are you in the truth?"

The 144,000 who will serve in heaven with Christ are referred to as the "mystery class" or the "little flock." Christ told his disciples that this group would "know" the "mysteries" of the Kingdom of Heaven. More commonly, the 144,000 are called the "little flock," derived from Luke 12:32, in which Christ said, "Have no fear, little flock, because your Father has approved of giving you the kingdom."

Jehovah's Witnesses believe that they will survive Armageddon, should they be alive when the battle takes place. They refer to this survivor-class as "Jonadabs" or "other sheep." It is thought that this group, along with Witnesses returned from the dust, will be the leaders and teachers in the "new system." The "new system" is defined as Jehovah's Kingdom on earth under theocratic law.

The Meetings

In general, Witnesses consider group membership the most important aspect of their lives. Most spend as much time as possible in organizational activity. The structure of these meetings is not left to local congregations; a printed format outlining what is to be done during the entire year is sent from the Society in New York, and local congregations must not deviate from the plan. Only meeting hours may vary from one congregation to the next.

Witnesses have five formal meetings each week, and each represents an important support of faith. All Witnesses are expected to attend as many meetings as possible. Sickness and secular employment are acceptable excuses for missing, but if too many meetings are missed, a flagging Witness can expect a visit from a group of brothers.

The first hour each Sunday is labeled a "Bible Educational Talk." The talks range from denouncing "the evils of the United Nations" to "how to communicate within one's family." The speaker, an elder, always relates his topic to Scripture. In urban areas, the speaker is sometimes a visiting elder from another congregation in the city; rural congregations as well will occasionally exchange speakers.

The second hour of the Sunday meeting is spent reading the current issue of the *Watchtower*. After a reader has read a paragraph from the text, the congregation is asked to respond to a question printed at the bottom of the page. The questions are numbered and correspond to the numbered paragraph in the *Watchtower* containing the answer. Many hands are raised. Ushers, usually teenage and always males, carry microphones on metal poles, and when the reader calls on one of the congregation to respond, an usher extends his pole down the aisle so the responder can read back the paragraph that has just been read. When a question appears easy enough, the reader will occasionally call on one of the children in the congregation to answer. If the child responds correctly, everyone beams approvingly.

Pioneers and Publishers   To be a Jehovah's Witness is to surrender one's self to the group. Proselytizing—Witnessing for Jehovah—is expected, and almost every Witness is involved in the activity. Proselytizers are divided into four categories: special pioneers, pioneers, auxiliary pioneers, and publishers.

Special pioneers commit themselves to a minimum of 150 hours each month in active fieldwork. Those in this category receive ninety dollars per month from the Society, the same as Bethel workers. This, of course, does not begin to cover their expenses. Special pioneers are often retired or are the wives of working men who can economically support the activity.

The pioneers in the congregation committed themselves to a minimum of ninety hours per month in the field. There were also auxiliary pioneers working sixty hours per month. During the winter, there had been a drop in the latter category and when the presiding elder of the congregation was asked about the drop in numbers, he winked and said, "The numbers will improve again when cold weather sets in. Many Witnesses have lawns and gardens to take care of."[35] Witnesses who dropped from the rank of auxiliary pioneer for the summer, of course, did not stop proselytizing altogether; they became publishers.

Most members of the Minnesota congregation were publishers and worked ten to fifteen hours per month in the field. Most male Witnesses worked at low-income blue-collar jobs, and many had working wives. It was difficult for these people to attend all the Witness functions and also make field calls, but they did so remarkably well.

[35]Zellner, "Of Another World," pp. 103–4.

Concluding Observations

Adult Witnesses are convinced that their religion is the only true religion, and salvation is possible only through Jehovah's plan as revealed by the Society. All other religions are false religions, and the Witnesses do not want their children associated with nonbelievers. But they have no choice. The Society does not maintain schools of its own, and Witness parents are required by law to send their children to secular schools. At a tender age, their young are forced out of the microcosm and into Satan's world.

The Witnesses do everything possible to isolate their children from the contaminating effects of a public education. Their children are not allowed to salute the flag, vote in school elections, run for class office, or sing the national anthem or school songs. They are not allowed to celebrate holidays, participate in extracurricular activities, date, attend school dances, or join school clubs. The Society in 1983 published a thirty-two-page booklet, *School and Jehovah's Witnesses,* setting out what their children can and cannot do in school. Witness children are instructed to give the publication to their teachers.

Despite efforts to isolate their offspring from mainsteam activities, children do not always share the religious zeal of their parents. But while the Society does lose some of its children, membership loss appears to be small. The Witness "socialization" process is effective, and although some do stray, it is usually only for a short time. Children raised in a close-knit social group often come to find life outside the group intolerable.

Kate Williams responded to the survey question "Are they [your children] members of the group?" that she was concerned for her children; she may well have been overly concerned. Although five of her eight children were living outside the Kingdom, this does not mean that they had joined other religious organizations. To be fully part of the "new system" means that meetings must be attended regularly and field commitments met. Young people sometimes find it difficult to meet these obligations. The best guess is that Kate Williams's children will return to full-time Witness activity.

The Society is an established sect. Witnesses are "of another world," and it appears that they will remain so. The believers are uncompromising; they refuse to acknowledge the legitimacy of any other religious organization, and believe the direction that they have taken is the only path to salvation. The Society continues to grow, because the members work long and hard, with Matthew 24:14 always in mind: "And this good news of the kingdom will be preached in all the inhabited earth for a witness to all the nations; and then the end will come."

KEY TERMS

Anomie, p. 230

Argot, p. 233

Armageddon, p. 219

Deformation thesis, p. 212

Disfellowship, p. 221

Eschatology, p. 218

Millenarian movement, p. 206

SOURCES ON THE WEB

www.watchtower.org
The official Web site of the Watchtower Society, the publication arm of the Jehovah's Witnesses.

http://www.jw-media.org/
The official Web site for public information.

www.ajwrb.org/
The Associated Jehovah's Witnesses for Reform on Blood actively argues against the Witnesses position on blood transfusions and related medical procedures.

SELECTED READINGS

Abrahams, Kyria. *I'm Perfect, You're Doomed: Tales from a Jehovah's Witness Upbringing.* New York: Touchstone, 2009.

Alfs, Matthew. *The Evocative Religion of Jehovah's Witnesses: An Analysis of a Present-Day Phenomenon.* Minneapolis: Old Theology Book House, 1991.

Beckford, James A. *Trumpet of Prophecy.* New York: Wiley, 1975.

Blackwell, Victor V. *O'er the Ramparts They Watched.* New York: Hearthstone, 1976.

Bowman, Robert M., Jr. *Understanding Jehovah's Witnesses: Why They Read the Bible the Way They Do.* Grand Rapids, MI: Baker Book House, 1991.

Franz, Raymond. *In Search of Christian Freedom.* Atlanta: Commentary Press, 1991.

Gaylin, Willard. *In the Service of Their Country: War Resisters in Prison.* New York: Viking, 1970.

Harrison, Barbara Grizzuti. *Visions of Glory.* New York: Simon & Schuster, 1978.

Hoekema, Anthony A. *Jehovah's Witnesses.* Grand Rapids, MI: Eerdmans, 1974.

Holden, Andrew. *Jehovah's Witnesses: Portrait of a Contemporary Religious Movement.* London: Routledge, 2002.

Insight on the Scriptures, vol. 1. New York: Watchtower Bible and Tract Society of New York, 1988.

Insight on the Scriptures, vol. 2. New York: Watchtower Bible and Tract Society of New York, 1988.

Manwaring, David R. *Render unto Caesar: The Flag Salute Controversy.* Chicago: University of Chicago Press, 1962.

Penton, M. James. *Apocalypse Delayed: The Story of Jehovah's Witnesses.* Toronto: University of Toronto Press, 1985.

Pike, Edgar Royston. *Jehovah's Witnesses: Who They Are, What They Teach, What They Do.* New York: Philosophical Press, 1954.

Reasoning from the Scriptures. New York: Watchtower Bible and Tract Society of New York, 1985.

Reed, David A., ed. *Index of Watchtower Errors,* comp. Steve Huntoon and John Cornell. Grand Rapids, MI: Baker Book House, 1990.

Rogerson, Alan. *Millions Now Living Will Never Die: A Study of Jehovah's Witnesses.* London: Constable, 1969.

Sterling, Chandler. *The Witnesses: One God, One Victory.* Chicago: Regency, 1975.

Stevens, Leonard A. *Salute! The Case of the Bible vs. the Flag.* New York: Coward, McCann & Geoghegan, 1973.

Stroup, Herbert Hewitt. *The Jehovah's Witnesses.* New York: Columbia University Press, 1945.

White, Timothy. *A People for His Name: A History of Jehovah's Witnesses and an Evaluation.* New York: Vantage Press, 1968.

Your Youth: Getting the Best Out of It. New York: Watchtower Bible and Tract Society of New York, 1976.

CHAPTER SEVEN

THE FATHER DIVINE MOVEMENT

The Peace Mission movement is extraordinary for a variety of reasons. Its founder and spiritual leader was a black man, Father Divine. Members of the Mission were very proud to be Americans and advanced the principles of democratic government, but they remained steadfastly antiwar, even during World War II. His followers in urban United States were primarily African American, but there was a substantial White membership. At the height of the movement's success, Father Devine was more ardently praised and revered by his followers than any other religious leader in the United States. To those who believed, he was more than just an exalted person. He was, quite simply, God.

Father Divine has now been dead for forty years and for all that time the head of the Peace Mission Movement has been Mother Divine. Mother Divine, a White woman born Edna Rose Ritchings, is the Father's second wife. They married in 1946 when she was not yet twenty-two. I visited her in 2005 at the Woodmont estate in Pennsylvania.[1]

[1]This account is based on Richard Schaefer's two meetings with Mother Divine and visit at the Woodmont estate of the movement, Gladwyne, Pennsylvania, August 14, 2005.

Meeting Mother Divine

A Rosebud led me to the study for my opportunity to meet the faith's leader. Reflecting the nationalistic pride of Peace Mission, she was wearing a blue skirt, white blouse, and a red blazer embroidered with a large V—a uniform unchanged for over seventy years. When I asked her what the V stood for she said "virtue" or "victory." But I know that the letter originally stood for "virgin," since Rosebuds, the choir and communion attendants of the faith, take a lifelong pledge of celibacy.

Within a few minutes I met Mother Divine, who, at age eighty, makes a striking, handsome presence, dressed in a white dress and speaking in a very engaging, alert demeanor. She was interested in knowing where I was from; upon learning that I was from Chicago, she recalled the woman who had led the Peace Mission there that had been closed now for a generation. She was pleased to know I was familiar with the teachings of Father Divine and said that they had ceased producing their publication *New Day* and were now reaching so many more through their Web site. One of the Rosebuds made sure I had a card with the site's address (www.libertynet.org/fdipmm/) before I left the estate.

As I talked with her in the sunlit study of Father Divine, which has remained relatively undisturbed since his death in 1965, I noticed she sat in a chair next to his large oak desk—his desk chair and his chair at the head of the table in the dining room are never sat in by anyone, since his spirit remains with the faithful. Outside the study windows I could see the Shrine to Life that I had earlier been allowed to enter, in which the earthly remains of Father Divine are entombed in a crypt said to resemble the Ark of the Covenant—the chest that Christians say holds the Ten Commandments.

Not all the visitors were able to enter the Shrine through the doors called the "Portal of Life Eternal," much less were permitted to speak with Mother Divine. Those dressed with bare shoulders or women in short skirts or pants were kindly escorted around the mansion by a Rosebud, but went barely farther than the Great Hall entrance, with its large picture of Father and Mother Divine. They were allowed to view the Shrine to Life only from the outside and at a distance of about a hundred yards.[2]

As different Rosebuds showed me around the serene estate, it was difficult to think that I was at the headquarters of a religious faith rather than immersed in a historical tour of a 32-room mansion dating back to 1892. The religious commitment among the five or so followers present was evident, and their continued devotion to Father Divine was palpable, but the energy of thousands of followers coming together at one time as had occurred in the past was but a memory on this warm August afternoon in 2005.

[2]A description of the Shrine to Life and limited interior photographs appear in D. Roger Howlett, *The Sculptures of Donald De Lue: Gods, Prophets, and Heroes* (Boston: David R. Godine, 1990), pp. 159–65.

Let's imagine what the scene might have been in one of the many Circle Mission churches across the United States in the 1950s when members of the Peace Mission Movement awaited the arrival of Father Divine.

The Communion Banquet

The U-shaped banquet table is decked in spotless linen, shining silverware, and fresh flowers. Each place setting includes a goblet with a cone-shaped napkin, in the center of which stands a small American flag. Just above the head table is a neon sign, FATHER DIVINE'S HOLY COMMUNION TABLE, and underneath the sign there are three large American flags. On the left wall is a felt banner with PEACE embroidered in large, even letters. On the right wall is a printed sign with the unsurpassable message: FATHER DIVINE IS GOD ALMIGHTY. All in all, it is a striking scene, and the 250 assembled guests—a mixture of Blacks and Whites—seem well aware of the fact.

The room itself vibrates with excitement and anticipation. Suddenly the tempo increases. There are several screams and shouts. From somewhere, a female voice rings out, "He's here! Father's here!" There is mass movement toward the doorway, where the curtains are parting. Then Father Divine—accompanied by Mother Divine on his right—breaks into the room with no uncertain step.

He is an African American man, short of stature, with smooth skin. His head is shiny bald, and while at the moment his face is impassive, his eyes are quick and penetrating. He wears jewelry: a diamond ring, an expensive-looking wristwatch, a gold chain across his vest, and two emblematic lapel buttons. Yet the overall effect is not one of pomp or flash. Father Divine's suit is dark and well cut, his tie is a conservative stripe, and his shoes are black.

Despite his diminutive size, it is apparent—to those present, at least—that he is a commanding personality. Every step of his buoyant walk, every gesture, every nod of his head brings gasps of delight from the onlookers. Several of the women jump high into the air.

Although Father Divine appears to be of indeterminate middle age, Mother Divine is clearly much younger. She is immaculately dressed. Almost a head taller than her husband, she gazes at him from time to time with genuine adoration. In addition to being his wife, she obviously is also one of his most devoted followers.

Together they make their way to the head table. Although the throng presses in closely, no one so much as touches Father. On his part, Father Divine seems to take the adulations for granted. Neither condescending nor overbearing, he acts with good-natured dignity and restraint. It is apparent that he is in command of the situation at all times.

Father and Mother Divine are seated, and because Father's feet do not reach the floor, a cushioned stool is placed under them. His followers return to their tables, and the noise subsides. The communion banquet is about to begin.

And what a banquet it is! A dozen different vegetables, roast beef, fried chicken, baked ham, roast turkey and duck, meat loaf, steak, cold cuts, spareribs, liver and bacon, four different kinds of bread, mixed salad with a choice of dressing, celery and olives, coffee, tea, and milk, and a variety of desserts, including layer cake, pie, pudding, fresh fruit, and great mounds of ice cream.

A corps of waitresses—immaculately clad in white—stands by, ready to help with the food. Each dish is first placed in front of Father Divine, who blesses it by touching the dish or adding a serving fork or spoon. The dishes are then passed on to the guests. The waitresses enthusiastically pour coffee, refill empty plates, help circulate the dishes, and otherwise encourage the diners to enjoy what Father Divine calls "the abundance of the fullness."

With so many courses, so much food, and so many people, the serving and eating process takes a good deal of time—two and a half hours, to be exact. There is never a dull moment, however; in fact, there is so much happening that it is difficult to follow it all.

A thickset Black woman suddenly jumps to her feet and thrusts both arms upward. "I was paralyzed!" she shouts in a throbbing voice. "No movement in the legs—none at all. And then I met you, Father, and you cured me. I am yours forever, Father, with true devotion!" She sits down and buries her head in her arms.

A middle-aged White woman stands up. "I had tuberculosis real bad. It was consumption. I coughed all day, and I coughed all night, and they told me I was a goner. Then you came into my life, Father, and made me well again overnight. I love you, Father, truly love you."

A thin Black man with gray-white hair gets up slowly. "Before I was twenty, I was put in jail twice for stealing. Each time, I told the judge I didn't do it, but in my heart I knew I did. I was a bad boy, and I grew up to be a bad man. I set my neighbor's car on fire and never told nobody—till now. It was only when God came to me in the form of Father Divine that I was able to resolve myself. Thank you, Father."

Festivities   The Rosebuds break into song at this point. They range in age from about ten to thirty-five, and all are dressed in red jackets and navy blue skirts.

There are approximately forty Rosebuds in the choir, and they sing their hearts out on every song. Their spirit is indomitable, inexhaustible. Although they are accompanied by a pianist, they have no sheet music to read. All their songs—dozens of them—are memorized. The words are original, although some of the songs are well-known melodies like "White Christmas" and "Anchors Aweigh."

During many of the songs the chorus is repeated, at which point the young women clap their hands and stamp their feet. When this happens, the audience joins in—and the chorus is likely to be repeated several more times. Unmistakably, the room is filled with happy singers. The only person not visibly affected is Father Divine himself, who acts as though the festivities were a routine part of his life. (Which indeed they are.)

Following the Rosebuds' songs, there are more confessions of sin and some additional tributes to Father Divine. One woman stands on a chair and shouts, "I love you, Father! Truly!" There is a chorus of agreement, after which individual testimonials are heard from all parts of the room.

"Blessed is the Lord!"

"I owe you everything, Father! Thank you, Father!"

"Bless his heavenly body!"

"Father Divine is *God Almighty!*"

At this point, the Lilybuds stand up and render a song. Dressed in attractive green jackets with white trim, the Lilybuds are an older version of the Rosebuds. There are perhaps fifty of them, and their ages seem to range from thirty-five up. Although they are not as vivacious as the Rosebuds, they do not lack enthusiasm. And their devotion to Father Divine is obviously unsurpassed. Their song has the ring of utmost sincerity.

> We want to be a real true Lilybud,
> Basking in our FATHER'S LOVE every day.
> We want to be a real true Lilybud,
> Obeying and doing what our precious FATHER says.

Now, for the first time, people are beginning to dance in the aisles. The dancing is unrehearsed, spontaneous, and individualistic. No two steps are alike, and no two people touch one another. Subdued at first, the movements and gesticulations accelerate as the evening wears on.

It is time now for a song from the Crusaders—the men's group. Although they include men of all ages, the Crusaders are a much smaller group than the Rosebuds or the Lilybuds. In fact, a large majority of those present at the banquet, both uniformed and nonuniformed, are female. There are about fifteen Crusaders, and they are dressed in powder blue coats, white shirts, and dark trousers. They sing lustily and—like their predecessors—with obvious devotion.

> I want to love YOU, FATHER,
> A little bit more each day,
> I want to love YOU, FATHER,
> In all I do and say.
> For the wondrous works YOU do,
> For I know YOU'RE GOD ALMIGHTY,
> And I've given this heart to YOU!

At the end of the song, the audience erupts with an outburst of clapping and shouting. There are more testimonials and dances, and more of the women leap into the air. One elderly gentleman lies down across three chairs, sobbing uncontrollably. But all such behavior appears to be taken for granted by the group itself. There seems to be a tacit sequence of events, and if the activity is becoming more feverish, it is because the sequence dictates that the program is coming to a climax. And sure enough, there is a stirring at the head table. Father Divine is getting up to speak.

The Sermon   As Father Divine looks into the eyes of his followers, there are shouts of "God! God! God!"; "Peace, Father!"; "Thank you, dear one!"; "Hallelujah!"; "I love you, Father!"; "God Almighty!" Once he commences to speak, however, all noise stops. For the duration of his talk, the audience gives him their full attention.

As he speaks, twenty-five young female secretaries take up their notebooks and write down Father's words in shorthand. As a matter of fact, everything Father Divine says—sermons, discourses, speeches, interviews, extemporaneous remarks—is recorded by the ever-ready secretaries. Their shorthand is then transcribed and appears in *New Day*, the movement's biweekly newspaper, thus preserving Father Divine's words for posterity.

Father Divine speaks in a strong, resonant voice, with a distinctive tone quality. Though he starts slowly—almost methodically—his audience is spellbound from the very first word. The sermon itself is a combination of the practical and the profound, the esoteric and the absurd, yet his phrasing is such that it is often difficult to tell which is which.

> Though we have Blessings unlimited economically, and though we have physical comfort and convenience for ourselves and for millions of others, yet back of all of it is IT, which said, "Let there be light, and there was light."
>
> Back of all of it was, as it is, the same, that while on the water, as so to speak, invisible, and spoke into visibility the earth upon which we are living, the beginning of the material and economic things of life![3]

Several times during his sermon, Father Divine punctuates an affirmation with "Aren't you glad!" And each time the audience answers with a resounding "Yes, so glad!" or "So glad, Lord!"

When the sermon is finished, there is a tumultuous burst of applause, and shouts of "So true, Father!"; "Thank you, Father!"; "Lord God Almighty!" People jump and whirl, and a number have tears in their eyes. Almost all are visibly moved. One woman clutches herself and screams, "I love you, sweetheart!" Another lies on the floor motionless, scarcely

---

[3]Full texts of sermons such as this one were reprinted periodically in the *New Day* until the printing operation closed in 1992. The Divinites have a Web site, as Mother Divine proudly told Schaefer in his August 14, 2005 interview.

noticed by the others. An elderly man takes his cane and whacks it against the table as hard as he can, the vibrating silverware adding to the din.

In the midst of all the exuberance, the Rosebuds rise and sing one of their inimitable songs, and there is more stamping and clapping. Additional testimonials and confessions follow—and further expressions of adulation for Father. Then the Lilybuds rise and sing. Then the Crusaders. Genuine ecstasy. Genuine rapture. No doubt about it. Only Father Divine manages to take it all in stride. In a few minutes, he and Mother Divine—with their entourage of secretaries and others—will leave and, quite possibly, visit another of their "heavens," where a similar spectacle will unfold.

"God in a Body"   Although it may read like fiction, this description of a Father Divine communion banquet is based on fact. The foregoing scene is a composite picture of actual happenings. Father Divine died in 1965, and while the movement continues, the enthusiasm has been necessarily dampened. Nevertheless, while he was alive, he was a phenomenally successful leader.

Who was this man, this superman, this "God in a body"? When and where was he born? What was his youth like? When did he first aspire to be God? Where did his financial support come from? How did his movement get to be worldwide in scope? Can it survive, now that "God" is no longer on earth?

Some of these questions are answerable; some—at the moment, at least—are not. From World War I to the present, the Father Divine story is traceable. It is far from complete, but the broad outlines are known. The period prior to World War I is the stickler. Here the picture is murky and tantalizing, and this is unfortunate. For if we knew the real origin and background of Father Divine the man, we would have a much better understanding of Father Divine in his role as a religious leader.

The George Baker Story

Relatively few books have been written about Father Divine, and most of them are out of date.[4] Moreover, the various accounts have been journalistic

---

[4]See Robert Allerton Parker, *The Incredible Messiah* (Boston: Little, Brown, 1937); John Hoshor, *God in a Rolls Royce: The Rise of Father Divine* (1936; reprint, Freeport, NY: Books for Libraries Press, 1971); Sarah Harris, *Father Divine: Holy Husband* (1953; reprint, New York: Macmillan, 1971). See also the series by St. Clair McKelway and A. J. Liebling, "Who Is This King of Glory?" *New Yorker*, June 13, 1936, pp. 21ff; June 20, 1936, pp. 22ff; and June 27, 1936, pp. 22ff. There have been hundreds of articles about Father Divine in publications such as *Time*, *Newsweek*, and the *New York Times*.

in nature, and some gross differences in reporting exist. In recent years, fortunately, there has been some scholarly interest in the subject, and during the 1980s and 1990s several revealing works have appeared.[5]

Although our knowledge of Father Divine's early years is admittedly spotty, it seems that there was once a man named George Baker. His date of birth has been reported as anywhere between 1860 and 1880, depending on who is doing the reporting. According to the most recent of these accounts, he was born in 1878 in Monkey Run, a Black ghetto at the northern edge of Rockville, Maryland.

His parents were Nancy and George Baker, Sr., two former slaves. Both were hard workers; in fact, as a house servant, Nancy was called on to work day and night. Unfortunately, her heavy schedule did not prevent her from gaining weight, and eventually "her obesity rendered her incapable of working."[6]

The episode is mentioned in some detail because it seems to have had a bearing on young George Baker's subsequent actions. Watts writes: "One day not long after his mother died, George Baker vanished from Rockville. He fled the poverty and agony of Monkey Run, leaving behind relatives and friends puzzled over his disappearance. He rejected destitution, his obese mother, his struggling family, and the white racism that promised to imprison him in Monkey Run for life."[7]

The Peace Mission offers little information about Father Divine's early life, viewing it largely irrelevant to his spiritual mission. They do emphatically deny his name was George Baker, and instead present his full name as Major Jealous Divine.

The whereabouts and activities of the man who would become Father Divine remain unknown for the next two or three years. There are isolated reports of his refusing to attend Jim Crow schools, of being jailed for riding in the Whites-only section of a trolley car, of being a Sunday school superintendent, and of spending six months on a chain gang. None of the accounts have been proved—or disproved. It is not until around 1900 that the various biographical accounts tend to converge.

By that year, George Baker had settled in Baltimore, working as a gardener during the day and as an assistant preacher at night and on Sundays. He was neither more nor less successful than other Black ministers of the

[5]See Stephen Zwick, "The Father Divine Peace Mission Movement" (Senior Thesis: Princeton University, 1971); Roma Barnes, "Blessings Flowing Free: The Father Divine Peace Mission Movement in Harlem, New York City, 1932–1941" (Ph.D. diss., University of York, England, 1979); Kenneth E. Burnham, *God Comes to America: Father Divine and the Peace Mission Movement* (Boston: Lambeth, 1979); Jill Watts, *God, Harlem U.S.A.: The Father Divine Story* (Berkeley: University of California Press, 1992); and Robert Weisbrot, *Father Divine and the Struggle for Racial Equality* (Urbana: University of Illinois Press, 1983).

[6]Watts, *God, Harlem U.S.A.*, p. 6.

[7]Watts, *God, Harlem U.S.A.*, p. 6.

period who were forced to take outside jobs—until fate intervened one Sunday morning in 1907, in the form of one Samuel Morris.

Although reports differ on how the two men met, the meeting itself had a profound and lasting effect on George Baker. Samuel Morris rejected the usual hellfire-and-damnation approach to salvation and instead taught that God dwells within every person. One report has it that Morris proclaimed himself to be God and, upon being evicted from the church where he was preaching, was befriended by George Baker. Another report makes no mention of this episode but states simply that Baker was drawn to the religious philosophy of Samuel Morris, returning "again and again" to hear him preach.

In any case, it may have been at this time that George Baker caught the idea of becoming God. Prior to his association with Morris, his sermons had given no inkling of heavenly aspirations, but by 1907 he seems to have become intertwined—apparently forever—with the Deity.

Although the details at this point are not clear, Samuel Morris and George Baker evidently worked out an arrangement whereby they shared the godship. Also, at this time, both men apparently changed their names (or were "reborn"). Samuel Morris was henceforth known as Father Jehovia, and George Baker became known as the Messenger.

In 1908 they were joined by a third man, John Hickerson, a tall, African American minister with an imposing voice. Not to be outdone by his companions, Reverend Hickerson also adopted a more spiritual name, St. John the Vine. Although Father Jehovia (Samuel Morris) seems to have been number one, the three men were somehow able to share their divinity, and for the next several years they were as flamboyant a preaching team as the area had ever seen.

The Messenger   In 1912 the triumvirate broke up. Presumably, they were no longer willing to share their divine authority, and in any case they went their separate ways. St. John the Vine Hickerson traveled to New York City,

The Father Divine Movement

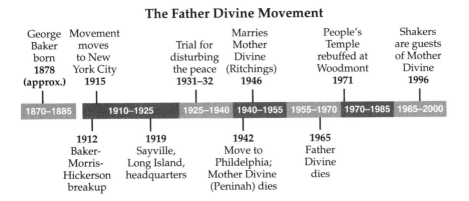

George Baker born 1878 (approx.)	Movement moves to New York City 1915	Trial for disturbing the peace 1931–32	Marries Mother Divine (Ritchings) 1946	People's Temple rebuffed at Woodmont 1971	Shakers are guests of Mother Divine 1996

| 1870–1885 | 1910–1925 | 1925–1940 | 1940–1955 | 1955–1970 | 1970–1985 | 1985–2000 |

1912 Baker-Morris-Hickerson breakup	1919 Sayville, Long Island, headquarters	1942 Move to Phildelphia; Mother Divine (Peninah) dies	1965 Father Divine dies

where he founded his own church. Father Jehovia passed from the picture and for all intents and purposes was never heard from again. The Messenger (George Baker) turned southward, gained some converts, and—if we can believe his biographers—ran into a pack of trouble.

At Valdosta, Georgia, in 1913, the Messenger was preaching the gospel in his own unique style. The townspeople were entranced and turned out in large numbers to hear the man who called himself God. While reports vary, there were some in the audience who were not impressed. Among the skeptics were a number of local pastors, who had the Messenger arrested and taken to court. The charge: being of unsound mind, as anyone proclaiming himself or herself to be God must be.

For reasons best known to themselves, the jury upheld the charge, and the Messenger was declared insane. Instead of committing him to a mental institution, however, the court ordered him to leave the state of Georgia forthwith. He did so, and as far as we know, he never returned.

In spite of the resistance and harassment he met in the South, however, the Messenger did succeed in gaining converts. They were few, to be sure—probably not more than a dozen—but they were dedicated believers, and they would form the nucleus of his forthcoming religious organization. One person is worthy of particular mention: a stout, African American woman called Peninah, or Sister Penny. Before the group left the South, Sister Penny was reportedly the Messenger's chief angel.

The New York City Period

In 1915, the Messenger and his disciples arrived in New York City, undaunted by their troubles and apparently none the worse for wear. After a brief stay in Manhattan, the little group settled in Brooklyn. Starting in a rooming house, they began to develop the format for what would one day be a worldwide religious organization.

As they struggled to survive in the big city, the Messenger himself was in touch with his old friend and fellow deity, St. John the Vine Hickerson. Hickerson's own church—the Church of the Living God—had been fairly successful. The Messenger attended Hickerson's services, checked his methods, asked questions, and otherwise borrowed from St. John the Vine's repertoire.

Along with modest success, however, Hickerson was also having some difficulty. Like his mentor, Father Jehovia (Samuel Morris), St. John the Vine taught that God was not in heaven but within every person. This meant that although Hickerson could be God, there could be any number of auxiliary gods—and this is exactly what was happening. Wearing "gold" and "silver" crowns and royal purple robes, these deities clogged the path to Hickerson's church.

Before long, St. John the Vine's church fell under the weight of its own gods. Although he did not pass into oblivion like Samuel Morris, John Hickerson became a relatively obscure figure. Following World War I, he was heard from less and less.

The Messenger himself severed all connection with John Hickerson and never referred to him publicly again. The little group in Brooklyn, meanwhile, was holding its own—perhaps even growing a bit. A few of the original members had left, but new ones kept joining. The Messenger was a persuasive speaker, and his followers genuinely revered him. He ran a tight ship, however, and unlike St. John the Vine, permitted only one God—himself. He made all the rules and brooked no interference, and he followed that practice all his life.

As to its living arrangements, the group operated communally. The Messenger himself did no work outside the church—nor would he, ever again. Instead, he ran an employment service, supplying domestics and menial workers to those who were looking for honest, reliable help. Whether or not they got their jobs through his employment service, however, the Messenger's followers presumably turned their wages over to him. He then paid the rent, bought the food, and took care of the necessary bills.

Peninah was in charge of the actual household management—including shopping and food preparation—and from all accounts she was an indefatigable worker. In fact, some observers believe that the Messenger

Father Divine at Thanksgiving Dinner in 1939 with his first wife, Sister Penny, and members of the movement, when its headquarters were in New York City.

married her during this period, though others set the date much earlier. But whatever the date, the marriage was spiritual in nature. It may also have been legal—though no marriage license has been uncovered—but it was not sexual.

Quite early in the movement, the Messenger declared that sex was unclean, a mark of depravity, and hence was forbidden. Neither he nor his followers have been known to violate the decree. We will return to this issue of sexual abstinence later in the chapter.

During the New York period, another interesting phenomenon occurred: the Messenger underwent further name changes. The reason is not entirely clear, but presumably he felt the need for a more appropriate title. In any case, just as George Baker evolved into the Messenger, so the Messenger evolved into Major Jealous Devine, which was eventually shortened to M. J. Devine, and finally—over a period of years—*M. J. Devine* became *Father Divine*. These latter changes, though gradual, are a matter of record and are not really in dispute. The dispute arises over the earlier sequence: the transition from George Baker to the Messenger, and from the Messenger to Major Jealous Devine. These name changes, along with Father Divine's stubborn refusal to acknowledge his heritage, created a genuine mystery that did not unravel until years after his death. Whenever he was asked when he was born, he might reply, "I wasn't born. I was combusted." He also answered queries about his birth with a scriptural "Before Abraham was, I am."

Sayville—The Turning Point

In 1911, Father Devine and his little group, numbering not more than two dozen, moved from Brooklyn to Sayville, Long Island. The house they moved to—an attractive, twelve-room dwelling at 72 Macon Street—still stands. It is used by the followers as a kind of shrine, for it was here that the movement first gained national and international recognition.

Things started off peacefully enough. If the White community was less than enthusiastic at the prospect of Blacks setting up in their midst, no overt reaction was initially apparent. In fact, for several years Sayville and its environs made good use of Father Divine's services. Operating an employment office—as he had in Brooklyn—Father Divine was able to supply reliable domestics for the many nearby estates.

From all accounts, Father Divine was a good neighbor. He kept 72 Macon Street spic-and-span. He worked in the garden. He was polite and friendly, with a ready smile. His followers did not inundate the neighborhood, as some had feared. The group did manage to grow in number—but slowly. They were not loud or unruly. There was no drinking. And there were never any sex problems.

Things went on this way for ten happy years.

Father Divine appeared to be consolidating his position. He was, in effect, learning how to combine the role of businessman with that of deity. On both counts, he was successful. As a businessman, he had the confidence and respect of the community—in spite of the general racial situation. And in his role as deity, he was superb.

African Americans of the 1920s were likely to be disadvantaged individuals. Faced with both social and economic discrimination, they often had a low level of aspiration and—more than occasionally—a feeling of hopelessness. Father Divine succeeded in imbuing his followers with a sense of hope and purpose.

He gave them economic security in the form of lodging, food, and employment. One source of jobs were Peace Mission-operated stores including shoe stores, grocery outlets, and hardware stores. He encouraged self-respect by insisting that workers give their employers an honest day's work for a day's pay. He forbade them to accept tips. He gave them a sense of self-discipline by prohibiting smoking, drinking, swearing, and "immodest behavior." And—above all else—he gave them spiritual security. For if he, Father Divine, was God Almighty, then his followers were assured of everlasting life.

To be sure, his followers had to make certain sacrifices. They had to renounce sex and marriage. They had to abide by Father Divine's rules and regulations, for he did not tolerate backsliders. And again, they presumably all turned their wages over to him. But these were small sacrifices compared to the economic and spiritual benefits involved.

Slowly but surely the fame of Father Divine spread. As the 1920s wore on, membership increased steadily. On Sundays, busloads of visitors would arrive at 72 Macon Street to see and hear God and partake of the mighty meals—thirty to forty courses every week, and all free! No collection plate was ever passed; no request for donations was ever made. When—invariably—the question was asked, "But where does the money come from to pay for it all?" the answer was always the same: "It comes from God."

In 1930, the Sunday bus excursions were joined by private automobiles—first dozens, then hundreds. To local residents, it seemed like an endless caravan. The banquets also grew in size and vigor. There were testimonials and increasing reports of miraculous cures. Then came the songs and the clapping. And the sermon. And the hallelujahs. And so on. To the citizens of Sayville, at least, things seemed to be getting out of hand. It was time that something was done.

At first there was police harassment. Many tickets for traffic and parking violations were issued in wholesale lots. When this tactic failed, the district attorney planted a female undercover agent at 72 Macon Street. Dressed as a poor African American working woman, the agent tried to verify rumors of sexual relations between Father Divine and his female followers. When this also failed, she tried to seduce Father Divine, but—by her own account—he ignored her. The only thing she could report was that everyone treated her with sympathy and kindness.

Next there were town meetings, with groups of angry residents demanding Father Divine's ouster. A committee of leading citizens was selected to visit 72 Macon Street and make their demands known. Father Divine received the group and listened patiently while they explained their point of view. Then he explained his. He and his followers were good citizens. They had broken no laws. He himself had helped Sayville economically by providing an employment service and by buying large quantities of food and supplies from local merchants. Furthermore, Father Divine pointed out, the Constitution guaranteed freedom of religion. So he was not going to leave Sayville. On the contrary, he was quite likely to expand his activities.

Father was polite, speaking in an even tone. But something in his manner told the committee that further discussion was futile, and they left. A short time later—during one of the Sunday services—police broke into 72 Macon Street and arrested Father Divine and eighty of his followers for disturbing the peace. The Sunday in question was November 15, 1931, a date that quite possibly marks the real beginning of the Father Divine movement. While the arrest itself was peaceful enough, the entire episode was a shot heard round the African American world.

Judge Lewis J. Smith   Despite the flimsiness of the case, Father Divine was indicted by the grand jury and held (on $1,500 bail) for trial. The Black press—and a sizable segment of the White press as well—took up the cry of racial discrimination, and the fight was on. News stories made the front pages, and publicity grew by leaps and bounds. Within a few weeks, Father Divine had become a *cause célèbre*. He himself, though not visibly perturbed, vowed to fight the case—and, if necessary, to "rot in jail" rather than succumb to the forces of intolerance and bigotry.

John C. Thomas, an African American lawyer who had been an assistant U.S. district attorney, offered his services to Father Divine, who accepted. The presiding judge in the case was Lewis J. Smith, who was White, and who—the record would show—was clearly antagonistic in his attitude toward the defendant. One of the judge's first acts was to cancel Father Divine's bail and remand him to jail for the duration of the trial. This action, based on a legal technicality, set the tone for the entire trial.

The actual proceedings were fairly clear-cut. The prosecution contended that Father Divine and his followers had annoyed the neighbors, disturbed the peace, obstructed traffic, and were a public nuisance. The defense naturally denied the allegations. Most of the witnesses were either neighbors (prosecution) or Father Divine's followers (defense). The only thing really noteworthy during the trial was the antagonism shown by Judge Smith toward several of the defense witnesses. It was easy to see where his sympathies lay.

Even in his charge to the jury, the judge showed partiality. He stated that Father Divine was a bad influence in the community, that his real name was not Father Divine but George Baker, that Mother Divine was not his legal wife, that he was not an ordained minister, and that he was able to induce others to turn their wages over to him.

After deliberating a short while, the jury—not unexpectedly—returned a verdict of guilty. They did, however, recommend leniency. Judge Smith adjourned the court for several days while he contemplated the sentence. The defendant, meanwhile, stayed in jail.

Public reaction was mixed. Some felt that Father Divine was in fact guilty as charged. Many fair-minded people, however, had come to the conclusion that he was innocent, a victim of unadulterated race prejudice.

Undaunted, Judge Smith reconvened the court and imposed the stiffest sentence the law allowed: one year in prison and a fine of five hundred dollars. Also undaunted, Father Divine went to prison, a quizzical expression on his face.

Three days later, Judge Lewis J. Smith was dead!

Only fifty years of age and apparently in good health, he reportedly had died of a heart attack.

When asked—in his cell—whether he had any comments regarding Judge Smith's demise, Father Divine replied, somewhat mournfully, "I hated to do it."[8]

Afterward, the appellate court overturned Father Divine's conviction, basing its decision on the "prejudicial comments" voiced by (the late) trial judge. The fines levied against Father Divine and his codefendants were also rescinded.

Why They Joined

The death of Judge Smith had an overwhelming effect on large segments of the African American community. Although most White newspapers carried the story in routine fashion, the Black press used banner headlines. In some neighborhoods, African Americans held parades and rallies. On June 26, 1932, for example—the day after Father Divine's release from prison—a "Monster Glory to Our Lord" rally was held at the Rockland Palace in Harlem. Lines started to form at five A.M., even though

---

[8]This statement has been reported countless times by various researchers, although Hoshor may have been the first (*God in a Rolls Royce*). Watts, in a more recent account, questions whether Father Divine ever "claimed direct responsibility for Smith's death" (*God, Harlem U.S.A.*; see her footnote 6, p. 211).

Father Divine wasn't scheduled to appear until noon. Over 7,000 persons jammed the auditorium, and thousands more were turned away.

Father Divine did not let his followers down. Shunning his usual figures of speech, he delivered one of the clearest talks of his career. Among other things, he said:

> You may not have seen my flesh for a few weeks, but I was with you just the same. I am just as operative in the mind as in the body. There were many who thought I had gone someplace, but I'm glad to say I did not go anywhere.
>
> I held the key to that jail all the time I was in it, and was with you every time you met. They can prosecute me or persecute me, or even send me to the electric chair, but they can never keep me from you or stop me from doing good![9]

When Father Divine finished his talk, the human explosion almost tore the roof off Rockland Palace. Eruptions of "Hallelujah!" "Sweet Savior!" "Father Divine is God Almighty!" rocked the auditorium. People jumped, screamed, shouted, shook, and whirled. Most were ecstatic, but some were overcome and wept. Harlem had never seen anything like it before.

After the waves of acclaim had passed, testimonials were heard. One woman had been cured of cancer through Father's intervention; another, of arthritis. A cripple had been healed and had thrown away his crutches. On and on they went, a spontaneous cascade of miracles.

Then the tone of the audience changed, and people began to complain not of their physical afflictions, but of their social oppression. They were poor and hungry. They lived in squalor and could not get jobs. They had no hope, no future. They needed help, and they needed it now—from God! Little by little, louder and louder, the chant was taken up: "Need you, Father! Need you! Need you! Need you!"[10]

What were the sociological factors that accounted for this mass attraction? To answer the question in generalized terms is easy: the right person was in the right place at the right time—with the right people. A more specific answer would involve a number of points.

Manifest versus Latent Function   As we noted with the Shakers, sociologist Robert Merton first proposed the concept of manifest versus latent function.[11] Many social processes and institutions have a dual function: a conscious, deliberate, or "manifest" function, and an unconscious, unrealized, or "latent" function. And so it was with the Father Divine movement. Men and women joined manifestly because they believed in the religious orientation of the group, but in a latent sense, the Divine movement provided them with certain rewards not otherwise attainable.

---

[9]Harris, *Father Divine*, pp. 42–44.
[10]Harris, *Father Divine*, pp. 42–44.
[11]Robert K. Merton, *Social Theory and Social Structure* (New York: Free Press, 1968).

Bettmann/Corbis

Members of the Father Divine movement were provided economic assistance through mission outreach programs in many cities, such as this one in Denver, Colorado, in 1937.

The nation was in the grip of the Great Depression, and as low persons on the economic totem pole, African Americans were the hardest hit. In many African American neighborhoods the housing was dreadful: run-down buildings, congestion, rats and roaches, three and four families sharing one toilet, no hot water, inadequate heat in the winter—year after year after year. Sickness, ill health, inadequate medical facilities, poor sanitary conditions, and a high death rate persisted, as did unemployment, desertion, drug addiction, and hopelessness. African Americans—particularly those in the lower class—did indeed need someone. And in the absence of a more appropriate candidate, it looked as though that someone might be Father Divine.

Of particular relevance here is the food factor. Social security, unemployment compensation, Medicare and Medicaid, Aid to Families with Dependent Children (AFDC), United Way, old-age assistance—such programs were still many years away. One of the first problems facing an unemployed person, therefore, was hunger. It is easy to see why Father Divine—whose daily services included huge quantities of free food—had such ready appeal. And whenever the question was asked, "But where does all the food come from—who pays for it?" the answer was always the same: "It comes from God, and God don't need money." Peace Mission grocery stores provided both employment for movement members and reasonably priced food to movement followers.

Indeed, the manifest reason most joined the movement was to be in God's inner circle. For many, the latent function was an escape from abject poverty.

The Racial Stereotype   The depression was not the only cause of African Americans' economic difficulties. Prejudice and discrimination were so widespread that even when jobs were available, African Americans were likely to be excluded. In the 1930s, even clerical and semiskilled occupations were generally closed to black applicants. One did not see Black sales-clerks in stores or Black secretaries in offices. One did not see Black bus drivers or mechanics or tradespeople.

In fact, in the 1930s, racial stereotyping was the order of the day. Originally defined as "pictures in the head," a **stereotype** can best be described as an unreliable generalization about all members of a group that does not recognize individual differences within a group. Thus, the belief by Whites that Blacks are lazy or inferior is a racial stereotype. And while sociologists are well aware that stereotyping still occurs, it is probably not so prevalent as it was two or three generations ago. In the 1930s, certainly, it was commonly believed by prejudiced Whites that Blacks were listless, unreliable, happy-go-lucky, and largely incapable of holding a job.

Because so much of Father Divine's program was aimed at the elimination of racial stereotyping and job discrimination, it is easy to see why he had such an impact on the African American community. It is no accident that his appeal was greatest in those areas where congestion, unemployment, and discrimination were rampant: Brooklyn, Manhattan, Newark, Jersey City, Philadelphia.

Alienation   Things were so bad for African Americans in the 1930s that a feeling of alienation often prevailed. As the term is used by sociologists, **alienation** is the condition of estrangement or dissociation from the surrounding society. Alienated persons feel that those in power have neglected them, and that there is nothing they can do about it. They believe that they have little or no control over their own destiny, and that—in effect—they have become dispensable.

More than any other leader of his time, it was Father Divine who fought against the spread of alienation, and he was a superb practitioner. He understood the masses. He could talk to them. He could engender feelings of self-respect, and he could play the role of God. Most important, he never lost sight of the two basics: food and jobs. These were the bedrock. As long as he was at the helm, Father Divine's followers would have ample food at little or no cost. And—through his employment service or within his own economic establishment—they would have jobs.

Food, jobs, and a joyous war against racism and alienation—no wonder large numbers of African Americans flocked to Father Divine's banner. Add to these his personal magnetism, his heavenly claims and obvious knowledge of the Bible, his penetrating voice and allegorical speech, his presumed healing powers, his spontaneous and vibrant manner, his intense concentration on goodness and fairness—for his followers, the result spelled God.

The Economic Structure

Over the years, there has been a good deal of misunderstanding regarding Father Divine's economic operations. His followers tended to believe that because he was God, he could "materialize" all the money he wanted, a notion that Father took no steps to dispel. The Internal Revenue Service, which had some genuine doubts about his deification, wondered why he never paid any income tax. After all, they reasoned, a man who wore expensive suits and diamond rings, who rode in Cadillac limousines and ate lavishly—such a man must also have a lavish income. Father Divine denied the imputation, and in a series of showdowns between church and state, the state lost.

During his long career, Father Divine never paid a penny in income taxes. His critics contended that, under the mantle of the Lord, he used his workers' salaries to line his own heaven with gold. His supporters countered with the argument that Father Divine had never asked anyone for money in his life, and that even in his own churches there was no such thing as a collection plate.

Actually, Father Divine's economic operations were not so complicated—or so secretive—as his critics claimed. While much of the day-to-day procedure never became public knowledge, enough is known to permit a reasonable description. The basic economic principle was remarkably simple: to feed and house ten people communally did not cost ten times as much as it would cost to feed and house a single individual, especially if the ten were willing to let the Lord handle the fiscal details. This was the principle Father Divine (as the Messenger) had followed in Brooklyn during World War I, and he adhered to it throughout his entire career.

The Hotel Business   Of all the economic enterprises under the aegis of Father Divine—and there were many—none was more successful than the hotel business, the structural network around which the movement revolved. For example, although the organization had a number of churches, or missions, many of the meetings and rallies were held in the hotels. Communion banquet services, like the one described earlier, were held in the hotels.

When it came to labor, problems were minimal. Instead of being staffed by employees demanding union wages, the hotels would employ Father Divine's followers, who would work for no wages whatsoever. Instead, they received room and board and the eternal care of a loving God, whom they were privileged to serve on a regular basis. And, of course, because they served outsiders, the hotels were profitable. This in turn enabled the movement to feed thousands of needy people virtually free of charge. One further point should be mentioned. Father Divine and his followers did not build their hotels; they bought them. Often in run-down condition, the buildings were refurbished—with the help of the faithful—and then opened for business. Father Divine had a remarkable eye for real estate values, and much of his success stemmed from his uncanny ability to ferret out bargains. Once he made his intentions known, it was not difficult to find the necessary backers. Large urban hotels such as the Divine Tracy (Philadelphia), the Divine Hotel Riviera (Newark), the Divine Fairmount (Jersey City), and the Divine Lorraine (Philadelphia) were all acquired in this manner, and all were operated successfully initially, but none are in operation today.

Father Divine was a strong believer in racial integration, and his hotels gave him the opportunity to practice what he preached. Blacks and Whites not only worked together side by side but—as a matter of policy—were assigned to the same room. Father Divine said the hotels were his "demonstrators of democracy in action."

Employment Service   Father Divine first started his employment service during the New York period (1915–1919). He had an obvious knack for placing domestic workers, and throughout his career the employment service remained his most successful operation, with the possible exception of the hotels.

The reason for his success is that, as previously mentioned, Father Divine insisted on an honest day's work for a day's pay. Over the years, his workers' reputation—for honesty, reliability, and devoutness—grew. Indeed, as many housewives in the New York–New Jersey–Philadelphia area can attest, the demand for domestics was greater than the supply. Father Divine forbade his workers to accept tips or gifts. The following announcement was printed and reprinted in *New Day* hundreds of times:

To Whom It May Concern

A true follower of Mine does not want or desire a gift, or present, or any-thing of that type for Christmas or any holiday, and considers it to be unevangelical, unconstitutional, and not according to scripture. . . . MY true followers, as long as they receive just compensation for their labor, will not accept tips, gifts, or presents. . . .

This leaves ME Well, Healthy, Joyful, Peaceful, Lively, Loving, Successful, Prosperous and Happy in Spirit, Body and Mind, and in every organ, muscle, sinew, joint, limb, vein, and bone, and even in every ATOM, fiber, and cell of MY BODILY FORM.

Respectfully and Sincere, I AM
Rev. M. J. Divine
(Better known as *Father Divine*)

The ending is one that Father Divine used in his written communiqu és. The message in the body of the letter is self-explanatory and is another example of how he could be crystal clear—when he wanted to be.

Father Divine's followers could work inside or outside the movement. If they worked inside—in a hotel, restaurant, or larger business establishment—they toiled in the service of the Lord, without wages. If they worked outside—as domestics, for example—what they did with their wages was up to them. Presumably, many of them did turn their wages over to the movement, but they were not forced to do so.

Social Organization and Nomenclature

All the groups discussed in the present volume are, in one way or another, outside the mainstream of American life. To help in their adaptation to the larger society, each of the groups has used certain techniques aimed at enhancing internal solidarity. The Father Divine movement has employed a combination of the sacred and the secular. Their churches, for instance, not only serve as places of worship but are designed to house and feed people.

Formerly known as "heavens," the churches and their branches are officially designated as "kingdoms, extensions, and connections," and many of the followers live in these buildings. Not all of the followers, to be sure: it is permissible to live at home. But the dedicated followers—sometimes called the "inner circle" or "holy family" of Father Divine—do live within the walls of the kingdoms. (It is from this group that the Rosebuds, Lilybuds, Crusaders, and secretaries have traditionally been drawn.)

Actually, the kingdoms, extensions, and connections are no more—and no less—than hotels, apartments, rooming houses, and other buildings used for all-purpose quarters by the faithful. Outsiders may also live in the kingdoms, but while they are on the premises, they are subject to the same strict rules of living as the followers. When the movement was at its peak—which is the historical present we are now discussing—there were over 175 kingdoms, extensions, and connections.

Followers who live in one of the kingdoms are closely knit and—like the Oneida Community, discussed in Chapter 5—would constitute a genuine primary group. Describing an assembly of followers who were waiting for the appearance of Father and Mother Divine, Kenneth Burnham writes: "It was here that it was possible to experience the primary-group nature of the rank and file of the Movement. They have known each other from five to forty years. They have worked together, traveled together in the church cars, lived together in buildings they own jointly, and eaten together at Communion served by fellow believers, and in restaurants owned and staffed by 'brothers' and 'sisters.'"[12]

Dedicated followers are united in ways other than by living and working together. They also believe together. They are convinced that Father Divine is God and that all his statements are literally true. They believe in the Bible, but for spiritual guidance they frequently turn to the community newsletter, which carries the sermons of Father Divine over and over again.

No Sex—No Marriage—No Family

Sociologists use the term **norm** to describe an established standard of behavior maintained by a society. In the Father Divine movement, the norm that celibacy is preferable to marriage pervades the entire organization. True followers do not believe in sex, marriage, or family. Married couples can join, but if they live in one of the kingdoms, they must separate. (The usual procedure is for males to live on one floor, females on another.) If there are children, they must be reared separately.

With regard to family life, dedicated followers see themselves as children and Father and Mother Divine as parents, and they believe that this type of relationship is more gratifying—and more exalted—than normal family arrangements. Point seven of "The Crusaders' Declaration Concerning God" shows the intensity of their feelings:

> I believe that FATHER DIVINE is my Real FATHER, and that MOTHER DIVINE is my Real MOTHER, and that I never had another.

True followers also abstain from all sexual relationships. In fact, men and women have very little to do with one another. Before and after communion banquets, it is quite common to see the men talking among themselves and the women among themselves. There is no hostility or antagonism, merely a gentle avoidance.

The "International Modest Code," formulated by Father Divine, is the behavioral guide used by all dedicated followers. The code—in whole or in part—is prominently displayed in the various kingdoms, extensions, and connections. It was reprinted in issue after issue of *New Day* as follows:

---

[12]Burnham, *God Comes to America*, pp. 81–82.

International Modest Code
Established by Father Divine

*No Smoking * No Drinking * No Obscenity*
*No Vulgarity * No Profanity*
No Undue Mixing of the Sexes
No Receiving of Gifts, Presents,
Tips or Bribes

True followers adhere to the code, word for word, almost by second nature. But they seem to give special attention and credence to the section "no undue mixing of the sexes." Celibacy, virginity, purity, chastity, virtue—by whatever term, the followers seem almost to flaunt the idea of sexual abstinence.

Shakers and Divinites   The practice of celibacy is shared by the Father Divine movement and the Shakers. Father Divine's growth came as the Shakers' numbers were diminished from their historical heights of the nineteenth century. Though Father Divine spoke of their organization in his speeches in positive terms, he did feel that he held to a higher level of morality. He observed that since Mother Ann Lee had succumbed to "sexual indulgence" (i.e., she had been married and pregnant), she did not achieve immortality. We do not have confirmation if he ever met with Shaker members, but after his death there was some interaction between the two groups.

In the mid-1990s, a delegation of Divinites from Woodmont went to the Shaker community at Sabbathday Lake, Maine. While no specific record is made of commentary on sexual abstinence, the followers of Father Divine commented on "how close they were to each other" and that they shared a "life of virtue." A Shaker delegation visited Philadelphia on at least two occasions. One was the festive celebration of Mother and Father Divine's fiftieth wedding anniversary in 1996—although Father Divine had passed away over thirty years earlier. By all accounts these meetings were heartfelt.[13]

Just as the Shaker sisters continue to wear the modesty kerchiefs across their chests, the Rosebuds wear a white V on their jackets, and of their "Ten Commandments," number six reads, "We will endeavor to let our every deed and action express virginity." The Lilybuds' "Endeavor" says

---

[13]Frances Carr, "Home Notes," *The Shaker Quarterly* 24 (Nos. 1-4, 1996), pp. 153–62; "Father Divine Follower of Sabbathday Lake Shakers Experience," at http://fdipmm. libertynet.org/word2/94shaker.html, accessed on October 15, 2009; Watts, *God, Harlem U.S.A.*, p. 218, fn. 45.

that they will "live pure, holy, virtuous, and clean." And the Crusaders pledge to "live a righteous, useful, consecrated Life which is devoted to holiness, purity, . . . self-denial."

The Rewards

The followers of Father Divine do not lead a completely sacrificial life. Far from it. They must renounce normal marital and familial relationships and abjure the profit motive, but the rewards—from their point of view—are far greater than the sacrifices.

Dedicated followers will never get rich, obviously, but then they have no need for riches. Their expenses are near zero. They have no family to support, no parents to look after. They pay no rent, have no mortgage or other expenses connected with a house. Their recreational and travel costs are minimal. They have no food bill. What need have these followers for wealth? The movement will care for their material needs as long as they live. And they in turn will provide the movement with a lifetime of dedicated service.

In the intangible sphere, dedicated followers' rewards are even greater. They have the day-to-day satisfaction of serving and being close to their God. They have the comfort of living and working with like-minded people. They are spared the worries of family living. They have no financial woes. They have peace of mind and a sense of spiritual well-being that outsiders often envy.

This last point is perhaps the most important, for no one can be around the group very long without being intrigued by their spiritual outlook. They give the impression of inner security because they *understand.* Their love of God—Father Divine—is so great that it has given them an understanding, both of themselves and of the outside world.

Nowhere in Father Divine's teachings is any provision made for the hereafter, for the dedicated follower has everlasting life. Father Divine spoke literally, not symbolically, on this point. Over and over again, he promised his followers that if they adhered to his teachings faithfully, they would have perfect health and eternal life. On the basis of these pronouncements, followers refuse to buy insurance of any kind.

Goodwill toward all people, racial integration, righteous government, international modesty—all these things are desired *now,* in this world, not the next. It is on this premise that the plans, policies, and actions of the movement are based. And it is this "here and now" philosophy that gives true followers a sense of abiding satisfaction. They feel that if they can unashamedly express their love for Father, put his teachings into practice, and show that the system works, then human salvation will be at hand.

But is it really true that Father Divine's followers do not get sick or die? Of course not. Their morbidity and mortality rates seem to be the same as for the population at large. When followers do die, however, it is attributed to the fact that they somehow failed to live up to the principles set forth by Father. Had they abided by those principles, they would not have died.

Present-day followers are realistic on this point. They realize full well that their members die. The point they make, however, is that Father Divine's teachings represent a *goal,* and that while the goal is difficult, it is not impossible. Successful or not, the true follower is one who devotes his or her life to the attainment of that goal. Mother Divine writes as follows on the subject:

> In the Peace Mission Movement there are no funeral services. Followers of Father Divine believe in giving flowers to the living. . . .
>
> If a follower dies in the faith, the body is taken care of in a very simple, legal, unobtrusive way. Followers believe that the body returns to the dust from whence it came, and that the Spirit goes back to the GOD that gave it. HE will give it another body as it pleases HIM.
>
> A true follower who brings his body into complete subjection to the Law of the Spirit of Life that gave JESUS CHRIST the victory *will not die.* This goal of Perfection is something great to which to aspire, but nevertheless it is Jesus' command: "Be ye therefore perfect, even as your Father which is in heaven is perfect." (Matthew 5:48)[14]

Enemies and Defectors

Despite his phenomenal success as a religious leader, Father Divine experienced considerable opposition. Segments of the African American community have been scornful of the fact that one of their members had the audacity to play God. The popular press has often ridiculed the movement, and serious scholars—with some exceptions—have remained largely aloof.

In the early period, much of the opposition came from the outside clergy. There was, of course, St. John the Vine Hickerson, who contended that "God" was none other than little George Baker from Baltimore. Daddy Grace was a more formidable opponent. Wearing colorful costumes and denouncing Father Divine as a false god, he set up "houses of prayer" along the East Coast and—at a dollar a head—performed special baptismal rites on thousands of enthusiasts. He was apparently more adept at baptism than he was at filing his income tax, however, and after running afoul of the Internal Revenue Service, he fled to Cuba.

---

[14]Mother Divine, *The Peace Mission Movement* (Philadelphia: Imperial Press, 1982), p. 51 (italics added).

The next opponent was Bishop Robert C. Lawson. Unlike so many of the others, Lawson was not an exotic or a cult leader, but a legitimate— and fairly well known—African American minister. He denounced Father Divine in the press and on the radio, calling him an unscrupulous faker. On and on he railed, week after week, month after month. But in the end, the result was the same. He was forgotten, and Father Divine's followers increased by the thousands.

And so it was with all Father Divine's competitors. Decade after decade they sallied forth, only to be whirled back like pursuers before the Pillar of Fire. In retrospect, none of Father Divine's outside antagonists gave him much cause for concern. His real grief came from those who were within the gates. Of all his flock, however, Verinda Brown probably caused Father more trouble than all his other "problem children" combined.

An Apostate   All religions have to deal with **apostates**—people who have renounced their beliefs and allegiances. For faiths like Father Divine's Peace Mission, apostates are a special challenge, since outsiders are more likely to believe the claims of an apostate of a faith generally viewed as marginal compared with more mainstream faiths, like the Presbyterian and Roman Catholic. Verinda Brown had a respectable background. She had no vices, no jail record, no physical debilities. In fact, when she first met Father, she was a happily married woman. She and her husband, Thomas, worked as domestics for a wealthy New York family. They made good money, and one would not have expected them to join the celibate world of Father Divine. But join they did.

Somehow—they could never explain why—they were drawn to Father, and after attending several communion banquets, they were ready to accept him as God. To put aside temptations of lust, Thomas Brown relinquished his job and went to work in one of the kingdoms. Verinda Brown kept her outside job as a domestic.

A short while later they adopted new names: Thomas Brown became Onward Universe, and Verinda became Rebecca Grace. To show their allegiance to the movement, they began to convert their insurance, their building-and-loan holdings, and their real estate to cash. Some of the cash they gave to Father Divine outright. With the rest they bought him gifts. At least, that is what they said they did.

Then Father Divine began to treat them coolly. Apparently, he was not convinced that they had kept lustful thoughts out of their minds. At first Verinda Brown felt hurt, then resentful, then bitter. After thinking things over, she decided to leave the movement, and a short while later her husband followed suit.

But Verinda Brown was not finished. She had, in effect, given Father Divine nearly $5,000—and she wanted it back. She hired a lawyer and took the case to court. Father denied the claim, and produced a host of followers who swore that he never took money in any way, shape, or form. The judge ruled in favor of Verinda Brown, and Father Divine was ordered to pay the full amount plus court costs. Father refused and promptly appealed the case, but to no avail. The appeals court upheld the original verdict, and the decision stands to this day.

The decision stands legally, that is. Not morally: Father Divine refused to pay—not a dollar, not a dime, not a penny. Instead, he simply left New York, and in July 1942 moved his headquarters to Philadelphia, where it has been ever since. The only time he returned to New York was on Sundays, when, according to state law, process papers cannot be served.

Father Divine's refusal to obey the court order was strictly a matter of principle. Over and over, he proclaimed: "The charge was false. The decision was unjust. I would rather rot in jail before paying one cent." Even his lawyers were never able to get him to change his mind. It was their view that the $5,000 was little more than a nuisance claim, and that paying it was preferable to the onus of moving. But Father never budged from his position.

There is no doubt, however, that Father Divine was hurt by the court decision—in a number of ways. For one thing, adverse publicity always hurts, especially in the case of a religious movement. For another, the subsequent move to Philadelphia led to a noticeable decline in numbers, and while other factors were involved, the move itself was probably instrumental.[15] Many of the key personnel moved with their leader to Philadelphia. A number of the kingdoms, extensions, and connections closed down, and today only a handful remain in New York. (It was for these very practical reasons that Father Divine's attorneys advised him to pay the claim.)

But there is another side to the story, for if Father Divine was hurt, was not New York hurt even more? After all, as Weisbrot points out, "The stress on independence, honesty, and self-discipline all contributed to a dramatic lowering of the crime rate wherever new Peace Missions established themselves."[16] A number of judges and police officials attested to this fact.

In a similar vein, because of their honesty and reliability, true followers were in great demand as workers. Additionally, Father Divine was feeding tens of thousands of unemployed New Yorkers every year, virtually free of charge. And, of course, none of his followers were permitted to go on welfare or relief of any kind. In brief, he was saving New York taxpayers a good sum of money on a more or less regular basis. Ironically enough, therefore, it looks as though New York's loss was Philadelphia's gain!

[15]Weisbrot, *Father Divine*, p. 211.
[16]Weisbrot, *Father Divine*, p. 94.

The Tommy Garcia Story   Tommy Garcia, at age fifteen, ran away from the Kingdom of Father Divine to find his natural father. Raised at Woodmont by Father and Mother Divine, Garcia believes he was being groomed to lead the Peace Mission movement. When Father Divine died in 1965 there was a power struggle in the church and Tommy was sent to a boarding school. Today, with his wife, Lori, Garcia operates an equipment leasing business in Las Vegas, Nevada. The following is excerpted from a telephone interview conducted by William Zellner in October 1999:[17]

Zellner: How did you become part of Father Divine's family?

Garcia: I was born in Los Angeles in 1954. My birth mother, Georgia Garcia, was a photographer of some merit. My father, Tomas Garcia, is a legal immigrant from Mexico. Pop worked days in a music store and attended night school studying television technology. I had a sister, Susan, born in 1959.

Zellner: Philadelphia is a long way from Los Angeles.

Garcia: Yes it is. In 1962, my mother was taking pictures of me at a temple in Los Angeles. A woman named Louise Schell approached my mom and asked her if she would like to attend a meeting at Jefferson Mission, a Divine satellite.

Zellner: Did you go?

Garcia: Yes. I was very young, but I remember the first time well. People there were seated alternating Black and White, men on one side, women on the other side. They were attentively listening to a voice recording of Father Divine. When I asked who was talking, I was told it was God—Father Divine. It didn't mean much to me at the time. I had been confirmed a Catholic when I was six years old, and the Black man in the picture next to the tape recorder looked nothing like the God that existed in my mind's eye.

Zellner: How did you get from Jefferson Mission to Woodmont?

Garcia: Mom told pop that she wanted to take me and Susie to visit her family in New Hampshire. (By the way, it is very difficult for me to call her mom. She has disowned me in favor of the movement.) He gave us the car and cash for the trip. Louise went with us. When we got to Philadelphia, we went directly to the Divine Lorraine hotel. Susie and I were separated. I was escorted upstairs to a room where I stayed, alone, all night. The next morning I was delivered to Father Divine's study at Woodmont. It was there that he said the words that haunt me to this day.

Zellner: And those words, Tommy?

Garcia: He said, "It has come to my attention, Tommy, that no one wants you. I want you. I care about you. If you agree, you will live with me here, and I will take care of you for the rest of your life."

[17]The Garcias maintain a Web site: http://www.tommygarcia.com.

Zellner: What were you thinking?

Garcia: I was thinking that there was something terribly wrong. In my mind's eye, I pictured the orphanages on the TV program *East Side Kids.* I feared going to a place like that. I looked at everything and everybody in the room. Then I looked back at Father Divine and said yes. He kept his word. From that time forward until his death, he treated me as his son.

Zellner: And Susie?

Garcia: I asked about her many times, and I was always told she had been taken to a different place. It was two years before I saw her again.

Susie was only three years old when she was put in that environment. I don't think she got the kind of nurturing young children need. She got what I call "disinterested caretaking." She was confused and hurt and her tragic death in 1993 may have brought her the only peace she would ever know.

Zellner: How did she die?

Garcia: She developed a drug habit and was thrown out of the extension when she was sixteen. She returned to Los Angeles where she went from the frying pan into the fire. She continued her addiction, and in 1993 she was raped and murdered on her way to a convenience store.

Zellner: That certainly is a tragic story.

Garcia: Her death is one of the reasons I feel obligated to tell my story. Many children ended up in the Peace Mission movement, effectively abandoned by their parents. I don't know how much of this goes on today, but I understand that it still does. To the extent that it does, it is publicly supported kidnapping. People who patronize the movement's restaurants, hotels, and other businesses are contributing to criminal behavior and the personal enrichment of Mother Divine.

Zellner: What part did you play at the banquets?

Garcia: I was often asked to give testimony. I was given many gifts and made to feel special. I would simply thank Mother and Father for the most recent gift. For example, I had my own TV. It's quite common for children to have TV's in their rooms today, but it was a real rarity in the 1960s. I even had a go-cart and a tractor.

I had every reason to feel special. I was the only person, other than Father and Mother Divine, to have a chauffeur-valet-bodyguard.

Zellner: How do you account for your special treatment?

Garcia: I believe that Father Divine had tremendous foresight. He thought that some of the higher-ups had their own agendas. He was aware that many of the followers did not see Mother Divine as a Goddess.

He knew he needed someone from outside the movement to be his successor. Just as Father Divine chose Mother Divine, he chose me. And, even at this time, if called, I will serve.

Indeed, there were many children raised in the Divine movement, but he was the only one raised at Woodmont. It was true, too, that he was given gifts and he was loved. But Mother Divine insisted that he was not being groomed for a leadership role, stating: "No one would be groomed for that purpose. We are all striving to develop Christ from within. If there is any position of authority to be filled—at that time the person would be selected."[18] She went on to say, "He could do anything he made up his mind to do. People recognized early that he's a leader. I think he needs more opportunity to lead. I don't know what it would be."[19]

Scope and Operation of the Movement

Most of his followers worshiped Father Divine, and it seems that the closer they were to him, the greater was their reverence. Indeed, it is a tribute to his leadership that there were so few Verinda Browns. But how, specifically, did the organization operate? How did one go about joining? Was Father the sole executive and administrator, or did he have deputies and assistants? How large was the membership? In how many states and countries?

Some of the above questions are answerable; some are not. The most difficult ones are those pertaining to numbers, for membership lists were never kept, and neither Father nor Mother Divine has ever given any figures, even though they have been asked hundreds of times. The ban on published statistics extends to financial transactions, bank statements, tax returns, and other fiscal records.

The actual procedure for joining Father Divine's organization must have been extremely informal. Several years ago, when the movement was closer to its peak, a follower was asked how one went about joining. "Well," the man replied, "you come to the meetings and services, and show them you're really interested. You keep meeting people and, like, you give them a chance to size you up. Then if you want, you can stay on and try it for a while. It all works out. The wrong kind don't last long."

Actually, there are two classes of members: the true or dedicated followers, who live and work within the movement, and the adherents, who

---

[18]Suzanne Gordon, "Life After Heaven," *Philadelphia Inquirer*, December 18, 1989.

[19]Gordon, "Life After Heaven." Garcia announced May 15, 2009, to the Palm Springs, California, television station (KESQ) his intention to take legal action to "re-start" the International Peace Mission Movement so its funds are used for charitable purposes. See video clip of the newscast at http://www.youtube.com/watch?v=lBqaxB87R2U or http://www.kesq.com/Global/story.asp?s=10371157. A local Philadelphia television station repeated his claim and while the Peace Mission movement did not directly respond, it did state in a news release that they continue to have "publicity seekers."

live at home. The latter group has always had varying degrees of affiliation and loyalty, and it is this group that has made it difficult to estimate
numbers.

The magnitude of the Father Divine movement has likely been exaggerated. True, in its heyday, substantial numbers were involved.
Standing-room-only crowds were in evidence almost every place that
Father spoke, and there was often danger that fire laws were being broken. The demands on his time were such that he could scarcely keep up
with his schedule.

But there was another side to the vociferation. Many of the standing-
room-only crowds included quasi-members, or simply spectators who
were eager to see what "God" looked like. On many occasions, busloads
of Father's followers accompanied him from place to place, adding to the
impression that there were followers everywhere.

Bettmann/Corbis

Followers of Father Divine were not bashful about
expressing their displeasure at what they regarded
at harassment of their leader. Here they march in
1938 showing their allegiance to a man who,
according to their banners, they equate with Jesus
Christ.

Nevertheless, by World
War II, traces of the movement could be found in
some twenty-five states,
although many of the organizations were short-lived.
Although Father Divine
himself continually stressed
the international flavor of
the organization, member-
ship abroad never amounted
to much numerically. A limited number of countries
were involved—Australia,
British West Indies, Canada,
Switzerland, England, Germany, and Panama. Today,
the foreign branches are
defunct. The hub of the
movement was always New
York, New Jersey, and
Philadelphia.

The peak period for the
Father Divine movement
came in the 1930s and 1940s.
It was during these years
that membership reached a
maximum, that the move-
ment became national and

international in scope, and that Father Divine became a renowned religious leader. The organization remained moderately strong during the 1950s and early 1960s, although the vigor was clearly waning. After 1965, however—the year of Father's death—the movement seemed to go downhill rather sharply. Today the organization survives, reduced in both numbers and energy.

How large was the membership during the peak period? No one can say for sure. The number never approached the 22 million repeatedly claimed by Father Divine or the "millions" regularly headlined in the press. If the hangers-on and the spectators are excluded, it is doubtful whether the figure even ran to the hundreds of thousands. Membership probably could be counted in the tens of thousands, but only at the height of the movement. Today the number of followers is quite small, perhaps a few hundred dedicated believers, perhaps less.

Even when Schaefer visited the Woodmont estate in 2005 and would ask the Rosebuds present how many people were necessary to maintain the sprawling complex, they would respond, "we don't count our blessings." While estimates abound, there has been no real authoritative estimate of the Father Divine movement, whether it was fifty years ago or today.

There have always been more Blacks than Whites in the movement. During the peak period, the Black–White ratio was about 90:10 or 80:20. Also, females have always outnumbered males, by perhaps four or five to one. And—predictably—the movement has had more appeal to the middle- and older-age groups than to the young.

Leadership   Not too much can be said about the subject of leadership. Writing in the period when the movement was at its peak, Arthur H. Fauset contends that "in the Father Divine Movement, Father Divine is the organization. There are no assistant leaders, nor directors, vice-presidents, vice-chairmen, or elders. Whatever directive is carried out is assumed to have been issued by Father Divine."[20]

The contention is largely true. It was Father Divine—and no one else—who formulated policy, gave talks, bought property, established businesses (although not in his own name), counseled the followers, dealt with the public, made the major decisions, and otherwise controlled the destiny of the movement. None of the other religious leaders discussed in the present volume had anything like the authority vested in Father Divine. Father Divine was exuberant in everything he did and extremely self-confident. Speaking and leading meetings were his strengths.

[20]Arthur H. Fauset, *Black Gods of the Metropolis* (Philadelphia: University of Pennsylvania Press, 1944), p. 56.

In the case of any orator, two essential ingredients are voice power and word power. And to anyone who ever heard him, there was no doubt that Father Divine had both. He had a mighty voice, which seemed even more compelling because of the small body that housed it. And when it came to words and sentences, he was a veritable magician.

Unheard-of expressions rolled off Father Divine's tongue like counterfeit bills off a high-power press. Words such as invisibilate, unfoldment, contagionized, convincement, transnipotent, physicalate, convictable, omnilucent, and tangibilated enlivened both his writing and his oratory. And when he was not tangibilating new expressions, he was, as Hoshor puts it, "tossing out words that never before had been used in the same sentence."[21]

The Rosebuds, Lilybuds, Crusaders, and secretaries have generally been drawn from the inner circle of the movement, and—in terms of helping Father and Mother Divine—they can be counted on to do whatever has to be done. The secretaries (whose numbers have dwindled from a high of around twenty-five to a mere handful today) have always had high status in the movement. Their duties include handling appointments, greeting visiting dignitaries, taking care of correspondence and other paperwork, and, of course, recording and transcribing the various talks given by Father (and now by Mother) Divine.

This, then, is the leadership structure of the movement. On the one hand, there is no doubt that Father Divine had some much-needed help; after all, he was running an organization of thousands. On the other hand, when the movement was at its peak, there was scarcely a person in the organization who could make a significant move without prior approval from Father. This was the way he wanted it, and this was the way his followers wanted it.

The current leader of the movement is Mother Divine, who has proved to be a remarkable woman. Because she has always occupied a special place in the leadership structure, let us examine both her socio-historical and her present role.

Mother Divine

In spite of tribulations, the movement continued to grow and prosper all during the 1930s. Father Divine was emerging as a a man to be reckoned with, and a variety of political figures—including the mayor of New York—courted his favor. But what of Sister Penny, Father's first wife? She was seen at his side less and less often. Finally, her appearances ceased altogether, and she was not heard from after 1940.

---

[21]Hoshor, *God in a Rolls Royce*, p. 50.

Second Marriage   It was not until August 1946, however, that Father Divine broke the sad news to his followers. Peninah had died six years earlier. She had had a protracted illness, had grown old and weary in body, so—acceding to her wishes—Father Divine had permitted her to "pass." He had been reluctant to do so. He had also been reluctant to tell his followers the sad news and had waited until the right time to do so. But the right time had come, and on April 29 he had taken a new bride: Sweet Angel, one of his young, White secretaries. As was previously noted, Father Divine's followers were not allowed to marry. Father felt he was the only one strong enough to marry and keep sexuality out of the bargain.

As might be expected, the announcement of Father Divine's second marriage came as something of a shock, both to the public at large and to those within the movement. Most Americans in the 1940s were intolerant of interracial marriages. In sociological terminology, such marriages were against the **mores** of the time, that is, those customs or beliefs about which the majority of people have strong emotional feelings.

In fact, at the time, interracial marriages were illegal in no fewer than thirty states. (It was not until 1967 that the Supreme Court declared such laws unconstitutional.) At any rate, the public was shocked and angered at Father Divine's action. Even for some of the followers, the announcement of Peninah's death plus the second marriage was too much. They simply left the movement.

After the first shock waves had passed, however, the new marriage proceeded to work out remarkably well. The public grew accustomed to seeing the couple together, true followers soon took Sweet Angel to their hearts, and Sweet Angel herself proved to be more of a help than even Father had foreseen.

So successful was the marriage that at the end of the first year a giant wedding anniversary banquet was held. From all accounts, it was something to behold. Indeed, it just may have been the most lavish ever given in the United States: 60 different kinds of meat, 54 vegetables, 20 relishes, 42 hors d'oeuvres, 21 different kinds of bread, 18 beverages, 23 salads, and 38 different desserts. All told, there were some 350 different kinds of food served, with the marathon meal lasting a full seven hours. Since then, the wedding anniversary celebrations have become one of the movement's most important yearly events, with followers attending from across the nation.

For the record, Mother Divine was born Edna Rose Ritchings, in Vancouver, Canada. Her father was a well-established florist, who would have been able to send Edna Rose to college. But her interest lay more in religion, particularly in Father Divine's brand. She became acquainted with the movement in Canada, and when she was twenty-one, she came to Father's headquarters in Philadelphia. A few weeks later, she was made one of the secretaries. At the time of her marriage, Sweet Angel had not yet reached her twenty-second birthday. She would eventually carry heavy responsibilities.[22]

According to the pronouncement made by Father Divine, Mother Divine was the reincarnation of Sister Penny, his first wife—and this is the view of all true followers today. But reincarnated or not, Mother Divine, formerly Sweet Angel, formerly Edna Rose Ritchings, has worked out very well indeed. When Father Divine was alive and in good health, she was at his side during virtually all the communion banquets, meetings, and interviews. During his declining years—roughly 1961 to 1965—she and the secretaries took over more and more of the movement's managerial duties.

Jim Jones   Mother Divine has been more than a caretaker of a movement she inherited. In 1971 Jim Jones, the American leader of the People's Temple, came with two hundred of his followers to the Woodmont estate. Jones had declared that he felt inspired by Father Divine and had actually met with him at Woodmont in 1957.[23] It was clear that his intention was to gain the allegiance of all the Peace Mission followers at the headquarters and perhaps even begin to take over their assets. Eventually leaving the grounds after several days, Jones contacted Father Divine's followers to try to persuade them to leave for his People's Temple.

Only one member is documented to have left, and her appeals to Mother Divine to recognize Jones as the reincarnation of Father Divine were rejected. While the general public took little notice of these events in 1971, the world became aware of Jones's power over people in 1978, when he led hundreds of his followers to mass suicide in Guyana.

There is no doubt that the Peace Mission movement has been going downhill, a trend that today appears irreversible. But under Mother Divine's leadership, the Woodmont estate continues to be beautifully preserved, as recognized in 2003 when she received a historic preservation award.[24] If it were not for the efforts of Mother Divine and a small group of followers who work closely with her, the entire organization would already have dissolved.

---

[22]The marriage proposal itself is of interest. Watts (*God, Harlem U.S.A.*, p. 168) writes that "one day while working with him, Sweet Angel boldly approached the minister and announced, 'I want to marry you because I know you are God.' Surprisingly, Sweet Angel's proposal did not offend him. He had observed the young woman as she worked and was impressed with her devotion to the movement. On April 29, 1946, he whisked Sweet Angel to Washington, D.C., and married her in a secret ceremony."

[23]Watts, *God, Harlem U.S.A.*, pp. 174–75. This meeting was portrayed in the 1980 television miniseries, *Guyana Tragedy: The Story of Jim Jones* with James Earl Jones playing the role of Father Divine. It can be viewed online at http://video.google.com/videoplay?docid=-2162288600433153789#.

[24]"Mrs. M. J. Divine Wins Magazine Award." June 2003. http://www.preservation alliance.com/news/news-motherdivine.php.

The Movement: Weaknesses and Strengths

Weaknesses   The basic weakness of the movement was that it developed as a one-person operation. Like the Oneida Community—but unlike the Jehovah's Witnesses and the Mormons—the movement made virtually no provision for succession. It was assumed that Father Divine would go on forever. Although present followers may deny it, his illness and death apparently decimated the movement. Father himself taught that true followers would not experience illness or death—and when he died, large-scale disaffection followed.

Granted, Father Divine's death would have created problems even if provisions for succession had been made. But the problems could have been solved. Other groups have faced and overcome similar obstacles. Oddly enough, however, the movement seems to be compounding the error in the case of Mother Divine: her death is not contemplated, and no successor has been designated. When the question of succession was raised with one of the followers, the answer was unmistakably clear: "But Mother Divine will always be with us, just as Father has always been with us . . ."

The movement's position on celibacy is related to its belief in immortality; that is, if dedicated followers live forever, there is no need for procreation. Of course, the fact that they do die means that the movement has no effective means of growth.

Exactly why Father Divine invoked the celibacy rule is not clear. Some writers feel that because the movement was interracial and because—at that time—attitudes toward miscegenation were decidedly negative, Father solved the problem neatly by prohibiting both sex and marriage. This explanation seems a little far-fetched. If he thought he was in the right, Father Divine would never have been deterred by public opinion. A more likely explanation is simply that he desired his followers to live the life of Christ, a position that was—and is—expressive of the very heart of the movement.

Irrespective of the reason, celibacy must be listed as one of the weaknesses of the organization. All groups grow by natural increase and/or by proselytizing. The Mormons have used both methods, and they have grown rapidly. The Amish have rejected all forms of birth control, and they have also shown rapid growth. The Shakers embraced celibacy and, in later years, made few attemps to proselytize—and they are now near extinction. One might guess that the same fate is in store for the Father Divine Movement.

Strengths   The movement has already made some positive contributions. During the Great Depression, the various branches fed thousands of destitute people at little or no charge. The homeless were provided with a clean room at a dollar or two a week. Prostitutes, beggars, thieves—all were welcomed into the movement and given respectable jobs.

Once they joined, followers were taught the value of honesty and hard work, and the importance of building self-respect. They were forbidden to accept gifts or gratuities, and they were admonished to dress moderately, eschew vulgarity, and act kindly toward others.

In race relations, Father Divine was clearly a generation ahead of his time. The movement of the 1930s and 1940s was pressing for reforms that would not be enacted until the 1960s and 1970s: laws prohibiting segregation in schools and public places, establishing fair employment practices, removing "race or color" designation on personnel forms and official records, outlawing restrictive covenants in housing, and so on.

In the political field, also, Father Divine proved to be a seer, for many of the planks in his "righteous government" platform came into being in the decades following World War II: affirmative action programs, changes in welfare policy, changes in tariff schedules, expansion of civil service coverage, and the like.

It may be true that the various reforms would have come about with or without the assistance of Father Divine. But it is equally true that he spoke out in no uncertain terms when many others were silent. Without the impetus of the Father Divine movement, these reforms might have been slower in arriving.

One other feature of the movement should be mentioned: the great emphasis on peace. Father Divine probably desired peace as fervently as any other person who ever lived: peace between nations, peace between races, peace between ethnic groups, peace among people, and peace with oneself. This is what he stood for, and this is what he preached. He called his organization the Peace Mission movement, a name it is known by even today.

The Present Scene

The Peace Mission movement provided large numbers of Black Americans with an escape from the dismal reality of a White world. It gave them a sense of physical and spiritual well-being. And it tried to develop self-pride. On a societal level, the movement served as the tip of the spear, penetrating into the murky areas of civil rights and international peace. It also served as a reminder that righteous government principles could be adopted by persons other than politicians.

Yet today the Peace Mission movement is in trouble. Times change, and the 1930s are a far cry from today. The societal context has shifted, and a new set of societal problems has emerged. But the movement has not changed. Its goals, organization, and method of operation are much the same today as they were seventy years ago.

In the 1930s, the urban masses—both Black and White—needed food, and Father gave it to them. During recent decades in the United States, fewer people suffered from starvation or lack of housing, and not many people sought the services of Father Divine's organization.

Eighty years ago, African Americans, particularly those in the lower classes, needed an inspirational leader who could stand up to the White world and show some results. And Father Divine filled that role. Today, leadership in the Peace Mission movement is White. African Americans today can readily find inspiration in many recognized Black leaders, even the president of the United States.

Sayville, Judge Lewis Smith, and the days of retribution are far behind. Father himself is no longer physically present to spark the membership and expand the organization. As a group, the followers are aging. Many have already died, and others have left the movement. The social climate that spawned the Peace Mission program has changed drastically. In brief, aside from self-perpetuation and the continuation of traditional rituals— such as publication of a newsletter, convocation of communion banquets, and the observance of holidays—there doesn't seem to be a great deal for the organization to do.

In some ways, the movement is still going. Thanks to Father Divine's vision, the organization is well endowed financially and owns a number of valuable properties. True followers can still put on a spirited performance at their get-togethers. They are absolutely devoted to Mother and Father Divine, and to the movement itself. Inexorably, however, celibacy continues to block the main arteries of growth. New converts are hard to come by, and—numerically—the membership appears to be at an all-time low. There are no churches, stores, or missions outside the Woodmont headquarters.

However, the movement shows little concern to their small numbers. Even in the 1980s, as the group probably dropped to below one thousand, Mother Divine compared the movement to the Shakers and contended that it was the quality, not quantity, of the followers that was important.[25]

This, then, is the present status of the movement. It is rapidly reaching the point—if it has not already—where the entire membership will consist of a small, spiritually elite group.

To an objective observer there is nothing on the secular or spiritual horizon to suggest a rejuvenation. The tours continue to be led by Rosebuds at Woodmont, but if there is some successor to Mother Divine or some learned council prepared to emerge, this is not known to even the closest outside observers. Father Divine will remain one of the indelible figures

[25]Watts, *God, Harlem U.S.A.*, p. 176.

in the history of twentieth-century religious thought. He was—with the possible exception of Brigham Young—the most remarkable of all the leaders discussed in this book. He was also a person of infinite goodness.

KEY TERMS

Alienation, p. 256
Apostates, p. 264
Norm, p. 260

Stereotype, p. 256
Mores, p. 272

SOURCES ON THE WEB

http://peacemission.info/www.libertynet.org/fdipmm/html
Web sites of the Peace Mission movement.

http://www.meta-religion.com/New_religious_groups/Groups/Christian/
peace_mission_movement.htm
Metareligion provides concise summaries of a vast array of religious groups, including the Peace Mission movement of Father Divine.

http://www.taylorstresststudio.com/divine/
The Father Divine project includes color video clips of Father Divine, the celebration in 1996 of the fiftieth wedding anniversary of Mother Divine and Father Divine, and an interview with Mother Divine.

SELECTED READINGS

Braden, Charles. *These Also Believe: A Study of Modern American Cults and Minority Religious Movements.* New York: Macmillan, 1949.

Burnham, Kenneth E. *God Comes to America: Father Divine and the Peace Mission Movement.* Boston: Lambeth, 1979.

Calverton, V. F. *Where Angels Feared to Tread.* New York: Bobbs-Merrill, 1941.

Fauset, Arthur H. *Black Gods of the Metropolis.* Philadelphia: University of Pennsylvania Press, 1944.

Galanter, Marc. *Cults: Faith, Healing, and Coercion.* New York: Oxford University Press, 1989.

Harris, Sarah. *Father Divine: Holy Husband.* 1953. Reprint. New York: Macmillan, 1971.

Higginbotham, A. Leon. *In the Matter of Color*. New York: Oxford University Press, 1980.

Hoshor, John. *God in a Rolls Royce: The Rise of Father Divine*. 1936. Reprint. Freeport, NY: Books for Libraries Press, 1971.

Hostetler, John. *Communitarian Societies*. New York: Holt, Rinehart and Winston, 1974.

Kephart, William M. *The Family, Society, and the Individual*. Boston: Houghton Mifflin, 1981.

Mabee, Carleton. *Promised Land: Father Divine's Interracial Communities in Ulster County, New York*. Fleischmanns, NY: Purple Mountain Press, 2008.

Moseley, J. R. *Manifest Victory*. New York: Harper & Row, 1941.

Mother Divine. *The Peace Mission Movement*. Philadelphia: Imperial Press, 1982.

Ottley, Roi. *New World A-Coming: Inside Black America*. Boston: Houghton Mifflin, 1943.

Parker, Robert Allerton. *The Incredible Messiah*. Boston: Little, Brown, 1937.

Staples, Robert, ed. *The Black Family: Essays and Studies*. Belmont, CA: Wadsworth, 1978.

Stinnett, Nick, and C. W. Birdsong. *The Family and Alternative Life Styles*. Chicago: Nelson-Hall, 1978.

Washington, Joseph R. *Black Sects and Cults: The Power Axis in an Ethnic Ethic*. New York: Doubleday, 1973.

Watts, Jill. *God, Harlem U.S.A.: The Father Divine Story*. Berkeley: University of California Press, 1992.

Weisbrot, Robert. *Father Divine and the Struggle for Racial Equality*. Urbana: University of Illinois Press, 1983.

CHAPTER EIGHT

Nation of Islam

Consider the 1965 remarks of Elijah Muhammad, leader of the Nation of Islam (NOI), to his African American followers about the "so-called Negro."

> Today you are begging the master, the slave-masters' children for what? You are begging them for a job. You are begging for complete recognition as their equals. Let us be honest with ourselves. According to history, we cannot find where the master made his slave equal until the servant made himself worthy of equality.
>
> I am with you to go on top. We cannot go on top with weight that is hanging on us. We cannot charge the white man with our faults. We are supposed to be, according to his own teachings, free. We are supposed to have been freed from him approximately 100 hundred years ago. Have we exercised that freedom? We must answer that we have not availed ourselves of that freedom. If we have not availed ourselves of that freedom which he says he gave

us, why should we think hard of him about the way he treats us? This may be a little hard to swallow.[1]

Who is this man? And how do people become dedicated to his teachings?

To begin to grasp the influence of the Nation of Islam, let's consider the conversion to the NOI of one man—arguably the most famous Muslim in the United States.

Case Study in Conversion: From Clay to Ali

Muhammad Ali for many years was one of the most globally identifiable persons worldwide. Born in 1942 in Louisville with the birth name Cassius Clay, Ali was guided into boxing by a White policeman who befriended him at age twelve. Soon he won two national Golden Gloves titles followed by a gold medal at the 1960 Olympic Games. His professional success continued. In 1964 he captured the heavyweight crown and became heavyweight champion of the world.

Immediately after becoming "the champ," Clay shocked the sports world and the general public by announcing that he believed in "Allah and in peace," was "not a Christian anymore," and embraced the teachings of the Nation of Islam. He also rejected his birth name, taking on briefly the name of Cassius X and soon assuming the name given to him by Elijah Muhammad of Muhammad (for one worthy of praise) Ali (name of one of the early heads of state under Islam).[2] How did Ali come to adopt Islam?

Clay's transition to the Islamic lifestyle was not as difficult as it was for many. A health nut, he did not smoke or drink. His father had been receptive to the message of early Black Nationalist Marcus Garvey's, whose United Negro Improvement Association flourished in the Black neighborhoods of the 1920s.

Clay first encountered NOI in 1959 when he traveled as a seventeen-year-old to Chicago for a Golden Gloves tournament. He came back home carrying a record album of sermons by Elijah Muhammad (the leader of the NOI at the time, to be discussed in depth later). Still in high school, he asked to write a term paper on Black Muslims but his teacher refused to let him. He was attracted to the message of self-respect for Black people. After moving to Miami in 1961, Clay started to associate with the chief NOI minister in town and delved deeper into the faith. He began reading the official

[1]"The So-Called Negro Must Do Something for Himself" is from Elijah Muhammad message to the Black Man in America (1965) and appeared in *The Final Call*, October 27, 2009. Accessed November 10, 2009 at "http://www.finalcall.com/artman/publish/Columns_4/What_The_So-Called_Negro_Must_Do_For_Himself_by_the_2579.shtml.

[2]David Remnick, *King of the World: Muhammad Ali, and the Rise of an American Hero* (New York: Random House, 1998), p. 207.

Bettmann/Corbis

Muhammad Ali is shown speaking to the Annual Convention of the Nation of Islam in Chicago in 1968. Obviously pleased by what he is hearing, we see the smiling leader Elijah Muhammad seated behind the famous professional boxer.

newspaper of NOI, *Muhammad Speaks.* By the next year he began to live by the dietary restrictions of Islam, such as the prohibition against consuming pork. Reporters began to see him at NOI events but he refused to confirm his interest.[3]

Clay began to revere Elijah Muhammad but like many converts found it difficult to comprehend his long speeches and his version of Muslim cosmology. However, NOI spokesman, Malcolm X, easily connected with the rising boxing star when they first met in 1962. Clay reached out and invited Malcolm X's entire family to vacation at his Miami home. It was shortly thereafter that Clay confirmed the press rumors that he was now a member of the NOI.

In light of his abandonment of his Christian upbringing, professional boxing organizations threatened to strip him of his title for "conduct detrimental to the spirit of boxing"— a true stretch of the imagination given the history of the sport. In 1965, Ali defeated former champion Floyd Patterson, who refused to call him by the name Ali, instead referring to him as Cassius Clay. Ali perceived this as an insult to Islam and to him as a man. During Ali's illustrious career as world champion (1964–1967 and 1970–1979), he came to symbolize the nation's frustration over race and the Vietnam War. Hostility toward him was not so much against Islam, which most Americans did not understand nor wish to learn about, but his boastfulness about his embrace of the NOI and the black pride movement.[4]

In 1967, before much of the country had more boldly turned against military involvement in Vietnam, Ali refused to obey an induction order and was subsequently sentenced to five years in prison. He never served time but his boxing license was suspended and he was stripped of his

[3]Ibid, pp. 125–43.
[4]Jeffrey T. Sammons, *Beyond the Ring: The Role of Boxing in American Society* (Urbana: University of Illinois Press, 1988).

heavyweight title. It wasn't until 1971 after appeals to the Supreme Court that Ali's status as a conscientious objector was finally recognized. The government had held the position that Ali was willing to be a soldier based on wire taps of Elijah Muhammad that Ali would serve in a "holy war" or a "Muslim war." But defense successfully argued that such a war was Armageddon of good and evil and the same war that a Jehovah's Witness would fight.[5]

It should be noted that Ali at the time was fully aware that as reigning heavyweight champion, he would never have seen combat. He would spend his time in army-mounted boxing exhibition bouts and moral-building work for the military. However, he would not compromise his principle.

Ali's acceptance of Muslim teachings contributed to his divorce from his first wife, who refused to accept dictates about modest attire for women and was suspicious about the NOI using her husband for their own purposes. To his credit, Ali did not tone down his association with Islam even though it cost him millions in endorsements, appearances, and media contracts.

Though he continued to support the organization, Ali grew more interested in traditional Muslim teachings and disenchanted with NOI's separatist rhetoric and, at times, anti-White rhetoric. Upon Elijah Muhammad's death in 1975, Ali followed a more traditionalist Islam position that he continues to hold today.[6]

Black Muslims: Label, Not a Religion

The Nation of Islam (NOI) is the longest continually functioning approach to Islam that is uniquely American and unapologetically centered on the Black experience. The NOI is the best known example of what the public often calls "Black Muslims."

The term **Black Muslim** refers to an African American who accepts many tenets of Islam but in the specific context of being Black in the United States. Black Muslims do not form a specific group, much less an organized religious group. Rather, Black Muslims is a label outsiders use to refer to Black-American-led groups with a distinctively American interpretation of Islam.

The groups so described do not accept the label "Black Muslim" and aim to distance themselves from it. Notably Malcolm X in his autobiography explained that for two years he tried "to kill off that 'Black Muslim.'" While we are Black people, "our religion is Islam: We are properly called 'Muslims'!"[7]

[5]Bob Woodward and Scott Armstrong, *The Brethren* (New York: Avon Books, 1979), pp. 159–60.
[6]Remnick, *King of the World*, pp. 239–40.
[7]Malcolm X, *The Autobiography of Malcolm X*, written by Alex Haley (New York: Ballantine Books), 1964 (revised with Epilogue by Alex Haley and Afterword by Ossie Davis. New York: One World, Ballantine Books, 1999), p. 247.

Groups labeled "Black Muslim" are part of global Islam, but as we will see, their teachings are very distinct from Islam of Africa and Asia. This situation is no different from that of Hasidic Jews, whose religious practice is part of Judaism but very different from the practice of Reform Jews. The difference between them is that Hasidic Jews celebrate this distinction, while Black Muslims have historically sought to minimize it.[8]

Before turning to a uniquely Black American interpretation of Islam we will first provide an overview of Islam, a religion that while so often in the news is still so misunderstood, and then consider the long history of Islam in the Americas.

Islam: An Overview

In order to understand the Nation of Islam and the Black Muslim movement it is necessary to understand the faith that underlies Islam in most of the world. Islam, with approximately 1.3 billion followers worldwide, is second only to Christianity among the world's largest religions.

Commonalities between Islam and Judeo-Christian Traditions Although news events suggest an inherent conflict between Christians, Jews, and Muslims, the faiths are similar in many ways.

The commonalities between Islam, Christianity, and Judaism are not merely incidental but central to Muslim faith. Islam reveres both the Old and New Testaments as integral parts of its tradition. Muslims recognize the Old and New Testament prophets and their divine Revelations—Moses (Torah) and Jesus (Gospels). Not surprisingly, Musa (Moses), Isa (Jesus), and Maryam (Mary) are common Muslim names. Indeed the headquarters of the Nation of Islam today is Mosque Maryam in Chicago, named after Mary, mother of Jesus. Similarly, Muslims learn many of the Old and New Testament stories familiar to Christians and Jews, such as Noah's Ark, the Ten Commandments, and David and Solomon.

All three religions are monotheistic (i.e., based on a single deity) and indeed worship the same God. "Allah" is the Arabic word for God used by practioners of Islam and refers to the God of Moses, Jesus, and Muhammad. Both Christianity and Islam include a belief in prophets, an afterlife, and a judgment day. In fact, Islam recognizes Jesus as a prophet (though not the son of God). All three faiths impose a moral code on believers, which varies from fairly rigid proscriptions for fundamentalists to relatively relaxed guidelines for liberals.

---

[8]Richard Brent Turner, *Islam in the African American Experience*, 2nd ed. (Bloomington: Indiana University Press, 2003), pp. 199–200; and Algernon Austin, *Achieving Blackness: Race, Black Nationalism, and Afrocentrism in the Twentieth Century* (New York: New York University Press, 2006), pp. 27–28.

Beliefs Unique to Islam   Islam is guided by the teachings of the Qur'an (or Koran), which Muslims believe was revealed to the seventh-century Prophet Muhammad. The Qur'an includes the collected sayings, or *hadeeth*, and deeds of Muhammad, which are called *Sunnah*, or the way of the Prophet. Muhammad grew up an orphan and became a respected businessman who rejected the widespread polytheism of his day and turned to the one God (Allah) as worshiped by the region's Christians and Jews. Islam says that he was visited by the angel Gabriel, who began reciting the word of Allah, the Qur'an. Muslims see Muhammad as the last in a long line of prophets; he was preceded by Abraham, Moses, and Jesus.

Islam is a communal practice, encompassing all aspects of one's life. Consequently, in countries that are predominantly Muslim, the separation of religion and the state is not considered necessary or even desirable. In fact, governments in Muslim countries often reinforce Islamic practices through their laws. Muslims do vary in their interpretation of several traditions, some of which—such as the requirement for women to wear face veils or **hijab**—are disputed.

Like other religious systems, certain rituals referred to as the "pillars of wisdom" characterize Islam. Muslims fast during the month of Ramadan, which marks the revelation of the Qur'an to the Prophet Muhammad; they pray to Allah five times a day facing Mecca (the birthplace of Muhammad and the holiest site in Islam); they make charitable donations; and when possible, they say Friday afternoon prayers with their community. They also undertake the **hajj,** the pilgrimage to Mecca, at least once in their lifetime. The city of Mecca in contemporary Saudi Arabia is the home of the House of Allah, or Ka'aba, which was built by Abraham and his son Ishmael. Muslims perform the hajj in accordance with the Qur'an and in the manner prescribed by the Prophet Muhammed in his Sunnah.

Diversity in the Islamic World   Islamic believers are divided into a variety of faiths and sects. These divisions sometimes result in antagonisms between the members, just as there are religious rivalries between Christian denominations, such as Roman Catholics and Protestants in Northern Ireland. The large majority of Muslims in the United States (and 85 percent globally) are Sunni Muslims—literally, those who follow the Sunnah, the Way of the Prophet. Compared to other Muslims, they tend to be more moderate in their religious orthodoxy. The Shi'is or Shiites (primarily from Iraq, Iran, and southern Lebanon) are the second-largest group. Sunnis and Shi'is historically disgreed on who should have been the *caliph,* or ruler, after the death of the Prophet Muhammad. This disagreement led to different understandings of beliefs and practices, resulting in the Sunni and Shi'is worshiping separately from each other.

In addition to Sunnis and Shi'is, there are many other expressions of Islamic faith. Furthermore there are divisions within Sunnis and Shi'is. To speak of Muslims as Sunni or Shi'i would be akin to speaking of Christians as Roman Catholic or Baptist, forgetting that there are other denominations as well as sharp divisions within the Roman Catholic and Baptist faiths.

Verses in the Qur'an prescribe Muslims to engage in the religious duty of **jihad,** or struggle against the enemies of Allah. Typically, Muslims take jihad to refer to an internal struggle for spiritual purity. Today, however, a very small but visible minority of Muslims view the prescription for jihad as a call to carry out an armed struggle against what they view as the enemies of the Palestinians, such as Israel and the United States. Such interpretations, even if held by a few, cannot be dismissed, because Islam is a faith without an established hierarchy; there is no Muslim pope or authority figure to deliver the one true interpretation, and there is no provision for excommunication. So while such interpretations are not representative of Islam, neither is there a single, recognized voice to denounce them. Individual *imams,* leaders or spiritual guides of a mosque, can offer guidance and scholarship, but Islam's authority rests with the scripture and the teachings of the Prophet.[9]

Islam in America

The history of American Islam begins in the seventeenth century, when members of some Muslim tribes were forcibly brought to the American colonies as slaves. Islam had spread to Africa over time, perhaps as early as Prophet Muhammad's lifetime. It is estimated that 10 percent of African slaves were Muslim. Slave owners discouraged anything that linked them culturally to Africa, including their spiritual beliefs. Furthermore, many in the South saw making slaves Christians as part of their mission in civilizing the enslaved people. Enslaved Muslims in the colonies and elsewhere often resisted the pressure to assimilate to the dominant group's faith and maintained their dedication to Islam.[10]

[9]Don Belt, "The World of Islam," *National Geographic* (January 2002), pp. 76–85. Please note that the reader will find here different spellings of words related to Islam because of different transliterations from the Arabic. Muhammad, the sixth-century prophet, appears occasionally as Mohammed or Muhammad; Shi'i as Shia or Shi'a; and so forth.

[10]Iluas Ba-Yunus and Kassim Kone, "Muslim Americans: A Demographic Report," in *Muslims' Place in the American Public Square,* Zahid H. Bukhari et al., eds. (Walnut Creek, GA: AltaMira Press, 2004) pp. 299–322; Karen Isaksen Leonard, *Muslims in the United States: The State of Research* (New York: Russell Sage Foundation, 2003); and Aminah Beverly McCloud, *African American Islam* (New York: Routledge, 1995).

It was exceedingly difficult for a collective Muslim community to survive slavery. Today's Muslims in the United States, whether African American or not, are not, figuratively speaking, descendants of this early Muslim presence in America. Today's Muslim population is a mix of the twentieth-century development of Islamic thought among African Americans and the Muslims immigrating from abroad in the last one hundred years. This contributes to a rich diversity of beliefs and practices among Muslims in America that is typically not found in predominately Muslim nations where one faith or sect dominates.

The most recent studies suggest that there are at least 1.3 million and perhaps as many as 3 million Muslims in the United States. About two-thirds are U.S.-born citizens. In terms of ethnic and racial background, the more-acceptable estimates vary widely. Estimates range as follows:

- 20–42 percent African American
- 24–33 percent South Asian (Afghan, Bangladeshi, Indian, and Pakistani)
- 12–32 percent Arab
- 15–22 percent other (Bosnian, Iranian, Turk, and White and Hispanic converts)

There appears to be total agreement that the Muslim population in the United States is growing rapidly through immigration and conversion. The number of U.S. adults who identify themselves as Muslim nearly tripled between 1990 and 2008.[11]

The number of mosques in the United States has grown to more than 1,700. Mosques (more properly referred to as a *masjids*) do not maintain identifiable membership rolls as some churches do, but scholars have observed that mosques and their imams today are taking on some of the characteristics of a congregation. To maintain their tax-exempt status, mosques are forced to incorporate boards and bylaws. Imams in the United States are more likely to take on a pastoral role relating to non-religious functions, such as helping immigrants adjust, and representing the Muslim community to other nonprofit groups serving the larger community.

Black Nationalism

The views of The Nation of Islam that we will be considering can be seen as a religious expression of Black Nationalism. **Black Nationalism** refers

[11]Cathy Lynn Grossman, "Muslim Census a Difficult Court," *USA Today* (August 6, 2008); Barry A. Kosmin and Ariela Keysar, *American Religious Identification Survey* (Hartford, CT: Trinity College, 2009), accessible at http://livinginliminality.files.wordpress.com/2009/03/aris_report_2008.pdf; and "Pew Forum on Religion and Public Life," *U.S. Religious Landscape Survey* (Washington, D.C.: Pew Forum), 2008a. Online at religions.pewforum.org/pdf/report2-religious-landscape-study-full.pdf .

to a consciousness that sees African Americans as a cohesive group whose collective experience and heritage are to be celebrated. Autonomy, dignity, and self-reliance are key tenets of Black Nationalism. Historically, Black nationalism has a component of speaking to Black people worldwide and especially seeing links between the interests of Blacks in the Americas and of those in the African continent. It has been manifested in efforts to encourage Black Americans to resettle in Africa expressions of Black Power during the civil rights movement, and to encourage and frequent Black-owned businesses.

A component of much, but not all, Black Nationalist thought is to promote a bridge between black cultural expression in the United States and the rich cultural traditions of Africa. As Malcolm X observed at a 1964 Harvard Law School gathering,

> When you hear a black man playing music, whether it is jazz or Bach, you still hear African music. The soul of Africa is still reflected in the music by black men. In everything else we do we still are Africans in colour, feeling, everything and we will always be that whether we like it or not.[12]

The religious expression of Black Nationalism is not limited to The Nation of Islam, its predecessors, and splinter groups associated with it. Many Christian denominations that are overwhelmingly African American present the "Black is Beneficial" message along with the Biblical teachings. The idea that Jesus Christ was a man of color akin to being a Black person is front and center in many of these churches. Their outreach efforts seek to empower the local Black community and chide their middle class members for avoiding the challenges still being felt by parishioners in slums.[13]

Universal Negro Improvement Association   While not a religious organization, one of the most visible Black Nationalist groups of the early twentieth century was the Universal Negro Improvement Association (UNIA). Jamaican-born Marcus Garvey promoted race pride and international unity through the UNIA, which he founded in 1914. He brought his organization to the United States in 1917 and it became one of the few Black-headed organizations working for Black Americans in the entire nation.

White America was not ready for a Black man gathering support and bringing together thousands of cheering African Americas in the 1920s. Like Father Divine, Garvey became the focus of intense scrutiny by government officials.

---

[12]Cited on p. 238 in Edward D. Curtis IV, "Why Malcolm X Never Developed an Islamic Approach to Civil Rights," *Religion* 32 (2002), pp. 227–42.

[13]Alphonso Pinkney, *Red, Black and Green: Black Nationalism in the United States* (New York: Cambridge University Press, 1976).

Garvey advocated economic independence for Black Americans, but unlike other groups, like the National Association for the Advancement of Colored People (NAACP), he promoted racial separation. The separation went beyond an ideological level. Speaking of the natural union with the people of Africa, he encouraged Blacks to migrate to Africa aboard his Black Star shipping line, which was established to promote commerce between Africa and the Americas. Garvey likened his emigration proposal, which was popularized by slogans like "Back to Africa" and "Africa for Africans," to the Jewish recovery of Palestine.

Criticism of the UNIA came from all quarters—established Black leaders like W. E. B. DuBois, integrationists both White and Black, and notably the federal government, which launched numerous investigations. Found guilty of mail fraud in 1925, Garvey was deported to Jamaica in 1927, never to return before his death in 1940.[14]

In Garvey's absence, the organization survived but rival splinter groups or "Garvey Clubs" surfaced. Without the founder there to unify those yearning for Garvey's message of self-reliance and uplift, organizational meetings filling Madison Square Garden in New York City did not repeat themselves. Yet for decades, aspects of the UNIA's message and Garvey's appeal persisted as evidenced by Mohammed Ali's recollection of his father's allegiance to Garvey.

Double Consciousness   Being Black in White America is a challenge even for someone who was supported by the majority of voters in a national election, as will be discussed later. Famed sociologist W.E.B. DuBois coined the phrase **double consciousness** a century ago to refer to the dual awareness of being both American and African. The descendants of Africans left a twoness and often conflicted identity. DuBois describes the twoness of being Black and American as two souls, two identities that cannot be fully reconciled. This is something African Americans experience from birth.

While Malcolm X did not make explicit reference to DuBois' teaching, he did acknowledge the burden he felt to advocate an Islamic worldview while also promoting the much more narrow goals for African Americans.[15] It is against this backdrop of Black Nationalism, double consciousness, and the long tradition of Islam that we can best understand the Black Muslim movement.

---

[14]William Van Deburg, *Black Nationalism: From Marcus Garvey to Louis Farrakhan* (New York: New York University Press, 1997).

[15]W. E. B. DuBois, *The Souls of Black Folk: Essays and Sketches*, 1903, reprint (New York: Façade Publications, 1961; and Curtis, "Why Malcolm X Never Developed an Islamic Approach to Civil Rights," *Religion* 32 (2002): 227–42.

Moorish Science Temple

One of the earliest expressions of the Black American approach to the Islamic faith is the Moorish Science Temple of America (MST). Founded in 1913 by self-proclaimed Prophet Noble Drew Ali (born Timothy Drew), the MST gained support in Chicago and other urban centers of the Midwest and East.

The background of Prophet Noble Drew Ali has not been successfully documented. He may have been educated in Egypt as a youth. He was clearly impressed with Asian philosophy and proclaimed American Blacks to be "Asiatics," using the term "Moors" or "Moorish Americans" to describe Black Americans. Followers presented their Asiatic status by wearing "nationalist" colors—men wore red or black fezzes and women wore turbans. Followers grew to as many as 20,000 at its height.

The Moorish Science Temple while identifying as Muslim retains Christian elements, including the prominence of Jesus and use of familiar Christian hymns. Yet in keeping with Islamic tradition, worshippers are segregated by sex, pray facing Mecca, and such rituals as baptism and Communion are not practiced. In the writings of Noble Drew Ali and MST ritual there is heavy reliance on aspects of fraternal organizations of the day, such as the Masons and Shriners. There are also elements of mysticism and spiritualism in MST descriptions of Jesus in Egypt, India, and Tibet during the years of his life not specifically recorded in the New Testament.

The scriptural basis of the MST is a sixty-page document titled "The Holy Koran of the Moorish Science Temple." This text, regarded as sacred, was written by Noble Drew Ali in 1927. It includes elements of the Qur'an, Bible, Masonic rituals, and other materials. Despite his conscious use of "Koran," the document does not cite the Qur'an. In fact, most of it is taken from early non-Muslim publications.

In the Holy Koran of MST, the idea that there is a Black race is rejected, and instead African Americans are viewed as members of the Moorish nation, the Asiatic race, and the Islamic religion. In Ali's teachings, the Moors or Asiatics are placed at the very center of human evolution and history. Ali identified African Americans as Moorish Americans. Quite significantly the Holy Koran of MST described Black heritage as very noble and removed from the stereotyped image of the African savage.[16]

---

[16]Noble Drew Ali, "The Holy Koran of the Moorish Science Temple," in Edward E. Curtis IV, ed., *The Columbia Sourcebook of Muslims in the United States* (New York: Columbia University Press, 2008), pp. 59–64; and Susan Nance, "Mystery of the Moorish Science Temple: Southern Blacks and American Alternative to Spirituality in the 1920s Chicago," *Religion and American Culture: A Journal of Interpretation* 12 (No. 2, 2002), pp. 123–66.

Most important to the MST, and objectionable to most traditional Muslims, the Holy Koran indentified Noble Drew Ali as the last Prophet who had been prepared by Allah (that is, God), following in the footsteps of Jesus and Mohammad.

The unexpected death of Ali in 1929 at the age 43 without any successor in place caused the organization to splinter into a variety of factions. Already in the 1930s there was evidence of the police and FBI deliberately organizing campaigns to break up the Moorish Science Temple movement. (This is an aspect of the history of the Black Muslim movement that continues throughout the 1900s and will be discussed later.) Nevertheless temples of the Moorish Science Temple still exist today. [17]

The Moorish Science Temple is regarded as the first mass religious movement in the history of Islam in the United States. One of the splinter organizations formed out of the Moorish Science Temple was the National of Islam, founded by former MST member, Wallace D. Fard Muhammad. His successor, Elijah Muhammad, is also thought to have been a Moorish Science Temple member.[18]

Nation of Islam: Early Years

As we learned in our discussion of the Father Divine movement, the depression led to a rapid deterioration in the experience of Black people. With the stunning deportation of Marcus Garvey in 1927 and death of Ali in 1929, there was no dynamic leader speaking to the spiritual side of Black Nationalism. W. D. Fard filled this void.

As with other early leaders of the extraordinary groups considered in this volume, relatively little is known about the founder of arguably the best-known Black Muslim organization. W. D. Fard first appeared in Detroit as a door-to-door peddler of silks and Asian and African wares. He is thought by some to be Arab and perhaps to have been born in Pakistan, although later accounts contend he was born in Mecca. As he peddled his products, he enthralled people with accounts of the Black homelands.

It is known that he was a member of the Moorish Science Temple and indeed claimed to be Noble Drew Ali reincarnated. When the MST fragmented in the 1930s, some followed Fard and accepted him as leader of a new religious organization, the Nation of Islam (NOI). In 1930 Fard

---

[17]FBI infiltration of Moorish Science Temple of America is discussed in Turner, *Islam in the African-American Experience*, pp. 104–08.

[18]C. Eric Lincoln, *The Black Muslims in America*, 3rd ed. (Grand Rapids, MI: William B. Erdmands Publishing Company, 1994), pp. 48–52; Tasneed Paghdiwala, "The Aging of the Moors," *Chicago Reader* (November 15, 2007), accessed October 28, 2009 at http://www.chicagoreader.com/chicago/the-aging-of-the-moors/content?oid=999633; and Turner, *Islam in the African-American Experience*, pp. 71–108.

founded the Nation of Islam and opened its first temple, named Temple No. 1, in Detroit, Michigan.

Without mentioning double consciousness by name, Fard dismissed any notion that Black people should be conflicted and defiantly declared that they were Asiatics, not Americans. Further, he emphasized that Black people had consistently been ill served by Christians, whether slave owners in the past or politicians today.

An early member of Fard's following of perhaps 8,000 by 1931, was Elijah Robert Poole. Then thirty-four years of age, Poole quickly became an enthusiastic student. A migrant from Georgia, Poole, his wife, and their eight children were among tens of thousands of Southern Blacks who sought opportunities in the industrial North. Just as Noble Drew Ali did earlier, Fard struck a responsive chord in many of these disillusioned migrants, whose experiences in the industrial North had not lived up to their expectations.

The spiritual message that Fard shared with Poole and other disillusioned Black Americans like him is universally referred to as "the hidden truth" or "secret wisdom." Numerous converts to the Nation of Islam over the last century, such as the great boxer Mohammed Ali, have acknowledged that hearing this wisdom was a life-changing event. So, what is this truth?

Black and White people did not come from the same God. Black people were to be "righteous and divine" while White people were naturally wicked. Blacks originally inhabited the holy city of Mecca trillions of years ago. White people emerged much later, a result of a series of genetic experiments by a mad and evil scientist named Mad Yacub. The White man lived on meat, inhabiting the caves of Europe, but eventually came to violently take power from the noble leaders of Black civilizations. While this narrative promotes racist thought, it can also be viewed as "ethnic therapy" in which a shocking new and, most importantly honorable, identity is presented to Black Americans in sharp contrast to the old, shameful identity that then prevailed. The Secret Wisdom holds that the stereotype of the African Savage was imposed by the White man to serve his own interests.[19] This turns the notions of Nordic racial superiority on its head and places the legacy of centuries of enslavement of Africans, or as Noble Drew Ali would say, the enslavement of Moors or Asiatics, in the Americas in a totally different light. Remember that as the followers of Detroit listened to this message in the 1930s, they lived in a city where White members of the Ku Klux Klan greatly outnumbered them.

---

[19]Abubaker Y. Al-Shingiety, "The Muslim as the 'Other': Representation and Self-Image of Muslims in North America," in Yvonne Hadddad, ed., *The Muslims of America* (New York: Oxford University Press, 1991), p. 55.

From its beginnings the racial message of the NOI was different from that of White supremacists. True, the NOI's membership was closed to non-Blacks, but their position of racial supremacy was a defensive reaction to White racism and its accompanying violence.[20]

Soon after Elijah Poole became a follower of the Nation of Islam, Fard acknowledged his high status and renamed him Elijah Muhammad. Fard's organization grew and he created the Muslim Girls Training Class, which instructed young women in home economics and how to be proper wives and mothers. In order to deal with trouble from unbelievers and police officers, he founded the Fruit of Islam—a military-type organization demanding allegiance of its male members—to provide self-defense as necessary. Both of these groups have operated continuously into the twenty-first century.

Elijah Muhammad: Emergence of a Prophet

Mysteriously Fard, now referred to simply as The Prophet or Master, disappeared in June 1934. At the time, and from subsequent investigative efforts, no explanation for his disappearance has been found. Even the contemporary members of the NOI refer to this incident as merely the Master's "departure."[21] Schisms that were already present intensified with the absence of The Prophet. Elijah Muhammad and a group of his followers established Temple No. 2 in Chicago in 1932, maintaining ties and allegiances to The Prophet.

Over time, the teachings of Elijah Muhammad have been rejected and dismissed, emotionally and intellectually, by many. However, as with the teachings of Joseph Smith, John Humphrey Noyes, and L. Ron Hubbard, lack of popularity of an underlying thesis behind an extraordinary group almost makes any success the faith enjoys more compelling.

Muhammad's teachings are disarming in two broad ways: (1) its portrayal of Whites in general and in the United States in particular, and (2) its sharp deviance from Islamic tradition.[22]

The Honorable Elijah Muhammad, the Messenger, deified The Prophet as Allah and mixed aspects of Islam with Christianity. It was not lost on his listeners that by declaring Fard to be Allah, Elijah Muhammad was explicitly declaring that God was Black. This accommodation was not totally unlike what Arab Muslims did in North and

[20]Turner, *Islam in the African-American Experience*, p. 158.
[21]"A Brief History on the Origin of The Nation of Islam in America A Nation of Peace and Beauty," accessed November 6, 2009 at http://www.noi.org/history_of_noi.htm.
[22]Lincoln, *The Black Muslims*, p. xvii.

West Africa beginning in the eighth century, incorporating the local spiritual and cultural beliefs.

Muhammad's early leadership years were not easy. Rivals questioned and threatened his authority. Fearing for his life, Muhammad left Chicago and preached the tenets of the NOI movement along the East Coast. If this were not enough, the Communist Party in the U.S. and a pro-Japan group attempted to infiltrate the NOI and other splinter groups. While the Honorable Elijah Muhammad was never directly linked to the Communist or pro-Japanese elements, the federal government heightened its surveillance. Finally in 1942, Muhammad was arrested for refusing to register for the draft and encouraging others to do the same. While Elijah was in prison, his wife, Clara Muhammad, became the effective leader of the NOI.

When Elijah Muhammad was freed from prison in 1946, most of the rivals vying for his position were no longer a significant threat. The Honorable Elijah Muhammad, the Messenger, was stronger than ever and now a martyr. During the 1950s, the NOI expanded its reach in urban centers. His appearances at Temples or arenas were greeted with a mix of excitement, awe, pride, and reverence. His remarks were punctuated throughout by affirmations from the crowd, "That's right! That's right." The Messenger at this time relied on a close-knit inner circle of Muslim leaders. In 1954 he bestowed one member of this inner circle, Malcolm X Shabbazz, with his highest appointment to date, Chief Minister of the prestigious New York Temple No. 7.[23]

During his more than four decades as leader of the NOI Elijah Muhammad saw over a hundred temples founded and numerous groceries, bakeries, and other small businesses form. Open to all–Muslim, non-Muslim, and people of all racial backgrounds—these enterprises enjoyed sporadic success but typically lasted only a few years at any given location. In some respects the NOI resembled the economic empowerment model of Father Divine. But they also encountered the same challenges: small business owners are very vulnerable economically and the NOI businesses specifically were intended to serve communities with little disposable income.

Elijah Muhammad and Islam   Are the teachings of the Nation of Islam Islamic? It may be strange for an outsider to think that a group whose very name includes "Islam" could not be considered Muslim. Yet to many Christians, groups like Christian Scientists or the Church of Jesus Christ of Latter-day Saints are *not* considered Christian.

Elijah Muhammad argued he was achieving orthodoxy in Muslim beliefs for the NOI. As already noted, Islam has been long marked by

[23]Ibid., p. 185.

The Nation of Islam

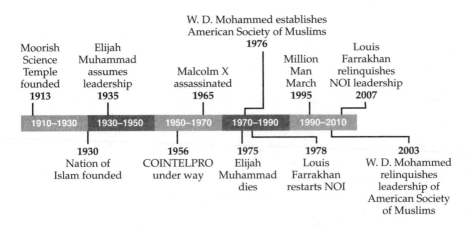

different sects and divisions, so there is not a simple normative universal definition of Islam or even any collective agreement among its adherents as to its boundaries. Still, given this qualification, one would have to conclude that the NOI represents a significant departure from Sunni or Shi'i Muslim thought. This should not be surprising given that NOI has its roots in the Moorish Science Temple and other Black Nationalist thinking. The emergence of NOI also predates any significant immigration to the United States from the predominately Muslim nations of Asia and Africa. Therefore, locally—that is, in the United States—there was not a visible or widespread Islamic presence for which the NOI could takes its cues.

NOI direct reference to the Qur'an was limited and often faulty. For example, Malcolm X, while national spokesman for Elijah Muhammad in 1962, attempted to use Islam scriptures to support the position of White people as devils. He cited the Qur'an where it says that "we shall gather the guilty, blue-eyed," and equated "blue-eyed" with White people. Commentators quickly noted the faulty interpretation and that "blue-eyed" should not be taken as referencing White people.[24]

While Elijah Muhammad played a decisive role in Islam's penetration into the Judeo-Christian bastion of the United States, it is also accurate to say that within a generation of his death, Muhammad's brand of Muslim faith no longer defines Islam in the United States.[25]

[24]Curtis, "Why Malcolm X Never Developed an Islamic Approach to Civil Rights," p. 228.
[25]Lincoln, *The Black Muslims;* and Wesley Williams, "Black Muslim Theology and the Classical Islamic Tradition: Possibilities of a Rapprochement," *American Journal of Islamic Social Sciences* 25 (No. 4, 2008), pp. 61–89.

Malcolm X: Spokesman for Black Muslims

Malcolm X was one of the most powerful and brilliant voices of the Black Nationalist movement and the Nation of Islam. He was an authentic folk hero to his sympathizers. Besides his own followers, he commanded an international audience, and is still referred to in a manner befitting a prophet. Few twentieth-century religious leaders have their lives so well chronicled as Malcolm X. Just after his death, *The Autobiography of Malcolm X*, written with Alex Haley, became a best seller and in 1992 director Spike Lee's motion picture, *Malcolm X*, reintroduced the Black Muslim leader to a new generation.

Born Malcolm Little in 1925 in Omaha, Nebraska, his family moved several times, settling in the Detroit area by 1929. These were not casual moves and were often the result of antagonism from White neighbors—most notably, White men, perhaps Ku Klux Klan members, burned down their home in Lansing, Michigan, when Malcolm was just five. The next year Malcolm's father died in a streetcar accident and then, a few years later, his mother experienced a complete nervous breakdown. In his early teens Malcolm was placed in various foster homes and even a juvenile home.

In 1946 Malcolm was caught and convicted of burglary charges and of carrying firearms. He began his prison sentence in Boston, where he was introduced to the teachings of Honorable Elijah Muhammad. The fact that Malcolm X converted to the NOI in prison is significant. The NOI found success in prison ministries because it did not stigmatize the prisoner but saw him as a lost soul and victim of the ravages of modern, White-dominated society.

In prison, Malcolm received letters from his brother Philbert in Detroit, which were filled with descriptions of the "holiness" that he had encountered there. Philbert wrote that he would pray for Malcolm. Malcolm dismissed these overtures at first but in time was intrigued by his brother's advice to "pray to Allah" and not to eat pork, drink alcohol, or smoke cigarettes. Eventually Malcolm began to follow the advice of his brother and family members and wrote to Elijah Muhammad. Reading anything he could find from the NOI voraciously, Malcolm X introduced The Messenger's teachings to other inmates. He passionately recounted in his *Autobiography* how he enjoyed telling his Black brother inmates the glories of past Black civilizations and the continuing treachery of the White man.

Upon his parole in 1952, Malcolm immersed himself in the NOI, using his charismatic personality to recruit new members. As mentioned, in 1954 he became minister of successively larger, bigger temples culminating in the prestigious Temple No. 7 in Harlem. He founded the newspaper *Muhammad Speaks* in 1961, which Black males sold on street corners, furthering the reach of the NOI. Membership of NOI mushroomed to an estimated 500,000. With the blessings of the Prophet Elijah Muhammad, Malcolm X became the face, the spokesperson, of the Nation of Islam.

At this time the Nation of Islam was known to most Americans, although not necessarily understood. In 1959, famed news analyst Mike Wallace conducted a five-part series about the NOI, titled "The Hate That Hate Produced." Followers of The Nation of Islam were captured on screen saying things about the Christian religion and White people in general that shocked the general public.[26] Unsurprisingly, criticism of the NOI abounded. Martin Luther King, Jr., in his famous 1963 "a letter from a Birmingham Jail," cited the NOI as a primary example of the dangers inherent in doing nothing to change the inequalities of segregation in the South. According to King, the anger of the Black separatist movement closed the dialogue between Whites and Blacks and "nourished" the "continued existence of racial segregation."[27]

However, Malcolm X saw it differently. In his autobiography, he explained what he understood to be the difference between segregation and the separatism of the Nation of Islam:

> *Segregation* is when your life and liberty are controlled, regulated, by *someone else*. To *segregate* means to control. Segregation is that which is forced upon inferiors by superiors. But *separation* is that which is done voluntarily, by two equals—for good of both![28]

Malcolm X ends his relationship with the Messenger   Some members of the Nation of Islam, such as Malcolm X, who eventually turned to more orthodox teachings of Islam, were not necessarily defensive about narratives such as Mad Yacub creating White people. As Malcolm X noted, the real fault for any misunderstanding lay with the Muslims of the East, who had failed to make real Islam known in the West and therefore allowed any "religious faker" (that is, Elijah Muhammad) to prosper.

Despite Elijah Muhammad's provocative speeches, he avoided speaking about everyday events, including the growing civil rights movement. When President John F. Kennedy was assassinated in November 1963, Malcolm X famously said that Kennedy never foresaw that the chickens would come home to roost so soon. Muhammad immediately indicated that he saw this as a direct defiance by Malcolm X of his orders not to make any statements regarding political events. The relationship between the top two figures in the NOI was deteriorating beyond repair.

---

[26]The two hours of this television special can be viewed (although of modest quality) at Google videos, specifically at http://video.google.com/videoplay?docid=6140647821635049109#'.

[27]"Letter from a Birmingham Jail," April 16, 1963, accessible at http://www.africa.upenn.edu/Articles_Gen/Letter_Birmingham.html.

[28]Malcolm X, *Autobiography*, p. 268. Emphasis is in the original.

In 1964, Malcolm X had begun to have serious conflicts with Elijah Muhammad. These centered on (1) Muhammad's position that the NOI stay out of taking positions on the growing civil rights movement, (2) the NOI's consistent distancing itself from more traditional Muslim groups that strictly followed the teachings of the Qur'an, and (3) Malcolm X's own doubts about the personal morality of Elijah Muhammad, as the latter's extramarital affairs came to Malcolm X's attention. This friction grew stronger following Malcolm X's well-publicized participation in a hajj to Mecca. At this time he took the Muslim name of el-Hajj Malik el-Shabazz. He disavowed Fard's divinity and the other NOI doctrines not accepted by mainstream Muslims, specifically Sunni believers.

As Malcolm X traveled to the Middle East he had been struck by the racial diversity among Muslims, which caused him rethink his frequent reference to "white devils." During his pilgrimage in 1964 to Mecca, the holy city of Islam, he wrote Alex Haley, his collaborator in his *Autobiography*, that he had "eaten from the same plate with fellow Muslims whose eyes were bluer than blue, whose hair was blond, blonder than blond, whose skin was whiter than white." Malcolm X began embracing a global Islamic faith.[29]

Interestingly, Elijah Muhammad had taken a pilgrimage and completed a hajj in 1960. Obviously he was introduced to orthodox Islam in Mecca, but unlike Malcolm X he did not reconsider his racial separatist teachings. He continued in the years following his hajj to maintain his primacy as the final authority of Islam in the United States.[30]

COINTELPRO

The Nation of Islam throughout its history has often been attacked by outsiders as secretive and overly clannish. This is a frequent charge we have seen with other extraordinary groups. However, there has been a legitimate reason for the NOI limiting access to outsiders.

The NOI was the subject of covert systematic government investigation with the intention of destabilizing the group. Beginning in 1956 and not ending until 1971, the FBI conducted **COINTELPRO** (COunter INTELigence PROgram) with the aim of protecting the national security. COINTELPRO prospered at a time when many Americans and federal officials were suspicious of dissident groups, seen as "un-American." Most of its resources were used to infiltrate, marginalize, or subvert

---

[29]David Gallen, *Malcolm X: As They Know Him* (New York: Carroll and Graf, 1992), p. 71. Malcolm X used the "white devils" reference many times. On national television, he made the remark in an interview with Black journalist Louis Lomax. Transcript accessed November 9, 2009 at http://teachingamericanhistory.org/library/index.asp?document=539.

[30]Turner, *Islam in the African American Experience*, pp. 194–95.

groups that various administrations identified as being subversive. Among those targeted were Communist organizations, but also civil rights groups and individuals such as Martin Luther King, Jr.

One category of targeted groups were Black Nationalist groups such as the Nation of Islam and the Black Panthers. While NOI leaders suspected government undercover work, the range and scope of COINTELPRO was, by its nature, secret and not understood until relevant FBI files were made public after a burglary of an FBI office in 1971. It became known that specific efforts were undertaken to create and exploit "splits" between Elijah Muhammad and Malcolm X. The NOI was to be discredited within the African American community. Furthermore, COINTELPRO had the Department of State in 1960 contact embassies in African, Arab, and Muslim nations to "discreetly" discourage foreign nationals "who express particular interest in the Islamic movement among U.S. negroes (SIC) . . . from making contact with . . . Elijah Muhammad." Such efforts should "avoid the impression that the U.S. Government has any prejudice against either Islam or negroes" (sic).[31]

Given that so much of COINTELPRO remains classified, it is impossible to determine how much this covert activity altered the experience of the followers of the Nation of Islam, but most likely it altered some of its history.

A Tumultuous Period: 1965–1975

In an eleven-year period, the Nation of Islam experienced tragedies and dissension that left followers less unified than they had been since the earliest years of Elijah Muhammad's leadership.

Increasingly distanced from the NOI, Malcolm X's appeal was still strong among Black American Muslims. Under the names Muslim Mosque and the Organization of Afro-American Unity, he sought to lead African American Muslims who were looking for a more traditional belief system. His efforts barely under way, Malcolm X was assassinated on February 21, 1965; there were charges of inadequate police protection.

Assassination of Malcolm X   Malcolm X's murder in a crowded auditorium before some 400 people, including his wife and children, created shock waves nationally and worldwide, especially in Muslim countries. While Malcolm X had increasingly spoken about nonviolence and had set aside the Black Nationalist rhetoric, he often spoke of the likelihood of an

---

[31]The February 15, 1960 Department of State instructions were declassified October 27, 2005, and can be viewed at http://www.adl.org/main_Nation_of_Islam/what_is_the_nation_of_islam.htm. The 1976 Church Committee was officially called the Select Committee to Study Government Operations with respect to Intelligence Activities, United States Senate.

attempt on his life, but generally avoided taking those steps personally that might have protected him from violence.

Who killed the longtime spokesman of the Nation of Islam? At least three firearms were responsible for the ten bullet wounds and two shotgun blasts. One person was arrested at the scene and people in the crowd identified two others. All three Black men said to be the shooters were members of the Nation of Islam. One confessed and all three were subsequently tried and convicted.

Their motivation and whether others had pushed them to commit the crime have been the subjects of speculation ever since. Malcolm X's tireless efforts to rid Harlem of narcotics, crime, alcohol, and prostitution have led some to question the role of organized crime in his assassination. In addition, the growing awareness of COINTELPRO's role to create dissension among Black Muslim groups has encouraged the argument that the federal government created an atmosphere where Malcolm X's murder was inevitable.

Millenarian Movement   Like the Jehovah's Witnesses, the Nation of Islam was a millenarian movement. Earlier we had presented Elijah Muhammad's teaching that White people were the outcome of a Black scientist named Mad Yacub thousands of years ago. Muhammad, drawing upon earlier predictions by Fard, also maintained that rule by Whites was destined to end in a cataclysmic war he termed "the Fall of America," similar to events described in the Book of Revelation. Scholars of Muhammad's writing and speeches contend that the victorious apocalypse was specified for the late 1960s. This would qualify the NOI as a **millenarian movement** in that its membership anticipated a dramatic change that will bring about a perfect time.

As we see, the period beginning in the mid-1960s was definitely a time of change, with Malcolm X's independence from NOI followed by his assassination. Some leaders such as Minister Louis Farrakhan saw it as a time of opportunity for the Nation of Islam.

Unlike the Jehovah's Witnesses, the anticipation of the millennium was not a major part of the belief system of the followers of Elijah Muhammad. Probably many were even unaware that a specific time for the Fall of America and the restoration of Black greatness had even been prophesized. The early 1970s saw fewer and fewer references in speeches and publications to whether the United States was in the process of an upheaval and whether the followers of Elijah Muhammad would play any special role.[32]

---

[32]The significance of the millenarian prophecy in the NOI is advanced by Martha F. Lee, *The Nation of Islam: An American Millenarian Movement* (Syracuse, NY; Syracuse University Press, 1996), but this significance is questioned by Lawrence Mamiya in his review of the book that appeared in the *American Journal of Sociology* (January 1997), pp. 1224–25.

Death of Elijah Muhammad In 1975, Elijah Muhammad passed away, leaving what appeared to outsiders an impossible void to fill, but this proved not to be the case. A successive leader was quickly identified as W. D. Mohammed, a son of Elijah Muhammad. (W. D. Mohammed was at various times known as Warith Dean). Before the death of his father, W. D. Mohammed had drifted in and out of the NOI's inner circle as he became more supportive of the Sunni view of Islam.

Birth of American Society of Islam

Upon assuming leadership, W. D. Mohammed boldly rejected the racial separatism once and for all, departing from the organization's legacy of Black Nationalism. He moved to abolish the paramilitary Fruit of Islam, invited Whites to join, and emphasized traditional Muslim teachings. To underscore this break, he renamed the religious organization the World Community of Islam in the West. The name eventually became the American Society of Muslims. The American Society of Muslims sought to become an integral part of American Islam, and no longer emphasized the race of its followers. W. D. Mohammed became the most prominent spokesman for the African American and immigrant Muslim communities. Despite his bold choices, Mohammed was more soft-spoken than his charismatic father. He chose to go by the more modest title "imam," a title typically associated with the leader of a single mosque, rather than lofty titles of "messenger" or "prophet" used by his father, Elijah Muhammed.

W. D. Mohammed's desire to move African Americans to more traditional Muslim practices would seem to have succeeded. About half (48 percent) of native-born African American Muslims in a 2007 national survey identify as Sunni. Another third (34 percent) identify solely as Muslim and 15 percent have another affiliation, including Shi'i and NOI.[33]

A significant reform enacted under the leadership of W. D. Mohammed was to decentralize the authority that had been present in the old NOI under his father. He encouraged local communities, temples, and mosques to create their own course. This move to greater autonomy made it increasingly difficult to generalize, much less specify, what the followers of W. D. Mohammed believed, except that they were prepared to reject the more racialized teachings of Elijah Muhammad. W. D. Mohammed declared that African American Muslims needed to become more faithful to the traditions of Islam.[34]

[33]Pew Forum on Religion and Public Life, 2008a, *U.S. Religious Landscape Survey*, p. 22.
[34]Michael Vicente Perez and Fatima Bahloul, "Wareeth Muhammad's last interview," September 14, 2008, accessed November 8, 2009, at http://mafatihulhikmah .blogsport.com/2008/09/wareeth-muhammads-last-interview.html.

While setting aside the Black Nationalist aspects of the faith, W. D. Mohammed still held that being Black and Muslim in the United States had social significance. In his last interview before his death, he explained this:

> Mainly it's the history: how we became Muslims, the strange routes that we took, the feeling we have in our hearts and minds, our outlook on everything. I am not saying it is negative. It is positive. It encouraged us to become independent thinkers. And if we can become independent thinkers, then we can make a contribution to Islam in America.[35]

W. D. Mohammed stepped down as spiritual leader of the American Society of Muslims in 2003, criticizing other imams and leaders in the African American Muslim community for not taking orthodox Islam seriously enough, including not dedicating themselves to mastering Arabic and studying the Qur'an. His resignation marked a period in which numerous factions developed and individual mosques and temples within the Black community were exerting more and more autonomy.[36]

W. D. Mohammed died in 2008. His followers in individual temples have not maintained a uniform organization or even a collective accepted name. However, they continue to study his past speeches and align themselves generally with Sunni teachings.

Nation of Islam Persists

Not all NOI followers were pleased with W. D. Mohammed's decisions. Most notably Minister Louis Farrakhan, who had led the Boston temple, left Mohammed's group in 1978 and reintroduced the "Nation of Islam." Farrakhan embraced the divinity of Fard and principles of Black Nationalism, along with references to the "white devil." While being viewed as a national leader, Black Muslim mosques often operate independently of each other today even when paying homage to Minister Farrakhan.

Farrakhan (originally Louis Wolcott), born in 1933, had joined the NOI in 1955, recruited by Malcolm X. He rose through the ranks, eventually heading Malcolm's old home Temple No. 7 in New York. Farrakhan reminds many outsiders of Malcolm X. A fiery speaker, willing to excite followers and incite critics, Farrakhan became the new public face of Islam among African Americans even if most, arguably, were moving toward more traditional Sunni teachings.

The issue of succession once again faced The Nation of Islam in 2007, as it had many times before with Fard's mysterious departure, Elijah

---

[35]Perez and Bahloul, "Wareeth Muhammad's last interview."
[36]Monique Parsons, "The Most Important Muslim You've Never Heard Of," September 2003, accessed November 8, 2009 at http://www.beliefnet.com/faiths/islam/2003/09/the-most-important-muslim-youve-never-heard-of.aspx?print=true

AP Photo/Charles Rex Arbogast

Mosque Maryam in Chicago, Illinois, which served as the headquarters for the Nation of Islam and Minister Louis Farrakhan.

Muhammad's death, and W. D. Muhammad's embracing Sunni beliefs. Acknowledging his advanced age and recovery from cancer surgery, Farrakhan gave up control of the NOI to an executive committee with senior Minister Ishmael Muhammad, a son of Elijah Muhammad, playing a key role.

Still, today little happens in the NOI headquarters without Farrakhan's involvement. He continues to appear and speak at major events such as the 2008 renovation of NOI's national Maryam Mosque in Chicago. He also was present at the funeral of W. D. Mohammed the same year.[37]

Later, we will consider the Million Man March, led by Minister Farrakhan, which generally received positive attention by the general public. More typically, however, the headlines concerning Farrakhan have been unflattering for the NOI. In 2009, Louis Farrakhan welcomed Mu'ammar al-Gadhafi, Libya's head of state, on his arrival to speak at the United Nations in New York City. This was not a greeting that endeared Farrakhan to the general public. This came just after Gadhafi himself welcomed back to Libya, as a hero, the man convicted for placing bombs aboard Pam Am Flight 103, resulting in 270 passengers losing their lives. Nonetheless, Farrakhan spoke amidst the national outcry that Gadhafi,

[37]Neil MacFarquhar, "Nation of Islam at a Crossroad as Leader Exists," *New York Times* (January 26, 2007), pp. A1, A16; and Ashahed M. Muhammad, "Life and Ministry of Imam W. Deen Mohammad Remembered," *The Final Call* (September 21, 2008), accessed at http://www.finalcall.com/artman/publish/National_news_2/life_and_ministry_of_imam_ w_deen_mohammad_remember_5222.shtml.

viewed by many as a sponsor of anti-American terrorism, should be permitted to enter the United States.

> You may ask why we feel honored and privileged to welcome him; it is because ever since we have know him, he has been a friend of the struggle of Black people all over the World for true liberation . . . While Brother Gadhafi's visit to America may attract protestors, which is the right of any American to do . . . I hope it will also attract those of us who have honored and respected Brother Gadhafi over the years for his tireless efforts in Black liberation and the struggle of the masses.
>
> On a personal note, years ago I told some revolutionary brothers in Africa that I too am a revolutionary but the revolution that I am concerned with is not fostered by the use of carnal weapons. The revolution that I was then involved in and am involved in now is fostered by the Divine Light found in the Bible and the Holy Qur'an. There is no real revolution as long as we remain mentally enslaved by our former colonial and slave masters. We must be made new and that can only happen if the veil of ignorance is removed and replaced with that knowledge that will bring up a new idea and vision. This kind of revolution will change Africa and the World.[38]

These are strong words, especially when delivered in the post 9/11 world.

The Nation of Islam and Jewish Americans

Starting with the Moorish Science Temple, the unique presentation of Islam among Black Americans has sought to distinguish itself from the Judeo-Christian heritage of the United States. Furthermore it has often denigrated Christians and particularly Black men and women who accept its beliefs. Noble Drew Ali declared that "Allah is God, the white man is the devil and the so called Negroes are the Asiatic Black people, the cream of the planet earth."[39]

Jewish Americans have been particularly identified among Whites as the focus of the rhetoric of the NOI. Why was this? Jews had long championed the antislavery cause, the creation of the NAACP, and later civil rights. However, on a daily basis, the Jews that many urban Black Americans encountered were landlords and inner city merchants. This led Black Muslim leaders to build on the anti-Jewish sentiment already present in larger society to rally anti-White feelings.

---

[38]Address entitled "The Nation of Islam Welcomes Muammar Gadhafi," reproduced in *The Final Call* (September 22, 2009), accessed November 10, 2009, at http://www.finalcall.com/artman/publish/featuredFarrakhanArticle/article_6445.shtml (p. 29).

[39]The Anti-Defamation League (ADL) of B'nai Brith has been particularly vigilant in identifying what the organization argues are anti-Semitic statements or positions within the NOI; see http://www.icdc.com/~paulwolf/cointelpro/islamic%20Negro%20Groups%20in%20the%20US%Feb%2015%201960.htm.

Anti-Semitic statements have been an occasional part of Nation of Islam rhetoric and literature despite occasional calls by some leaders for reconciliation. For example, the NOI's 1991 publication *The Secret Relationship Between Blacks and Jews* advances the argument that slavery in the Western Hemisphere was initiated by Jewish shipowners and merchants and that Jews have continued to seek domination of African Americans in the contemporary world. There is no support for such arguments and such a book only served to inflame Jewish–NOI relationships. Elsewhere, the NOI argues that Jewish organizations control the Federal Reserve.

Given such positions, the NOI, and Louis Farrakhan in particular, have been termed **anti-Semitic**—defined as being prejudice and discriminatory against Jews, whether secular or observant.

Almost as often as the NOI is charged with being anti-Semitic, statements are made by the organization contending the charges are nonsense and that allegedly anti-Semitic quotations have been taken out of context. For example, Malcolm X told religion scholar C. Eric Lincoln in an interview that "we make no distinction between Jews and non-Jews so long as they are all white." In other words, anti-Jewish expressions are a subset of anti-White feelings.[40]

Jewish Americans do not accept such explanations, noting that much NOI rhetoric resorts to using Jewish stereotypes, minimizes the Holocaust, and overlooks support of Jews and Jewish organizations for the cause of civil rights. The fact that the NOI has taken a strong position favoring Palestinians and Arab states over Israel's right to exist further inflames the back and forth between NOI and Jewish Americans.

Statements that are viewed as anti-Semitic in nature are not relegated to a generation ago. Upon the death of Michael Jackson in 2009, Farrakhan delivered a three-hour address titled "The Crucifixation of Michael Jackson and All Responsible Black Leadership." At one point he cited Zionist Jews as primary perpetrators for crucifying influential African Americans like Jackson and Martin Luther King. He also contended that Jackson had been forced to remove anti-Semitic lyrics from songs and went on to detail Jackson's alleged failed attempt to work with Jewish filmmakers like Steven Spielberg. While most of Farrakhan's speeches past and present are devoid of anti-Semitic references and speak of the need for his followers to reach out to all, his statements continue to distract from his leadership role.[41]

[40]Lincoln, *Black Muslims,* p. 161.
[41]Anti-Defamation League, "Farrakhan's Michael Jackson Speech Marked by Anti-Semitism" (July 20, 2009), accessed October 28, 2009, at http://www.adl.org/main_Nation_of_Islam/farrakhan_michael_jackson_speech.htm.

Family Life and Gender

As with most people, the family plays a central role in the lives of followers of the Nation of Islam. Indeed the importance of family, emphasis on morality, and modesty are attractive aspects of the NOI. Many converts find their lifestyle a refuge to the chaotic lives they may have left behind.

Traditionally, Islam worldwide permits men to have multiple wives—a maximum of four. The Qur'an admonishes Muslim men to do justice economically and emotionally to their wives, and if they cannot, then they should have only one wife. In some non-Islamic countries, this practice of multiple marriages is legal, but it is exceedingly rare for Muslim households in countries where the law is not supportive. Followers of the Nation of Islam, as well as other groups adhering to Islam in the Untied States, have never endorsed the practice of multiple wives.

The NOI generally has taken conservative views on many social issues. Members of the Nation of Islam are to make marriage work and while divorce is permitted, it is frowned upon. Adultery is severely punished and homosexuality is frowned upon.[42]

Nation of Islam leadership encourages its members to marry other Black American Muslims. Interracial marriages are forbidden. The NOI places an emphasis on large families. Elijah Muhammad saw birth control as part a conspiracy "directed at so-called Negroes and not at the American whites . . . . They are seeking to destroy our race through our women."[43]

Islam does stress that women need to be protected and should present themselves modestly in public. This code is operationalized very differently within countries where Muslims dominate, and it varies within Muslim populations in the United States as well as among members of the Nation of Islam.

The sixth-century Prophet Muhammad indicated in his Sunnah that the female body should be covered except the face, hands, and feet. Hence, traditional Muslim women should wear head coverings. The **hijab** refers to a variety of garments that allow women to follow the guidelines of modest dress. The wearing of a hijab is expected among female followers of the Nation of Islam. It may include head coverings or a face veil and can take the form of a headscarf rather than something that actually covers the face; the latter would be dictated by a cultural tradition, not Islam. U.S. Muslims select from an array of traditional garments from Muslim

[42]Louis Farrakhan, *A Torchlight for America* (Chicago: FCN Publishing, 1993), pp. 104–05; and "Pew Forum on Religion and Public Life," 2008a, *U.S. Religious Landscape Survey*, pp. 45–46.
[43]Cited on p. 31 of Lee, *Nation of Islam*.

Alex Wong/Newsmakers/Getty Images

A family of members of Fruit of Islam take in the 2000 Million Family March on the Capitol Mall in Washington. The march marked the fifth anniversary of the Million Man March and was organized by the Nation of Islam to celebrate family unity and racial and religious harmony.

countries. These garments include long, loose-tailored coats or a loose black overgarment along with a scarf and perhaps a face veil. U.S. Muslim women are just as apt to wear long skirts or loose pants and overblouses that they may buy at any local retail outlet.[44]

While precise data are not available, African Americans are more likely to be converts to Islam than are people of Asian or Arab background. A 2001 national study of mosques identified about 20,000 converts annually to Islam, of whom 70 percent were African Americans. This leads us to conclude that when it comes to African American adherents to Islam generally, and NOI households more specifically, they are following a religious path not necessarily taken by their own parents or in-laws. This inevitably places tension on African American Muslim families as they attempt to maintain ties with their larger kinship group.[45]

Education

Educating young people, whether formally through schools or informally through day-to-day social interaction, is a common theme among

[44]Shaykh Fadhilalla Haeri, *The Thoughtful Guide to Islam* (Alresford, UK: O Books, 2004).
[45]Ihan Bagby, Paul M. Perl, and Bryan T. Froehle, *The Mosque in America; A National Portrait* (Washington, DC: Council on American-Islamic Relations, 2001).

extraordinary groups. The Nation of Islam is no exception. Followers of the Nation of Islam value formal instruction and many private schools have been created by their members. Initially few in number, there are now several hundred elementary and secondary schools, the majority attached to mosques, that offer what has been referred to in other religious contexts as a parochial school education. Some of these are affiliated with Black Muslim groups. Increasing numbers of Muslims are turning to home schooling either out of a desire to adhere to their customs in a way that is difficult to do in public schools, or out of a concern over the prejudice their children may experience.

Children attending public schools encounter the type of adjustment experienced by those of a religious faith different from the dominant one in society. Although public schools are intended to be secular, it is difficult to escape the orientation of many activities of Christmas and Easter or dietary practices that may not conform to the cultural tradition of the children's families. In some public school districts with larger Muslim student populations, steps have been taken to recognize religious diversity. A few have granted Eid-al-Fitr, the day marking the end of Ramadan, as an official school holiday for all students.

Arabic is important in both youth and adult education. NOI members typically greet each other *"As-salaam a laikum"* (peace be unto you) and are greeted in return by *"Wa-alaikum salaam"* (and unto you be peace). Opening prayers are often said in Arabic, but most NOI followers know little Arabic beyond those ritualistic uses.

The Clara Muhammad schools, named after Elijah Muhammad's wife, are a network of schools founded by the NOI in 1932. Originally called the University of Islam, these schools were (and are) at the elementary and secondary level. At this writing, in early 2010, there are thirty-two schools located in at least nine states, the District of Columbia, and Bermuda.[46] Each school today is independently governed and administered although they draw upon a common curriculum.

These pre-K through eighth-grade schools involve study of the Qur'an and the Arabic language and also seek to redress the social and economic disadvantages of being Black in a predominantly White society. While the schools are not restricted to Black youth, they are overwhelmingly populated by African Americans. Some non-Muslim parents do send their children to Clara Muhammad schools, attracted by their more disciplined nature.

Since the 1975 break between NOI and W. D. Mohammed, the schools have moved "from a Black Nationalist organization" to "a global,

---

[46]Austin, *Achieving Blackness,* p. 31; Oscar Avila, "Muslim Holiday Testing Schools," *Chicago Tribune* (November 24, 2003), 1, 16; Yvonne Y. Haddad, Farid Senzai, and Jane I. Smith, eds., *Educating the Muslims of America* (Oxford: Oxford University Press, 2009); Michael S. Merry, *Culture, Identity, and Islamic Schooling* (New York: Palgrave Macmillan, 2007).

multi-ethnic, multi-linguistic, multi-cultural, universal Islamic philosophy."[47] Despite this outreach, relatively few Muslim immigrant households make use of Clara Muhammad schools even when they are available. Typically, immigrant Muslims and their descendants frequent full-time or after-school programs organized along Muslim sect and nationality lines.

The Million Man March

The high point, both in visibility and generally positive response, in the recent history of the Nation of Islam came with its sponsoring the Million Man March (MMM) in 1995. While not religious, much less Black Nationalist, in rhetoric, the call for Black men to gather on the Mall in Washington, D.C. by Minister Farrakhan received international attention. He called for "a million sober, disciplined, committed, dedicated, inspired black men to meet in Washington on a day of atonement." In his address at the Million Man March, Farrakhan alternated between citing verses from the Qur'an and the Bible. Free of advocacy for the NOI, Farrakhan asked men to make the MMM pledge, which included a vow against crime, wife and child abuse, and drug use.[48]

The mass gathering, on October 16, 1995, was greeted with admiration but also some criticism. Some of the latter was accompanied by stereotyped fear of so many Black males gathering in one place. Critics mocked a broad call for moral behavior by Farrakhan for African American men in a tone, for example, not directed at similar gatherings by evangelists such as Billy Graham. Most of the controversy was a continuation of the debate swirling around Farrakhan and his more contested positions.

Interestingly, the biggest headlines in the immediate aftermath involved the debate over the size of the gathering. Critics contended that anything less than a million signaled a failure for the NOI leader. Obviously in the months leading up to MMM, Farrakhan created the very explicit goal of at least one million. The U.S. (National) Park Police issued its official estimate, as it did for mass gatherings, of 400,000. That figure put it much larger than the 1979 Papal Mass or the 1963 March on Washington ("I have a dream") Rally but fell short of Farrakhan's announced goal and pronouncements on that day and subsequently that millions gathered. In the furor over numbers, Congress prohibited

---

[47]Clara Muhammad Schools, "About Us," accessed November 1, 2009, at http://www.claramuhammadschools.org.

[48]Charles Bierbauer, "Its Goal More Widely Accepted than Its Leader," CNN News (October 17, 1995), http://www.cnn.com/us/9510/megamarch/10-17/notebook/index.html; and Frances Murphy, "The MMM Pledge," http://www.afro.com/history/million/pledge.html.

the Park Police from publicizing its estimates of demonstration sizes ever again.[49]

Regardless, the legacy of such an event is hard to measure. There is evidence that appeals to the assembled masses did lead to thousands of new registered voters. Perhaps the most tangible legacy has been the creation of new organizations for Black men to serve their communities. Mentoring efforts continue years after the mass gathering before the United States Capitol.[50]

Black Nationalism in Obamaland

The notion of Black Nationalist thought being greeted with such hostility by most White Americans may seem outdated in light of the recent election of President Barack Obama. But even a mainstream politician like Obama ignited the fear of many voters because of his connections with both Black Nationalism and Islam. During the 2008 campaign, Obama had to assure voters he would represent all Americans. This need largely grew out of adverse reaction to his own affiliation with a church proud of being Black in the United States. Indeed, he dedicated a speech, "A More Perfect Union" for that purpose, declaring his unyielding faith in the decency and generosity of the American people.[51]

In his autobiography, Barack Obama reflects on the ambivalence that many people felt when they first heard of Black Nationalism: "I had tried to untangle the twin strands." He accepted the message of "solidarity and self-reliance, discipline and communal responsibility" but rejected that it depended on "hatred of whites."[52]

Obama's religious background fueled some of the controversy surrounding his candidacy. The son of a nonpracticing Kenyan Muslim immigrant, he was raised in the Christian church. As an adult he became a member of the predominately White denomination, the United Church of Christ (UCC). The long time pastor of the particular UCC church in Chicago where Obama attended, was married, and had his children

[49]Clark McPhail and John McCarthy, "Who Counts and How: Estimating the Size of the Protests," *Contexts* 3 (Summer 2004), pp. 12–18.

[50]"A movement or just a moment?" *USA Today* (October 10, 1996), accessed at http://www.usatoday.com/news/index/nman001.htm; and "Big Brothers Big Sisters, Essence Magazine," accessed at http://www.bbbs.org/site/c.dijkkpljvh/b.1539813/apps/s/content.asp?ct=7227917 on October 29, 2009.

[51]Barack Obama, "A More Perfect Union," Constitution Center, Philadelphia, Pennsylvania, March 18, 2008, in T. Denean Sharpley-Whiting, ed., *The Speech: Race and Barack Obama's 'A More Perfect Union* (New York: Bloomsbury, 2009), p. 237; also accessible at http://www.huffingtonpost.com/2008/03/18/obama-race-speech-read-th_n_92077.html.

[52]Barack Obama, *Dreams from My Father: A Story of Race and Inheritance* (New York: Three Rivers Press, 1995), p. 197.

baptized, was Reverend Dr. Jeremiah A. Wright, Jr. Wright reflected the Black Nationalist tradition in some of the contemporary African American protestant churches. Wright declared, "Racism is how this country was founded and how this country is still run!" Notwithstanding that Rev. Wright was an ex-Marine and earned a doctoral degree from the prestigious Divinity School at the University of Chicago, video clips of controversial segments of his sermons went viral on the Internet, creating an image of Obama's pastor as a racist. Wright was unashamedly Black in the Black Nationalist tradition, but that does not mean he was anti-White.[53]

Rev. Wright can be seen as a part of the Christian movement that trumpeted Black Nationalist thought. Black liberation theology goes back to the mid-1960s, when African American pastors advocated an aggressive use of Christian principles to overcome racism. This theology developed both as a means to further the civil rights movement and also in response to the Nation of Islam's charges that Christianity was a White man's religion. Pastors and congregations, like those of Rev. Wright, try to make Christianity a means for African Americans to demand justice.[54]

Obama's Christianity was not only suspect, but so were the Muslim roots of his father. To some American Muslims, his constant campaign assertions that he was not a follower of Islam was akin to committing treason. On the other hand, despite Obama's public devotion to Christianity, some non-Muslims saw him as the "wrong kind" of Christian, and believe that in fact he is a Muslim. In March 2009, after he was inaugurated, 12 percent of the general public reported their belief that he was a Muslim.[55]

Concluding Thoughts

Islam among African Americans is diverse. The Nation of Islam should be viewed as a segment of the Black Muslims, and Black Muslims should never be considered as typical of all African American Muslims, especially in the twenty-first century.

However different the beliefs and practices of the various Black Muslim groups may have been, they all shared one commonality. As a scholar of African Americans and Islam summarized it, "All communities saw Islam

[53]Derrick Z. Jackson, "Wright Stuff, Wrong Time," T. Denean Sharpley-Whiting ed. *The Speech*, pp. 19–24.

[54]James H. Cone, *Risks of Faith: The Emergence of Black Theology of Liberation, 1968–1998* (Boston, MA: Beacon Press, 1999).

[55]Pew Research Center, "No Decline in Belief that Obama is a Muslim," national survey, March 9–12, 2009, accessed at http://pewresearch.org/pubs/1176/obama-muslim-opinion-not-changed on April 2, 2009.

as the 'true' religion of black people and the only way to establish them-
selves as humans in the world and especially America."[56]
A legacy of Black Muslims lies in the positive influence on many
African Americans, especially those trapped in the inner city, self-hatred,
confusion, and inferiority, to aspire to and succeed in self-determination,
ethnic pride, and dignity.[57]
Curiously, given all the antagonism, actually venom, directed at the
NOI and its central figures—Elijah Muhammad, Malcolm X, and Louis
Farrakhan—most Americans now have directed their fears of Muslims
toward more traditional Islamic groups—whether here or abroad. African
American Muslims share this concern. In the post-9/11 world, Muslim
Americans are concerned that they have been stereotyped as terrorists
and are singled out by government's antiterrorism efforts. According to a
2007 national survey, this view is shared by African American Muslims
(72 percent) and native-born Muslims who are not Black (74 percent).
Of course, anti-Muslim feelings that are directed toward African
American Muslims are confounded by racism. Not surprisingly, African
Americans who are adherents to Islam see themselves facing both racial
and religious intolerance. In the same 2007 national survey mentioned
above, overall half of all Muslims who are African American say they
have been the target of bigots in the past twelve months, compared with
28 percent of White Muslims and 23 percent of Asian immigrant
Muslims.[58]
Despite the controversy over Elijah Muhammad's positions, his teachings can be credited with the spread of Islam among African Americans.
He represents the benchmark that faiths either distance themselves from
or embrace. His continued relevance makes it seem as if he just emerged
at the beginning of the twenty-first century rather than a hundred years
earlier.

KEY TERMS

Anti-Semitic, p. 304

Black Muslims, p. 282

Black Nationalism, p. 286

COINTELPO, p. 297

Double consciousness, p. 288

Hajj, p. 284

Hijab, p. 305

Jihad, p. 285

Millenarian movement, p. 299

---

[56]Pages 18–19 in Aminah Beverly McCloud, "African Americans and Islam," in Gary
Laderman and Luis León, eds., *Religion and American Cultures* (Santa Barbara, CA: ABC,
2003), pp. 17–19.

[57]Williams, *Black Muslim Theology*, pp. 75–76.

[58]"Pew Forum on Religion and Public Life," 2008a, *U.S. Religious Landscape Survey*,
pp. 37–38.

SOURCES ON THE WEB

www.noi.org
The official Web site of the National Organization of Islam, whose chief
spokesperson is Minister Louis Farrakhan.

www.finalcall.com and http://www.muslimjournal.net/mj_home.htm
The newspapers, which serve as the primary communication outlets for, respectively, the Nation of Islam and the successive publication of *Muhammad Speaks*
(under Elijah Muhammad and then W. D. Mohammed).

http://wdmministry.com
The Mosque Cares is a charitable organization begun by Imam W. D. Mohammed,
son of The Honorable Elijah Muhammad, that continues following his death in
2008.

SELECTED READINGS

Austin, Algernon. *Achieving Blackness: Race, Black Nationalism, and Afrocentrism in
the Twentieth Century.* New York: New York University Press, 2006.
Bukhari, Zahid H., Sulayman S. Nyana, Mumtaz Ahmad, and John L. Esposito.
Muslim's Place in the American Public Square: Hope, Fears and Aspirations. Walnut
Creek, CA: AltaMira Press, 2004.
Curtis IV, Edward E. *Black Muslim Religions in the Nation of Islam, 1960–1975.*
Chapel Hill: University of North Carolina Press, 2006.
Farrakhan, Louis. *A Torchlight for America.* Chicago: FCN Publishing, 1993.
Gardell, Mattias. *In the Name of Elijah Muhammad and the Nation of Islam.* Durham,
NC: Duke University Press, 1996.
Haddard, Yvonne Yazbeck, and John L. Esposito, eds. *Muslims on the
Americanization Path?* Oxford: Oxford University Press, 2000.
Jackson, Sherman A. *Islam and the Black American: Looking Toward the Third
Resurrection.* Oxford: Oxford University Press, 2005.
Jenkins, Robert L. *The Malcolm X Encyclopedia.* Westport, CT: Greenwood Press,
2002.
Lee, Martha F. *The Nation of Islam: An American Millenarian Movement,* revised ed.
Syracuse, NY: Syracuse University Press, 1996.
Lincoln, C. Eric. *The Black Muslims in America,* 3rd ed. Grand Rapids, MI: William
B. Erdmands Publishing Company, 1994.
Marsh, Clifton E. *From Black Muslim to Muslims: The Resurrection, Transformation
and Change of the Lost-Found Nation of Islam in America, 1930–1995,* 2nd. ed.
Lanham, MD: Scarecrow Press, 1991.

McCloud, Aminah Beverly. 1995. *African American Islam*. New York: Routledge, 2004. *Transnational Muslims in American Society*. Gainesville: University Press of Florida, 2006.

Turner, Richard Brent. *Islam in the African-American Experience*. 2nd. ed. Bloomington: Indiana University Press, 2003.

Walker, Dennis. *Islam and the Search for African-American Nationhood*. Atlanta, GA: Clarity Press, 2005.

X, Malcolm. *The Autobiography of Malcolm X* (written by Alex Haley). New York: Ballantine Books, 1964 (revised with Epilogue by Alex Haley and Afterword by Ossie Davis. New York: One World, Ballantine Books, 1999).

CHAPTER NINE

CHURCH OF SCIENTOLOGY

- L. Ron Hubbard
- David Miscavige
- Dianetics: An Overview
- Converting to Scientology
- Organization, Headquarters, and Splinter Groups
- Scientology as a Religion

- Positions on Social Issues
- Scientology Enemy No. 1: The Government
- Condemning the Condemners
- The Death of Lisa McPherson
- Hollywood Connections
- The Last Words

Although all contemporary faiths have their unique aspects, the Church of Scientology is in a class by itself. Its roots are in a self-help therapy that was developed by a science fiction writer. The Church of Scientology has little, if any, relationship to any other organized religious group, historically or ideologically. Indeed, its detractors, and there are many as we will see, question whether it even deserves to be referred to as a religion; some say the label "religious cult" would be more accurate.

Despite enjoying a devoted following of hundreds of thousands, if not millions, worldwide, the Church of Scientology has been sharply criticized and has been a continuing subject of derision, humor, and ridicule. Another characteristic that distinguishes Scientology from other religions is that popular awareness of Scientology is based mainly on either its Hollywood celebrity adherents or the name of its founder. Let's first consider the remarkable life of L. Ron Hubbard, the founder.[1]

---

[1]The core publication of the Church of Scientology is L. Ron Hubbard's *Dianetics* (Los Angeles: Bridge Publications, 1991). Depending upon the printing, this book carries the subtitle "The Modern Science of Mental Health" or "A Handbook of Dianetics Procedure." The companion book is Hubbard, *What Is Scientology?* (Los Angeles: Bridge, 1998). Although the latter formally bears Hubbard's name as the sole author and states it is "based on the works of L. Ron Hubbard," it is obviously a composite volume because it covers Hubbard's death and developments in the organization of the Church of Scientology following the founder's death. Relatively speaking, the most objective book on the Church of Scientology is sociologist J. Gordon Melton's *The Church of Scientology* (Toreno, Italy: Signature Books, 2000). However, many critics of the Church of Scientology see Melton as an apologist and prefer more critical treatments. A balanced collection of scholarly essays can be found in James R. Lewis (ed.),

(continued)

L. Ron Hubbard

Lafayette Robert Hubbard was born in Tilden, Nebraska, in 1911. The town, with a population of 1,000, takes pride in its location on the Cowboy Trail but makes no effort to acknowledge being the birthplace of a religious founder. Indeed, former Philadelphia baseball player Richie Ashburn, born sixteen years after Hubbard, was recognized with his name on a park and a small museum in a local pharmacy while plans to similarly honor Hubbard went unrealized.

In 1997 a group of Scientologists donated $50,000 to Tilden to build a park in Hubbard's honor. As park plans grew grander, Scientologists pledged another $800,000. The City Council gratefully accepted the offer until they became aware of public perceptions of the Church of Scientology. The money was returned and the park was not built. The Tilden link is forgotten except by historians of Scientology.[2]

Early Life   Tilden was not an important part of Hubbard's development. Hubbard's father was a naval officer, and his family moved often; they left Tilden while Hubbard was an infant. As far as can be determined, he never returned. His youth was spent on the move. When he was a teenager he took two trips to Guam to visit his father, who was stationed there.

Typical of accounts of founders of religious faiths, devotees and critics concur on broad outlines of Hubbard's life but diverge dramatically over details. This is further complicated because the Church of Scientology has yet to release an official biography of Hubbard—very strange given the voluminous publications funded by the Church of Scientology. In some released materials, Hubbard himself and, after his death, the Church of Scientology, gave great significance to his travels as a young man to Asia. These accounts speak of encounters with Chinese magicians and

---

Book-length critiques by former Scientologists include those by famed novelist William S. Burroughs (*Ali's Smile: Naked Scientology* [Bonn, Germany: Expanded Media Editions, 1991]) and Jon Atack (*A Piece of Blue Sky: Scientology, Dianetics and L. Ron Hubbard Exposed* [New York: Lyle Stuart, 1990]). The general absence of serious treatment of this important movement in spiritual thought was the subject of a scholarly paper by Douglas E. Cowan, "Researching Scientology: Academic Premises, Promises and Problematics" (paper presented at the Annual Conference of the Center for Studies on New Religions, Waco, TX, 2004). The Church of Scientology is said to be the most demonized cult on the Internet, according to Massimo Introvigne, "So Many Evil Things" (paper presented at the Annual Meeting of the Association for Sociology of Religion, Chicago, August 5, 1999).

[1](continued) *Scientology* (London: Oxford University Press, 2009). There is no lack of sharp criticism, ranging from a *Penthouse* magazine interview (June 1983) with the founder's eldest son to a cover story in *Time* (May 6, 1991). Any criticism is met with a sharp rebuttal as evidenced by a twelve-page "correction" of the *Time* cover story. (See "Fact vs. Fiction: Church of Scientology International" by the Church of Scientology and posted at http://www.solitary-trees.net/pubs/facvsfic.htm.).

[2]Mike Wilson, "Tilden, Nebraska: Scientology Crooks Thrown Out of Town," *St. Petersburg Times*, May 11, 1997.

Yves Forestier/CORBIS SYGMA

L. Ron Hubbard was not only the founder of Scientology, but he wrote virtually all the documents that Scientologists continue to follow a generation after his death.

Buddhist monks that involved an openness not usually available to foreigners. This exposure to Eastern religion and mysticism is said to have sparked the young Hubbard's thinking about new ways of exploring one's inner self. However, detractors of the faith point to documentation that they believe shows that Hubbard spent little time in Asia. These detractors argue that they have uncovered notes of the young man speaking very disparagingly of the Chinese in particular.[3]

There does appear to be consensus that Hubbard graduated from Woodward School for Boys near Washington, D.C. He then attended George Washington University while at the same time serving a brief stint in the Marine Corps Reserve. Records from the Church of Scientology hold he was a "commander" and coordinated "intelligent activities" in Australia, although independent verification of this is lacking. In college, he had poor grades and left after two years while on academic probation. Nonetheless, the Church of Scientology publications sometimes refer to him as a civil engineer. More commonly they assert Hubbard was frustrated with formal learning and that the academics and scientists failed to appreciate his scientific experiments and the understandings he had gained earlier from "Philippine pygmies" and "shamans of Borneo."[4]

[3]Atack, *A Piece of Blue Sky;* Chapter Two, "Hubbard in the East"; and Douglas E. Cowan and David G. Bromley, *Cults and New Religions: A Brief History* (Maiden, MA: Blackwell, 2008), p. 28.

[4]L. Ron Hubbard, *What Is Scientology?;* and Cowan and Bromley, *Cults and New Religions,* p. 29.

Church of Scientology

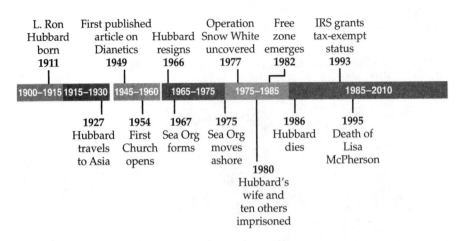

Writing Career   In the 1930s Hubbard's writings began to appear in fiction magazines with titles like "Final Blackout" depicting war-ravaged, disease-infested Europe in the future and a psychological horror story, "Fear."[5] These and his other writings were enormously popular and created a ready audience for Hubbard's output.

In 1933, at the age of twenty-two, Hubbard married Margaret "Polly" Grubb in Washington State. Soon their two children were born (L. Ron Jr. in 1934 and Katherine May in 1936). Hubbard would later have two other wives. Mary Sue Hubbard, his third wife, played a significant role as the First Lady of Scientology from the beginning of their marriage in 1952.

With American involvement in World War II approaching, Hubbard joined the U.S. Navy in June 1941, continuing on active duty until 1945. As with his youthful sojourns to Asia, there exist parallel yet different accounts of his military service. Some accounts depict Hubbard's constant reassignments due to quarrelling with superiors while the Church of Scientology's account describes his critical role in naval hospitals helping unresponsive patients get past "mental blocks" that were impeding their recovery.[6]

In 1949, Hubbard is said to have written to the American Psychological Association about his process *narcosynthesis*. This process involves helping a patient recall repressed memories and emotional traumas through the use of narcotics. This controversial and disputed technique has advocates independent of Hubbard or the Church of Scientology. Undeterred by critics of the technique, Hubbard, then thirty-nine, made his views

[5]L. Ron Hubbard, *Final Blackout* (Hollywood: Galaxy Books, 2005 [1940]), and *Fear* (Los Angeles: Bridge, 1991).
[6]Atack, *A Piece of Blue Sky*; Hubbard, *Handbook of Scientology*; and Melton, *The Church of Scientology*, p. 2.

public in the popular magazine *Astounding Science-Fiction* in 1950. In addition to narcosynthesis the article described Dianetics, a system of thought, described in a later section of the chapter. The next year Hubbard published Scientology's foundation text *Dianetics: The Modern Science of Mental Health*.[7]

Hubbard became a popular lecturer as people wanted to learn more about a do-it-yourself way to improve mental health. By all accounts he was a charismatic individual, attracting people to his message much like Joseph Smith and Father Divine.[8]

In contrast to the psychology establishment in general and psychotherapy in particular, Dianetics was more accessible, according to Hubbard, to the average man and woman. Indeed, Hubbard told his audiences that users of Dianetics could then become practitioners and help others.

By 1954, Hubbard oversaw the establishment of the first Church of Scientology. What was to be referred to as the Founding Church of Scientology was opened in 1955 in Washington, D.C. Hubbard had clearly taken the position that Dianetics was no longer just a secular self-help therapy but was religious-based counseling.

L. Ron Hubbard passed away on January 24, 1986. Mystery surrounded his death as it did the last ten years of his life, which he spent as a recluse in a series of homes in rural Southern California. Hubbard had signed a statement forbidding an autopsy for religious reasons, which is binding in California. So when he died at age seventy-four, the sheriff's office photographed his body and took fingerprints to confirm his identity. Shortly thereafter his ashes were "scattered at sea," according to the Church of Scientology.[9]

Hubbard never claimed to be a divine figure nor does the Church of Scientology today view him that way.[10] He is regarded by the faithful as an extraordinary man who has no successor. There is no expectation of any future prophetic clarifications, rather it is the prolific writings of Hubbard to which Scientologists continue to turn for understanding and inspiration.

[7]Hubbard had privately published *The Original Thesis* in 1948 and then expanded these ideas about Dianetics for the limited audience of *The Explorers Club Journal* ("Terra Incognita: The Mind," Winter/Spring 1948) of New York City. Therefore, the newsstand appearance of "Dianetics: The Evolution of a Science," *Astounding Science-Fiction* 45 (No. 3), 1950, pp. 43–87, is considered the unveiling of Dianetics. The successive publication of *Dianetics* and Hubbard's many other writings is now overseen by the Church of Scientology's publication arm, Bridge Publications of Los Angeles.

[8]Simon Locke, "Charisma and the Iron Cage: Rationalization, Science and Scientology," *Social Compass* 51 (No. 1): 111–31, 2004.

[9]Associated Press, "L. Ron Hubbard, 74, Founder of Scientology Church Dies," *New York Times*, January 28, 1986, and Robert Lindsey, "L. Ron Hubbard Dies of Stroke; Founder of Church of Scientology," *New York Times*, January 29, 1986.

[10]Douglas E. Cowan and David G. Bromley, "The Church of Scientology," in Eugene V. Gallagher and W. Michael Ashcraft, eds., *Introduction to New and Alternative Religions in America*, vol. 5 (Westport, CT: Greenwood Press, 2006), p. 172.

David Miscavige, at age twenty-six, was named the head of the Church shortly after Hubbard's death, a position he continues to hold as of 2010.

David Miscavige

L. Ron Hubbard is the founder, the definer, and the ideologue of Scientology, but David Miscavige has been the driving force behind the Church of Scientology for the past two decades. Although the Church explicitly states that Miscavige is not an official spokesperson, he publicly represents the faith on special occasions. He is the person who typically answers for the Church of Scientology in rare public interviews. Miscavige's biography and speeches are second only to Hubbard's in dominating the official Scientology Web site.[11]

Miscavige's official title is Chairman of the Board of the Religious Technology Center (RTC), a nonprofit organization aimed at maintaining and promoting Scientology. He is acknowledged as the ultimate ecclesiastical authority regarding the standard and pure application of L. Ron Hubbard's religious theories.[12]

Miscavige was raised a Roman Catholic in New Jersey but followed his father's encouragement to become a Scientologist. The elder Miscavige had struggled with asthma and credits the faith with ending his symptoms. Shortly after his father's conversion, the family moved to the Church of Scientology's retreat in England. By age twelve, David Miscavige was introducing others to Scientology through a process called *auditing* (described later in the chapter).

Miscavige dropped out of high school in 1976 at the age of sixteen, joining the elite branch of Scientology known as the Sea Org (discussed later in the chapter). He became an assistant to Hubbard, who was then sixty-six. The young Miscavige, called Misc (pronounced "Misk") by his friends, quickly became known as skilled in developing film recordings of Scientology activities. Miscavige rose within the organization while handling legal, financial, and public affairs. He began efforts, that continue today, to have the Church of Scientology hold the copyright to all of Hubbard's voluminous nonliterary writings.[13] By the mid 1970s, he was

---

[11]Since 1982 to the present, the president of the Church of Scientology International is Heber C. Jentzsch. Born in Utah, raised a Mormon, Jentzsch was caught up in the Snow White scandal and sentenced to prison, but he continuously held the title of President. See "Heber C. Jentzsch," accessed October 25, 2009 at http://www.scientology.org/news-media/biographies/jentzsch.html; and CNN, "Larry King Live: Guest, the Reverend Heber Jentzsch," December 20, 1993.

[12]Church of Scientology, "David Miscavige," posted at www.scientology.org/scnnews/miscavige.htm and accessed on January 11, 2007.

[13]The fiction writings are handled by an independent outlet, Galaxy Press in Hollywood, a few blocks from the Church of Scientology Celebrity Centre.

the most significant figure in Scientology with the exception of Hubbard and his wife.

In the late 1970's controversies over Scientology teachings and the Church's efforts to squelch government investigations sent Hubbard into reclusion and his wife to prison. At this time Miscavige became the organizational rock that got the Church of Scientology through the embarrassments.[14]

Dianetics: An Overview

The Church of Scientology is based on the writings of L. Ron Hubbard. By some estimates, he has written 40 million words and has had more than 3,000 lectures transcribed. In addition he wrote 560 novels and short stories. Although the teachings of Scientology do not explicitly exclude following other belief systems, typically Scientologists do not perceive themselves as being both a Scientologist and, say, a Lutheran or Buddhist at the same time.[15]

Scientology affirms the existence of a Supreme Being but does not describe a divinity figure or specify its relationship to man or woman. Hence, one cannot approach Scientology by building upon even the basic elements of any other faith. It is truly a unique dogma.

Dianetics strives to have the individual achieve a heightened, positive state. The word *Dianetics* comes from Greek words meaning "through" and "soul." It is a method to alleviate unwanted emotions, irrational fears, and psychosomatic illnesses.

The word *Scientology* did not appear in the initial presentations of Dianetics by L. Ron Hubbard. Dianetics was first advanced by Hubbard as a means to gain control of one's life. While Dianetics outlined the process and philosophy behind the Church of Scientology, Hubbard did not start using the word publicly until 1952 and a few years after that came to view Scientology as a religion. Critics then and now argue that claims by the Church of Scientology to be a religion were no more than a marketing device to make money and to avoid federal taxes.[16] The Church presents the word *Scientology* as literally meaning "the study of truth." The term reflects Hubbard's efforts to bring scientific devices or strategies to resolve philosophical and personal issues.

---

[14]Thomas Tobin, "The Man behind Scientology," *St. Petersburg Times*, October 25, 1998.

[15]The presentation of Dianetics is based on Hubbard, *Dianetics*, and Hubbard, *What Is Scientology?* A significant amount of detail has been set aside here; it is impossible to summarize an entire religious doctrine in a couple of pages.

[16]Stephen A. Kent, "Scientology—Is This a Religion?" *Marburg Journal of Religion* 4 (July 1999). Accessed February 11, 2007, at web.uni-marburg.de/religionswissenschaft/journal/mjr/frenschkowski.html.

Auditing   Essential to Dianetics is a process known as **auditing.** This is usually the first step one takes to become a Scientologist. It is a form of personal counseling in which the auditor, always a Church member, measures a person's mental state using an Electropsychometer, or E-Meter, a device developed by Hubbard. As Scientology progressed or matured and come to be presented as a religion, the E-Meter was viewed as a "religious artifact" and auditing as a "confessional" or "spiritual counseling."[17]

The E-Meter uses low voltage to measure a person's emotional state by registering skin conductivity (or galvanic responses). A dial with a fluctuating pointer registers "rises" and "falls" of emotional change and is said to assist the auditor in helping the person heighten his or her ability to think clearly. The recipient of this audit is referred to as a **Preclear** because he or she is on the way to becoming a **Clear.**[18]

The Clear, a highly valued state within the Church of Scientology, refers to a person free from the ill effects of his or her own mind. The Preclear is attempting to reach this desired state through auditing. The goal of the auditing process is for the Preclear to become aware of and eliminate **engrams.** An engram is described as a particular type of stored mental image or memory that is harmful and usually the result of a painful or traumatic experience. A Clear is free of any engram. Obviously, the vocabulary of Scientology, mostly from the works of Hubbard, is rather strange to an outsider. Converts are introduced to it slowly. As with other extraordinary groups, the argot of Scientology, well-known to insiders, provides a sense of shared understanding. Minimally, there are a hundred of these types of terms and acronyms used regularly by Scientologists.[19]

To lay people the auditing process seems akin to psychoanalysis, but the Church of Scientology observes that the auditors never evaluate what the Preclear says. Preclears are guided but their responses are not placed in any context; for example, any role played by their early upbringing, dreams, or sexual fantasies does not come into play. Auditing bears no relationship to psychology and the Church of Scientology typically is critical of psychological therapies or treatments, with or without prescriptive drugs. Furthermore, anyone could become an auditor. This, of course, contrasts with the long training involved in becoming a psychotherapist.

The antagonism that Scientology shows toward psychiatry gained national attention when devotee Tom Cruise appeared on national

[17]Cowen and Bromley, *Cults and New Religions,* pp. 32–33; and Gail M. Harley and John Kieffer, "The Developmental Reality of Auditing," in James R. Lewis, ed., *Scientology* (Oxford, England: Oxford University Press, 2009), pp. 183–2005.

[18]Capitalization of terms like *Clear, Preclear,* and *Thetan* is inconsistent in Scientology writings. They are capitalized throughout this chapter to bring attention to the reader of their special usages and definitions of the Church of Scientology.

[19]Scientology maintains an online glossary at http://www.scientology.org/gloss.htm.

Scientologists employ the Electropsychometer, or E-meter, during audits. A counselor monitors the device, which the Church says can detect mental tension or stress levels of a person holding the cylindrical electrodes while being asked questions.

television in 2005 proclaiming psychiatry to be a "pseudoscience." Cruise criticized actress Brooke Shields for taking Paxil, a prescribed antidepressant, to treat her postpartum depression after the birth of her daughter in 2003. He claimed there was no such thing as chemical imbalances and saw the drug as masking a more underlying problem; he said Shields should take vitamins, exercise, and do "various things."[20]

The auditing process has been critiqued not only because it stands apart from traditionally accepted methods of therapy, but also because of the financial cost to the individual. The Church of Scientology charges for most of the auditing process, which can run into hundreds if not thousands of dollars. Auditors, typically full-time employees of the Church of Scientology, collect these fees. Indigent Preclears are provided for through some form of assistance, but most pay for the sessions over the length of the auditing process.

Some scholars have likened auditing to multilevel sales organizations like Amway and Herbalife. Preclears pay for auditing, but in time can become practitioners themselves and become employed by the Church.

---

[20]NBC Television, "Today Show," June 24, 2005; American Psychiatric Association, "APA Responds to Tom Cruise's Today Show Interview," News Release, June 27, 2005; and Brooke Shields, "War of Words," *New York Times*, July 1, 2005. Cruise was introduced to Scientology during his marriage to Mimi Rogers (1987–1990) and credits Dianetics with helping him overcome his dyslexia.

Media accounts describe people mortgaging all they own to continue paying for their audit sessions. Adherents to the Church of Scientology however say these claims are exaggerated or downright false.[21]

Training In addition to auditing a person must also complete training to become a Clear. Training involves learning the laws of life as written by Hubbard to maintain the freedom said to be gained through auditing. The training and auditing processes are displayed in a Scientology chart called "The Bridge to Total Freedom," subtitled a "classification and gradation chart." This chart outlines the steps a Scientologist takes to reach the state of Clear, as first presented by Hubbard in 1965 and since refined.[22]

The Thetan According to the Church of Scientology, there were already 750 groups by 1950 applying the techniques described here. Hubbard read their reports of Preclears reporting previous lives or incarnations. Drawing upon these reports, he advanced the discovery of the "Thetan."

Thetan is the Church of Scientology term for a person's immortal spiritual being and can be thought of as similar to a soul. The Thetan has an existence apart from one's body. But unlike the usual concept of a soul, a Thetan can be associated with more than one person over the millennium. By becoming one with a Thetan, Scientology believes that a person crosses a chasm and moves to a brighter, happier world.

By becoming Clear, one reaches the Operating Thetan (OT) level, which means literally you truly are able to act. To be OT does not mean you become God; it means to Scientologists that you become wholly one. To be OT is a significant step for a Scientologist, worthy of personal celebration, and the Church of Scientology allows one to acknowledge it by wearing an OT bracelet.

MEST The existence of Thetans—the spiritual essence—goes back trillions of years, according to the Church of Scientology. This spirit of collective Thetans is responsible for the material universe—matter, energy, space, and time, commonly referred to by Scientologists with the acronym MEST.

Since one's Thetan extends well beyond a single lifetime, a person needs to confront engrams suppressed not only from his or her life but from previous lifetimes of the Thetan. The Thetan has been embodied many, many times—a belief commonly called reincarnation. However, Scientologists avoid using this term and do not believe, as do some

[21]Richard Behar, "The Thriving Cult of Green and Power," *Time* 171 (May 6, 1991); and Cristina Gutiérrez, "Religious Aspects of Multilevel Sales Organizations," paper presented at the Annual Conference of the Center for Studies on New Religions, London, 2001.

[22]"The Bridge to Total Freedom" can be accessed at http://www.whatisscientology .org/html/Part02/Chp06/pg0181_1.html.

believers of reincarnation, in transmigration—that is, Scientologists do not believe the Thetan takes any animal form other than human.

How do Scientologists believe that we can be affected by something we ourselves have not experienced in *our* lifetime?

Scientologists illustrate this with "a pinch test." Early in the auditing process the practitioner will lightly pinch the Preclear. The E-Meter records this response, which the Church of Scientology interprets as measuring the engram created by the pinch. At a later point or even at another session, the practitioner will ask the Preclear if he or she recalls the pinch. At this time the E-Meter elicits the same response as when the person was pinched even though the Preclear was not touched.

Engrams generated by past events more traumatic than a mild pinch may be at the root, according to Hubbard, of diseases ranging from arthritis to measles to tuberculosis as well as kidney trouble, the common cold, high blood pressure, and underdeveloped genital organs. A key concept in Dianetics is that engrams may predate one's own lifetime and that auditing raises one's consciousness to deal with them effectively.[23]

Once a Scientologist recognizes the engram from the pinch, the event will no longer produce the negative impact. It will be remembered in the traditional notion of memory, but this engram will be cleared.

Auditing is an ongoing, lifetime process to be cleared of engrams. At some point a person assumes control for his or her own audit; it is at this point that the person is said to have attained the level of Clear. This status is reported to the Church in a manner analogous to a Christian being "born again": the Clear makes joyous pronouncements and looks forward to future enlightenment.

According to Church teachings, Scientologists who become Clear are more self-determined, less vulnerable to engrams. By 1995, the Church reported 50,000 practitioners had reached a state of Clear. In time, the Church of Scientology believes, as more people reach this state, global problems such as pollution, drugs, crime, and war will be eliminated. Scientology is presented literally as a bridge to a better life, for the individual, for all.

Converting to Scientology

Where do members come from? The Church of Scientology makes effective use of distributing its publications and maintaining an informative Web site. The publicity it receives, whether positive or critical, keeps it before the public.

---

[23]Hubbard, *Dianetics*, pp. 123–47.

Since Scientology is so new, few followers are born into the belief system. According to the Church's data, nearly 40 percent are introduced to Scientology through a personality test—the Church's widely disseminated Oxford Capacity Analysis—or a Hubbard book.[24]

The Internet is a major vehicle to reach the uninformed, but it is also a source for anti-Scientology appeals. Inflammatory attacks come from groups that the Church of Scientology refers to as "cyber-terrorists." Hackers sometimes succeed in taking down Scientology's main Web site. Anonymous criticism is not new, but, the speed of the Web gives Scientology a special way to reach potential converts and critics an immediate forum for their campaign.[25] The Internet has emerged as a very important arena for the Church of Scientology.

The Church of Scientology, like many other religious organizations, mounts significant social outreach, especially in campaigns aimed at drug abuse, illiteracy, and human rights.[26] As with so much of Scientology, none of this is without controversy. The Church of Scientology is proud of its efforts to help people free themselves of drugs. But its Narconon Program, founded in 1966, has been criticized by those who argue for better external verification of its effectiveness despite personal statements of assistance by such celebrities as actress Kirstie Alley, a former cocaine user.[27]

Scientology "volunteer ministers" are often available at disaster sites around the world. For example, members of the Church of Scientology speak highly of their ministers' role assisting recovery workers following the 9/11 attacks in New York City. However, their assistance is not always welcomed, especially in cultures suspicious of new religions. The volunteer ministers were in South Asia following the 2005 tsunami, but they were asked to leave when their techniques of counseling survivors were seen as too religious in nature.[28]

[24]Unfortunately the Church of Scientology gives no information about their statistical data which appears to be collected sometime after 2002. See "Statistics" at http://www.scientology.org/news-media/stats/index.html.

[25]David Sarno, "Web Awash in Critics of Scientology" (*Los Angeles Times*, March 3, 2008), pp. E1, E8; and Douglas E. Cowan, "Researching Scientology: Perceptions, Premises, Promises, and Problematics," in James R. Lewis, ed., *Scientology* (Oxford, England: Oxford University Press, 2009), pp. 53–79.

[26]Melton, *The Church of Scientology*, pp. 44–46; Church of Scientology, "This Is Scientology," DVD, Golden Era Productions for the Church of Scientology, 2004; and Religious Tolerance, "About the Church of Scientology," accessed January 7, 2007, at www.religioustolerance.org/scientol2.htm.

[27]Joel Sappell and Robert W. Welkos, "The Courting of Celebrities," *Los Angeles Times*, June 25, 1990, p. A18.

[28]Peter S. Goodman, "For Tsunami Survivors, a Touch of Scientology," *Washington Post*, January 28, 2005.

Despite the criticism, the Church of Scientology's nonreligious outreach activities attract attention, curiosity and, eventually, adherents to the faith. Also, as with most religions, family and friends have supplied an important source of converts. According to the Church of Scientology, family and friends introductions account for half of the new adherents. According to Church data, 56 percent of members in the early 1990s joined the Church when they were between the ages of twenty-one and thirty. Hence Scientology is able to present a more youthful image than many other established faiths.[29]

As previously discussed, counting followers of a faith is a difficult task. First, it must be acknowledged that some "members" of a religion rarely have any relationship to the organization or even to other members. Second, the number of followers is subject to fluctuation, especially during times of growth and decline. Third, and most important, given the absence of external counts in a census, it is the organization itself that offers the "official number."

In the case of the Church of Scientology, the Church does not make official announcements regarding membership. Independent national surveys show fewer than 50,000 members, but even critics of Scientology agree that many people are reluctant to indicate, even to a researcher, their attachment to a faith so stigmatized in the media. From survey estimates (or perhaps "guesstimates" is a better term), membership ranges somewhere between 3 million and 9 million.

Moving to global estimates is even more difficult, especially given, as we will see later, that in some countries the Church of Scientology experiences significant governmental criticism. Worldwide membership estimates range from 5.6 million to 10 million.

It is probably accurate to say that the largest following of the Church of Scientology is in the United States, and that both in North America and worldwide the religion is growing rapidly.[30]

It should be noted that despite what one might think given the nature of antagonism against Scientology, it is possible to be a casual member. Many come and go and come back again across a fluid boundary without facing the antagonism that one would encounter as a member of the Amish community, for example.[31]

---

[29]David G. Bromley and Mitchell L. Bracey, Jr., "The Church of Scientology: A Quasi-Religion," in William W. Zellner and Marc Petrowsky, eds. *Sects, Cults, and Spiritual Communities: A Sociologial Analysis,* (Westport, CT: Praeger, 1968), pp. 151–52.

[30]The estimate ranges come from the respected, independent Internet resource Adherents.com; Religious Tolerance, "Religious Affiliations: Comparing the U.S. and the World," posted August 10, 2008, accessed October 26, 2009, at www.religioustolerance.org/compuswrld.htm.

[31]James R. Lewis, ed., *Scientology* (Oxford, England: Oxford University Press, 2009), p. 135.

Organization, Headquarters, and Splinter Groups

The Sea Org   In 1967, shortly after Hubbard set aside the day-to-day operations of the Church of Scientology bureaucracy, he founded an elite branch of the Church of Scientology members called the Sea Organization, or simply Sea Org. This branch is staffed by advanced, dedicated members of the Church who pledge to work full time.[32] The name *Sea Organization* comes from the fact that the unit initially was housed on three oceangoing ships, in one of which Hubbard lived for a short time. In 1975, the Sea Org moved onshore to Clearwater, Florida.

Today the Sea Org remains a dedicated community of Scientologists headquartered in Church complexes around the world. Scientologists entering the Sea Org sign what has come to be known as the "billion-year contract." One agrees to enter full-time employment and go where one is needed by the Sea Org "for the next billion years."

Members of the Sea Org have some similarities to a community of monks or nuns. Life revolves around the faith. There are married couples but typically if they have children they are encouraged to move to staff positions outside the organization. When members' children reach age six, they may return to the Sea Org, with their children being schooled at the Church of Scientology Cadet School.[33]

Rehabilitation Project Force   In any religion, people's dedication often wanes. They may become disenchanted for a time, but may return to reassert their commitment later. Typically this pattern, common to all faiths, occurs informally and with little fanfare and virtually unnoticed by the religion's hierarchy. For Sea Org members, disenchantment with the faith is totally different.

In 1974 the Church of Scientology began the Rehabilitation Project Force (RPF) to address members of the Sea Org who perform unsatisfactorily. Just exactly what this means and what the RPF does to rehabilitate members is the subject of fierce debate between skeptics and followers of Scientology. There appears to be consensus that theft and lying within the Church may bring one to the attention of the RPF for discipline, but matters for the RPF can also include violations such as adultery and severe derelictions of duty. Officially the Church sees the RPF as a means toward spiritual recovery. Intense daily counseling and isolation from

[32]J. Gordon Melton, "A Contemporary Ordered Religious Community: The Sea Organization," paper presented at the Annual Conference for the Center for Studies on New Religions, London, 2001.

[33]According to Private Schools Report the Cadet School had 169 students ranging from third through twelfth grades. See http://schools.privateschoolsreport.com, accessed November 2, 2009.

others are techniques used by the RPF to address "burn out" among Sea Org members.

Critics contend that the RPF processes amount to forced labor and describe people identified by the RPF as inmates. Some people going through rehabilitation choose to leave the Sea Org or are dismissed from the faith altogether.[34]

Clearwater, Florida It is not too much of an overstatement to refer to Clearwater as the capital, if not Mecca, of the Church of Scientology. In fact, Clearwater is explicitly referred to as the Flag Service Organization and the "spiritual headquarters of the Scientology religion."[35]

For reasons that are unclear and may not be particularly spiritually important, L. Ron Hubbard was attracted to the Tampa Bay area. In 1975, the land base of the Scientology Organization (the Sea Org) was located here and when much of those operations were moved ashore, growth of the Church of Scientology infrastructure in the deteriorating old downtown area of Clearwater exploded. Dozens of buildings now make up the Church of Scientology official presence and an estimate placed at two hundred the number of stores, restaurants, service operations, and small businesses owned by Scientologists in Clearwater. The 2010 city election had council candidates criticizing Scientology for its empty storefronts downtown and failure to participate with city planners.

One proud devotee declared, "You can't separate Salt Lake City and the Mormons and you can't separate Clearwater and Scientology." Indeed, today the Church of Scientology officially proclaims Clearwater as the "spiritual headquarters" of the faith. Church employees number at least 1,200, and estimates of numbers of followers in this city of 100,000 range from 7,000 to 12,000. No city in the world has such a high proportion of Scientologists.

Clearwater has economically benefited from Scientology. However, like Linden, Nebraska, birthplace of L. Ron Hubbard, this Florida city does not publicize its role in the contemporary Church of Scientology. Indeed, careful perusal of any official literature of the history or attractions of this Florida city will mention it as the birthplace of the Hooters Restaurant chain in 1983 but no mention is made of it as a virtual pilgrimage destination for Church of Scientology elites.[36]

---

[34]Cowan and Bromley, "The Church of Scientology"; Kent, "Scientology—Is This a Religion?"; and "What Is the Rehabilitation Task Force?" accessed January 13, 2007, at www.scientology.org.

[35]"Scientology in Clearwater," accessed October 26, 2009 at http://scientology.fso.org.

[36]"Scientology in Clearwater," accessed January 7, 2007, at http://Scientology.fso.org; Robert Forley, "Scientology's Town," *St. Petersburg Times,* July 18, 2004; and Mike Brassfield, "Stances define Clearwater City Council candidates," *St. Petersburg Times,* February 21, 2010.

Splinter Groups   Despite being a relatively new organization, the Church of Scientology already has had to denounce splinter groups, including sects that claim to practice Dianetics complete with E-Meters independent of the Church. Members of the sects refer to themselves as the "Free Zone." The sects appear to have emerged over disagreements beginning in 1982 with the operation of the Religious Technology Center, the arm of the Church of Scientology headed by David Miscavige.

Early in its history, people attracted to Dianetics came and went, of course, some returning to their traditional faiths and others striking out on their own. Most notable among the latter was Werner Erhard. He was a Scientologist in the 1960s and went on to create Est (Erhard Seminars Training) in 1971, which itself became to many a quasi-religion.

These splinter groups, while embracing some of Hubbard's writings or worldview, have developed their own principles. Especially significant among the Free Zone are the thoughts of William "Captain Bill" Robertson, who broke from the Sea Org and the Church of Scientology hierarchy in 1983. Although the size of the splinter groups is difficult to assess, especially since Robertson's death in 1991, the Free Zone appears to be most active in Europe, especially in Germany, and relatively insignificant in North America.

The very existence of break-away organizations reflects that Scientology is moving into a more mature stage.[37]

Scientology as a Religion

At the outset, we noted that many outsiders refuse to view Scientology as a religion. Later we will consider the legal skirmishes between the Church of Scientology and various governments concerning their official religious status, but first we want to consider its status as a religion within the scholarly community.

The Church of Scientology contends that it is "the only major new religion to emerge" in the twentieth century.[38] Scientology presents itself as not unlike Judeo-Christian religions and Eastern religions, particularly Buddhism.

However, because an organization declares its doctrine to be a religion does not make it so. Some scholars straddle the fence and place the Church of Scientology in the category of **quasi-religion,** which includes organizations that may see themselves as religious but are seen as "sort-of religious" by others. Included in this classification system are New Age

[37]"Free Zone Association," accessed January 14, 2007, at www.freezone.org; "Ron's Org," accessed January 14, 2007, at www.ronsorg.org; and "Larry King Live," December 20, 1993.
[38]Hubbard, *What Is Scientology?*, p. 561.

movements and Transcendental Meditation as advanced by Maharishi Mahesh Yogi and introduced in 1958.[39] A particular challenge to academics, trying to maintain an impartial view, is the Church's tense secrecy. While Scientology speaks of openness, it has not to date permitted the kind of systematic research that other controversial groups—the Unification Church or The Family International—have long permitted.[40]

Academic scholarship related to the Church of Scientology, limited as it is, is moving toward accepting Scientology as a religion. This does not mean scholars regard Scientology as presenting an accurate worldview, any more than religious studies scholars call such diverse doctrines as those of Episcopalians or Hindus as "accurate" and the "last word." Organizationally, many religious scholars find Scientology's method of financing operations problematic. Most religions seek voluntary contributions and payment for services (e.g., child care programs and youth activities) as secondary to doctrine. In the Church of Scientology, the doctrine speaks of "reciprocity" and expects people to pay for the spiritual benefits they receive through auditing and training.

Scientology can be viewed as a religion because it has a body of beliefs as expressed in *Dianetics,* offers an explanation of the world and a purpose for humankind, and addresses issues like salvation and afterlife.[41]

Let's consider aspects of Scientology to see how they may, or may not, resemble those of more conventional religious organizations.

Doctrine   Salvation is a common religious theme. But in Scientology, in contrast to other religions, salvation is more immediate as one proceeds through auditing.[42]

Also in contrast to other religions, within Scientology you do not find the general membership offering new interpretations of Hubbard's teachings. Rather his message is accepted and the only public interpretation is how one may apply it to one's own existence.

Worship   Members of many religions gather together to worship. Do Scientologists gather? Scientology contends it does not mandate a particular relationship with God. Whereas communal prayer may be logical for others, it is not appropriate for Scientologists.

"Auditing and training are the two central religious services of the Scientology faith."[43] This declaration may be hard to get past for those

---

[39]A. Greil and D. Rudy, "On the Margins of the Sacred," in T. Robbins and D. Anthony, eds., *In Gods We Trust* (New Brunswick, NJ: Transaction, 1990), p. 221; and David C. Bromley, "Making Sense of Scientology: Prophetic, Contractual Religion," in James R. Lewis, ed., *Scientology* (Oxford, England: Oxford University Press, 2009), pp. 83–101.

[40]Cowan and Bromley, *Cults and New Religions*, p. 46.

[41]Bromley and Bracey, Jr., "Church of Scientology," p. 142; Melton, *Church of Scientology.*

[42]Hubbard, *What Is Scientology?*, p. 562.

[43]Ibid., p. 563.

accustomed to clergy addressing groups of people. Scientologists do not gather in sizeable collective groups on a regular, scheduled basis.

However, every Scientology center does offer working services where Hubbard's sermons are delivered verbatim. The rooms are not dedicated for this purpose but are multipurpose and serve other functions during the week. Typically they have a central table, lectern, conspicuous images of Hubbard (often a sculpted bust), and the Scientology cross—a cross with two short diagonal lines or rays emitting from the intersection of the conventional vertical and horizontal lines. Scientologists will often wear this cross, which has become a trademarked symbol.[44]

Although ceremonies of birth, marriage, and death (funerals) are outlined in Scientology, it is auditing and training that are the core services.

There are Sunday services in the Church of Scientology but they are not critical to one's self-identification as a Scientologist. At the service, principles of Scientology are read and an audio lecture by L. Ron Hubbard is played. Those in attendance may ask questions or engage in a discussion.

The Church of Scientology has naming ceremonies akin to baptism and funeral rites that are not unlike mainstream Protestant ceremonies. However, of course, no Biblical references are made. Rather, the naming ceremony is described by the Church of Scientology as a means to helping orient the Thetan in its new body. Unlike many religions, the ceremony is not performed for converted adults, as their Thetan is presumed to have gained awareness through their embracing of Scientology teachings.[45]

Given that Thetans are described as living billions of years, human life is a relative passing aspect of existence. Hence funerals are relatively simple ceremonies that are largely for the benefit of the deceased. The Church of Scientology does not dictate whether bodies are viewed during a wake, burial versus cremation, or nature of grave markers. As discussed previously, Hubbard, by his request, was cremated and his ashes scattered at sea. Funeral services often include readings from Hubbard's works and non-Scientologists are welcome to attend.

There are also ordination ceremonies for Church of Scientology ministers who have passed an examination of their knowledge of the organization and Dianetic beliefs.

Holidays   The identifiable high points of the Church of Scientology's calendar are the Scientology holidays; these include L. Ron Hubbard's birthday on March 13 and the Auditor's Day celebration on the second Sunday of September. Celebrants at local churches may see prerecorded or live

[44]Cowan and Bromley, *Cults and New Religions*, p. 39; "Religions and Technology Center," accessed October 26, 2009, http://www.rtc.org/guarant/pg006.html.

[45]Regis Deriquebourg, "How Should We Regard the Religious Ceremonies of the Church of Scientology?" in James R. Lewis, ed., *Scientology* (Oxford, England: Oxford University Press, 2009), pp. 116–82.

broadcasts prepared at one of the main centers of Scientology, such as those in Los Angeles or Clearwater, Florida. Hubbard's birthday is an opportunity for devotees to pay tribute to their founder and usually involves Church statements speaking in positive terms about the organization's future.[46]

The second red-letter day, Auditor's Day, is a tribute to the hard work of the thousands of auditors. Opponents of Scientology often use the occasion to mount protests or information pickets outside Church of Scientology's buildings.

Disconnection   Although the practice is not unique to the Church of Scientology, the group has been broadly criticized for asking its members to distance themselves from its detractors. **Disconnection** is the Scientology practice of members discontinuing association, or even communication, with anyone considered a threat. The fact that disconnection may include breaking off even with one's family make the practice unusual in most faiths, although the Old Order Amish practice of *Meidung* is another example of this deeply disconcerting practice.

The practice, while widely hinted at, came to the public's attention as a result of a 2008 book about Scientologist Tom Cruise documenting incidents that Scientologists would of their own free will write letters "disconnecting" from loved ones who are not Scientologists and especially those who disparage their beliefs. The implication is that pressure to disconnect is significant but not technically an official policy.

The Church has issued a formal statement denying the practice of disconnection and arguing that Scientology promotes reaching out across faiths. But the controversy did not stop there. Jenna Miscavige Hill, niece of Scientology leader David Miscavige, entered the fray, claiming that at the age of sixteen she was disconnected from family members, including her parents—former leaders in the Sea Org—when they left the Church in 2000. Jenna eventually reconnected with her parents after she left the Church of Scientology in 2005. Fueling the controversy in 2009, filmmaker Paul Haggis (*Crash* and *Million Dollar Baby*) broke with the Church after 35 years of membership. Haggis left Scientology because of the San Diego's branch's public support of California's Proposition 8 to end same-sex marriage. At this time, Haggis publicly recounted how his wife had been ordered to disconnect from her parents years earlier.[47]

---

[46]For example, see David Miscavige, "Opening Address in Honor of L. Rom Hubbard's Birthday," March 2002. Posted at www.lronhubbard.org.

[47]Andrew Morton, *Tom Cruise: An Unauthorized Biography* (New York: St. Martin's Press, 2008), p. 206; "Scientology Disconnection," Accessed November 10, 2009 at http://www.scientologydisconnection.com; "Paul Haggis," accessed November 10, 2009, at http://markrathbun.wordpress.com/2009/10/26/paul-haggis; Laurie Goldstein, "Breaking with Scientology: Defectors Say Church Hides Its Abuse of Staff Members," *New York Times* (March 7, 2010), pp. 1, 24.

Positions on Social Issues

The Church of Scientology's positions on social issues are neither consistently conservative nor consistently liberal. As with any spiritual faith, devotees conform and deviate from accepted practices. Still, we can consider the Church of Scientology's official position in several areas.

Gay Marriage and Homosexuality   Initially the Church placed homosexuality in the same category of "sexual perversions" as sexual sadism. However, Hubbard cautioned that punishment of gays and lesbians was as bad as acceptance. Homosexuality was regarded as an illness to be overcome; the Church taught that people with preference for same-sex partners needed therapy through Dianetics.

Hubbard's early pronouncements came at a time when professional psychiatry still saw homosexuality as a disease. As new research and conclusions emerged, Hubbard, to his credit, renounced his earlier positions. In 1967, he declared that it was not his intention to regulate people's private lives and therefore "all former rules, regulations and policies relating to the sexual activities of Scientologists are cancelled." However as we discussed the San Diego Scientology branch did work to end gay marriage in California. Despite the fact that Paul Haggis brought this effort to the attention of national Scientology leadership, nothing was done to end what he viewed as hate-mongering.[48]

Abortion   As described in *Dianetics*, abortion and attempted abortion can traumatize the mother and unborn child physically and spiritually. Scientologists believe the fetus has already been occupied by a spiritual being. Hubbard writes of the aborted child condemned to a "life" with "murderers." However, in some instances, abortion might be chosen because of health concerns of the mother or other personal factors.

Birth Control   Procreation and child rearing are considered part of one of the eight dynamics of existence. Couples are free to decide the size of their families, and do so by determining the greatest good across the dynamics. Personal and social circumstances, profession, and income are part of this decision, as with members of any faith.

Afterlife   Scientologists believe the Thetan (spirit) has lived lifetime after lifetime. An individual experiences in his next lifetime the civiliza-

---

[48]Hubbard, *Dianetics*; "About Scientology," *St. Petersburg Times*, July 18, 2004; and Religious Tolerance, "The Church of Scientology and Homosexuality," posted December 2006 and accessed January 7, 2007, at www.religioustolerance.org.; and "Paul Haggis," accessed November 10, 2009, at http://markrathbun.wordpress.com/2009/10/26/paul-haggis.

tion he had a part in creating today. With this knowledge comes more responsibility to help make that tomorrow a good one to return to.[49]

Scientology Enemy No. 1: The Government

As highlighted in Chapter 6, religions often engage in adversarial relationships with the central government. In the United States, for example, organized religions are in conflict with the government over the display of sacred symbols such as nativity scenes in public areas. In the context of these typical secular–sacred tensions, the confrontational experiences of the Church of Scientology in its short history with many governments are unprecedented in modern times.

Healing Under Attack   In 1958 the Food and Drug Administration (FDA) began investigating the healing practices of the Church of Scientology. The FDA seized quantities of Dianazene tablets, which the Church of Scientology marketed as a means to prevent and treat radiation sickness. E-Meters were seized because the FDA felt that they were being presented as treatments for physical ailments.

After appealing the actions, the Church of Scientology agreed to make such items available only for religious practices and agreed to carry labels stating they were not effective at preventing or treating physical illnesses.[50]

Operation Snow White   The adversarial relationship between the Church of Scientology and the U.S. government is also reflected in an episode that has come to be known as Operation Snow White.

Acting on suspicions that Scientologists were trying to infiltrate federal agencies to uncover and remove reports unfavorable to the Church, the FBI raided Scientology offices in 1977. Specifically they raided the Guardian Office, which had been created in 1966 to monitor antichurch actions being taken by governments worldwide. They uncovered an elaborate espionage plan called by the Scientologists Snow White.

Hubbard himself was named an unindicted coconspirator. The exact extent of his knowledge of the undercover program could not be proved.

---

[49]"About Scientology," *St. Petersburg Times,* July 18, 2004.

[50]Current official publications of the Church of Scientology carry this disclaimer of Dianetics as a spiritual healing technology: "It is presented to the reader as a record of observations and research into the human mind and spirit and not as a statement of claims by the author [Hubbard]. The benefits and goals of Dianetics technology can be attained only by the dedicated efforts to the reader." The Hubbard Electrometer (or E-Meter) carries the disclaimer: "In itself, the E-Meter does nothing. It is not intended or effective for the diagnosis, treatment or prevention of any disease, or for the improvement of health or any bodily function." Source: L. Ron Hubbard, *Dianetics,* p. vi.

However, a number of high-ranking officials, including his wife, Mary Sue Hubbard, were convicted of conspiracy against the U.S. federal government and actually served prison time.

Needless to say, this was a very embarrassing event in the history of the Church of Scientology. Typically when officials mention the events, it is usually asserted they were set up by the government or others trying to destroy the faith. The leaders who were imprisoned have been effectively written out of Scientology. Mary Sue Hubbard, once the First Lady of Scientology, was removed from all Church positions while her husband was still alive. They were separated at the time of her ouster. Eventually her name was removed as coauthor of publications she wrote with L. Ron Hubbard.[51]

U.S. Milestone: Recognition   Although Scientology has never been banned in the United States, the government for decades questioned its legal status, as a religion when it came to tax matters and official consideration as a charity. The Internal Revenue Service (IRS) recognized it as a tax-exempt charity as far back as 1957 but this status was revoked in 1967, at least in California.

After much legal action, in 1993 the IRS granted the Church of Scientology full status, recognizing that it was organized and operated exclusively for religious and charitable purposes. As a part of this announcement, the Church of Scientology agreed to pay the IRS $12.5 million in settlement of disputes over payroll, income, and estate taxes. Although this was a significant amount of money, the Church of Scientology was exceedingly pleased with the outcome. David Miscavige took the podium at the Los Angeles Sports Arena and announced in a two-and-a-half-hour speech, "The war is over!" The Church of Scientology was officially a tax-exempt church, at least in the United States.[52]

A World Religion   Government hassles have not been limited to the United States. Typically countries outside the U.S. have been reluctant to grant the Church of Scientology legal status. Church authorities often have had to make legal arguments that can be very protracted; some continue into the present.

After actually being banned from Australia, the Church was granted religious status there in 1982. Other countries have granted religious status including South Africa, Sweden, and relatively recently, Italy in 2000, New Zealand in 2002, and Taiwan in 2003. Scientology still has no official

[51]Cowan and Bromley, "The Church of Scientology," pp. 185–86; and Melton, *The Church of Scientology*, pp. 19–20.

[52]Derek H. Davis, "The Church of Scientology: In Pursuit of Legal Recognition," paper presented at Center for Studies on New Religions, Waco, TX, 2004; Douglas Frantz, "The Shadowy Story Behind Scientology's Tax-Exempt Status," *New York Times*, March 9, 1997.

recognition in Canada, and Great Britain continues to reject its application to be considered a charity. Belgium and Austria have created official lists of suspect religious groups that include the Church of Scientology.

The most official opposition is in France and Germany. Since 2001, France has officially designated the Church of Scientology as an "aggressive cult." In 2009, a French court found the Church guilty of fraud because of the money it charged for auditing. Basically calling the practice a scam, the court imposed a fine of nearly $900,000.

Earlier during the 1990s, several of Germany's states labeled Scientology as a threat to the constitution. For a period of time Scientologists were prohibited from elected office and from entering into government contracts.

More recently, while the German government did not need anything to further its anti-Scientology stance, Tom Cruise managed to do it. In 2007, protests grew over the casting of the actor in the film *Valkyrie* to play the role of the revered hero Colonel Claus Schenk Graf von Stauffenberg, who was executed after trying to kill Adolf Hitler in 1944. Casting a non-German for the role was bad enough, but Cruise established Scientology information/hospitality tents for the film crew at the filming sites.

To support their position in the face of government opposition, Scientologists cite Article 18 of the Universal Declaration of Human Rights from the Charter of the United Nations, which guarantees freedom of thought, conscience, and religion. They argue that the attempts to curtail their organization are no different from the hostility that Communist countries today and in the past have shown to religions. Beginning in 2003, the Church of Scientology opened its International European Office of Public Affairs and Human Rights in Brussels, Belgium, home of the European Parliament. Scientology leaders are increasingly active in allying themselves with the broad issue of religious freedom. For example, they point to the persecution they experience in some European countries as similar to that experienced by Muslims.[53]

Scientology's ability to extend worldwide may be limited in ways unrelated to government hostility. As we noted in discussing whether the Church of Jesus Christ of Latter-day Saints was emerging as a global faith, truly cross-cultural religions need to adapt to different cultures. To date, Scientology has not adapted. For example, its stress and personality tests

---

[53]Davis, "The Church of Scientology"; John Lichfield, "Churches in France Oppose Anti-Cult Law, *The Independent* (London), June 25, 2000; Robert A. Seiple, "Discrimination on the Basis of Religion and Belief in Western Europe," testimony before the House International Relations Committee, U.S. House of Representatives, June 14, 2000; Andrew Gumbel, "Scientology Faces a Week of the Wrong Kind of Revelation," *The Guardian Weekly* (June 11, 2009), p. 6; James T. Richardson, "Scientology in Court: A Look at Some Major Cases from Various Nations," in James R. Lewis, ed., *Scientology* (Oxford England: Oxford University Press, 2009), pp. 283–94; Susan J. Palmer, "The Church of Scientology in France: Legal and Activist Counter attacks in the War of Sectes'," Lewis, *Scientology*, pp. 295–322.

are administered the same way throughout the world with the same unambiguous American cultural meanings, even if translated. Hubbard and his successors have rejected the idea that Scientology's practices have any specific American cultural meanings, and admittedly engrams and Thetans know no national boundaries. Perhaps, in time, the Church of Scientology will have to adjust its message if it is to be effectively delivered outside the United States.[54]

Condemning the Condemners

Scientology's detractors, as we have just seen, range from governments to the press to ex-members. Typically the Church of Scientology takes these critics head-on rather than ignoring them. For example, when British writer Andrew Morton wrote an unauthorized biography of Tom Cruise, the Church of Scientology issued a multipage news release responding to the book's lengthy indictment of the religion.[55]

The Church of Scientology's approach is not unusual and is an example of what sociologists Gresham Sykes and David Matza refer to as a **technique of neutralization.** In their 1957 work, *The Technique of Neutralization: A Theory of Juvenile Delinquency,* they investigated how juvenile delinquents see their antisocial behavior as right and justified— that is, how they neutralized the critical mainstream perspective. Similarly, Scientologists deflect the perspective that they are engaged in strange or bizarre behavior. One technique of neutralization is the **appeal to higher loyalties,** as in one's friends and other social obligations. Scientologists employ this technique when they justify behavior ridiculed by outsiders as required by the teachings of L. Ron Hubbard, or through encouragements from the Church hierarchy.

Another technique of neutralization is **condemnation of the condemners,** or rejecting the rejectors. The rule-violators shift the focus from their own behavior to the motives and behavior of those who disapprove of their delinquency. Scientologists see their detractors as ignorant of the faith and are convinced, if their Church was given a fair hearing, the critics would be won over. Detractors who lead competing faiths or seek media attention are seen as self-serving.[56]

---

[54]Bernadette Rigal-Cellard, "Scientology Missions International (SMI): An Immutable Model of Technological Missionary Acting," in James R. Lewis, ed., *Scientology* (Oxford, England: Oxford University Press, 2009), pp. 325–34.

[55]Andrew Morton, *Tom Cruise* and "Church of Scientology Statement," accessed January 15, 2008, at http://www.msnbc.msn.com/id/22658115/print/1/displaymode/1098/.

[56]Gresham M. Sykes and David Matza, "Techniques of Neutralization: A Theory of Delinquency" (*American Sociological Review,* December 1957), pp. 664–70.

Disguised members of a group called Anonymous protest Scientology near a building associated with the Church in Los Angeles, California.

Scientologists use the term **suppressive person** to describe people who belittle or try to thwart their activity. A suppressive person, according to Hubbard, has an antisocial personality and basically tries to undermine anyone doing "better in life." The challenge of these attackers is so great that "SP" is common shorthand in conversations within the Church. Scientologists believe than an SP's aim is to stop all those who do good and spread bad news rather than achieving anything positive. SPs are often the target of the practice of disconnecting, as Scientologists are expected to cut off all contact with them.[57]

The Death of Lisa McPherson

Reflecting upon Operation Snow White and being labeled a cult by the French government, it may be surprising that the most difficult controversy for the Church of Scientology in the twentieth century revolved around a car accident.

[57]"What does 'Suppressive person' mean?" Accessed October 25, 2009, at http://www .scientology.org/common/questions/pg77.htm.

Fort Harrison Hotel   Longtime Scientologist (after a Baptist upbringing) Lisa McPherson, age thirty-six, was involved in a relatively minor automobile accident on November 18, 1995. At the accident scene, paramedics observed signs of mental disorder in McPherson, one sign being that she voluntarily removed all of her clothes. They took her to a nearby hospital for psychiatric evaluation.

Church officials soon removed McPherson from the hospital and took her to the Fort Harrison Hotel, the Church of Scientology's headquarters in Clearwater. While there, her physical condition deteriorated and she died seventeen days after the accident. She never saw a licensed physician during this time and was allegedly force-fed vitamins, herbal remedies, and sedatives. The official cause of death was a blood clot that developed as a result of "severe dehydration" and "bed rest." At the time the Church of Scientology called the "circumstances" of her death "unfortunate," and contended that the Church had no "intent to do any harm" to its member.[58]

The Church was charged with practicing medicine without a license and criminal neglect. Two years later, McPherson's estate joined in a wrongful-death suit. For nearly ten years, Scientology nationally and worldwide, and particularly in Clearwater, Florida, came to be defined in the media by the criminal and civil cases surrounding the death of Lisa McPherson.

As the months and years dragged on, the McPherson death started to take on the aura of street theater. Memorial vigils occurred on the anniversary of her death. Critics of Scientology would picket Fort Harrison carrying signs saying "Scientology Kills." In one of the Clearwater mayoral races, an incumbent mayor supportive of the prosecution fought off an opponent backed by Scientologists.

A Legal Resolution   In this climate, how was the tragic death of Lisa McPherson resolved? Ultimately, the outcome of the criminal case was anticlimactic. The county medical examiner's records on this case were so poorly maintained that criminal prosecution had to be dropped.

Eventually, in 2004, the Church offered $20,000 to McPherson's estate as a settlement in the civil case. The estate countered with a demand for $80 million. The suit was settled before it went to trial with the amount remaining undisclosed by mutual agreement of the parties involved.[59]

Although the McPherson death is viewed generally as a dark moment in recent Scientology history, it also reflects a connection to more accepted

---

[58]Richard Leiby, "The Life and Death of a Scientologist," *Washington Post*, December 6, 1998, p. F1.

[59]Douglas Frantz, "Distrust in Clearwater," *New York Times*, December 1, 1997; Richard Leiby, "The Life and Death of a Scientologist," *Washington Post*, December 6, 1998, p. F1; "Scientologists Settle Lawsuit," *New York Times*, May 30, 2004, p. 25; and Thomas C. Tobin and Joes Childs, "Death in Slow Motion," *St. Petersburg Times* (June 21, 2009). An anti-Scientology Web page is still maintained at www.lisamcpherson.org.

religious faiths. To Scientologists, their intervention with ill devotees is no different than prayer as a supplement to, or even a replacement for, accepted medical treatment. The Church's relationship to the medical establishment is similar to that of Christian Scientists, who also prefer that believers follow a more spiritual route to healing. As discussed, Scientologists see the auditing process as a means of physical as well as spiritual healing.

The medical establishment often scorns Scientology practices, but the Church contends that if the word *Dianetics* were to be replaced with the word *faith,* or *auditing* with *prayer,* the Church of Scientology would receive the same benign skepticism with which the medical establishment regards other religions. To date, results of scientific studies of the impact of prayer on physical health are mixed and no independent researcher has published findings on Scientology's practices on health—either mental or physical.[60]

Hollywood Connections

Scientology's visibility is heightened by its connections with celebrities. Although this celebrity connection may not have been predictable, Hubbard was a creative person who showed a passion for artistic expression. The faith's large following in Los Angeles and separation from established religions made it attractive to those alienated from more conventional worldviews. Several celebrities who are identified as adherents of Scientology are very willing to express their support for the faith. Among those active proponents are actors Kirstie Alley, John Travolta, and Kelly Preston—all of whom lend their name to the faith.[61]

Also notable in his support was the late songwriter and musician Isaac Hayes. In 2006 he publicly and bitterly left the television show *South Park* after nine years of voicing the role of Chef in the popular Comedy Central animated adult series. He broke with the series over the November 16, 2005, episode, "Trapped in the Closet," which included a highly satirized synopsis of Scientology beliefs and sarcastic attacks on Tom Cruise, John Travolta, and others. Although some embraced his taking the "high road," others noted that he seemed to have no problem with the show's ridicule of Jesus, Muslims, Mormons, Roman Catholics, Jews, and gays.[62]

[60]Religioustolerance.org, "Prayer as a supplement to, or a replacement for medical treatment," accessed January 7, 2007, at www.religioustolerance.org/medical.htm.
[61]Among other notable Scientologists are Nancy Cartwright (voice of "Bart Simpson"), singer Chaka Khan, jazzman Chick Corea, skateboarder Jason Lee, actor Mimi Rogers, singer Lisa Marie Presley, actress Priscilla Presley, FOX-TV personality Greta Van Sustern, and the late singer and congressman Sonny Bono.
[62]Ben Sisario, "Citing Religion, Isaac Hayes is Leaving South Park," *New York Times,* March 14, 2006.

Celebrity Centres   L. Ron Hubbard, himself a celebrity independent of Scientology, understood the creative spirit. Therefore, in 1969 he created the Church of Scientology Celebrity Centre to utilize the full body of Dianetics and Scientology on behalf of the creative individual.

Another of the Church of Scientology alliances with Hollywood was through the Warner Brothers production in 2000 of *Battlefield Earth*. The motion picture, based on the L. Ron Hubbard 1982 novel of the same name, is set in the year 3000 and follows the actions of enslaved earthlings trying to break free of the tyrant Psychlos, played by Scientologist John Travolta. Although the motion picture plot does not embrace Scientology teachings, anti-Scientologists were quick to find parallels. In any event, this cinematic treatment of Hubbard's writing was a failure both among film critics and at the box office.[63]

The Scientology Wedding   Weddings are important events and most religions take them seriously, attaching devotional readings and significant statements of commitment by the two involved. However, Scientology, as it often has, faced worldwide scrutiny when Scientologist Tom Cruise married Katie Holmes. Before considering "TomKat," as the celebrity press came to call the couple, let's consider the role of weddings Scientology.

Scientology provides for weddings conducted by an ordained Scientology minister. Marriage is viewed as essential to the life of a Scientologist, as is procreation and the rearing of children.

Scientology marriage ceremonies, as in other religions, can vary in their degree of formality. Although marriage and weddings are fundamental to the Church of Scientology, the Church does not require that nonbelieving partners convert. Scientology weddings may include traditional rituals such as those involving rings and statements of commitment, and the Church does not prohibit customs from other religious faiths at their weddings.[64] In summary, one could attend a "Scientology wedding" and be oblivious to any influence of the teachings of L. Ron Hubbard.

Cruise–Holmes   The most famous Scientology wedding was between Tom Cruise and Katie Holmes on November 18, 2006, in Italy. Although it may seem frivolous to focus on such an event when considering an extraordinary group, this wedding for much of the world brought Scientology to the front page.

Cruise, twice divorced, and the Roman Catholic Katie Holmes gave birth in April 2005 to a girl, Suri Cruise, and then announced their engage-

---

[63]Rick Lyman, "'Battlefield Earth': Film Doggedly Links to Scientology Founder," *New York Times,* May 11, 2000.

[64]Nadine Brozan, "For Mrs. Cruise, Perhaps a Cat," *New York Times,* November 12, 2006.

ment in June 2005. The significance of Scientology to Cruise was underscored by his selection of David Miscavige, head of the Church of Scientology since the death of L. Ron Hubbard, as his best man. (Matron of honor to Holmes was her sister.)

As a part of the ceremony, Cruise in his vows promised to provide Holmes "a par, a comb, perhaps a cat"—a phrase that comes from a 200-line poem authored by Hubbard. However, probably unless one was really looking, most Scientology weddings would appear indistinguishable from many nondenominational, open-air ceremonies.[65]

A Scientology minister officiated at the Italy ceremony. Was this legal in Italy? The issue is moot because the couple reportedly made their marriage official in Los Angeles at a civil ceremony prior to heading for Italy.[66]

Death of Jett Travolta   While Lisa McPherson's death in 1995 had direct ties to Scientology leadership, the 2009 death of Jett Travolta resonates much more with today's generation. The 16-year-old son of John Travolta and Kelly Preston died at the family's vacation home in the Bahamas.

The medical examiner listed the cause of death as "seizure." In the following weeks, representatives of the Travolta family disclosed that the boy had autism. Speculations mounted that Jett's health may have been in jeopardy because the family had refused early medical intervention and relied instead on treatments approved by Scientology. The Church of Scientology explicitly rejects the existence of autism. They similarly warn people against moving to pharmaceutical solutions for Attention Deficit hyperactivity disorder, schizophrenia, and bipolar disorder.

Critics and former members of the Church hope that the realization of his son's autism and the possible role of Scientology's teachings in his son's death will lead Travolta to leave Scientology or even denounce his faith of many years. Neither has occurred to date.[67]

The Last Words

Scientology, despite its apparent success and growing membership, is not popular. Perhaps even more distressing to Scientologists than the low esteem with which the general public holds their faith, is that it continues to be ridiculed and parodied. In October 2006, a French acting troupe

[65]Cusack, Carole M., "Celebrity, the Popular Media, and Scientology: Making Familiar the Unfamiliar" in James R. Lewis, ed., *Scientology* (Oxford, England: Oxford University Press, 2009), pp. 389–409.

[66]"Tom Cruise and Katie Holmes Marry," People.com, posted November 19, 2006.

[67]Kim Masters, "Travolta's Scientology Turning Point?" *The Daily Beast* (September 27, 2009), accessed August 30, 2009, at http://www.thedailybeast.com/blogs-and-stories/2009-09-27/travoltas-scientology-turning-point/.

staged the off-Broadway play *A Very Merry Unauthorized Children's Scientology Pageant,* complete with a depiction of Katie Holmes as a sock puppet on the hand of an actor playing Tom Cruise. The Church of Scientology was not pleased to say the least.[68]

All religions are subjected to criticism and humor, but what makes the Church of Scientology different is that virtually all popular media treatments of any aspect of it are critical. Despite this social context, the Church of Scientology remains supremely confident of what it has to offer the individual and what its adherents collectively can offer society.

Given his voluminous literary output, it is appropriate to close with the words of L. Ron Hubbard, which are often read during weddings: "Happiness and strength endure only in the absence of hate. To hate alone is the road to disaster. To love is the road to strength. To love in spite of all is the secret of greatness. And may well be the greatest secret in this universe."[69]

KEY TERMS

Appeal to higher loyalties, p. 338
Clear, p. 322
Condemnation of the condemners, p. 338
Disconnection, p. 333
Engram, p. 322

Preclear, p. 322
Quasi-religion, p. 330
Suppressive Person (SP), p. 339
Technique of neutralization, p. 338
Thetan, p. 324

SOURCES ON THE WEB

www.scientology.org
The official site for the Church of Scientology.

www.religioustolerance.org/scientol1.htm
www.cesnur.org/testi/se_scientology.htm
Two sources of relatively objective information about this faith and its symbols, history, belief, and practices.

[68]Ben Brantley, "A Guided Tour of Hell, With an Appearance by Satan," *New York Times,* October 14, 2006; and "A Very Merry Unauthorized Children's Scientology Pageant," *New York Times,* December 15, 2006.

[69]Religious Tolerance, "Interesting Quotes: On Topics from Justice to Morality," accessed January 17, 2007, at www.religioustolerance.org/quotes1.htm.

www.xenutv.com
A major anti-Scientology site, with extensive news articles, analyses, and criticism of the faith, Dianetics, and L. Ron Hubbard.

www.lisamcpherson.org
www.lisamcpherson.com
Sites highly critical of the Church of Scientology surrounding the death of Lisa McPherson.

SELECTED READINGS

Burroughs, William S. *Ali's Smile, Naked Scientology.* Bonn, Germany: Expanded Media, 1985.

Cooper, Paulette. *The Scandal of Scientology.* New York: Tower Publications, 1971.

Cowan, Douglas E., and David F. Bromley. *Cults and New Religion: A Brief History.* Maiden, MA: Blackwell, 2008.

Hubbard, L. Ron. *Dianetics.* Hollywood, CA: Bridge Publications, 1950.

_____. *Scientology: The Fundamentals of Thought.* Hollywood, CA: Bridge Publications, 1997.

_____. *What Is Scientology?* Hollywood, CA: Bridge Publications, 1998.

_____. *The Modern Science of Mental Health,* 1995.

_____. *Scientology: A New Slant on Life.* Hollywood, CA: Bridge Publications, 1997.

Kin, L. *Scientology—More Than a Cult.* Wiesbaden, Germany: Edition Scien Terra, 1991.

Lewis, James R., ed. *Scientology.* Oxford, England: Oxford University Press, 2009.

Melton, J. Gordon. *The Church of Scientology.* Torino, Italy: Signature Books, Center for Studies on New Religions, 2000.

Miller, Russell. *Bare-Faced Messiah: The True Story of L. Ron Hubbard.* Toronto: Key Porter Books, 1987.

Wallis, Roy. *The Road to Total Freedom: A Sociological Analysis of Scientology.* New York: Columbia University Press, 1977.

Whitehead, Harriet. *Renunciation and Reformation: A Study of Conversion in an American Sect.* Ithaca, NY: Cornell University Press, 1987.

CHAPTER TEN

WICCA

- Witchcraft: An Introduction
- Anti-Witchcraft Efforts
- Gerald Gardner
- Organization of Wicca
- Coven vs. Solitare
- Magick
- The Life Cycle

- Coming out of the Broom Closet
- The Goddess
- Wicca as a Religion
- Media
- Contemporary Patterns

Sgt. Patrick Stewart was in his Chinook helicopter when a rocket-propelled grenade shot him down in 2005 in Afghanistan. The military awarded him the Air Medal, the Bronze Star, the Purple Heart, and the Combat Action Badge. His widow requested that the U.S. Department of Veteran Affairs furnish a headstone, provided at no cost to veterans. Permission denied! Why? Stuart's widow had requested a religious emblem on the marker, but not a Christian Eros, the Star of David, or the Muslim Crescent and Star. Reflecting the sergeant's beliefs, they sought the symbol of Wicca and Witches, the pentacle. "No way," declared the federal government.

The **pentacle** is a ring or circle surrounding a five-pointed star (called a pentagram). The points represent the elements of Wicca and witchcraft: fire, air, water, earth, and spirit.

Over three dozen religious symbols were permitted on the headstones of fallen soldiers at the time, including the nine-pointed star of Bahi'a and something akin to an atomic symbol for atheists. Other approved symbols included those for Sufism, Seicho-No-Ie, and the United Moravian Church, but no pentacle. Family members protested but the government would not budge.

In 2006, the state of Nevada argued that it had authority over the Northern Nevada Veterans Memorial Cemetery, where Patrick Stewart was buried, and ordered the plaque bearing the Wiccan symbol be installed on the grave marker. It was installed just before Thanksgiving. Meanwhile, legal action proceeded against the Department of Veterans

IN MEMORY OF
PATRICK DANA STEWART
SGT US ARMY
AFGHANISTAN
OCT 21 1970 ⬟ SEP 25 2005
BSM PH

AP Photo/Cathleen Allison

After several years of legal maneuvering, the U.S. Department of Veteran Affairs finally permitted the Wiccan symbol of a pentacle to appear on military headstones, as requested by the family of a deceased veteran from the conflict in Afghanistan.

Affairs. In 2007, the VA finally added the pentacle to the list of approved symbols. By 2009, more than a dozen military graves in national cemeteries bore the pentacle.[1]

Witchcraft: An Introduction

Before exploring Wicca, it is helpful to understand the terminology generally accepted among practitioners. This is not easily done because many aspects of Wicca seem to be, but are not necessarily, related to fanciful and imaginative activities.

By comparison, first let us imagine you had not even a casual knowledge of Christianity but you had heard of such things as Noah's Ark, Charlton Heston (rather, Moses) parting the Red Sea, the virgin birth, colorful Easter eggs delivered by rabbits in baskets, and the fiery flames of hell. Second, a knowledgeable Christian tells you that he or she cannot dismiss all these events but can explain and, in some cases, embrace

[1]Samuel G. Freedman, "Paganism, Slowly, Triumphs Over Stereotypes," *New York Times* (October 31, 2009), p. A13; Jeremy Leaming, "Pentacle Quest." December 2006. Accessed December 2, 2009 at http://www.au.org/media/church-and-state/archives/2006/12/pentacle-quest.html. A visual display of approved symbols can be seen at United States Department of Veteran Affairs. "Available Emblems of Belief for Placement on Government Headstones and Markers," http://www.cem.va.gov/hm/hmemb.asp.

selected elements. Third, this is the only Christian you have ever seen, much less talked with in your life. You may at this moment be very puzzled at the legitimacy, much less the attractiveness, of Christian beliefs. This imaginary scenario reflects some of the challenges people encounter both when trying to learn about Wicca and when trying to teach others about the Wicca religion. Before delving into the history of witchcraft, we will first review some of the concepts commonly associated with Wicca in the public eye.

Pagans? Yes   Pagan worship or paganism has come to mean those who worship divinity other than the God of Judaism, Christianity, or Islam. Literally the word **pagan** means "hearth or home dweller," so paganism came to be associated with rural people, people who were less likely to have come into direct contact with organized churches. Precisely speaking, paganism would include any polytheistic religions (that is, religions that incorporate belief in more than one god), including Hinduism, Confucianism, Buddhism, and Native American traditions. Many people globally follow an earth-based or nature-oriented religion. Sometimes one encounters the term "neo-pagan," which is generally synonymous with pagan, although some writers reserve the term neo-paganism to refer only to *contemporary* manifestations of paganism.

Some pagan worshipers practice witchcraft, which means reliance on magic or, more precisely, *magick* (more on that later). Witchcraft is also referred to as the Craft and the Old Religion to underscore that it predates monotheism. Paganism includes the practice of witchcraft, but it is a broader category that includes other practices as well. Within the practice of witchcraft there exist many forms and expressions such as voodoo or shamanism.

The focus of this chapter is on Wicca. Wicca is a modern (i.e., the last hundred years) form of practicing the Craft. Wicca, the word, is the Anglo-Saxon root for such words as witch and wizard. All believers in and practitioners of Wicca, both male and female, are referred to as Witches. (Note that throughout this chapter we will capitalize "Witch" when referring to Wiccan members.) However not all Witches are necessarily practitioners of Wicca and practitioners of other forms of witchcraft such as voodoo are not necessarily witches.

Satanists? No   Wicca, or witchcraft for that matter, should not be confused with Satanism. There is no place in the Craft for worship of devil figures including Satan or the Antichrist. Further there is no "black mass" or defamation of Christianity or its symbols. In fact, the devil and hell are parts of Christian theology and do not exist in Wicca. Christians at different times have argued that the Craft was invented by Satan to frustrate the spread of Christianity and the salvation of the world, but the Craft itself does not recognize the devil.

The Satanist charge is frequent. In 2004, Thomas Jones and Tammie Bristol were granted a divorce in Indiana. The state reported that while the couple's nine-year-old attended Roman Catholic school, both Jones and Bristol were practicing Wiccans. During the case, Judge Cale J. Bradford inquired about the couple's rituals and beliefs. Upon hearing their response, he declared, "people might think that you worship Satan" and ordered them to shelter their child from their beliefs. However, in August 2005, Jones and Bristol successfully had the order overturned after bringing their case to the Court of Appeals of Indiana.[2]

Occultists? Perhaps   The final concept we will discuss that is often associated with Wicca is the occult. Occultism is a broad category with some elements overlapping with witchcraft and Wicca. Generally speaking, occultism refers to a belief in the supernatural or so-called hidden wisdom. Occultism includes some of the elements of magic embraced by Wiccans. But it also includes astrology, numerology, spiritualism (communication with the deceased), and extra-sensory perception (ESP). Some of these occult practices may be embraced by individual Wiccans but they are not fundamental to being self-identified as a practicing Wiccan.

So what are the ties between contemporary practice of Wicca and those things viewed as witchcraft across the centuries? There is no simple, or at least, unaminously agreed upon answer. Certainly some Wiccans see no relationship between what they practice today and what was known as witchcraft in the past. Others, reflecting on their spiritual connections to the earth paramount to their beliefs, feel connected to that which early people saw as sacred—be it mountains or constructed monuments like Stonehenge. Virtually no one engaged in Wicca today sees a coherent, continuous tradition emerging from ancient times or those things labeled pagan in the early days of Christianity to contemporary Wicca.

Anti-Witchcraft Efforts

Throughout this text we have often observed how extraordinary groups are subjected to prejudice and discrimination and, at times, even persecution by national governments. In this regard, witchcraft is in a category by itself.

Beginning in 1542, Britain under Henry VIII regarded witchcraft as a crime punishable by death. British law provided that death was spared if

---

[2]Americans United for Separation of Church and State, "Discriminatory Divorce Decree Overturned Indiana," August 18, 2005. Accessed December 2, 2009 at http://blog.au.org/ 2005/08/18/discriminatory_/.

the alleged practitioner was able to read a passage from the Bible. Successive acts of the crown or Parliament created and mantained anti-witchcraft laws into the twentieth century. In 1951, the last Witchcraft Act was repealed in England. This law was intended to prosecute mediums (that is, persons who communicate with spirits of the deceased) who defrauded their clients.

The Puritans   The most well-known and respected study of society's reaction to Witchcraft is *Wayward Puritans* by sociologist Kai Erikson, whose research on the topic began in the late 1950s. Erikson's research focused on how the Puritans in the Massachusetts Bay Colony in the seventeenth century came to identify people as witches and punish them accordingly. The term "puritan" is controversial in itself, but as used here it generally refers to a person who is extremely strict in practicing religious discipline.

The subtitle of this classic text is "a study in the sociology of deviance." As defined in Chapter 2, **deviance** is behavior regarded as violating the expectations or norms of a group or society. Sociologists emphasize that deviance is subject to time and space. For example, smoking has only recently been banned in some public areas. Hence, cigarette smoking moved from an accepted social practice to, in some contexts, decidedly deviant. Power dynamics within society also affect the perception of deviance in that the privileged can more easily manipulate what is viewed as improper than those with less power. For example, while assistance to the poor is often stigmatized, assistance to the more privileged through college loans and home purchase guarantees are protected.

In *Wayward Puritans* Erikson describes how people create social boundaries that define their community. With repression of their religious beliefs growing in England, groups of Puritans, as they came to be called starting in 1630, totaling as many as 20,000, immigrated to New England. The government of Massachusetts Bay emerged first along the lines of a business-oriented model to exercise control over land. But quickly the many day-to-day societal issues began to draw upon the common law of England with a good dose of Biblical vigor. However, the Puritans were unwilling to abide by the strict Word of God. For example, Puritans would not impose the law against adultery to a settler found lying with an American Indian woman.[3]

Puritans, like all people, came to develop a common understanding of deviance. Efforts by the English Crown to establish the Anglican Church in Massachusetts and friction with other religious communities such as the Quakers threatened their consensus on what constituted deviance and

[3]Kai T. Erikson, *Wayward Puritans: A Study in the Sociology of Deviance* with a new Foreword and Afterward by the Author (Boston: Allyn and Bacon, 2005).

what did not. In America in the late 1600s, the Puritan future seemed more fragile than ever.

In 1692, several Salem girls spent their afternoons with a slave girl in the kitchen of a minister. Soon neighbors began to speculate about this assemblage of anywhere from nine to twenty girls with a slave born in Barbados who had a reputation for skills in magic. Quickly Salem residents reported seeing the girls engaged in bizarre behavior—screaming for no reason, falling into convulsions, or barking like a dog. They seemed like they were hardly developing into quiet Puritan maidens. Worse yet, their behaviors seem to be contagious.

Controlling Witchcraft   As is true today, residents first turned to medicine to solve the "problem." The one town physician soon exhausted his remedies and it was consequently believed that the problem lay outside medicine. It seemed obvious to the community that the Devil had come to Salem. Ministers quickly rose to the challenge and asked the afflicted girls who their tormentors were. Three were identified as responsible for the girls behavior and accused of Witchcraft—the slave girl, a pipe-smoking woman who neglected her children, and a woman known to have engaged in premarital sex. Note that all of the accused were women. At the time, being a woman made you a vulnerable target.

What was to be a quick trial turned into a broadening hysteria as the suspects identified many other people in the colony who were engaged in the "Devil's conspiracy." The Massachusetts Bay Puritans felt their sense of community threatened, both by the growing hysteria and the simultaneous arrival of non-Puritans to the colony. Some Puritans left seeking opportunities inland. Other Puritan communities, fearing they were vulnerable, actually asked the trial suspects to assist them in identifying witches. Happy to oblige, they named dozens. Ultimately nineteen people and two dogs were hanged, seven more condemned, and one pressed to death under a pole of rocks for refusing to speak at his trial. Two died in prison, bringing the number of deaths to twenty-two. No one, once officially labeled deviant as a witch in court, was ever acquitted.

Quickly, but not quickly enough, the Puritans began to reflect on the hysteria. The shocking death toll inspired restraint. Some saw the witchcraft charges as outrageous: upstanding pastors and even the president of Harvard University stood accused. So who was deviant in this society? Pondering this question, famed Puritan thinker Cotton Mather noted that witches engaged in many rituals characteristic of the accepted faith of the Bay Colony, including baptism.

The witch trials ended and so did the Puritan experiment in America. Puritans no longer felt a cohesive sense of community or as members of a public movement. As some moved West and non-Puritans arrived, a shared consensus based on a shared religion had vanished.

The consequence of the Salem witch trials, and other efforts by authorities to outlaw similar activities, was that anything even resembling witchcraft came to be generally regarded as a deviant activity. This label stuck well into the twentieth century. Witchcraft was not allowed to be viewed as an alternative spiritual system. By having trials, not to mention public hangings, the community established the limits of religious expression.

More recently, in the last several decades, attacks on Wicca and other activities led to defensive cries of "never again the burning times," with reference to the practice of executing witches in the past. Interestingly, this emotional call of victimization obscures the fact that the witches of Salem were not executed by burning. Wicca today, while increasingly visible, offer no threat to mainstream religions like the alleged witches did to the fragile Puritan community. Regardless, today's Wiccans feel their spirituality is a gentle and peaceful one and find any violence (physical or verbal) difficult to understand.[4]

Gerald Gardner

The central figure behind modern witchcraft is the Englishman Gerald Brosseau Gardner, born in 1884 near Liverpool, England. Gardner is not the creator of Wicca in the way that Jacob Amman, Joseph Smith, or L. Ron Hubbard were of their extraordinary, spirited belief systems. Obviously aspects of witchcraft and, more generally, the occult predate Gardner. Gardner, however, drew upon past rituals and described new ones that he put into print and publicized. For example, one of the precepts that Gardner articulated was the importance of "working" **skyclad**. Skyclad means literally "clothed by the sky." Working as used here refers to the spell work witches do when gathered in a circle (to be discussed in more depth later). So Gardner maintained that witches gathered naked. Gardner was firm about nudity but defends the custom against any notion that it was meant to lead to lust. Gardner believed and argued that being skyclad helps a person to gain inner sight. Then, and now, not all witches participate in rituals skyclad, and those that do so may reserve it for special occasions.

Explanations for working skyclad notwithstanding, this practice contributes to the sensual allure of the Craft along with the call for the fivefold kiss in some Wiccan rituals. The fivefold kiss is described as the kissing of a person's feet (right side always first), knees, womb or phallus ("without which we would not be"), breasts, and, finally, the lips. The

---

[4]Ibid, pp. 21–22; and Robert Detweiler, "Shifting Perspectives on the Salem Witches," *The History Teacher* 8 (August 1975), pp. 596–610.

fivefold kiss serves as a blessing and may be used regularly by Witches or limited to special rituals.[5]

The Craft Emerges   As a youth, the severely asthmatic Gardner and his nanny spent winter months in Ceylon (now Sri Lanka). Later the self-taught young man moved on and settled in what today is Malaysia. During these travels, he became fascinated with South Asian culture, history, and especially folklore. Eventually he worked for the British government there until he retired in 1936 and returned to England. It was at this point that Gardner began to describe what we have come to view as Wicca. He continued to describe, practice, and develop Wicca beliefs and rituals until his death in 1964. His lifelong interest in folklore led to his interest in local accounts of Witch activity in the New Forest area of England where he had retired. He even joined a local theater group that often staged amateur plays with occult and spiritual themes.

Gardner's associations with the occult soon went beyond the stage. In 1939, he said he was initiated into a group who claimed to be hereditary Witches practicing a religion passed down to them as an oral tradition. He was eventually allowed to write down the rituals in the form of a novel called *High Magic's Aid*. Why did Gardner write about the rituals as fiction if he accepted the teaching? At the time, witchcraft was illegal in England, so the only permissible way for Gardner to discuss his beliefs was to market it as fiction. Writing *High Magic's Aid* was a very bold move at that time, even though it was presented as fiction.

Whether Gardner totally imagined the rituals he set forth or actually witnessed "traditional" initiations continues to be debated. Similarly, whether the practices are years or centuries old is in dispute. However, perhaps most importantly, followers of Gardnerian Wicca or related versions do not seem to be concerned. Their devotion to what they understand as Wiccan is far removed from the debate among historians of what did and did not occur in the first half of the twentieth century in England. Indeed, some Wiccans have pejoratively referred to those preoccupied with creating a "correct" history or narrative as "Wiccan fundamentalists."[6]

Gerald Gardner rightly carries the unofficial title of the "father of modern witchcraft" because he empowered people to go public with their beliefs and rituals, popularized the notion of casting spells, and created a sense of belonging among shared-believers. Most important, Gardner was successful in publicizing the Craft in a way that was nonthreatening and did not lead to adverse actions such as the reinstitution of anti-witchcraft laws by Britain's Parliament.

[5]Gerald Gardner, *The Gardnerian Book of Shadows* (c. 1949–1961, LaVerge, TN: Bibliobazaar, 2008), pp. 9, 24. There is no single authoritative version of BoS, since it has been passed down. An accessible version can be located at www.sacred-texts.com/pag/index.htm.

[6]Charlotte Allen, "The Scholars and the Goddess," *The Atlantic* (January 2001).

Isle of Man   In 1951, the same year that the last anti-witchcraft law in England was repealed, Cecil Williamson opened the Museum of Magic and Witchcraft on the Isle of Man, an island in the English Channel. Williamson had been a tobacco farmer in colonial Africa and had amassed a collection of objects associated with magic.

Gardner arrived and became Williamson's museum director and was known as the Resident Witch. The museum fell into financial problems and Gardner bought it and replaced the displays with his own collection. The museum came to be called The Folklore Centre of Superstition and Witchcraft and included a restaurant. The museum was hardly a collection of rare artifacts. It resembled what tourists might expect of a "Witch's college," complete with a manufactured unicorn.

Gardner's centrality to written Wicca ritual persisted and he worked to introduce the tradition to the United States. Upon his death, he bequeathed all his artifacts and copyrights of his publications to his last High Priestess, Monique Wilson. While she maintained the coven and museum for a short time, she eventually sold everything to the Ripley's Believe It or Not Company. The Company dispersed the materials to its many museums and sold some artifacts to private collectors. Gardner's hands-on shepherding of Wiccan thought ended amidst outrage in the Wicca community at what Monique Wilson had done.

Gardner's 1954 book, *Witchcraft Today*, declared that the Craft had survived continuously, presumably, from the Middle Ages. Raymond Buckland is generally credited with bringing the Gardnerian tradition to the United States. Son of a Gypsy father, he had studied aspects of the occult and was drawn to Gardner after reading *Witchcraft Today*. He studied with Gardner and established a coven in Long Island, New York, in 1963, when his job with a British airline company led to his move.

One should not dismiss the significance of Gardner and his immediate followers as well as those who separated from Gardner's traditions but still borrowed heavily from his rituals. The Gardnerian tradition changed the perception of Witches previously held for hundreds of years. Before Gardner a Witch was thought to be antisocial and capable of evil, and the term was only used to refer to women. Prior to contemporary Wicca, a Witch typically was seen as seeking harm to her neighbors. Yes, good Witches did exist, but they were largely a literary invention (as in L. Frank Baum's *The Wonderful Wizard of Oz* in 1900) and were not believed to be those who practiced witchcraft.

Book of Shadows   Gardner recorded the collection of rituals to be used by individual Witches or by a coven into the Book of Shadows (typical abbreviated as BoS). Today one cannot assuredly point to *the* Gardnerian Book of Shadows in the way one can definitively point to the King James Version of the Bible.

There is not such a thing as a single Gardnerian Book of Shadows. If one were to order the BoS from an online bookstore, check one out from a public library, and then compare them to fragments widely reproduced online, one would wonder if the original ever existed. Gardner's version evolved from a very limited printing in the beginning. Followers would hand copy, adapt, and add to those they could get their hands on. Indeed, Gardner never published the BoS. *Witchcraft Today* contained excerpts but it was not until after his death that the purported complete BoS appeared. Today, copies of versions of the Book of Shadows are handed down from Witch to Witch. Witches commonly adapt their copy of the BoS with their own innovations.

Generally, the BoS indirectly refers to ties to the Old Religion and the need to be on your guard at all times. For example, it reminds Wiccans that "in the old days many of us went to the flames laughing and singing, and so we may again."[7]

The specificity in Gerald Gardner's Book of Shadows at times appears like a training manual. "Mark the circle with chalk, paint, or otherwise . . . Furniture may be placed to indicate the bonds." Goddess position to arms crossed. Chant or sing "Eko eko, Azarak Eko . . . Samahac atha Famolas." Any elaborate explanations let alone justifications are absent from the BoS (but so too are they from the Bible and Qur'an).

Followers of Gardnerian Wicca were warned, not instructed, to write the BoS in their own hand and never let it out of their sight. Others were only to see handwritten versions. If danger, whatever that meant, threatened, Witches needed to be prepared to destroy their written versions.[8]

In the BoS are outlined the Sabbat rituals that are commonly recognized by even those not a part of the Gardnerian Wiccan tradition. **Sabbat** refers to festivals associated with the seasons—spring equinox, summer solstice, autumn equinox and winter solstice. Additionally the four midpoints between equinoxes and solstices are often observed. Since those events are loosely based on the Celtic agricultural year and Wiccans are worldwide, adaptations are made to fit local climate and time.

In addition to the Sabbat, another part of the ritual year for Wiccans is the **Esbat,** timed to the lunar calendar or the phases of the moon. Some Wiccan traditions emphasize the energy that comes from the moon. The full moon is thought to be the best time to seek visions and wisdom through meditation.

Contemporary Wiccans, while all acknowledging the importance of Gardner, do not all necessarily follow in his tradition. For example, Alex Sanders (1926–1988) encountered Gardner and developed his own BoS, which he later claimed was his grandmother's, suggesting his witchcraft

[7]Gardner, *The Gardnerian Book of Shadows*, p. 31.
[8]Ibid, pp. 24, 36.

Wicca

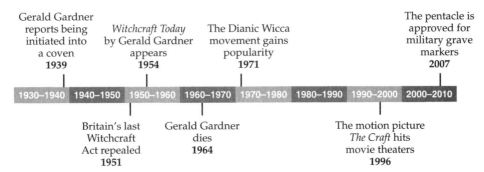

Gerald Gardner reports being initiated into a coven
1939

Witchcraft Today by Gerald Gardner appears
1954

The Dianic Wicca movement gains popularity
1971

The pentacle is approved for military grave markers
2007

1930–1940 1940–1950 1950–1960 1960–1970 1970–1980 1980–1990 1990–2000 2000–2010

Britain's last Witchcraft Act repealed
1951

Gerald Gardner dies
1964

The motion picture *The Craft* hits movie theaters
1996

was inherited. Sanders became a media darling in the "counterculture" years of the late 1960s and early 1970s, as he willingly allowed himself and his followers to be photographed skyclad. Openly bisexual, Sanders welcomed gays and lesbians to the Craft. In contrast, Gardner had stressed a male–female polarity in Wicca that tended to be hostile to same-sex relationships. While not as popular as Gardner, the teachings of Alex Sanders—termed the Alexandrian tradition—are widely followed.[9]

Wiccan ritual is not a dogma shared by all Witches. As summarized by a Religious Studies professor who has been a practicing Wiccan since high school, "Wiccan ritual takes on a dizzying variety of forms." It can be elementary or highly detailed and sophisticated. A Wiccan ritual, circle, or meeting can consist of a single heartfelt prayer or be highly complex and time-consuming.[10]

While some outsiders decry Wicca's lack of centrality or dogma as a "churchless religion," this openness is very attractive to many. As Christina Lombardi, who founded the Nassau Community College's Wicca/Pagan Society in New York in 2003, declared: "Wicca represents freedom, not needing a middleman between me and God."[11]

[9]Douglas E. Cowan and David G. Bromley, *Cults and New Religions: A Brief History*, pp. 197–98; and Jeffrey B. Russell and Brooks Alexander, *A History of Witchcraft*, 2nd ed. (New York: Thames and Hudson, 2007), pp. 167–71. The biographical portrait of Gardner is drawn upon Philip Heselton, *Gerald Gardner and the Cauldron of Inspiration: An Investigation into the Sources of Gardnerian Witchcraft* (Milverton, Somerset: Capall Bann Publishing, 2003); Shelly Rabinovich and James Lewis, eds., *The Encyclopedia of Modern Witchcraft and Neo-Paganism* (New York: Kensington Publishing Corp., 2002); Julia Phillips, "History of Wicca in England: 1939 to the Present Day," Revised 2004. Based on a presentation at the 1991 Australian Wiccan Conference in Canberra. Accessible at www.geraldgardner.com/history_of_Wicca_Revised.pdf.

[10]Nikki Bada-Frialick, *Coming to the Edge of the Circle: A Wiccan Initiation Ritual* (Oxford: Oxford University Press), 2005.

[11]Mary Reinholz, "An Alternative Rite of Spring," *New York Times* (May 9, 2004).

Gardner invited Doreen Valiente to become a part of his Isle of Man coven. Valiente played a critical role in editing Gardner's Book of Shadows. It was with Valiente's assistance that Gardner's BoS evolved into a new system of rituals that provided the foundation for Wicca. Valiente also put emphasis on Goddess worship. As Gardner's success and fame grew, splits developed in the Isle of Man coven. The most significant split was the departure of Valiente in response to Gardner's contention that "ancient" witchcraft gave precedence to the God over the Goddess.

Rede   There are some common almost universal rituals among Witches. In Wiccan rituals, reference is often made to the Wiccan Rede (pronounced reed), which, in effect, means Wiccan advice. The Rede is often expressed in a long verse or poem, which serves as a creed or statement of faith. Witches today, whether solitairy or coven-associated, often recite memorized versions of it. The Rede, however recited, typically expresses that short-term pain is regrettable but unavoidable in everyday dealings. Yet harm, permanent or long-term damage, must be avoided wherever possible.

In fact, sometimes the Rede is shortened to the point of: "If it harms none, do what you will." The origins of various versions are unclear and probably are rooted in several literary and oral traditions. Doreen Valiente popularized the Rede typically used today in 1964. In any event, the Wiccan Rede, whether expressed in twenty-six verses or simply the eight words noted above, is akin to the Golden Rule ("Do unto others as you would have them do unto you") that appears in the Gospel according to Luke, in the Bible's New Testament. The Wiccan Rede asks twenty-first-century Witches to consider how their actions impact others and the environment.[12]

Organization of Wicca

There is some organization within Wicca, as we will consider shortly, but there is no central authority. Beyond one's immediate like-minded friends, Witches generally follow independent paths and, to a large degree, follow traditions and rituals they choose.

To different degrees, all of the other extraordinary groups discussed in this volume have some hierarchy, or at least some central coordination or clearinghouse of activities with other believers. It also follows that they establish boundaries between who is in the fellowship and others who may claim membership but are excluded. This boundary maintenance is

---

[12]Rabinovich and Lewis, eds., *The Encyclopedia of Modern Witchcraft and Neo-Paganism*, pp. 278–279, 289; and Amethyst Treleven, *Seeker's Guide to Learning Wicca* (South Australia, Australia: Oak and Mistletoe, 2008), pp. 8–9.

absent among Witches. This is not to say that Witches accept any self-proclaimed Witch. A Witch is free to think of some as not really Witches or that they are, at the very least, misguided. Individual experience and expression are fundamental to Wicca.

A corollary to the absence of a central authority is that there is no central liturgy or agreed upon wisdom. There is no Bible, no Qur'an, not even a songbook. Autonomy in action and thought is the custom among Witches rather than the exception.

Commonality among Wiccans lies in a sense of "agreement on attitude, outlook, and perspective" rather than a detailed system of beliefs and practices. While there are *detailed* beliefs and practices of Wicca, these are not *commonly* shared details. It has even been argued that Wicca as a religion exists, in part, as a rejection of the widely held religious doctrines, rather than what it asserts as true. We will return to the variability of the Wiccan experience when we discuss whether Wicca is a religion or not, since the presence of central authority and liturgy is often the starting point of religion.

Coven vs. Solitaire

Once of the most important distinctions for a Witch is whether they practice alone as a *solitaire* or in a group of similarly minded Witches in a *coven*. It is not unusual for a person to move back and forth between the two lifestyles.

Coven   The **coven** is a membership group of Witches sharing common rituals. The number of Witches in a coven ranges from three or four to thirty, with people joining or leaving just like a church or temple. Coven life offers the in-group support that is typical of the other extraordinary groups. Shakers share a Shaker settlement. Jehovah's Witnesses obviously feel at home in their assembly centers. Similarly, being a member of a coven can reinforce one's beliefs. On the other hand, the very structure of a coven can be stifling to a Witch who has developed an individual belief system and rituals that may not conform to the demands of a particular coven.

Covens are usually of mixed gender, although some are restricted to women and a few to men. The assembly of Witches is typically governed by a High Priest or High Priestess and in a mixed coven, there is often one or both. The terms priest and priestess do not have the same meaning within a coven as they do in other organized belief systems. In Wicca, after a probationary period a coven will initiate a Witch as a priestess or a priest. Further study, time, and acceptance may permit initiation as High Priest or High Priestess, although some covens avoid such hierarchical language. So the Wicca community view themselves as a priesthood of

Wiccans practice their faith either as solitaires or in groups called covens, as shown here.

Rebecca McEntee/CORBIS SYGMA

believers. Wicca priests and priestess are not clerics who hold a monopoly on leading rituals. Leadership is shared.[13]

Solitaires   A **solitaire** has freedom that a coven member lacks. The lack of face-to-face support is less of an issue today than a generation ago. According to a 2005–2006 Internet survey of self-identified Wiccans, solitaires outnumber coven members two to one.[14]

Solitaires do reach out through the Internet to other Wiccans. This occurs through get-togethers or readings at bookstores that specialize in the occult or spiritualism. Research conducted at fairs and festivals indicate that Witches who have practiced only as solitaires or even members of small covens are overwhelmed when participating in rituals with eighty to 200 Witches present. In situations like these, solitaires describe typical routines as "powerful extraordinary" or "scary" or "odd." Solitaires also include Witches who want to gather with others but just "haven't met the right group of people" and look forward to connecting with others.[15]

[13]Graham Harvey, "The Authority of Intimacy in Paganism and Goddess Spirituality," Diskus 4 (No. 1, 1996), pp. 34–48.

[14]Covenant of the Goddess, "The 2005–2006 Wiccan/Pagan Poll Results." Accessed December 4, 2009 at http://www.cog.org/05poll/poll_results.html.

[15]Marian Bowman, "Nature, The Natural and Pagan Identity," Diskus 6 (2000); and Chas S. Clifton, *Her Hidden Children: The Rise of Wicca and Paganism in America* (Lanham, MD: Rowman and Littlefield, 2006), pp. 11–12.

While hard data are lacking, anecdotal evidence indicates a growing number of festivals and Witch camps that permit solitaires to interact with other witches. Sometimes organized by Pagan organizations, Wiccan activities or informational booths appear at spiritualism gatherings and women-orientated music festivals.[16]

The existence and recognition that one can be a solitary practitioner of the faith distinguishes Wicca and similar beliefs from the many other religious forms that require or at least expect occasional participation in collective worship and gatherings. Still, solitaires are sometimes viewed as second-class within the practice of Wicca since they have not been initiated. Furthermore, their knowledge and commitment have not been externally validated.

Magick

Most Wiccans make a point to speak of magick rather than magic. The term magic refers to the conjuring and illusions associated with show business. Magick is a central part of witchcraft. **Magick** is the art and science of causing change, transforming oneself as well as others. Stage magicians separate themselves from their tricks and are not personally altered in performing such acts. Witches, on the other hand, view magick as transformative for themselves.

So are there spells and potions and secret incantations in magick? Modern magick is founded on idealistic principles that a person can affect the world with study and practice. It is an ongoing discipline of "knowing oneself." It is not unusual for Wiccans in perfecting magick to draw upon conventional and secular aspects of psychotherapy or self-help programs.

However, unlike some "five weeks to a better you" program, magick embraces the extensive use of different materials. These materials range from those typical of many non-Wiccan households, such as candles or incense, to more unusual items. Some magick makes use of a **poppet**—a small cloth doll representing a person. In popular culture, Witches using a poppet are associated with anger and malignant magic. However, in actual Wiccan practice, poppets are also used in the giving of blessings or efforts to heal. Wiccans do not associate themselves with the stereotypical "voodoos dolls" portrayed in the mass media that are often used with evil intentions.

The term **spellwork** refers to the use of words to control the physical world or to petition spiritual beings. Since the premise of magick is to alter

---

[16]Helen A. Berger, "Learning about Paganism." In Eugene V. Gallagher and W. Michael Ashcraft, eds. *Introduction to New and Alternative Religions in America* (Westport, CT: Greenwood Press, 2006), pp. 200–215.

or change, spellwork is often called upon. There is no single set or book of blessings, healings, or curses that constitute the spellwork. The spells can be accompanied by the use of candles, incense, or herbs, or the elaborate deployment of colored cloth, cords, or ropes. The words used draw upon various sources, including the thousands of folkloric spells of oral tradition, or a single coven, a solitaire, or others engaged in witchcraft.

Spells are sometimes associated with the wearing of an amulet, which is worn like a necklace. It is thought to carry a particular energy for Witches and, therefore, is not unlike the St. Christopher medal worn for safe journeys by Roman Catholics.

Spellwork has become organized by purpose over time and includes:

> Blessings—to grant favors
> Binding—to control a person, a thought, or another entity for bad or good
> Curse—to bring misfortune
> Healing—to bring wellness or health
> Warding—to protect a person or place
> Hexes—general term for evil spells but can also include the use of symbols rather than spoken words

This listing should only be regarded as an overview. Individual witches in their spellwork may only draw upon some of these types and not necessarily use or even recognize all of them. Most notably, Wiccans do not embrace negative spellwork, so they would not endorse curses, hexes, or binding for bad. In addition, binding a person for bad or good is generally frowned upon within the Wiccan community.[17]

While Wiccans try to distance themselves from parlor tricks and the trivial use of magick, many approach the Craft fascinated by the prospects of magick. In a case study of an Atlanta coven, the researchers observed new members who boldly declared that their magick helped them create parking spots on campus and that they could cause pendants to mysteriously swing in the air. More experienced members would try to patiently teach that magick is not meant to manipulate or damage nature, but to work in harmony with nature to lead to useful results.

To explain spellwork, some Wiccans' use an analogy of "fervent prayer" among Christians, where if one or more people bring energy to a focal point, a desired goal will be achieved. To pursue this analogy further, just as with heartfelt prayer, Wiccans acknowledge that a Witch may will something but not wholeheartedly believe or deserve it to be attainable. When this is so, the magick will fail.

Is magick helped by herbal charms, candles, or a wand (such as Harry Potter's wand)? Experienced Witches tend not to use such accessories but

---

[17]Rabinovich and Lewis, *Encyclopedia of Modern Witchcraft and Neo-Paganism*, pp. 6–7, 212, 252–258.

recognize that the use of such elements emboldens or assists beginning practitioners. These tools help to focus energy or enable visualization of what they are trying to accomplish.[18]

In some Wiccan rituals an Athame is employed. An **athame** is typically a double-edged knife or handled blade. It has many uses but it is not used for actual physical cutting. It is often used when addressing the God and the Goddess or in the practice of calling to the quarters. We will later see how the athame played a role in a most important court case related to Wiccans in the United States.[19]

The Life Cycle

Wiccans, like members of more accepted religions, follow a number of rituals associated with the life cycle.

Wiccaning   A child is named by his or her parents at a **Wiccaning,** which includes a dedication to the Goddess and the God. The ceremony can be seen as the functional equivalent to naming among Jews and to baptism among Christians. Since people are initiated as adults into Wicca, the Wiccaning does not bind the child to the tradition nor are they regarded as a Witch until they initiate the process themselves. This is a significant departure from infant baptisms, since the Wiccaning parents are not making a religious commitment for their child.

The Wiccaning often has three elements. The first is the presentation of the child to the God and the Goddess with the name given by either the parent or the High Priest or Priestess. Second, the child is presented to the **quarters**—that is, physically to the north, south, east, and west so that the child will recognize and be known by the air, fire, wind and earth. Third, the child is presented to the community, which can physically include the passing of the baby from member to member who may extend individual blessings.

Despite the public associations of witchcraft with "evil doings," Wicca have no notion of "original sin," so unlike baptisms, which are also a purifying ceremony, the child of a Witch who has not participated in a Wiccaning is not regarded as less cleansed or with sin.[20]

Handfasting   Contemporary followers of Wicca enter into a wedding-like ceremony called a **handfasting,** typically performed by a High Priest

---

[18]Allan Scarboro, Nancy Campbell, and Shirely Stane, *Living Witchcraft: A Contemporary American Coven* (Westport, CT: Praeger, 1994), pp. 51–54.

[19]Gardner, *The Gardnerian Book of Shadows,* p. 21.

[20]Rabinovich and Lewis, *Encyclopedia of Modern Witchcraft and Neo-Paganism,* p. 288.

and/or a High Priestess. A separate legal wedding precedes or follows the handfasting unless the High Priest or Priestess has the civil (that is, legally recognized) authority to make the nuptials legally binding.

The term handfasting comes from the custom of tying the couple's hands together in a lover's knot until their vows are made and they sexually consummate the relationship, although this latter element is not necessarily adhered to. Often the couple will be required to jump the broom as part of the ceremony—an acknowledgment of the Old Religion.

In a coven where members concur, handfastings may occur with two men or two women. This acceptance of same-sex couples, when present, can make the Wicca practice very attractive to gay and lesbian people.

Handfasting binds the couple as long as they love each other and, therefore, **handpartings** are sometimes performed to symbolize the end of the partnership. This may involve the breaking of a chalice or the undoing of the lover's knot.[21]

Coven-led Wiccaning or handfasting may be held in an **open circle,** meaning that nonmembers can be present. Typically, covens gather in a **closed circle** with only those initiated into the coven present, and others, including other Witches, are not allowed.

Afterlife   Wiccans do not precisely agree on what happens when a person dies. Some see one's spirit continuing forever in what is often referred to as the **Summerland.** This afterlife is not a heaven or hell but a time to reflect on life lived and the future that yet awaits the spirit. In Summerland spirits coexist with the Goddess and God.

Reincarnation is a common part of Wicca with the belief that each soul may choose who it will be and the life it will pursue. Typically the reincarnated soul does not remember his or her previous Earthly existence. Some spirits choose not to be reborn and become spirit guides.

Cemeteries, so often associated in the public mind with witchcraft, generally are seen as rather insignificant to Witches. The buried remains do not represent the spirit. However, some Witches still see them symbolic ways to remember the departed.

Throughout its rituals across the life cycle, Wicca proudly claims to be all-inclusive in terms of welcoming people to the Craft. Having said that, there are debates about which specific rituals are to be followed at the time of death. Nonetheless, generally issues of race, age, and nationality are literally nonissues for Witches.

With regard to this openness, it is interesting to note that teachers of Wicca will often make explicit references to working with followers who have some physical impairment or disability. Rituals, whether in a coven or as a solitaire, often require the Wiccan to stand or kneel. Following the

[21]Rabinovich and Lewis, *Encyclopedia of Modern Witchcraft and Neo-Paganism,* p. 123.

dictates may be in candlelight or moonlight, rendering lip reading a challenge. Wiccans openly acknowledge such situations and explicitly provide that methods be arranged for people with disabilities and that, in the end, the ultimate connection is made between one and the God and Goddess.[22]

Coming out of the Broom Closet

Identifying oneself as a member of an extraordinary group to nonbelievers is always difficult. It may be especially difficult for a Wiccan to reveal their beliefs to others who hold strong but traditional religious ties. Among Wiccans this experience has been dubbed "coming out of the broom closet."[23]

Given that many Wiccans are young, many must come out of the broom closet to their parents. Reaction ranges from the extremes of cutting off contact with the offspring Witch to genuinely wanting to learn more about their son's or daughter's path with the Craft. Many will treat it as a "phase" in their child's spiritual journey and look ahead (hopefully) to when the child or even young adult return to the family's spiritual roots.

The Craft encourages to patiently counsel parents of children interested in becoming Witches by explaining that we may not like or agree with all our children's decisions. Suggestions are made for parents to meet with the leaders of a Wiccan/Pagan organization. Print resources have been developed for the Wiccan, as well as welcoming relatives and friends who want to learn more about the Craft.[24]

Covens typically allow people to join at age 16, although parental consent is sought for minors. To outsiders this seems very simplistic and is akin to responding to a teen's decision to join a glee club. However, decision to practice Wicca obviously would not go far with many parents.

As the advice to non-Wiccan parents of Witches grows, so does the literature for Wiccans raising their children to be Witches. Given how recently the contemporary practice of the Craft began, raising Witches does not have much of a tradition. Emphasis is placed on children finding themselves but a subtle transmission of values accompanies child

[22]Gary Cantrell, *Wiccan: Beliefs and Practices* (St. Paul, MN: Llewellyn Publications, 2002), pp. 199–209.

[23]The colloquialism of "out of the broom closet" is often used in the Wiccan and scholarly community. For example, see Gary F. Sensen and Ashley Thompson, "'Out of the Broom Closet': The Social Ecology of American Wicca." *Journal for the Scientific Study of Religion* 47 (No. 4, 2008), 753–66.

[24]Carl McColman, *When Someone You Love is Wiccan.* (Franklin Lakes, NJ: New Page Books), and Pagan Parents: Accessed December 4, 2009 at http://www.paganparenting.com/index.html.

development. Parents use chants for lullabies and lively Pagan music for dancing. Candles become as commonplace as Legos. Some covens entertain children of members, potential future Witches, with dragon imagery—almost analogous to Christians resorting to Santa Claus or the Easter Bunny. As the child grows older, he or she is introduced to the seasons and taught a profound respect for Nature. In the teen years, one becomes familiar with the Book of Shadows and starts full participation in rituals. A few covens have even managed to institutionalize the transmission of the Craft in what are termed "Sun Day School" or "Moon School," which are likely to meet in a monthly basis.[25]

The Goddess

Wicca stands out among most religions for the importance it gives to the feminine. Now, of course, not all feminists are Wicca and not all Wiccans are feminists, but the beliefs of Wicca raise the female form to a level not seen in other spiritual journeys—perhaps the twoness of God "he" and "she" among Shakers comes closest, but still falls short of Goddess worship.

The origins of seeing the divine in female form are as old as depictions of the supreme being as male. Given the dominance of Christian, Muslim, and Jewish thought with a male deity, the concept of Goddess can be jarring even to nonreligious people.

The Goddess movement should not be interpreted as a reversion to monotheism, or a movement away from the polytheistic roots of witchcraft. Goddess spirituality is still localized in the notion of multiple manifestations of the divine.

Wiccans view the Goddess as the giver of life and related to the sacredness of all living things. Mother Nature is not just a euphemism but also a salute to the earth that mankind and womankind have seriously wounded. Before environmentalism became popularized, Wicca communities gave more than lip service to the purity of the earth that deserved to be protected. Wiccans often recount that they recognized the divinity of nature and the earth well before taking the path to Wicca.

Wicca maintains that the God and the Goddess are equal and exist together—that is, the divine is not androgynous or a he/she but a divinity of the God *and* the Goddess. Whether it be because of the God and the Goddess aspect of the Craft, a 2006 national survey of self-identified Wiccans showed 74 percent to be female.[26]

[25] Ashleen P'Gaea, *Raising Witches: Teaching the Wiccan Faith to Children* (Franklin Lakes, NJ: New Page Books), 2002.
[26] Covenant of the Goddess, "The 2005–2006 Wiccan/Pagan Poll Results." Accessed December 4, 2009 at http://www.cog.org/05poll/poll_results.html.

Were the historical witch hunts actually attacks on women? People within the Wicca community specifically or those who practice witchcraft more generally have often raised this question. Witchcraft in Salem, Massachusetts, was an inverted model of power—women were determining men's behavior. This made the alleged witches' conduct even more unacceptable and deviant.[27]

This view holds that the empowerment of the female through the belief in a female divinity, the Goddess, and the prevalence of female witches exercising magick, is even more threatening to men than the existence of Wicca as an organized religion. Admittedly the institutions that seemed to threaten those labeled as witches throughout the centuries were male-dominated. Further evidence shows that, often, popular culture depictions of witchcraft and even Wicca today often borders on the pornographic both in words and artistic renditions of how some people imagine witches and covens behave.

The God and the Goddess duality are important to most contemporary Wiccans. However, for some, the Goddess has assumed a degree of centrality. For example, traditions have emerged such the Dianic Wicca, where only the Goddess is spoken of and membership is often limited to women. Indeed, Dianic Wiccans are sometimes described as "gender specialists." To emphasize this aspect, some followers of the Dianic approach speak of "wimmin" or "womyn" only—that is, they take the word "men" out of "women." The Dianic approach was popularized by the Hungarian immigrant Z (for Zusann) Budapest in 1971 in Los Angeles. She blended Wicca with the feminist politics of the time. She started the Susan B. Anthony Coven Number 1 and now has a national following.

Z Budapest claimed to have inherited an 800-year-old lineage of Hungarian witchcraft from her mother, an artist and psychic medium. Z Budapest put her feminist Wiccan view front and center, declaring "hands off woman's religion." In 1975, she was arrested in Los Angeles for violating the anti-fortune-telling law when she read tarot cards for an undercover policeman. She unsuccessfully tried to fight the charge on the grounds it was a science typical of her religion. More interestingly, many in the Wiccan and larger Pagan community did not rush to Budapest's defense, thinking her feminist politics overshadowed her embracing of the Craft.

Starhawk (born Miriam Simos) has broadened the more narrow Dianic movement. She has tried to "reclaim" the Craft by blending elements from Gardner's interpretations with feminist witchcraft but keeping it

[27]Russell and Alexander, *A History of Witchcraft*; and Isaac Reed, "Why Salem Made Sense: Culture, Gender, and the Puritan Persecution of Witchcraft," *Cultural Sociology* (No. 2, 2007), pp. 209–234.

open (and welcoming) to men. Acting on her beliefs, Starhawk is an active ecofeminist.[28]

Wicca as a Religion

As with Scientology, most outsiders refuse to view Wicca as a religion. Admittedly, just because a ban of people, however small or large, self-identifies as a religion does not make it so.

Most religion scholars place Wicca in the category of a **quasi-religion.** This category has been created to include organizations that may see themselves as religious but are seen as "sort-of religious" by others. Included in this classification system are New Age movements and Transcendental Meditation as advanced by Maharishi Mahesh Yogi and introduced in 1958.[29] To date academic scholarship related to Wicca is quite limited, and if historical treatments of its roots are not considered, is almost nonexistent.

Government Recognition   Often it is noted that the United States officially recognizes witchcraft or Wicca as a religion. Is this true? No, but it is not difficult to see why this is so often repeated, especially in publications outside the United States. As we have observed previously in this volume, the federal government does not have or maintain a list of religions. For tax purposes, it does stipulate nonprofit organizations, which include the Roman Catholic Church and the Salvation Army but also include in the same category the American Cancer Society and the Sierra Club.

So where did this notion of witchcraft being recognized by the U.S. government come from? At the beginning, it was noted that the U.S. Department of Veterans Affairs eventually approved the pentacle for use on the cemetery markers of fallen soldiers.

While prisons are not usually associated with spirituality in the public mind, an inmate has the hours of contemplation that can often be directed to investigating alternatives in religion. We have seen this quest for spirituality within prison walls in our discussion of the Nation of Islam. Herbert Dettmer was a prisoner in Virginia and a self-identified Wiccan. Dettmer requested access to objects when practicing his faith, including an athame. Prison authorities refused but not so much arguing on the

[28]More information on Dianic Wicca can be found at www.zbudapest.com and Starhawk at www.starhawk.org. Also see Clifton, *Her Hidden Children*, pp. 120–21; and Constance Wise, *Hidden Circles in the Web: Feminist Wicca, Occult Knowledge, and Process Thought* (Lanham, MD: AltaMira Press), 2008.

[29]A. Greil and D. Rudy, "On the Margins of the Sacred," in T. Robbins and D. Anthony, eds., *In Gods We Trust* (New Brunswick, NJ: Transaction, 1990), p. 221.

grounds of ensuring prison safety, given Dettmer did request a knife, but rather on the grounds that Wicca was not a religion.

Dettmer decided to sue the director of the Virgina Department of Corrections, Robert Landon. In the 1985 case of *Dettmer v. Landon*, the United States District Court for the Eastern District of Virginia found that Wicca was a religion and decided in Dettmer's favor. The state appealed the decision to the Fourth Circuit Court of Appeals.

In April 1986 the case was heard in the federal appellate court. The state argued that Wicca was not a religion but rather a "conglomeration" of "various aspects of the occult, such as faith healing, self-hypnosis, tarot card reading, and spell casting, none of which would be considered religious practices standing alone."

The appellate court rejected these claims and upheld the decision of the district court. The court found that Dettmer's beliefs were religious and he was therefore entitled to full First Amendment protections. However, the court ruled that Dettmer was not entitled to use the athame, since "[t]he decision to prohibit Dettmer from possessing the items that he sought did not discriminate against him because of his unconventional beliefs." This decision was momentous in the history of Wicca. For the first time, Wicca was recognized as a religion by a court of law.[30]

Just as paganism is an issue for many in larger society, it is also an issue in the military. The Chaplain Corps of the U.S. Army have recognized Wicca as "a nontraditional faith" since 1978. Still conflict persists.[31] For example, in 2006 a Pentecostal Christian Army chaplain, Don Larsen, applied to be reconsidered as a Wiccan chaplain after he became a member of the Sacred Well Wiccan congregation in Texas. Sacred Well is an organized coven that boasts over 950 members nationwide engaged in the Craft. Larsen's request was denied, first because he lacked a valid endorsement from a religion (his Pentecostal church rescinded its endorsement) and then, when they received an endorsement from the Sacred Well congregation, a Wiccan group, they rejected it, arguing that there were simply too few Wiccans in the military to justify a full chaplain.

Military estimates in 2007 placed the number of Wiccans in uniform at only 3,200. However, according to the Pentagon's own figures, several faiths with a small number of military followers have not only one chaplain but several. For example, in the military there are twenty-two rabbis for 4,038 Jews, eleven imams for 3,386 Muslims, six teachers for 636 Christian

[30]Herbert Daniel Dettmer, Appellee, v. Robert Landon, Director of Corrections, Apellant, United States Court of Appeals, Fourth Circuit,—799 F.2d 929. Accessible at http://cases.justia.com/us-court-of-appeals/F2/799/929/117777/.

[31]A excerpt on Wiccan from the 1990 edition of the Religious Requirements and Practices at Certain Selected Groups: A Handbook for Chaplains can be accessed at http://www.religioustolerance.org/wic_usbk.htm.

Scientists, and one Buddhist chaplain for 4,546 Buddhists. Along the same lines, one pagan Web site claimed that in the Air Force, Wiccans are the third largest non-Christian group behind Judaism and Buddhism.[32]

While Wiccans in the military wait for their first High Priest or High Priestess in uniform to be officially identified as a chaplain, they may find support with the Military Pagan Network. The Military Pagan Network has been underway since at least 1992. Its mission is to generally advocate for Pagans in the military in several different ways from providing a way to find others within the military pagan community to contacting military agencies about changes they could make to be more inclusive in their policies. Little wonder then that an online organization called Pagan Veterans of the USA is in the process of forming and Wiccans continue to seek recognition from the U.S. Department of Veteran Affairs.[33]

Another intersection with government, also with some controversy, was when pagan groups stepped forward to accept assistance from the federal government. In the early years of the administration of President George W. Bush, the White House launched the Office of Faith-Based and Community Initiatives to create partnerships with neighborhood groups, including those with explicit religious ties. When its director, James Towey, was asked in 2003 if pagans could participate, he said he was unaware of any pagan groups that performed charity. Almost immediately, twenty-nine different pagan groups came forward who did nature preservations, homeless assistance, food drives, ministry to at-risk youth, counseling for battered women, and maintained food and clothing pantries. It is not clear whether any of the pagan groups received support.[34]

Media

The continuing concern about anything related to Witchcraft helps to explain why the *Harry Potter* series ranks forty-eighth on the American

---

[32]Alan Cooperman, "For Gods and Country: The Army," *Washington Post* (February 19, 2007); Bob Smietand, "Buddhist Chaplain is Army First," *The (Nashville) Tennessean*, posted September 8, 2009; "The Army Chaplain Who Wanted to Switch to Wicca? Transfer Denied," *USA Today*. Accessed December 4, 2009 at www.usatoday.com/news/military/2009-09-08-buddhist-chaplain_n.htm; and Military Pagan Network, Inc., "Statistics and Facts about Military Pagans." Accessed December 4, 2009 at http://www.milpagan.org/media/statistics .html.

[33]Military Pagan Network can be accessed at http://www.milpagan.org/. See Yahoo Group site at http://groups.yahoo.com/group/Pagan-Veterans-USA/.

[34]Circle Sanctuary, "Pagan Groups Doing Charity Work." Accessed December 4, 2009 at http://www.religionlink.com/tip_091020.php; Religion Link, "Background and Resources." Accessed December 4, 2009 at http://www.religionlink.com/tip_091020.php.

Library Association's list of most frequently banned or challenged books of the 1990s.[35] This is really quite amazing when one realizes that the first *Harry Potter* book did not appear in England until 1997.

We have repeatedly described in this volume the misinformation that exists about extraordinary groups. While legitimate critiques can be made, they are often overwhelmed by spurious charges. If one were trying to learn about Wicca, the mass media would not be a good place to start. For example, consider the range of media images associated with witchcraft—from *The Blair Witch Project* to *Charmed* to *Sabrina* to *Rosemary's Baby* to the musical *Wicked*. There is clearly little commonality there. Wiccans readily admit to watching "witchy" visual media, but concede that the popularized witches do not represent what they regard as the real thing.

Obviously Hollywood and other media outlets seek to entertain rather than inform people about witchcraft, generally or specifically Wiccans. As one writer correctly observed, "Harry Potter has as much to do with Wicca as Easter bunnies do with Christianity."[36]

Nonetheless, opponents to Wicca argue that positive media portrayals of Witches serve to entice the unsuspecting to become curious about witchcraft. For example, Evangelist David Benoit argues that media depictions like *The Wizard of Oz* lull people into accepting witchcraft despite the Biblical injunction "Thou shalt not suffer a witch to live" (Exodus 22:18).[37]

Witches in Training   While we are rightfully dismissive of much in the mass media regarding Wicca or witchcraft, the mass media does serve as a major source for Witches to learn about the Craft. YouTube, as of mid-2010, had over 29,000 clips on Wicca and over 150,000 on witches. Of course, many are trivial, but many of the clips are instructional.

The 1996 motion picture *The Craft* stands out among contemporary films for its modern depiction of Wicca rather than presenting some medieval representation of sorcery. Through this movie, curious teen girls were drawn to the collection of ideas, rituals, and objects. While the motion picture was foremost an entertainment piece and sensationalized

[35]Rita Delfiner, "Is Harry Potter Too Wicca for Kiddies to Read?" *New York Post* (September 26, 2000). Accessible at http://www.cesnur.org/recens/potter_061.htm.

[36]Jan Glidewell, "Wiccans are not all that wild about Harry Potter," *St. Petersburg Times* (November 26, 2001). Also see Helen A. Berger and Douglas Ezzy, "Mass Media and Religious Identity: A Case Study of Young Witches," *Journal for the Scientific Study of Religion* 48 (No. 3, 2009), pp. 501–514.

[37]David Benoit, "Witches and Satanists Use the Media to Recruit." Accessed November 24, 2009 at http://heaven77.50webs.com/wizardoz03.html; and Ruth La Ferla, "Like Magic Witchcraft Charms Teenagers," *New York Times* (February 13, 2000).

witchcraft, the film's producers actually used a Witch from the Covenant of the Goddess in California as a consultant.[38]

A study of ninety Witches between ages 17 and 23 in the United States, Australia, and England found that films and television shows about witchcraft were a significant factor in their understanding of the religion. While few saw the media as responsible for creating their interest in the Craft, they felt it helped them to learn about it. Further, the study found many believed some media portrayals reflected the values important to Witches. The respondents were divided between whether media treatments helped to normalize Wicca as a religion or opened it to further attacks.[39]

The Internet   Today, one cannot talk about the media and any religion without considering the Internet. The Craft is alive and well online, but so too are its detractors. The various expressions of Wicca are present but, so too are those who take offense to how others choose to worship the God and the Goddess.

The Internet impacts Wiccans in two important ways. First, because many who find themselves drawn to particular pagan paths do so in isolation, networking online provides the connectedness that members of virtually all other religions take for granted. Second, due to the stigma associated with being a Witch, one is not likely to declare themselves to be one openly. Having an online group of seemingly like-minded folk is extremely important, as it allows Wiccans to express their religious identity.[40]

Thanks to the mass media, the general public is increasingly aware of Wicca believers even if unfamiliar with the name, much less the beliefs and rituals. With this greater familiarity may come tolerance. A 2009 national survey found that one in five find "spiritual energy" in mountains, trees, or crystals. Similar populations believe in astrology and reincarnation. According to the survey, women are somewhat more likely to hold these beliefs.[41]

---

[38]Russell and Alexander, *A History of Witchcraft*, p. 182. Also see the interview with Pat Decin, the Witch consultant, at http://www.cog.org/nextgen/thecraft.html.

[39]Berger and Ezzy, "Mass Media and Religious Identity: A Case Study of Young Witches"; and Peg Aloi, "A Charming Spell: The International and Unintentional Influence of Popular Media Upon Teenage Witchcraft in America." In Hannah Johnston and Peg Aloi, *The New Generation Witches: Teenage Witchcraft in Contemporary Culture* (Hampshire, England: Ashgate, 2007), pp. 113–27.

[40]Douglas E. Cowan, *Cyberhenge: Modern Pagans on the Internet* (New York: Routledge, 2005); and Cowan, "Wicca, Witchcraft, and Modern Paganism." In Eugene V. Gallagher and W. Michael Ashcraft, eds. *Introduction to New and Alternative Religions in America* (Westport, CT: Greenwood Press, 2006), pp. 176–99.

[41]Pew Research Center. Many Americans Mix Multiple Faiths (Washington, DC: The Pew Forum on Religion and Public Life), 2009.

Fluffy Bunny   An aspect of mass media coverage of most aspects of every-day life contribute to what scholars refer to as **commodification,** defined as placing an economic value on goods or services not previously viewed in economic terms. Getting advice, making friends, or even locating a life part-ner have all been commodified as people can pay for each of these services.

"Fluffy Bunny" is a term used among Wiccans as a shorthand way to refer to inauthentic attachments to witchcraft. Wiccans see this inauthen-tic attachment as propelled by the media, whether it is *Harry Potter, Charmed,* or *Buffy the Vampire Slayer.* The term is not used to describe new-comers but to describe adherents who are superficial or "posers" who chose not to become educated in the Craft. Commodification intensifies the fluffy bunny syndrome.

Many Wiccans have expressed concern over the unnecessary commodifi-cation of their faith. People interested in Wicca discussions and sharing meaningful Wicca writings are often targeted as customers for Wicca-related goods. Commodification in Wicca takes hold when objects for sale online, in retail stores, and at festivals overwhelm the quest for shared understand-ings. Reasonable interest in clothing, reading materials, objects, and artwork is taken over by entrepreneurs and sellers of crystals and jewelry and even items unrelated to Wicca, such as tarot cards and wands. In the last couple of decades, Witches or those interested in the Craft are increasingly involved in market exchanges through purchases of "how to" books, training courses, ritual tools, and other "necessary" accessories. Admittedly, without a central authority or even agreed-upon literature, Wicca followers, whether solitaires or coven members, are vulnerable targets. If an online source purports that a certain object is necessary for a ritual, it is slightly more difficult to recog-nize the salesmanship behind the claim.

Clearly the consumerism moves beyond the Craft. For example, in pro-moting the "Goddess of Love Potion" on her Web site, one Australian Witch assures the purchaser it has "magick powers" that have been "shrouded in mystery for thousands of years." Or a Teen Witch Kit can be yours for $50, complete with a "crystal" (a clear quartz), an easy-to-assemble plastic altar, a purple drawstring bag with yellow stars and cres-cent moons, a bag of salt, a pentacle pendant, and a gold-colored cord.

The very popularity of witchcraft, as manifested in books that focus exclusively on spells, concerns practicing pagans. A 2001 national survey found a significant minority—one-third—viewed this popularization as a problem. They fear such public representations do not reflect well on Wicca as a religion and further harms their image within interfaith coun-cils and the judicial system.[42]

---

[42]Helen A. Berger, Evan A. Leach, and Leigh S. Shaffer. *Voices from the Pagan Census: A National Survey from Witches and Neo-Pagans in the United States* (Columbia, SC: University of South Carolina Press) 2003.

In a related matter, many Wiccans are also concerned by the increasing number of people who charge money to teach the Craft, or who offer lectures but expect attendees to buy commodities from them. This is very reminiscent of issues that swirl around the Church of Scientology. As we considered in Chapter 9, Scientology practices, such as auditing, and some of its teachings (or knowledge) are only available for a price.[43]

Contemporary Patterns

The growth in interest regarding Wicca, as well as the growth in the number of people self-identifying as Witches, is a part of a larger pattern in the United States, where an increasing number of religious paths are becoming accepted. People in the United States are beginning to have a buffet approach to religion—picking and choosing from different religions to find the combination that fits them best. In this atmosphere, investigating the Craft seems more acceptable than it did even a generation ago.

Estimating the size of the Wicca faithful is decidedly difficult. Of course, there is no central office gathering information or issuing membership cards, and public expressions of concern and ridicule do not encourage Wiccans to come out of the "broom closet." Nonetheless, we do have some data.

National surveys allowing people to self-identify showed 8,000 Wiccans in 1990, 134,000 in 2001, and 342,000 in 2008. While these are estimates, the trend points to either more people being willing to self-identify as Wiccan or an absolute growth in the faithful. Probably both trends are operating.[44]

Some scholars of contemporary religion observe that whether by design or accident, Wicca is more inclusive than many other religions

[43]Douglas Ezzy, "The Commodification of Witchcraft," *Australian Religion Studies Review* 14 (No. 1, 2001), pp. 31–44; and Angela Coco and Ian Woodward, "Discourses of Authenticity Within a Pagan Community: The Emergence of the 'Fluffy Bunny' Sanction" *Journal of Contemporary Ethnography* (October 2007), pp. 479–504; Silver RavenWolf (www.silverravenwolf.com) who is a prolific author and hosts a popular Web site particularly aimed at teens. See Stephanie Martin, "Teen Witchcraft and Silver RavenWolf: The Internet and Its Impact on Community Opinion," in Hannah Johnston and Peg Aloi, *The New Generation Witches: Teenage Witchcraft in Contemporary Culture* (Hampshire, England: Ashgate, 2007), pp. 129–38. Silver is the person who produced the controversial Teen Witch Kit described above.
[44]Samuel G. Freedman, "Paganism, Slowly, Triumphs Over Stereotypes," *New York Times* (October 31, 2009), p. A13; Barry A. Kosmin, Correspondence to Schaefer, December 2, 2009; and Kosmin and Ariela Keysar, *American Religious Identification Survey* [ARIS 2008], Hartford, CT: Trinity College.

and therefore potentially more attractive to new members. The divine feminine—the God *and* the Goddess—was present in early publications of Gerald Gardner, but clearly feminization of Wicca built upon the tide of the feminist movement in the later twentieth century. The growing acceptance of gays and lesbians within the Wicca community is attractive to many and serves to distinguish many practitioners of Wicca from mainstream religions. Similarly, the embracing of earth and finding spiritual significance in all that surrounds us nicely complements the rising interest in environmentalism since the first Earth Day in 1970.[45]

The United States appears to have the most self-identified Wiccans nationally. However proportionately, numbers may be similar in countries such as Great Britain, Australia, Canada, and New Zealand. In these nations, government censuses ask people to identify their religion and these countries have shown increases in Wiccans, pagans, and "earth-based" and "nature" religions. Indeed, in Australia, four times as many people self-identify as Wiccan than Scientologist. Similarly in England, there are approximately 7,227 self-identified followers of Wicca compared to 1,781 Scientologists.[46]

While Wicca certainly has not entered the pantheon of the big three in the United States—Christianity, Islam, and Judaism—there is evidence that it is becoming more mainstream in the United States. Another sign of the maturing of Wicca is that dissent among Wiccans is not difficult to identify. Admittedly, this is ironic given that the Craft emphasizes autonomy and finding your own direction. Still, whether with the Department of Veterans Affairs or the media, Wiccans seek to engage the public and policy makers with their religion and find a place for covens alongside congregations.

So what does the future hold for Wicca? Will one or two collectives develop nationally to serve numerous covens or even organize solitaires? Will Wicca gain a measure of mainstream acceptability? It is difficult to say what might occur in the next twenty years, given all that has unfolded in just the last sixty. Perhaps it is fitting to close with an admonition used in initiations, as written in a Book of Shadows: "Encourage our hearts, Let thy Light crystallize itself in our blood, fulfilling us of Resurrection, for there is not part of us that is not of the Gods."[47]

[45]Lil Abdo, "The Baha'i; Faith and Wicca—A Comparison of Relevance in Two Emerging Religions," *Pomegranate: The International Journal of Pagan Studies* 11 (No. 1, 2009).
[46]James R. Lewis, "New Religion Adherents: An Overview of Anglophone Census and Survey Data," *Marbury Journal of Religion* 9 (September 2004); and Lewis, "The Pagan Explosion: An Overview of Select Census and Survey Data." In Hannah Johnston and Peg Aloi, *The New Generation Witches: Teenage Witchcraft in Contemporary Culture* (Hampshire, England: Ashgate, 2007), pp. 13–23.
[47]Gardner, *The Gardnerian Book of Shadows*, p. 21.

KEY TERMS

Athame, p. 363
Closed circle, p. 364
Commodification, p. 373
Coven, p. 359
Deviance, p. 351
Esbat, p. 356
Handfasting, p. 363
Handparting, p. 364
Magick, p. 361
Open circle, p. 364
Pagan, p. 349

Pentacle, p. 347
Poppet, p. 361
Quarters, p. 363
Quasi-religion, p. 368
Sabbat, p. 356
Skyclad, p. 353
Solitaire, p. 360
Spellwork, p. 361
Summerland, p. 364
Wiccaning, p. 363

SOURCES ON THE WEB

www.witchvox.com
Since 1997, this site has offered a broad range of nonjudgmental information on everyday Wiccan and pagan practices.

www.cog.org
The Covenant of the Goddess, based in northern California, offers a broad range of information.

www.geraldgardner.com
Insight into the Wiccan tradition viewed by the followers of Gerald Gardner.

SELECTED READINGS

Alder, Margot. *Drawing Down the Moon: Witches, Druids, Goddess-Worshippers, and Other Pagans in America Today.* Completely revised and updated. New York: Penguin, 2006.

Bado-Fralick, Nikki. *Coming to the Edge of the Circle: A Wiccan Initiation Ritual.* New York: Oxford University Press, 2005.

Berger, Helen A., Evan A. Leach, and Leigh S. Shaffer. *Voices form the Pagan Census: A National Survey of Witches and Neo-Pagans in the United States.* Columbia, SC: The University of South Carolina Press, 2003.

Blain, Jenny, Douglas Ezzy, and Graham Harry. *Researching Programs.* Walnut Creek, CA: AltaMira Press, 2004.

Cantrell, Gary. *Wiccan Beliefs and Practices.* St. Paul, MN: Llewellyn Publications, 2002.

Clifton, Chas S. *Her Hidden Children: The Rise of Wicca and Paganism in America.* Lanham, MD: Alta Mira Press, 2006.

Coleman, Kristy S. *Re-writing Woman: Dianic Wicca and the Feminine Divine.* Walnut Creek, CA: AltaMira Press, 2009.

Cowan, Douglas E. *Cyberhenge: Modern Pagans in the Internet.* New York: Routledge, 2005.

Erikson, Kai T. *Wayward Puritans: A Study in the Sociology of Deviance.* New York: John Wiley and Sons, 1996.

Gardner, Garald. *The Gardnerian Book of Shadows.* LaVerge, TN: Bibliobazaar, 2008 [c. 1949–1961].

Heselton, Philip. *Gerald Gardner and the Cauldron of Inspiration.* Milverton, Somerset: Capall Bann Publishing, 2003.

Howard, Michael. *Modern Wicca: A History from Gerald Gardner to the Present.* St. Paul, MN: Llewellyn Books, 2009.

Johnston, Hannah E., and Peg Aloi. *The New Generation Witches: Teenage Witchcraft in Contemporary Culture.* Aldershot, England: Ashgate, 2007.

McColman, Carl. *When Someone You Love is Wiccan.* Franklin Lakes, NJ: New Page Books, 2003.

O'Gaea, Ashleen. *Raising Witches: Teaching the Wiccan Faith to Children.* Franklin Lakes, NJ: New Page Books, 2002.

Parker, John. *At the Heart of Darkness: Witchcraft, Black Magic and Satanism Today.* New York: Citadel Press, 1993.

Rabinovitch, Shelley, and James Lewis, eds. *The Encyclopedia of Modern Witchcraft and Neo-Paganism.* New York: Citadel Press, 2002.

Russell, Jeffrey B., and Books Alexander. *A History of Witchcraft: Sorcerers, Heretics and Pagans,* 2nd ed. New York: Thames and Hudson, 2007.

Scarboro, Allen, Nancy Campbell, and Shirely Stave. *Living Witchcraft: A Contemporary American Coven.* Westport, CT: Praeger, 1994.

Starhawk. *The Spiral Dance: A Rebirth of the ancient Tradition of the Goddess.* 20th Anniversary Edition. San Francisco: Harper San Francisco, 1999.

Trekevan, Amethyst. *Seeker's Guide to Learning Wicca: Training First Degree in the Northern Hemisphere.* Hull Street, Australia: Oak and Mistletoe, 2008.

Wise, Constance. *Hidden Circles in the Web: Feminist Wicca, Occult Knowledge, and Process Thought.* Walnut Creek, CA: AltaMira Press, 2008.

GLOSSARY

Alienation The condition of estrangement or dissociation from the surrounding society. (p. 256)

Anabaptist A general term that was applied to those who rejected infant baptism practiced by Roman Catholics and early Protestants. (p. 39)

Anomie A sense of powerlessness or worthlessness, leading eventually to a feeling of alienation. (p. 230)

Anti-Semitic Prejudice and discrimination against Jews whether secular or observant. (p. 304)

Appeal to higher loyalties A Scientology technique of neutralization that appeals to loyalties, such as to one's friends and other social obligations, in order to justify behavior ridiculed by outsiders as required by the teachings of L. Ron Hubbard, or through encouragements from the Church hierarchy. (p. 338)

Apostate A person who has renounced his or her belief in and allegiance to a religion. (p. 264)

Argot A special language peculiar to a group. (p. 233)

Armageddon The final, decisive battle between good and evil. (p. 219)

Ascending fellowship The Oneidan practice in which older godly male members in a special group called the Central Committee could pick a virgin at about the age fourteen for whom they were spiritually responsible. (p. 187)

Assimilation The process through which a person forsakes his or her own cultural tradition to become part of a different culture. (p. 2)

Athame A double-edged knife or handled blade. (p. 363)

Auditing A form of personal counseling that is the first step one takes to become a Scientologist. (p. 322)

Black Muslims An African American who accepts many tenets of Islam but in the specific context of being Black in the United States. (p. 282)

Black Nationalism A consciousness that sees African Americans as a cohesive group whose collective experience and heritage is to be celebrated. (p. 286)

Blaming the victim The act of portraying the "problems" of racial, ethnic, and other groups as their fault rather than recognizing society's responsibility. (p. 33)

Bori In Rom culture, a new wife who lives with her husband's family and comes under the supervision of her mother-in-law. (p. 18)

Celestial marriage A Mormon marriage ceremony that serves to "seal" a man and woman not only for life, but also for all eternity. (p. 129)

Charismatic authority Power made legitimate by a leader's exceptional personal or emotional appeal to his or her followers. (p. 162)

Clear The most highly valued state within the Church of Scientology. (p. 322)

Closed circle A Wiccan gathering in which only those initiated into a coven may be present and others, including other Witches, are not allowed. (p. 364)

COINTELPRO (Counter INTELigence PROgram), A program carried out by the FBI in the 1950s with the aim of protecting the national security. (p. 297)

Commodification Placing an economic value on goods or services not previously viewed in economic terms. (p. 373)

Commune A form of cooperative living where community assets are shared and individual ownership is discouraged. (p. 87, 164)

Complex marriage A communal circumstance in which every man and every woman is married to each other. They can engage in sexual intercourse, but are not attached to one another as couples. (p. 183)

Condemnation of the condemners A Scientology technique of neutralization in which rule-violators shift the focus from their own behavior to the motives and behavior of those who disapprove of their delinquency. (p. 338)

Conspicuous consumption The tendency to gain attention through the overt display of one's wealth. (p. 43)

Counterculture Any group behavioral pattern that arises in opposition to the prevailing culture. (p. 3)

Coven A membership group of Witches sharing common rituals. (p. 359)

Cultural relativism The tendency to view people's behavior from the perspective of one's own culture. (p. 201)

Culture The totality of learned, socially transmitted customs, knowledge, material objects, and behavior. (p. 161)

Daro The traditional Rom payment by the groom's family to the bride's family in a marriage arrangement. (p. 17)

Definition of the situation A concept referring to the idea that a social situation is whatever it is defined to be by the participants. (p. 13)

Deformation thesis The term used by sociologists to describe the dynamic and rapid shifts in organizational form, and activities of groups and organizations in response to societal influences. (p. 212)

Deviance Behavior that violates the standards of conduct or expectations of a group or society. (p. 58, 351)

Disconnection The Scientology practice of members discontinuing association, or any communication, with anyone considered to be a threat. (p. 333)

Discrimination The denial of opportunities and equal rights to individuals and groups because of prejudice or for other arbitrary reasons. (p. 31)

Disfellowship The Witness term for excommunication. (p. 221)

Division of labor Divisions within society based on the manner in which tasks are performed. (p. 94)

Double consciousness A phrase coined by famed sociologist W.E.B. DuBois to refer to the dual awareness of being both American and African. (p. 288)

Endogamy The restriction of mate selection to people within the same group. (p. 60)

English (or Englishers) Non-Amish, as defined by the Amish. (p. 42)

Engram A particular type of mental image, as described by Dianetics. (p. 322)

Esbat A Wiccan ritual timed to the Lunar Calendar or the phases of the moon. (p. 356)

Eschatology A part of theology that refers to the final events of the world. (p. 218)

Ethnocentrism The tendency to assume that one's own culture and way of life represent the norm or are superior to all others. (p. 32)

Eugenics The study of human genetics and of methods to improve inherited characteristics. (p. 191)

Exogamy Marriage outside of one's group. (p. 61)

Familia The functional extended family that is the essential nucleus of Rom social organization. (p. 15)

Familiyi Plural of **famlia.** (p. 10)

Formal social control Social control carried out by authorized agents, such as police officers, judges, school administrators, and employers. (p. 27)

Gadje Romani word for non-Gypsies. (p. 3)

Gender roles Society's expectations of the proper behavior, attitudes, and activities of males and females. (p. 22)

Gentiles Non-Mormons, as defined by Mormons. (p. 130)

Hajj The Muslim practice of making the pilgrimage to Mecca at least once in a lifetime. (p. 284)

Handfasting For Wiccans, a wedding-like ceremony typically performed by a High Priest and/or a High Priestess. (p. 363)

Handparting A Wiccan ceremony sometimes performed to symbolize the end of a marriage or partnership. (p. 364)

Hijab A variety of garments that allow Muslim women to follow the guidelines of modest dress. (p. 305)

Ideal type A model for evaluating specific types, enabling the sociologist to compare an actual situation with a conceptualized ideal. (p. 93)

Informal social control Social control that is carried out casually by ordinary people through such means as laughter, smiles, and rituals. (p. 27)

In-group A group or category to which people feel they belong. (p. 33)

Jack Mormon The name commonly used by Saints to refer to a Mormon who is inactive or lapsed. (p. 140)

Jihad The struggle against the enemies of Allah as prescribed in the Qur'an. (p. 285)

Kris The Rom system of law and justice. (p. 29)

Latent function The unconscious, unrealized function of a social institution or process. (p. 88)

Magick The art and science of causing change, transforming oneself as well as others. (p. 361)

Male continence The method of birth control practiced by the Oneidans, in which the male willingly refrains from ejaculation. (p. 165)

Manifest function The conscious, deliberate function of a social institution or process. (p. 88)

Marimé The Romani word for defilement or pollution, used both as an object and a concept. (p. 10)

Meidung The shunning or avoidance of excommunicated members in the Amish community. (p. 39)

Melalo The Romani word for *dirty*, as opposed to *marimé*, or *polluted*. (p. 12)

Millenarian movement A movement made up of people who anticipate a dramatic change that will bring about a perfect future. (p. 206, 299)

Mores Customs or beliefs about which the majority of people have strong emotional feelings. (p. 272)

Mutual criticism The uniquely Oneidan practice in which a member who was being reprimanded was taken in front of either a committee or sometimes the whole community to be criticized for his or her action. (p. 177)

Norm An established standard of behavior maintained by a society. (p. 260)

Open circle A Wiccan gathering in which non-members of a coven can be present. (p. 364)

Out-group A group or category to which people feel they do not belong. (p. 33)

Pagan One who worships divinity other than the God of Judaism, Christianity, or Islam. (p. 349)

Pentacle A ring or circle surrounding a five-pointed star (called a pentagram). (p. 347)

Perfectionism The doctrine that, given the proper environment, people can lead perfect, or sinless, lives. (p. 163)

Polygamy The practice of taking multiple spouses; in the Mormon tradition, the practice of taking multiple wives. (p. 127)

Polygyny The practice of taking multiple wives. (p. 127)

Poppet A small cloth doll representing a person. (p. 361)

Preclear A member of the Church of Scientology who has received an audit but has not yet attained Clear status. (p. 322)

Prejudice A negative attitude toward an entire category of people. (p. 31)

Primary group Groups characterized by intimate, face-to-face association and cooperation, such as the family. (p. 168)

Quarters Part of a Wiccan ceremony recognizing air, fire, wind and earth. (p. 363)

Quasi-religion A category created by religious scholars to include organizations that may see themselves as religious but are seen as "sort-of religious" by others. (p. 330, 368)

Reference group The social group that people look to for standards of behavior and appropriate conduct, one that can bestow or withhold approval. (p. 107)

Relative deprivation The idea that people feel aggrieved not because of what they are deprived of in any absolute sense, but because of what they are deprived of in terms of their reference group. (p. 55)

Romaniya The Gypsy way of life and view of the world, embracing their moral codes, traditions, customs, rituals, and rules of behavior. (p. 26)

Rum springa A period of discovery during which Amish youth often test their subculture's boundaries. The term literally means "running around." (p. 71)

Sabbat Wiccan festivals associated with Spring Equinox, Summer Solstice, Autumn Equinox and Winter Solstice. (p. 356)

Sanctions Rewards or punishments employed by a group to bring about desired behavior on the part of its members. (p. 58)

Secondary group A formal, impersonal group in which there is little social intimacy or mutual understanding, such as a large corporation. (p. 168)

Skyclad A Wiccan practice of worshipping naked. (p. 353)

Social control Techniques and strategies for preventing deviant human behavior in any society. (p. 27)

Social distance The tendency to withdraw from a group. (p. 3)

Solitaire A Wiccan practicing her beliefs alone. (p. 360)

Spellwork The use of words to control the physical world or to petition spiritual beings. (p. 361)

Spiritualism The Shaker belief that the living could communicate with the dead. (p. 109)

Stake LDS geographical unit made up of five to ten **wards.** (p. 135)

Stereotype An unreliable generalization about all members of a group that does not recognize individual differences within that group. (p. 256)

Stirpiculture The selective breeding method employed for the biological improvement of the Oneida Community. (p. 191)

Subculture A segment of society that shares a distinctive pattern of mores, folkways, and values that differs from the pattern of the larger society. (p. 161)

Summerland The Wiccan concept of the afterlife as a time to reflect on life lived and the future that yet awaits the spirit. (p. 364)

Suppressive person (SP) A term used by Scientologists to describe people who belittle or try to thwart their activity. (p. 339)

Thetan The Church of Scientology term for the immortal spiritual being or soul. (p. 324)

Technique of neutralization A behavior described by sociologists Gresham Sykes and David Matza in which an individual justifies his or her actions by neutralizing the critical mainstream perspective; often employed by Scientologists to deflect the perspective that they are engaged in strange or bizarre behavior. (p. 338)

Tithing The LDS custom of members giving one-tenth of their incomes annually "for the support of the Lord's work." (p. 141)

Value The collective conception of what is considered good, desirable, and proper—or bad, undesirable, and improper—in a culture. (p. 68)

Vitsa A Rom unit of identity, or kin group, made up of a number of *familiyi*. (p. 16)

Ward The basic horizontal or geographical unit of LDS, roughly corresponding to Protestant congregation or the Catholic parish. (p. 134)

Wiccaning A Wiccan naming ceremony which includes a dedication of the child to the Goddess and the God. (p. 363)

INDEX

Ackley, Maria. *See* Russell, Maria
African Americans
    alienation of, 256–57
    Great Depression and, 255–56
    stereotyping of, 256
Afterlife
    Scientology and, 334–35
    Wicca and, 364
AIDS. *See* Auto-immune deficiency disorder
Ali, Muhammad
    background on, 280
    as conscientious objector, 281–82
    conversion case study, 280–82
    early NOI encounters of, 280–81
    Malcolm X and, 281
    traditional Islam position of, 282
Ali, Noble Drew, 289–90, 303
Alienation, 256–57
Allah, Fard as, 292–93
Alley, Kirstie, 326, 341
Amative sex, 185
American Gypsy: A Stranger in Everybody's Land (documentary), 13, 13n40
American Gypsy Organization, 35
American Society of Islam, 300–301
Amish
    AIDS and, 47
    appearance/apparel, 42–43, 42n6, 43n7
    Ausbund, 56
    ban on autos, xx, 53–54
    barn raising, 44–45
    Beachy, 54, 72
    challenges facing, 70–75
    child raising, 64–65
    clergy, 56–58
    clergy selection, 57
    courtship, 60–61
    early history, 40–41
    economic development and, 49
    education/socialization, 66–70
    faceless dolls, 69
    family, 63–66
    family functions, 65–66
    farming, 48

farmland scarcity affecting, 74–75
farmstead, 48–51
funerals, 47
future regarding, 75–76
government intervention and, 73–74
hex signs and, 50, 50n18
holidays regarding, 52
homes, 50–51
leisure/recreation, 52–55, 53n22
lifestyle, 43–44
manic-depression and, 46–47
marriage, 61–63
medicine/health and, 44–47
Meidung and, 39, 40, 59–60
modernization threat and, 71–72
Morton, Holmes, clinic and, 45–46
music, 56, 61
name origins, 39, 39n1
New Order, 72
nonviolence, 73–74
Old Order, 41, 41n4
overview, 39
pace of change and, 51
as "a peculiar people," 42–47
pictures/portraits regarding, 44, 44n8
politics and, 74
population statistics, 41
relative deprivation and, 54–55
religious customs, 55–58
rollerblading and, 51
rum springa and, 70–71
sanctions, 58–60
school, 67–68
singings, 61
socializing, 52–53, 53n22, 66–70
as "temporary visitors," 58
tourism and, 72–73
values, 68–70
Web sources, 77
women's' role, 64
Amish in the City (reality show), 71
Amman, Jacob, 40
Anabaptists, 39
Anne Lee. *See* Lee, Mother Ann
Anomie, 230